THE
REALMS
OF
OBLIVION

The Davies family's log home, 1875, Shelby County, Tennessee; William Little Davies in the foreground. DMA Archives

THE REALMS OF OBLIVION

AN EXCAVATION OF THE DAVIES MANOR HISTORIC SITE'S OMITTED STORIES

ANDREW C. ROSS

Vanderbilt University Press
NASHVILLE, TENNESSEE

Copyright 2024 by Vanderbilt University Press
All rights reserved
First printing 2024

Library of Congress Cataloging-in-Publication Data

Names: Ross, Andrew C. (Andrew Charles), 1982- author.
Title: The realms of oblivion : an excavation of Davies Manor historic site's omitted stories / Andrew C. Ross.
Description: Nashville, Tennessee : Vanderbilt University Press, [2024] | Includes bibliographical references and index.
Identifiers: LCCN 2024004421 (print) | LCCN 2024004422 (ebook) | ISBN 9780826506818 (paperback) | ISBN 9780826506825 (epub) | ISBN 9780826506832 (pdf)
Subjects: LCSH: Davis family. | Davies-Rodgers, Ellen, 1903-1994. | African Americans--Tennessee--Brunswick--Social conditions--History. | African Americans--Abuse of--Tennessee--Brunswick. | Slaveholders--Tennessee--Brunswick--Sources. | Slavery--Economic aspects--Tennessee--Brunswick. | Davies Plantation (Brunswick, Tenn.)--History. | Brunswick (Tenn.)--Race relations. | LCGFT: Biographies.
Classification: LCC F444.B85 R67 2023 (print) | LCC F444.B85 (ebook) | DDC 306.3/620976819--dc23/eng/20240214
LC record available at https://lccn.loc.gov/2024004421
LC ebook record available at https://lccn.loc.gov/2024004422

Front cover image: Girls in period dress in front of Davies Manor, 1951; courtesy of Special Collections Department, University of Memphis Libraries

To Richmond Bennett and Barbara Williams,
whose connection across time was the genesis of this story.

Contents

Preface   xi

Introduction. *Omitted in Mass*   1

PART I. 1700–1842

1. The Southside   19
2. God, Grace and Child, and Wonder   26
3. Laborers in God's Vineyard   41
4. A Mother and Grandmother of All the Others   52
5. Blood on the Fence, Blood on the Ground   59

PART II. 1843–1860

6. Garden Spot of the World   81
7. Storm Clouds   93
8. Morning Sun   100
9. The Time for Moderation Has Passed   112

PART III. 1861–1865

10. Goodbye Pa   133
11. Disposed of as Follows   142
12. His Erring Children   150
13. No-Man's-Land   159
14. Honorable Mention   166
15. Oh for a Better State of Things!!!   181

PART IV. 1865–1893

16. There Is Danger of Much Trouble   191
17. A Relic of the Old Barbarism   202
18. A Terrible State of Frenzy   210
19. Yearning for the "Days of Yore"   219
20. A Promising and Pleasant Little Village   229

Epilogue. *You Can't Tell All the Good Parts Unless You Bring in Some of That Bad Part*   253

Profiles of Enslaved People, 1773–1865   271
Davies Family Tree   304
Notes   307
Acknowledgments   351
Index   359

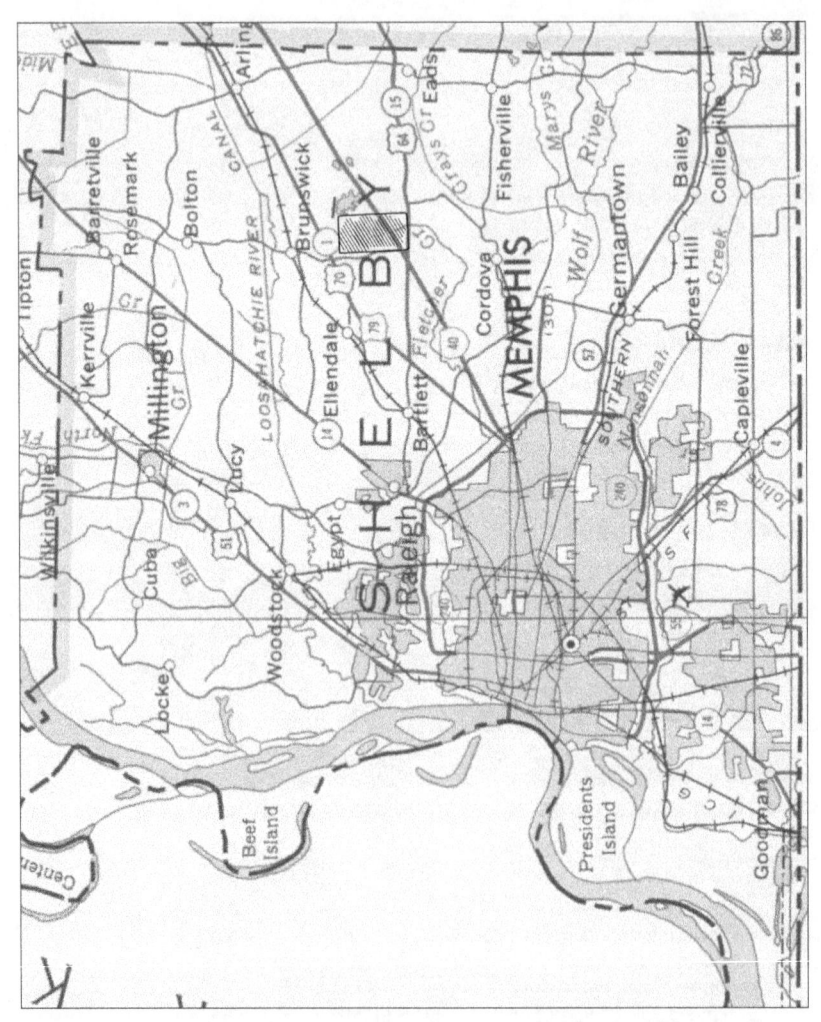

Shelby County, Tennessee, map with shaded area depicting the approximate boundaries of Ellen Davies-Rodgers's estate at its peak size in the mid-twentieth century. Detail from a map of the State of Tennessee by the US Geological Survey, compiled 1957, revised 1973.

But the story's complicated and hard to read
Pages of the book obscured or torn out completely . . .
> ——The Avett Brothers,
> "We Americans"

I asked in an earlier work, "In what universe could the humanity, family integrity, and honor of slave owners count for more than the humanity, family integrity, and honor of slaves?" My answer was that we Americans have lived in that universe since the founding of the country, and have only recently begun the process of moving beyond its boundaries.
> ——Annette Gordon-Reed,
> *The Hemingses of Monticello:*
> *An American Family*

Visiting—

80-Year-Old Caretaker Mose Fraser Stands Proud Guard Over The House Known To History As . . .

Davies Manor

Cover image for January 25, 1965, *Commercial Appeal Mid-South Magazine* article on Davies Manor. Courtesy of Memphis and Shelby County Room, Memphis Information Files, Memphis Public Library

Preface

When long-time Shelby County Historian Ellen Davies-Rodgers turned ninety on November 13, 1993, some five hundred people turned out to celebrate the milestone occasion at the historic plantation-turned-museum-site that she owned a half hour's drive east of downtown Memphis. The party that unfolded was a see-and-be-seen affair: throughout the afternoon, a who's who roster of local politicians, religious leaders, and other Memphis-area movers and shakers trickled into the former cattle barn that Davies-Rodgers had converted into the "Hill's Barn" event center (named after her late husband, Hillman Rodgers). Davies-Rodgers had long cultivated her identity as a "quintessential Southern lady," and for her birthday, she certainly looked the part. Wearing a black lace dress and a pair of her signature white gloves, she sat at the edge of the expansive room warmly greeting her guests—some of whom waited in line for upward of an hour to pay their respects.[1]

Few in attendance that day would have been surprised that the "Grand Dame" of Shelby County could attract such a turnout. Davies-Rodgers, or "Miss Ellen," as most called her, had spent the better part of the twentieth century cutting a wide swath of influence across life in Tennessee's largest and most populous county. Regarded as a "tough field general," a "trailblazer," and a "social powerhouse and political force to be reckoned with," she had held a place in local power circles dating back to the reign of Edward Hull "Boss" Crump Jr., the "Godfather of Tennessee politics" whose Memphis-based machine she had furthered as a "stalwart" supporter between the 1940s and early 1950s. Toward the end of the Crump era, she became the first woman from Shelby County to serve

Ellen Davies-Rodgers, portrait by John Clark, 1982. DMA Archives

as a delegate to the Tennessee State Constitutional Convention; later, in that same capacity, she engineered the defeat of a progressive-led movement hoping to consolidate Memphis and Shelby County government. Operating from the formidable home base that her two-thousand-plus-acre farm provided, Davies-Rodgers subsequently became a prominent voice against the encroaching forces of urbanization, fighting annexation efforts that threatened her estate, as well as the planned routes for a transmission line project and Interstate 40. In the latter case, she was not able to prevent the interstate from splitting her land. Yet she did manage to convince the Tennessee Department of Transportation to construct what amounted to her very own bridge linking the two sides of her estate.[2]

Davies-Rodgers was able to carry such clout due to her ambition and intelligence—not to mention her unique personality that combined disarming charisma with a "feisty" penchant for confrontation. As one writer who profiled her put it, she was a "supremely confident" woman who "descended from iron Southerners" and "takes on all comers with a velvet hammer and a cup of kindness." Her career as teacher, early childhood education specialist, and member of the Shelby County Board of Education garnered Davies-Rogers plenty of recognition as well. Yet the true source of her influence lay at the intersection of her inherited wealth and her lifelong work in public history. That work had begun in earnest in the 1930s after she came into possession of her family's sprawling estate following the deaths of both her father, Gillie Davies, and her older cousin, Dr. William Little Davies. The latter had been a passionate keeper of local history himself, who, recognizing his young cousin's inclinations, bequeathed her the two-story log home and surrounding land that had centered the Davies family's plantation since before the Civil War. Thus, Davies-Rodgers embarked on the project that would ultimately define her legacy: the transformation of her farm and ancestral story into a historic attraction that she successfully linked to larger origin narratives about Shelby County and West Tennessee.[3]

Davies-Rodgers's own residence, "The Oaks," became a key part of her estate's reputation. But the main draw was unquestionably the log home that she restored and took to calling "Davies Manor." By claiming that Davies Manor had originally been built by "an Indian chief" in 1807—a date that placed its beginnings more than forty years before her paternal grandfather, Logan Davies, and great-uncle James Davies had first come to own it (and one that also meant the home pre-dated by twelve years the creation of Shelby County)—Davies-Rodgers established the narrative that Davies Manor was the oldest surviving residence in the county and among the oldest in West Tennessee.* Likewise, throughout the mid-twentieth century, Davies Manor was used by its owner to host private tours, historical meetings, and a variety of social events—all of which had the dual effect of bolstering Davies-Rodgers's political clout. The home became a centerpiece of the popular "plantation pilgrimage" tours sponsored by the Memphis Cotton Carnival Association, as

---

* The undocumented claim about 1807 was questioned by some of Davies-Rodgers's own contemporaries. Among them was H. W. "Ida" Cooper, a local genealogist and historian for the Morning Sun Cumberland Presbyterian Church; in the 1960s, while corresponding with the Memphis historian and journalist Paul Coppock, Cooper wrote that Davies-Rodgers "tried too hard to claim that the old Joel Royster log country home is the oldest in Shelby Co." as part of her effort to make the home into "a shrine." Later, the National Park Service's Historic American Building Survey would also dismiss the 1807 origin date as "unfounded." In some instances, Davies-Rodgers even pushed the founding date claim further back in time. In her 1988 book, *Shelby Chapter: Sons of the American Revolution, The History*, she wrote that Davies Manor was "built before 1807 by an Indian Chief." Today, the Davies Manor Association uses circa 1830 as the origin date of the home.

well as the home base for the Zachariah Davies Chapter of the Daughters of the American Revolution. Organized by Davies-Rodgers in 1945 and named in honor of her great-great-grandfather, the chapter was for many years the largest DAR affiliate in Tennessee, with nearly three hundred members.* By 1965, when Davies-Rodgers was appointed the first-ever Shelby County historian—a position she would hold without interruption for the rest of her life—she had just self-published her first book, a religious history she titled *The Romance of the Episcopal Church in West Tennessee, 1832–1964*.[4]

Over the next twenty-plus years she produced a prodigious amount of research and writing on her family and community, publishing nine additional books through her own company, Plantation Press. Her establishment of the Davies Manor Association in 1976 ensured that the narratives she left behind would live on at the Davies Manor house museum, which officially opened to the public in 1982. Meanwhile, through all these years, Davies-Rodgers's estate remained a bustling agricultural operation, gradually transitioning from cotton-focused production to a more diverse crop schedule and cattle farm. This farm—or "fiefdom," as it was characterized by a reporter in 1973—is one that relied on the labor of African American sharecroppers, tenant farmers, and general farmhands, as well as domestic workers who worked in and around The Oaks and Davies Manor.[5]

Davies-Rodgers's indefatigable spirit and ability to remain so active late in life remained front and center themes during the 1993 birthday party that commemorated the opening of her ninth decade. Attendees like Sam T. Wilson, the former mayor of the nearby town of Arlington, marveled at her resilience. "I've always heard that people when they got old they

---

* Davies-Rodgers's paternal forebear Zachariah Davis (ca. 1746–1828) owned a sizable tobacco, wheat, and cattle farm in Lunenburg County, Virginia. (The family would later change their surname to "Davies.") Davies-Rodgers's claim about Zachariah's militia service in the Revolutionary War was central to the DAR chapter's establishment. Questions surrounding the evidence that Davies-Rodgers used to prove Zachariah's military service are discussed more in the footnotes of Chapter 1. Putting aside her claims about her great-great-grandfather, Davies-Rodgers consistently leaned into undocumented lore in the course of connecting Davies Manor and her own ancestral lines with prominent narratives about early Tennessee and United States history.

outlived their friends, but the older Miss Ellen gets the more friends she has," Wilson told a reporter on the scene. As the afternoon progressed and it came time for formal speeches, the women of the Zachariah Davies DAR presented their founder with a proclamation of thanks. More proclamations were read on behalf of the Shelby County Board of Commissioners and the Tennessee General Assembly. The bishop of the Episcopal Diocese of West Tennessee, Alex Dickson, read a formal resolution recognizing Davies-Rodgers's dedication to the church through her books and philanthropy. Finally, when Davies-Rodgers took the microphone, she thanked the packed room with her usual charm. "I used to look at old ladies who were 90 and wonder how they made it, and I look at myself and I ask the same question," she said. Still, she went on, "I'm here and I feel good.... We'll have another little party in ten more years."[6]

Despite her optimism, Davies-Rodgers would not live to see another birthday. A little over four months later, on March 17, 1994, she died of kidney failure at a hospital in Memphis. In response, Shelby County flags were ordered flown at half-mast, and the county mayor, Bill Morris, issued a statement calling Davies-Rodgers's death the "passing of an era." Morris went on to say, "She had an influence and significance in our history that spanned generations.... Long before women had assumed their rightful place in decision-making, Mrs. Rodgers was making her voice heard, and she was equally adept at talking to either a farm worker or a U.S. senator."[7]

Plenty of other public officials offered tributes in the coming days. Among them were those who had once clashed publicly with Davies-Rodgers. The mayor of the town of Bartlett, a man whom Davies-Rodgers had called "greedy" over his city's annexation plans, said, "In the strongest sense of the word she was a very determined person who would always see a good cause through." The mayor of neighboring Lakeland agreed, saying, "Shelby County has lost probably one of the most influential women of our time." Still other tributes balanced praise with acknowledgments of Davies-Rodgers's confrontational personality. The *Commercial Appeal* called her an "opinionated plantation mistress" and stated in the obituary it published, "She could serve charm with fried chicken and chocolate cake, and if that didn't work, she relied on her lawyers." A member of the Memphis City Council called her "a real

Scarlett O'Hara," while Dickson, the aforementioned bishop, said, "She was a genuine human being, no façade, right up front. She fought for her goals and her vision."[8]

The comments that perhaps got closest to articulating Davies-Rodgers's complexities came from a land developer and county commissioner named Clair VanderSchaaf. "She was a woman ahead of her time, and behind in time, constantly merging the past, present and always looking to the future," he said. The context behind VanderSchaaf's remarks lay in his extensive dealings with Davies-Rodgers through her final years. Somewhat ironically, given her battles against urbanization, she had agreed to sell VanderSchaaf almost all the farmland surrounding the historic core of her estate. The first phase of the subdivision that emerged, Davies Plantation Estates, was already established at the time of her death, and many more homes would soon be on the way. Yet as VanderSchaaf knew all too well, Davies-Rodgers had left her own distinct mark on the development, insisting on provisions aimed at preserving a semblance of the area's rural character. Anyone driving through the subdivision also saw her hand at work in the names of streets like Ellen Davies Cove, Zachariah Cove, Davieshire Drive, and William Little Drive. Less obvious historical tributes were left in the form of Moses Cove and Mary Tucker Cove—the former named after Mose Frazier, a one-time sharecropper who had become the official "caretaker" of Davies Manor until the 1960s, and the latter named after a formerly enslaved midwife and landowner who had delivered Davies-Rodgers at her birth in 1903.[9]

In 2017, more than two decades after Ellen Davies-Rodgers's death, I became immersed in the legacy of this one woman and her ancestors when I took a full-time position working for the historic site that she had created. At the time, I had just finished a graduate school detour and was in the midst of transitioning out of a journalism career and into museums. Given my prior experience with long-form research and reporting projects, I felt intrigued by the chance to dive into the DMA's unique archives and help develop fresh interpretative strategies for the organization. I was especially intrigued by the DMA's need to conduct new research into the community of people whom Davies-Rodgers's forebears had once enslaved. Despite my reservations about being the right person for such a job, I understood from the start that I had stumbled

Ellen Davies with her father Gillie Davies in 1925. Six years later, following the death of her older cousin Dr. William Little Davies, Ellen inherited much of her family's surrounding farmland, including the log home that she restored and began to promote as "Davies Manor." DMA Archives

By the late 1940s, Davies Manor had become a well-known historic attraction and a prominent feature of the annual "plantation pilgrimage" tours connected to the Memphis Cotton Carnival—the "South's Greatest Party." During these years, Edward Hull "Boss" Crump Jr. served as vice president of the Cotton Carnival Association and Ellen Davies-Rodgers chaired the Association's "Ante-bellum Plantation Pilgrimage Committee." Courtesy of Special Collections Department, University of Memphis

4E 23
DAVIES MANOR

Built near Old Stage Road about 1807, occupied by Logan Early Davies, James Baxter Davies & their descendants for over a century. Named for Zachariah Davies, soldier of the American Revolution. In the path of both armies, 1861-65, it was the scene of a dramatic episode between Frances Anna Vaughan Davies and a Union forager in 1863.

TENNESSEE HISTORICAL COMMISSION

Tennessee Historical Commission marker for Davies Manor shortly after it was erected in 1953. From the time she inherited and restored Davies Manor, Davies-Rodgers promoted the home's origin date as 1807, a claim that made it the oldest residence in Shelby County. Today, the Davies Manor Historic Site interprets the founding date as circa 1830. Courtesy of Special Collections Department, University of Memphis

Davies Manor

Built near the Old Stage Road about 1807, occupied by Logan Early Davies, James Baxter Davies and their descendants for over a century. Named for Zachariah Davies, soldier of the American Revolution. In the path of both armies 1861-65, it was the scene of a dramatic episode between Frances Anna Vaughn Davies and a Union officer in 1863.

Location: On the Old Stage Road (Highway 64) near Morning Sun, at Davies Plantation, South Gate.

Placed By

The Tennessee Historical Commission

Unveiling And Dedication Of Marker
Saturday Morning, 11:00 O'Clock

December 5, 1953

Sponsored by the Zachariah Davies Chapter N. S., D. A. R. and the Old Stage Road Society, N. S., C. A. R.

Program for the THC Davies Manor marker unveiling ceremony on December 5, 1953. Some four hundred people attended the event. Among the prominent speakers were Memphis mayor Walter Chandler and US congressman Clifford Davis, who gave the keynote address. Like Davies-Rodgers, both were aligned with the Boss Crump political machine. In 2022, congressional legislation was approved to remove Davis's name from the federal building in Memphis due to his segregationist career and one-time membership in the Ku Klux Klan. Courtesy of Memphis and Shelby County Room, Memphis Information Files, Memphis Public Library

Ellen Davies-Rodgers was widely known by her contemporaries as a "quintessential Southern lady." Here, she prepares to host a tea in 1957 inside her home, The Oaks, which was situated roughly a half-mile west of Davies Manor. Between The Oaks and Davies Manor, Davies-Rodgers regularly hosted social and political events, and the meetings of local "hereditary-patriotic" groups, including the Zachariah Davies Chapter of the DAR and the Shelby County Chapter of the National Society of Sons of the American Revolution. Courtesy of Special Collections Department, University of Memphis

Entrance sign for Davies Plantation in 1957. Hillman and Ellen Davies-Rodgers's estate encompassed more than two thousand acres in northeast Shelby County by the late 1950s. The plantation's approximate boundaries extended north to south between Memphis Arlington Road and US 64, and east to west between Canada and Brunswick Roads. Courtesy of Special Collections Department, University of Memphis

Mose Frazier in 1959 along with Sir Top, the collie belonging to Hillman and Ellen Davies-Rodgers. After sharecropping land in Walls, Mississippi, that was owned by Julius Augustus Davies, and later, William Little Davies, Mose moved to Shelby County and worked as a general caretaker for The Oaks and Davies Manor until the late 1960s. DMA Archives

Valerie Moss, one of the cooks and domestic workers for Ellen Davies-Rodgers, pictured in 1981 inside the kitchen of Davies Manor. DMA Archives

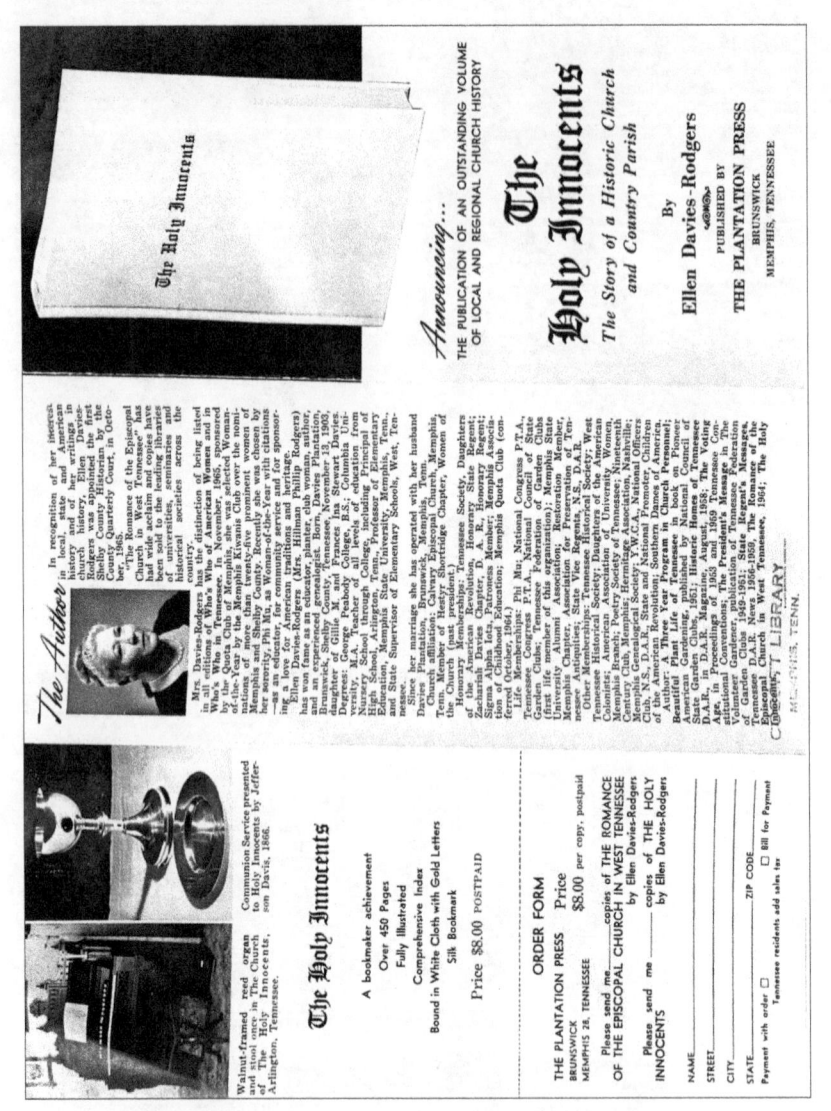

By the early 1960s, Davies-Rodgers had begun to author and self-publish full-length works of history. Seen here is the promotional brochure for *The Holy Innocents*, published in 1965 and promoted as a companion to her first book, *The Romance of the Episcopal Church in West Tennessee, 1832–1964*. Courtesy of Memphis and Shelby County Room, Memphis Information Files, Memphis Public Library

Davies-Rodgers in 1969 (foreground) leading a meeting of citizens fighting the planned route of a transmission line project through rural northeast Shelby County. Courtesy of Special Collections Department, University of Memphis

In 1965, Davies-Rodgers was named the first-ever Shelby County Historian. She is pictured here with two men inside Davies Manor during a Shelby County Historical Commission meeting in the late 1960s. DMA Archives

Scenes From The Suburbs of Memphis Today That Will Be The Heart of The City "Tomorrow."

On a hillock overlooking a lake 3 bedrooms, 2 baths, central air conditioning, 30' family room with fireplace, electric kitchen.

A natural focalpoint For a subdivision of 4 to 6 acre lots— The answer to a growing desire to own a few acres of land

FOR SALE
171 ACRES
ON
DAVIES PLANTATION RD.
TOM SPEARING
EDWARD LeMASTER CO.
527-8521
REALTORS   FALLS BLDG.

Call Tom Spearing about acreage in and around Memphis and Shelby County

Put your "lazy dollars" to work. 112 cultivable acres, 2 orchards, 2 lakes, 3 homes.

Park-like view from main residence overlooking Davies Plantation Road, steeped in the history of the past.

Through the late 1970s and 1980s, Davies-Rodgers sold large swaths of her agricultural land to developers capitalizing on the suburban growth in northeast Shelby County. Today, with the exception of the thirty-seven-acre Davies Manor Historic Site, virtually all of the land that the Davies family's estate encompassed has been developed into subdivisions. Courtesy of Memphis and Shelby County Room, Memphis Information Files, Memphis Public Library into a project with deep meaning and value. Similarly, I sensed early on, though I did not know the full extent of it then, that the DMA's knowledge base about the Davieses themselves had barely scratched the surface beyond the accounts that had come down from Davies-Rodgers. Surely, I suspected, there were deeper layers to this family's history waiting to be found.

It is important to note that prior to this point the DMA had made notable strides toward confronting the history of slavery and African American exploitation that had always been fundamental to Davies Manor's story. In the early 2000s, staffers and volunteers transcribed and loosely catalogued many of the surviving plantation records that directly pertained to slavery and sharecropping. Later, in 2008, the board of directors created a committee of volunteers and staffers to lead a research and oral history project focused on documenting narratives about the Black community who had lived on and around Hillman and Ellen Davies-Rodgers's estate through much of the twentieth century. That initiative, named the Mose Frazier Committee, resulted in invaluable interviews being recorded with more than two dozen African American participants. In a few cases, connections were also made with descendants of enslaved people whose histories directly intertwined with the Davieses'.[10]

Overall, though, the findings remained preliminary. Leads for new interview subjects and more potential descendants needed to be pursued. Sections of the DMA's archives had yet to be transcribed or analyzed at all. Genealogical threads and interpretive clues that connected certain records, names, and events through the generations had yet to be followed. Neither had historic newspapers, outside archives, and governmental records from Virginia and Middle Tennessee—places where Davies-Rodgers's ancestors had owned plantations prior to their move to Shelby County—been explored and cross-referenced with the DMA's papers. Nor had academic historians specializing in slavery and African American studies been consulted in depth or encouraged to research the archives with publication in mind. Crucially, Davies Manor's existing body of research into local African American history had not been integrated in a meaningful way into the site's docent-led tours. Instead, the story that the museum communicated to visitors continued to be told through a lens focused almost exclusively on memorializing the Davies family and their home itself. Along with talking points on architecture, furniture, and general aspects of nineteenth-century life, tours emphasized themes about the Davies family's grit and determination—their history "from the time of Zachariah ... as long-lived, tough, resilient pioneers," according to one booklet the museum printed in 2009. Meanwhile, perspectives about and from Black people were essentially nonexistent. Simply put, the visitor experience at Davies Manor was one that still, decades after Davies-Rodgers's death, appeared to me to remain very much under her control.[11]

This is not the place to give a detailed accounting of the research and development process that took shape between that point in time and 2019, when our small team of staffers and volunteers completed a twelve-panel exhibit we titled *"Omitted in Mass": Rediscovering Lost Narratives of Enslavement, Migration, and Memory through the Davies Family's Papers.* Nor is it the place to fully recount the interpretive and administrative changes that occurred after the exhibit's opening—and that have continued to evolve in a more inclusive direction since I left the organization in 2022. Rather, I feel it is most pertinent to highlight the fundamental understandings about Davies-Rodgers herself that came into focus during the exhibit's development, and later, through the years of additional research that culminated in this book.

On the most obvious level, what became abundantly clear are the dramatic differences between the historical narratives fashioned by Davies-Rodgers about her own family and community, and those that primary records show to be objectively true. Less obvious—and certainly more complicated to address in the museum space she founded—is a related truth: Dramatic differences also exist between how Davies-Rodgers is remembered by white Shelby Countians, and how she is remembered by African Americans whose lives she and her forebears either influenced tangentially, or, in many cases, directly touched.

I first began to glimpse these disparities through the firsthand memories about "Miss Ellen" shared by her former friends and acquaintances. Sometimes, the accounts came from people I met who were visiting the museum. In other cases, the memories had been documented years earlier through the Mose Frazier Committee's work. These stories told from white people's perspectives were usually carefully worded to avoid overt critiques. But the common thread had to do with Davies-Rodgers's anomalous attitudes and proclivities within a rapidly changing post-Civil

Rights-era society. Her requirement well into the 1980s that African American domestic workers wear formal white uniforms was commented upon frequently, for example. One individual who visited Davies Manor as a young man in the 1970s characterized Black domestic workers as having essentially been "displayed" by Davies-Rodgers during her social events; on some occasions when it was hot, he recalled, women working in the home even had to physically "fan [Davies-Rodgers], which made a lot of visitors uncomfortable." The interviewee went on to say, "Miss Ellen was not big on change, and I believe the status quo suited her just fine and she held onto it much longer than most other well-to-do whites.... [She] was definitely 'Old South' and she may very well have viewed the obvious presence of servants as something of a status symbol." Another interviewee, Edward Williams, who succeeded Davies-Rodgers as the Shelby County historian, recalled coming to Davies Manor for the first time in the 1960s for a West Tennessee Historical Society meeting; during that event, Williams overheard another attendee, referencing the domestic workers serving refreshments, remark that there seemed to be an "abundance of hot and cold running blacks." Beyond these sorts of accounts, so too did I personally hear multiple stories about Davies-Rodgers's inclination to verbally reproach Black people she encountered in her daily affairs or on her plantation who did not show her the deference she expected. The subtext behind such anecdotes spoke loudly.[12]

Reading her books proved even more revealing. The instances of troubling passages are numerous, but become especially apparent in "Back Porch Court," one of the chapters in her final book, *Turns Again Home: Life on an Old Tennessee Plantation Trespassed by Progress*, which she self-published in 1992. Although Davies-Rodgers intended the chapter as a tribute to the African American community who, "whether slave or free," lived and worked on her family's estate, her biographical sketches employ heavy doses of paternalism, consistently emphasizing people's "loyalty," and frequently veering into uncomfortable physical descriptions about certain individuals' appearances and "cleanliness." At one point, she explicitly states her opposition to interracial unions: "Whether sexual indulgence is a relationship by marriage or of illegitimacy, a child born of a race-mixed union always suffers a lack of identity—he never knows who he is!" she writes. "For life, such a child must bear the stigma which is the result of their parents' selfish behavior."[13]

As I encountered these sorts of things in my early days working at Davies Manor, I began to more fully understand just how deeply Davies-Rodgers had been guided, until the very end of her life, by a belief system based on white supremacy. Similarly, I recognized the extent to which she had pushed into the public arena interpretations of history that one of her contemporaries once described as "like magnolias pressed between the pages of *Gone With the Wind*." As Davies-Rodgers saw it, the past was a place characterized by "timely grace" and "days of innocence in America." Her family's home and plantation had been a "citadel of hope, of faith, of human well-being" that preserved "life's most worthy ideals and motives." Meanwhile, the subject of slavery, in the rare instances she referenced it at all, simply had no relationship to her family's ability to build and maintain intergenerational wealth and influence. Not surprisingly, neither did Davies-Rodgers ever give any indication in her writings that she recognized the connections between the legacies of slavery and Jim Crow segregation that remained in effect in the South through much of her lifetime. As for the actual people whom her family had enslaved, they had not been held in bondage and forced to labor for life against their will; rather, they were "faithful helper[s]" and "workers employed" by her ancestors. Moreover, they were people who had always remained "loyal" to the Davieses.[14]

But the clearest evidence of all that Davies-Rodgers had viewed the world through an unabashed "plantation mentality" came through the oral histories shared by African Americans who had worked for her and her husband. Time and again, in both the existing collection I read through, and in new recordings that were made, interviewees described a climate of anxiety, fear, and economic exploitation that characterized life at the estate. For instance, the entirely new claim emerged that Hillman and Ellen Davies-Rodgers had recruited newly released prisoners from the Shelby County penal farm to work as sharecroppers who could be easily manipulated. Similarly, repeated memories were shared that characterized Davies-Rodgers as aggressively coercing young Black people to work odd jobs for little to no pay. Andy Payne, a man whose parents sharecropped for Davies-Rodgers in the early 1950s, recalled being a teenager and frequently hiding in the bushes when he heard Davies-Rodgers's car approaching, fearful as he was that she would force him to do a job. On one occasion, after she convinced him to rake leaves behind her house for a full week, she paid him with a pack of gum and fifteen cents. "I was mad," Payne remembered in his 2010 interview, recalling how he had anticipated making ten dollars and going to the fair. "I would tell my mother and daddy about it and they would say 'well son, we can't do no better.'"[15]

In yet another damning interview, Annie Mae Frazier Blackwell Myles, daughter of the long-time Davies Manor employee Mose Frazier, revealed a series of especially painful memories about the treatment of her father. According to Myles's account, her father "was scared" of Davies-Rodgers and her husband, both of whom treated Frazier like he "was somebody's slave." The indignities Frazier endured included living in a bare-bones two-room cabin with no insulation or plumbing, being required to only use backdoor entrances to Davies Manor and The Oaks, and being subjected to regular intrusions from Davies-Rodgers into his personal affairs. These intrusions, such as when his Social Security checks were reportedly withheld by Davies-Rodgers against his will, were intended to keep her father dependent, Myles stressed. (Davies-Rodgers herself, in language that she apparently intended to be humorous, describes in "Back Porch Court" an episode in which she effectively prevented Frazier from marrying the woman he wanted to wed.) The final straw came when Frazier developed dementia in the 1960s and Davies-Rodgers would not let him leave to live with his own family in Memphis. At that point, Myles recalled, she "went and stole my dad off the plantation" under cover of night.[16]

What is recounted above is just a sampling of the evidence that complicates Davies-Rodgers's legacy and should be accounted for alongside the near uniform adulation that has defined her memorialization up to this point. The purpose of doing so is not to demonize her or fall into a reductive analysis of the past. Most of us, to varying degrees, are bound by the limitations of the times and places we inhabit, and Davies-Rodgers was certainly a product of a particular time and place. Still, a reevaluation of her life and legacy is long overdue. Because what *was* unique about her was the extent to which she revered—and made it her mission to promulgate through her writings, political influence, and the historic site she founded—the values of her ancestors' Old South world. Likewise, the lasting impact she had on the larger process of memory making in Shelby County and West Tennessee should not be underestimated.

Most books on Shelby County history penned in recent decades have prominently featured Davies-Rodgers, her forebears, and Davies Manor itself as central storylines. From Perre Magness's 1988 *Past Times: Stories of Early Memphis*, to John Harkins's 2008 *Historic Shelby County: An Illustrated History*, to *Early Families of the Memphis Area*, compiled and edited that same year by Paul A. Matthews, the Davieses' experience—and again, it is an experience whose narrative shape and scope were dictated almost exclusively by Davies-Rodgers—has repeatedly been presented as a defining aspect of the county's collective past. Harkins's book, which is among the most comprehensive and authoritative texts on the county yet to be written, weaves in discussion of multiple generations of the Davies family.* The book also concludes its final page with a tribute to the DMA for continuing to "fight the good fight to enliven local history," and for being "among the more fruitful organizations in preserving Shelby County history."[17]

As Harkins rightly noted, the physical preservation of the Davies Manor home and the establishment of the DMA to continue that project in perpetuity are indeed Davies-Rodgers's most tangible and far-reaching legacies. And in and of themselves, those *are* significant achievements. Today, in keeping with the DMA's mission to "create opportunities for the public to make meaningful connections between the past and the

---

* In his book, Harkins wrote that during the antebellum years the Davies estate "was not a large plantation by pre–Civil War standards and probably never employed more than fifteen or so slaves at any time." This characterization epitomizes the minimization of slavery's importance that has traditionally been at play in local historians' treatment of Davies Manor—in particular, their unquestioning deference to Davies-Rodgers's accounts. As this book will later examine, records show that at least twenty-six people were enslaved at the approximately eight-hundred-acre plantation by 1861. Furthermore, an evaluation of agricultural census data from 269 farmers and planters who surrounded the Davies estate prior to the Civil War (in Civil Districts Eight and Nine) shows only six estates that produced more cotton than what Logan and James Davies reported in 1860. In terms of sheer size, the Davieses' plantation was smaller than the very largest estates in the county that stretched into the thousands of acres. Yet relatively speaking, Logan and James Davies still owned a very sizable plantation, and they certainly owned more land and enslaved more people (who produced more cotton) than the vast majority of heads of household in Shelby County.

present," thousands of visitors, young and old alike, continue to step through the doors of Davies Manor every year. The historic site puts on a variety of educational programs and events, including the long-running Davies Manor Quilt and Fiber Arts Show, and for many years—most recently in 2022—Davies Manor hosted the annual Shelby County History Festival, an event that plays an important role connecting the groups and individuals dedicated to preserving local historical knowledge. It is also notable that between Davies-Rodgers's death and 2019, the two subsequent Shelby County Historians served as presidents of the DMA board, further cementing Davies Manor's reputation within the Memphis region as an important site where place-based education on the nineteenth century can be vividly brought to life. Without the foundation laid by Davies-Rodgers, none of that would be possible.[18]

Multiple things can be true at once, however, and in this case, it is also true that Davies Manor, even as it has persevered into the twenty-first century and made strides toward telling a more complete and nuanced history, has simultaneously demonstrated an inability to move beyond Davies-Rodgers's singular influence and fully grapple with the responsibilities that are inherent to being a space of place-based education *and* a former site of enslavement. The historic site, said another way, has traditionally failed to account for the vastly different ways that its visitors—specifically, its African American visitors—might perceive and find meaning in the ongoing memorialization of a space with such a painful past. As a result, the site has played a role at times as a welcoming environment for those whose agendas, either implicitly or explicitly, align with ideologies based in white supremacy and radical pro-Confederate history. From the annual Civil War battle reenactments that were held for years at Davies Manor, to the persistent influence of the Sons of Confederate Veterans organization, to the lack of diversity on the DMA board (or among its staffers), to the efforts by some on that very same board to downplay the legacy of slavery, the organization *does* have a history of failing at key moments to do the difficult work of honest reckoning, and forthright self-analysis. Likewise, the site has neglected to demonstrate that it values the perceptions of those who would view a plantation museum's ongoing connections to pro-Confederate history as deeply troubling.

The most glaring example of this failure in recent memory took place in the summer of 2018 when three DMA board members—each of whom were members of a local Sons of Confederate Veterans chapter—successfully pushed for Davies Manor to host that year's annual picnic celebrating the 197th birthday of the infamous slave trader, Civil War general, and Ku Klux Klan leader Nathan Bedford Forrest. The SCV's rationale for relocating the Forrest picnic to Davies Manor, rather than host it at its traditional location at Health Sciences Park (formerly known as Forrest Park), had to do with the City of Memphis's decision, seven months earlier (and shortly before the city's commemoration of the fiftieth anniversary of Martin Luther King Jr.'s assassination), to remove the long-controversial Forrest statue from the park. And so it came to be that an event celebrating one of the wealthiest slave traders in the antebellum South, and one of the most polarizing military figures in all of American history, was held on the grounds of a former slave-powered-plantation-turned-museum—one that at that very moment was attempting to reckon with its past through interpretive changes and outreach to African Americans with connections to the site. During the picnic—a scene that consisted of "Dixie" renditions, military reenactments, wreaths laid in honor of Forrest, and plenty of Confederate flags—the SCV raised money for litigation against the City of Memphis. At one point in the day, during a recorded interview with a National Public Radio reporter on hand, a picnic attendee casually stated that Memphis mayor Jim Strickland deserved to be "taken out and hung" over the statue's removal. The NPR story that later emerged remains to this day the only national-level media attention Davies Manor has ever received.[19]

Suffice it to say that the DMA board's decision to allow the picnic (a decision made over my objections as the site's then projects director and one that I have felt troubled by ever since for not disputing harder) constituted a low point in my time working for the organization.* Ironically, it also happened to occur in the middle of a new strategic planning initiative (and the *Omitted in Mass* exhibit project) and helped

---

* In 2019, two of the three SCV members who had pushed for and organized the Forrest picnic's relocation to Davies Manor resigned from the DMA board. In one case, the SCV member (who was also an assistant prosecutor for the town of Collierville) resigned after news articles emerged revealing his Facebook comments made in support of white nationalists at the 2017 Unite the Right Rally in Charlottesville.

facilitate a series of especially important board discussions about the DMA's mission, values, and long-term vision. By the following year, the board had approved a new strategic plan that featured revised mission and vision statements and prioritized creating a visitor experience and interpretive changes that would attract more diverse audiences. The exhibit completed soon afterward marked an important step in that direction. So did new programming events and partnerships that emphasized the site's African American history. More positive developments have continued since then. Looking to the future, only time will tell how Davies Manor will continue to explore its potential to further widen its interpretive possibilities, deepen its impact, and expand its community of stakeholders.

The basic idea for a book-length work that would interweave narratives about the Davies family with those of people they enslaved originated out of my recognition that the research connected to the exhibit project deserved to be expanded. What ended up developing over the ensuing years, however, was a manuscript that evolved far beyond what I'd originally envisioned as entirely new findings about the Davieses, Black families they enslaved, and other white and Black families they intersected with continually emerged in the primary records I encountered in courthouses, archival collections, census records, and newspapers spread between Virginia and West Tennessee. I should also stress that the project evolved in ways I did not originally anticipate as *I* evolved and gained more clarity, especially after moving on from the organization, about the overarching meaning of this rather obscure history and why I believe it carries so much relevance beyond the scope of Davies Manor itself.

In its completed form, *The Realms of Oblivion* (a title drawn directly from Dr. William Little Davies's writings about memorialization) is a book intended to operate on multiple levels, simultaneously telling an informative and engrossing bottom-up history, while also challenging readers to consider the complexities undergirding the survival of that history into the present day. Why exactly do we study the Davies family at all, we should ask? What forces, we should wonder, resulted in the home that they occupied becoming memorialized as a place of meaning? Furthermore, within an America that remains bitterly divided over the competing narratives we tell ourselves about our national story—and likewise, the identities and belief systems we forge out of that contested past—what can we learn by attempting to reconcile the competing versions of this one micro-history?

Ultimately, the book moves toward those questions by laying out a multigenerational story that I have become convinced is, for all its hyperlocal qualities, a "quintessential[ly] American" one.* It is so not only because of the themes and plot points that frame the narrative itself—a tale of western migration, consuming commercial ambition, and evangelical fervor; of the decline of tobacco, the rise of King Cotton, and the impact of those macrolevel forces on specific people; of trauma, exploitation, and untimely death; of agency, survival, and hope; of family and community bonds forged and then broken through forced separations, kidnappings, and sales; of domestic confrontations, contentious litigation, and a bloody family feud; of civil war and the breakdown of a slavery-based society; of resistance and emancipation; of political advances, political defeats, and the rise of mob violence (and coursing through all those things, the opposing forces of white supremacy and Black resilience)—but also because of the specific way that the full drama and scope of this narrative remained buried and ignored for so very long. The reasons behind the omissions are many. But the root cause, I contend, has to do with the deeply rooted American compulsion, manifested in this case through Ellen Davies-Rodgers and the historic site she created, to build our histories on the soft stuff of false nostalgia, rather than on harder foundations of unblinking truth.

This claim notwithstanding, I should go ahead and stress here that this is not a project that has been structured around academic arguments

---

* My use of "quintessential[ly] American" in this context is inspired by the writings of Lonnie G. Bunch III, the secretary of the Smithsonian, who has stressed the role that museums and historic sites have to play in "centraliz[ing]" African American historical narratives in ways that are "ripe with meaning, ambiguity, and complexity." In his essay "'All the Day, Every Day': Reflections on Thirty Years of Interpreting African American History," Bunch continues on this point, writing: "Far too frequently the interpretation of African American history is still viewed as exotic, ancillary, or a necessary palliative that shows a commitment to, or at least, the recognition of an understood audience. Rather than being viewed as a separate but equal presentation, the interpretation of this history, this culture must be seen as the quintessential American story: a history that profoundly shapes us all regardless of race or religion."

about the institution of slavery or the shifting interpretation strategies happening today at many plantation museums and historic sites around the country. Nor have I aimed to write a monograph-style case study focused primarily on the economic, social, and political conditions that dictated life in the communities inhabited by the Davieses and the people they enslaved. The book *does* speak to those things, and it's my sincere hope that scholars of Tennessee and Southern history will find the text revealing and useful. At bottom, though, I have taken an approach that emphasizes a blend of journalistic-oriented inquiry, genealogical excavation, and narrative writing intended to keep readers engaged. I wanted to see just how far the disparate and largely untapped paper trail connected to this one site's history could be followed, and what would happen when those findings were combined into a coherent story arc. In that sense, I wanted to juxtapose the story that revealed itself to me with the story as it has traditionally been told. Similarly, I wanted to expand the narrative lens where appropriate and connect the Davies family and the Black families around it to the larger historical events that dramatically impacted their lives. Just as importantly, I wanted to also call attention to the omissions in the evidentiary record, believing that those places—"the unnervingly silent gaps," to quote from the historian Tiya Miles—have a great deal to say in and of themselves about the evils of slavery and the tragically lopsided nature of American history that has been passed down to us as a result. Finally, at the most basic level, I simply wanted to do justice to a story that increasingly captivated and surprised me the more time I spent digging into it.[20]

All that being said, there is a straightforward but no less important assertion that undergirds the text: an objectively true accounting of the Davies family's story and the historic site created in their name *must* be one that is interwoven with narratives about the generations of African Americans who were intrinsically connected to the Davieses' experience. Said another way, this book seeks to make it clear that it was only through the intergenerational exploitation of Black people's bodies and labor that the Davies family managed to create and hold the intergenerational wealth and influence that they did. This point bears repeating: the institution of slavery, and later, the exploitative forces driving sharecropping and low-wage farm and domestic labor, were by no means peripheral to the Davieses' experience. Rather, and contrary to all that

Davies-Rodgers wrote, those forces were foundational, elemental—a defining thread woven throughout from beginning to end.

Ellen Davies-Rodgers was the sort of person who liked to employ her own distinctive sayings in her daily life. One of her favorites had to do with her passion for studying the past. "If you don't like history, you don't like yourself.... Each of us is history," she often said. Taking her at her word then, I have tried to tell as deeply researched and authoritative a story as possible about five consecutive generations of her own family. The main thrust of the book's narrative, I should be clear, is a corrective history of the Davieses themselves—and one that aims to accurately situate their reliance on enslaved labor at the forefront of their experience rather than at the margins. The book also follows the family beyond the Civil War, in the process tapping into newly discovered materials that reveal specific ways the legacies of slavery and white supremacy continued to manifest on and around their estate through the late nineteenth and early twentieth centuries. At the same time, the book aims to bring out of the shadows all that has been learned thus far about the generations of people whom the Davieses enslaved between the late 1700s and 1865. These flesh and blood people were not simply "slaves" whose experiences should be reduced to the condition that bound them. Instead, they lived lives that were complex and full of meaning, deserving of our efforts in the present, however fragmentary and incomplete those efforts might be, to sit with and reimagine them.

With respect to the latter goal, it is crucial to acknowledge that I have relied on records left behind by enslavers, government officials, census enumerators, and newspaper correspondents—by everyone, in other words, except the enslaved people in question themselves. At points in the book, I have incorporated the scholarship of historians whose groundbreaking work has unlocked new means for getting beyond the traditional archive and inhabiting enslaved people's perspectives—for moving away from the "external values" that their society placed on them as "property" and toward their "soul values," to borrow terminology from Daina Ramey Berry. I make no claim to have fully succeeded on this front, however, nor to have moved fully beyond the limitations of the especially obscure source material that guided the concept for this particular project and the large cast of specific people it attempts to follow. Likewise, the information presented in these pages on enslaved individuals and families should be understood more as beginning points and bridges to new knowledge rather than definitive. My greatest hope is that the biographical sketches of bondspeople pieced together in the book can help inform further interpretation of their experiences, as well as new genealogical discoveries by their descendants.[21]

INTRODUCTION

Omitted in Mass

By the early 1920s, when he finally retired from his long career as a rural physician, Dr. William Little Davies had sealed his reputation as a man who showed a distinct "kindliness . . . for the unfortunate and suffering." Davies, known by family and friends as Will, or Dr. Will, had spent his entire career caring for the people who lived in and around the adjacent rural communities of Brunswick and Morning Sun. Though located less than thirty miles northeast of Memphis, these two isolated hamlets were sparsely populated places that offered limited services—access to formally trained physicians like Davies among them. Although Davies regularly treated patients out of his two-story log home, he also made it his business to venture out on house calls through the "vast area" of the surrounding countryside; by doing so, he earned praise for being "a splendid example of the old type of Southern family physician now rapidly disappearing."[1]

The people Davies treated comprised a diverse lot that spanned the full spectrum of his society. They included the families of poor white tenant farmers and middle-class merchants. Other patients hailed from the wealthiest and most prominent local families. Like Davies himself, they were almost all either landowning cotton planters, or the children and grandchildren of landowning cotton planters, whose roots in the county dated to the antebellum period. Having originally built their wealth through commercial cotton production powered by enslaved labor, these families had continued to farm sprawling tracts of land after the Civil War, primarily utilizing sharecropping arrangements with freed-people and their descendants. African American farmers, field hands, domestic workers, and their extended families constituted the other segment of

Davies's patient base. Quite a few of these patients, and their descendants, had once been enslaved by the doctor's own father and uncle on the plantation that James and Logan Davies had jointly established in 1851. Although some formerly enslaved people and their families had come to own small farms in the decades after emancipation, most had remained deeply impoverished, struggling year in and year out to simply stay out of debt to white landowners—much less earn enough income to pay for regular medical care. In summary then, like many country doctors of his time, Dr. Will Davies's practice was "semi-lucrative" but by no means a source of great wealth. The wealth that he did possess, rather, came primarily through his inherited landholdings.[2]

Davies had not chosen his practice location without some inner conflict about it. Early on in his career, after returning to Morning Sun from medical school in Nashville, he had given real thought to starting over somewhere more lucrative. He debated Arkansas, where he had contacts, and at one point corresponded with a surgeon friend in Kentucky who told Davies he was "discouraged" to see him persist in a place that offered "so little compensation." During this same period, Davies spent close to half a year doing postgraduate work in New York City. The city must have been an intoxicating experience for the young Tennessee doctor; afterward, he briefly speculated about a relocation to Manhattan. Ultimately, however, he decided to remain in the place he knew best, in the process earning an important place in the memories of early twentieth-century residents of Brunswick and Morning Sun.[3]

A handsome, slightly built man whose inquisitive eyes indicated a deep well of feelings, Davies certainly possessed the ability to charm. Yet he also had an eccentric side—a "prolific imagination, quite visionary," he himself admitted—that set him apart to some degree from the more conservative elements of his society. This side of his personality seems to have contributed to a certain restlessness in his personal life. Throughout his twenties and thirties, Davies took full advantage of the bachelor lifestyle. He regularly attended picnics and dances, dated a number of "lovely ladies," and, when visiting Memphis, liked to stay at Duffy's European Hotel, a fashionable establishment that offered plenty of chances to socialize and meet women.[4]

Davies appeared ready to settle down for a brief period in the 1880s when he asked a woman named Suzy Gardiner for her hand in marriage.

Yet not long after the engagement began Davies broke things off, telling his fiancée that he was "mentally, physically, and financially a wreck." Although the explanation may have been truthful enough, it is also possible that other factors were at play. Years later, the doctor's younger cousin Ellen Davies-Rodgers would recall that Will had become "displeased and disturbed" by his bride-to-be's overzealous interest in his finances. Especially off-putting were Gardiner's apparent inquiries into the estate plan for the plantation land that Davies stood to inherit from his father James. Likewise, the doctor, being the "reserved gentleman that he was," decided to shoulder the blame for the breakup rather than bring matters to a head. Whatever the case may have been, the failed courtship hardly encouraged Davies to pursue the path of marriage and children. Instead, he passed into middle age, then beyond, resigned to his existence as a "lonely old bachelor," as some in his family only half-jokingly called him.[5]

If going it alone through life troubled him, he left no surviving record of such. More likely, bachelorhood suited him, providing him ample time and space to pursue his eclectic interests. A voracious reader, he devoured everything from newspapers and medical journals to poetry, novels, and works of philosophy. During his visits to Memphis, or when travelling to cities like New Orleans and Cincinnati, he attended theater. In a similar vein, music and radio became passions, leading him to follow the latest technological innovations of the day. Davies also maintained an extensive correspondence, penning wide-ranging letters that his recipients found "highly interesting." Writing an old friend or extended relative, Davies might veer from local politics in one sentence to the wonders of nature in the next. With colleagues he shared medical industry gossip and thoughts about the latest treatments for various ailments. And then there were matters related to history—maybe his favorite subject to think about and discuss.[6]

From an early age, Davies seems to have possessed a deep interest in the workings of the past. By at least the late 1870s, when he'd moved back home to begin his practice, he had become something of his family's unofficial historian. Along with saving business documents, correspondence, and other records of value, he interrogated older generations of his immediate and extended relatives about their knowledge of earlier times. So too did he pose questions to the African American community who worked on and around his family's estate.

Davies's own origin story, at least as he came to know it, could be traced as far back as his paternal great-grandfather (name unknown), who was said to have been a silversmith in Wales.* The historical picture from that point forward remained murky until a son of the silversmith, Zachariah Davis, emerged in the late eighteenth-century Virginia Southside.† There, in Lunenburg County, in the years preceding the Revolutionary War, Zachariah had married and begun a family with the daughter of a wealthier neighbor and slaveholding landowner. After the war, Zachariah became quite wealthy himself, buying and selling thousands of acres, raising cattle, and managing a thriving wheat and tobacco plantation powered by upward of two-dozen enslaved laborers at various points.[7]

Like countless other Anglo-American families of the time, the nineteenth century brought various members of the Davis clan into the Trans-Appalachian West. Among them were three of Zachariah's sons—including Dr. Will's grandfather, William Early Davis, who pursued dual careers as a Methodist minister and slaveholding planter and established successful plantations in both Middle and West Tennessee through the

---

* My interpretation of William Little Davies's knowledge about his family history comes from a holistic reading of his correspondence and notes in the DMA archives in conjunction with the "Hearts of Oak with Mortar" chapter in Davies-Rodgers's *Turns Again Home*. Although it is clear that Davies researched his great-grandfather Zachariah Davis at length and knew that he was a slaveholder, there is no evidence that he examined the legal and financial records in Lunenburg County that revealed the names and number of people Zachariah enslaved throughout his life. (These are the records that I have used to make the assertion about "upwards of two-dozen"—a subject that is given deeper consideration in Part I.) Picking up where her older cousin left off, Davies-Rodgers conducted even more extensive research into her great-great-grandfather, including travelling to Lunenburg County. Davies-Rodgers, like William Little Davies, certainly knew that Zachariah had enslaved people. However, neither did she explore the subject at any length. Furthermore, it should be noted that Davies did not provide citations for her sources in either *Turns Again Home* or *Along the Old Stage-Coach Road*.

† Between the mid-eighteenth century and the 1840s (and in some cases even after the 1840s) all known records of the Davies family employ the surname "Davis." For purposes of consistency, this narrative will use Davis until the early 1840s, the approximate time when Zachariah's descendants seem to have made a concerted effort to alter their surname to Davies.

antebellum period. In 1851, two of William Early's sons, Logan Early and James Baxter Davies, continued the family tradition when they established a plantation of their own in Morning Sun, Shelby County. Three years later, James married an orphaned girl named Almeda Little, and the following year, in the log home that he would eventually turn into a doctor's office and inherit, Will Davies entered the world.[8]

Such was the narrative that Davies made a concerted effort to preserve and pass down. Still, he remained keenly aware that a great deal about his family's past had slipped through the cracks of history. Once, in 1917, in the course of writing the genealogical editor at the *Richmond Times Dispatch* about a "Gordian knot" he was "endeavoring to untie," Davies expressed his disappointment that "we never heard from Virginia relatives after the postbellum period." These lost relatives, the doctor wrote, were "banished, either to other climes or extinct."[9]

But it wasn't just his own bloodline that drew his curiosity. The older Davies became, the more he engaged with the broader historical narrative of the Shelby County community that was so much a part of him. And nowhere could he do that more intimately than in local cemeteries— or as he called them, "scenes of repose." Wandering cemeteries allowed Davies to indulge in his "antiquarian propensity" to reflect on existential matters while also noting vital genealogical data—names, dates, epitaphs, symbols—etched into headstones and monuments. In Pleasant Hill Cemetery, in Brunswick, he studied the graves of the area's earliest settlers. A few miles south, in the cemetery attached to Morning Sun Cumberland Presbyterian Church, he commiserated over the graves of his late mother and father, and aunt and uncle. Buried there also were members of other planter families who had closely intersected with his own. Each of these clans—especially the Ecklin family, originally of North Carolina, and the Crenshaw, Feild, and Thurman families, all originally of Virginia—bore long-standing associations for Davies that were deeply bound to his own sense of identity.[10]

The final resting places of individuals his family had once enslaved interested him as well. A half mile west of Morning Sun, in the cemetery attached to Morning Grove Baptist Church, Davies walked among the gravesites of Wilcher and Mary Tucker, and their children—most of whom had originally been enslaved by his paternal grandparents. A short distance from the Tuckers were the plots containing the remains of one

Richmond Bennett and his family. Originally enslaved by the doctor's maternal grandfather, Richmond Bennett had passed into the control of James Davies through his marriage to Almeda. Later, after enduring most of the Civil War in the capacity of James's "body servant," Bennett had started a family of his own with one of Wilcher and Mary Tucker's daughters.[11]

But these deceased freed-people were only a fraction of those whom Davies's forebears had once held in bondage. Most former slaves, Davies knew, were buried on his own land in the "Davies Plantation Cemetery." Compared with Morning Grove, however, it was a less formal final resting place. Here, on the far southern boundary of Davies's landholdings, in a field scattered with trees, there were few if any headstones to document the basic evidence of people's lives. Instead, gentle depressions in the ground were typically the sole indications of the unknown men, women, and children buried below.[12]

In the years leading up to the Civil War, the plantation jointly owned by Logan and James Davies covered approximately eight hundred acres sandwiched between Morning Sun and Shelby Depot (the latter community was renamed Brunswick around 1880). From an acreage standpoint, it was a sizable, if not extraordinarily large, plantation relative to those owned by West Tennessee's "elite" class of planters. In terms of productivity, however, the Davies brothers undoubtedly ran a booming cotton operation. In early 1860, Logan and James recorded a total of eighty-six ginned bales—or roughly 34,400 pounds of cotton—that had been produced during the previous year's growing season; it was a figure that placed them in the top 10 percent of Shelby County's leading cotton producers. The approximately twenty-two people the brothers enslaved that year provided the raw power behind all that cotton.* Day after day, week after week, month after month, year after year, these individuals

---

* The twenty-two figure is drawn from the 1860 Shelby County Slave Schedule for Logan and James Davies. Those twenty-two people lived in five "slave houses" according to the same schedule's data. The Davies brothers' own plantation records from the following year would list the number of people they enslaved at twenty-six.

carried out the grinding labor necessary to wrench from the rich soil the cash crop that formed the bedrock of the brothers' wealth.[13]

Will Davies spent his earliest years immersed in this cotton-obsessed atmosphere built around enslaved labor. If we can imagine him as a young boy playing in the yard of his family's home, or walking to and from his first school with his older brother Gus Davies (perhaps accompanied by an enslaved caretaker), we can imagine just how frequently he must have interacted with bondspeople. By the time he was eight, the fundamental parameters of that world had changed with the demise of slavery. Yet his father's and uncle's plantation still relied—and would continue to rely—on the labor of Black sharecroppers and field hands, most of whom remained bound to the economic control of Logan and James in ways that were not dramatically removed from antebellum times. Such was the climate that formed Davies. And even as he made a career for himself in medicine and briefly left the plantation behind, such was the climate that he returned to and lived within for the rest of his life.

Davies did not leave behind writings that explicitly addressed his feelings about the legacy of slavery, or race relations more generally. Nevertheless, the surviving record does indicate that he reflected on these matters at length. Similarly, it is evident that he recognized the inextricable links between his family and certain Black families who had remained in the area long after emancipation. Along with his attention to the anonymous gravesites on his own family's land, Davies worked at various points to commemorate graves in Morning Grove. He became especially interested in memorializing the Black men who had been taken to the Civil War as "body servants." Beginning in 1916, when the seventy-two-year-old Richmond Bennett died, Davies began an annual ritual of placing flowers on Bennett's grave every Fourth of July. Davies also wrote about and attempted to recognize the gravesites of Randle Feild, Simon Crenshaw, Artie Ecklin, and Gabe Little—each of whom had been taken to the Civil War by other Morning Sun Confederates attached to the same infantry company as Davies's father. Late in life, when the doctor initiated an effort to place flags of both the Confederacy and the Union on the graves of these above-mentioned men every Memorial Day, he explained his reasoning as follows: "It is to be hoped that this the Old Morning Sun community is not oblivious of the kindly

8   THE REALMS OF OBLIVION

deeds and history of those interred in the Morning Grove Cemetery and will retain a personal attachment to whites as to colored."[14]

Judging by these sorts of actions, along with scattered evidence in other sources, Davies might be interpreted on the one hand as a man who held relatively forward-thinking views in his time. For instance, he wrote critically of the "provincialism and narrow-minded prejudice" that he observed around him. He also took pride that others considered him among the "broad-minded" and "progressive element of citizenship." On the other hand, Davies was very much a product of his era in the way that he romanticized the Old South world of his childhood. That lost society, he believed, was one that had been ruled by the "Southland's most chivalrous antebellum regime" and made better by the "loyal service" and "family attachments" of slaves. What he often yearned for, he wrote, was a "past oblivious to the present aggressions and progressive advances."[15]

Epitomizing some of the core contradictions and paternalism of his time, Davies could simultaneously acknowledge that the system of slavery had been doomed to fail while also viewing that same system through a wistful, almost bittersweet lens. To that end, he was a man who certainly seems to have adhered to the "Lost Cause" view of the war that had come to define so much of the collective historical memory within his generation. Along with holding prominent positions in the Sons of Confederate Veterans organization, he closely followed and financially supported the erection of statues around the South honoring heroes of the Confederacy. Within this context then, the doctor's interest in the subject of enslaved men in the Confederate Army assumes a more nuanced light: namely, as being part and parcel of a larger effort by ex-Confederates and their descendants to harness the narrative of "loyal" Black men happily serving Confederacy—the "Civil War's most persistent myth" one historian has called it—in order to soften understandings about the South's reasons for secession and setting off the war.[16]

Furthermore, there are still other clues about the doctor's perceptions about race—clues that are among the most troubling and difficult to decipher—that can be glimpsed in Davies's publicly stated support in the early 1890s for "one of the most remarkable instances of mob violence" in the history of the South, as one newspaper described the brutal lynching in Memphis of a Black man named Lee Walker. As this narrative will later examine, the circumstances leading to that particular lynching crime directly involved members of the doctor's own extended family and community.[17]

Taken in their entirety then, Dr. William Little Davies's historical footprints point toward a quite paradoxical figure on matters related to race. Davies's contradictions continued in another way as well: For all the "kindliness" that he showed others, for all his worldly interests and intellectual passions, he possessed a decidedly fatalistic streak. This streak seems to have become more prominent in the last years of his life. When Davies admitted to feeling haunted by mortality, when he wrote with sadness about the inexorable waves of time burying the "glory—the splendor of the past," when he mused about all those he'd once known who had "migrated to the realms of oblivion," it is evident that the darker shades of his personality were at hand.[18]

Davies officially retired from medicine at the age of sixty-three. But instead of slowing down, he devoted renewed energy to managing his farming interests across the more than six hundred acres he had inherited from his father. In 1924, when his brother Gus died, Davies inherited his late sibling's farm in Walls, Mississippi. He subsequently threw himself fully into commercial farming. He travelled regularly between his own estate and Walls, keeping tabs on the production schedules of sharecroppers and tenant farmers at both locations. On his way to and from Mississippi, he spent time in Memphis meeting with cotton factors, tracking his investments, and staying abreast of political developments. He had entered his twilight years as active and engaged as he'd ever been.[19]

Soon though, larger troubles arrived. By the late 1920s, Davies was dealing with worsening labor shortages on his farms. The economic picture darkened further in the fall of 1929 when the bottom fell out of Wall Street. Furthermore, his health was deteriorating. Along with a heart condition, he was slowed by rheumatoid arthritis, a condition that had also plagued his father.[20]

However much it must have pained him to witness his own body break down, it probably did not surprise him either. Davies, after all, was a man who had gained a lifetime of experience observing "the ravages of time" and "decrepitude" have their way with the human body. Surely then he understood that the forces at work inside him were inescapable.[21]

William Little Davies, date unknown. DMA Archives

An unidentified African American family stands on the porch of their home in this photo from the DMA Archives, likely taken in the late nineteenth century. "Our Plantation Miss," the only contextual information found on the image, gives reason to speculate that the family was photographed on the Walls, Mississippi, estate owned by Gus Davies, and later, William Little Davies. DMA Archives

An elderly William Little Davies sits outside his log home listening to a radio circa late 1920s. DMA Archives

Julius Augustus "Gus" Davies, older brother to William Little Davies, date unknown. DMA Archives

Monday, October 27, 1930, would turn out to be one of those days when Davies found himself wrestling with emotions of a heavy variety—the type that demanded to be worked out via pen and paper. Addressing a cousin in Virginia with whom he shared a close bond, he proceeded to scrawl out fourteen free-flowing pages that veered between rambling and coherent. More diary-like than actual letter, more philosophical in sections than concerned with the practical, the totality of what he penned on this fall day provided a revealing window into the psyche of the now seventy-three-year-old Davies.[22]

To be sure, not everything on his mind was depressing in nature. On the political front, he felt optimistic that the incumbent governor Henry Horton would secure a second term in the following week's elections. Davies also looked forward to serving as an elections' judge in the local contests—a tradition that had begun with his uncle Logan and continued with both him and his first cousin Gillie. The other subject he was happy to discuss was Gillie's twenty-six-year-old daughter Ellen. An early childhood education teacher at the West Tennessee State Teachers' College, Ellen had recently earned mention in Memphis newspapers for her lectures before teachers' associations. Will bragged that Ellen was fast becoming a woman of real standing in local society; her attendance at an "exquisite elaborate" dinner hosted the week prior by an "aristocratic" Memphis family offered a case in point.[23]

Yet more so than politics, or the pride he felt about his younger cousin's achievements, Davies acknowledged in his letter that he was feeling consumed by anxiety. Nearly a year had passed since the Great Crash on Wall Street, and though it had taken some time for the shockwaves to reach Tennessee, signs of widespread misery were now impossible to ignore. Bankruptcy announcements, he wrote, were being "mentioned in every daily paper." Just the week prior, that very fate had befallen Memphis's S. M. Williamson Investment Bank, "one of the most staunch firms in the city." Similarly, people were dealing with shuttered bus lines, railroad industry layoffs, and salary cuts across a range of other once stable professions.[24]

The economic pain had hit Davies on multiple fronts. With production levels down at the Walls property, he feared that his revenue that season would not even cover the farm's taxes. At his home estate, corn production was disappointing, one of his best mules had died, and low cotton prices and boll weevils were combining forces to wreak havoc on his leading cash crop. To make matters worse, he wrote, "Many negroes are now feeling a restless spirit, a characteristic trait developed in a disastrous crop year and wish to move on to some other farm." Davies continued by describing the "irresponsible" Black farmers whom he believed were only surviving "through the white man's sacrifice and assistance." Taken as a whole, he felt, "Problems of living [are] the feature of the day"—a situation that he feared was turning him into a "confirmed cynic, misanthrope and pessimist."[25]

But beyond his financial worries were even deeper, more esoteric anxieties. In a string of reflections related to death and impermanence, Davies dwelled at length upon the various tragedies that had befallen three formerly prominent Morning Sun-area families—the Feilds, the Crenshaws, and the Thurmans. Though they were once considered the leading "aristocratic families in this locality," Davies wrote, each of them had "disintegrated" beneath the weight of "tragic shadows." These shadows included deaths from disease and in the Civil War. There had been one death to suicide, and another to a gun accident rumored to be suicide. Other family members had suffered "domestic discord," "disastrous" business failures, and, in the case of a woman named Sallie Ecklin Thurman, death in an asylum. Yet another calamity had struck a sister of Sallie's, Charl Ecklin, whom Davies had dated in his younger days. Years later, long after their split, Charl had been struck and killed by a passing train in a freak accident when one of her feet became trapped in the tracks. "Not one of these names lives here now—dispersed or dead," he wrote.[26]

Davies recounted the bleakest chapters of these families' histories— histories that intimately overlapped with his own—as a way of emphasizing the fleeting nature of life. He marveled, for instance, that all evidence of people's well-lived lives—their "magnificent abode[s]" especially— could vanish so utterly into nothing but "corroding gullies" and "decrepit ruins." The precariousness of the physical past—or, as he put it, an understanding that "neglect must prevail"—clearly disturbed him. It was likely for this very reason that he had become so concerned with honoring the dead through monuments and headstones. Such commemoration might not last forever; but etchings in stone would at least allow a person's memory to survive a good long while. The idea of being laid to rest without any sort of marker bothered him greatly.[27]

On this point, Davies turned in his letter to a project that he had apparently been considering for quite some time: He told his cousin that he wanted to erect a stone memorial "in sentiments" to his family's former slaves and those people's descendants—the vast majority of whom had been "omitted in mass" through burials in anonymous graves. The cemetery where he intended to place this stone was located on the southern edge of his property on a hillside overlooking the old Memphis to Somerville Road. Davies knew that multiple generations of African American families had been buried there since at least 1855. He did not know exactly how many but he knew the figure was high.* As for the wording of the memorial itself, Davies now wanted a "revision of the original inscription contemplated." The specific changes he had in mind centered on the surnames that would appear on the stone. Instead of only acknowledging the people enslaved by his grandfather and father, he had decided that he should include mention of those people held in bondage by his maternal forebears also. Explaining his rationale, he wrote, "There are more descendants of the slaves bearing the names of our grandmothers families than those bearing our grandfather's names."[28]

After discussing a few additional semantic points about the memorial's inscription, Davies veered off in characteristic fashion to a range of other topics. But as he wrapped up the letter, he returned yet again to a matter related to historical memory. He had recently read an article by a well-known Tennessee politician praising the preservation of plantation homes in the city of Clarksville, northwest of Nashville. Some of the homes dated to the 1830s, and Davies, like the article's author, felt optimistic that this "town of culture and country" was preserving authentic glimpses of the pre-Civil War South. Davies loved the fact that Clarksville's "men of wealth and enterprise" had financed the restoration of homes with "broad piazzas" and "tall pillars." The city's "fidelity to antebellum architecture" had even extended to the decision to replace wire fences with split rail—a move intended to preserve fox hunting traditions.

---

* Writing about this same cemetery many years later, Ellen Davies-Rodgers would place the number at "probably fewer than a hundred unmarked graves."

"Recreating scenes of the Old South is the goal of this enterprise," he concluded.[29]

Interestingly—and revealing one more layer of his contradictory character—Davies had allowed his own nearly century-old home to fall into a state of disrepair even as he admired the distant preservation efforts in Clarksville. Why he had done so is unclear. Perhaps his financial struggles had contributed to the neglect. Or maybe Davies did not consider his residence especially worthy of preservation. For all its rustic charm, his log home was a humble structure compared to the grand plantation homes that he admired so much. But then again, it is hard to believe that Davies did not appreciate the significance of his residence. Just as he understood the power of a headstone etched with a name, he surely must have recognized all the stories contained within the hand-hewn walls of his birthplace.

The following May, less than a year after he penned his letter, Davies succumbed to myocarditis. Per his will, his home and surrounding agricultural holdings were bequeathed to Ellen. Under her hands, the story of the log house she named "Davies Manor" was in many ways just beginning to take shape. As for the land itself, it would remain a thriving farm, steadily expanding in size through the coming decades and reaching more than two thousand acres by the mid-twentieth century. Eventually, though, it would all be subsumed by modern development. Slowly at first, then quite rapidly, the Davies family's plantation, all the way out to the cemetery of unmarked African American graves, would be sold, built upon, and transformed into something irrevocably removed from its past.[30]

PART I
1700–1842

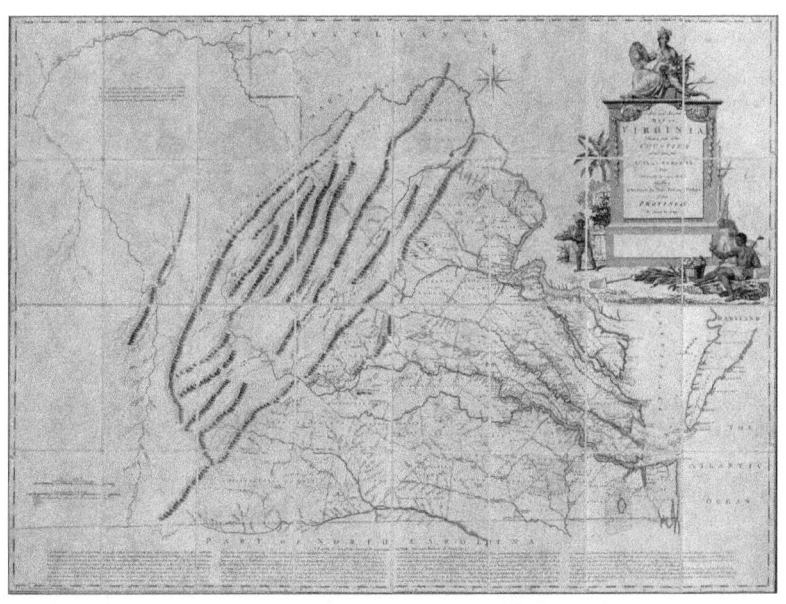

"A new and accurate map of Virginia wherein most of the counties are laid down from actual surveys. With a concise account of the number of inhabitants, the trade, soil, and produce of that Province," Thos. Jefferys, 1770. Library of Congress, Geography and Map Division

CHAPTER 1

The Southside

At the dawn of the eighteenth century, within Great Britain's Virginia colony, most of the English-speaking population remained concentrated in Tidewater communities surrounding the Chesapeake Bay and its tributaries. These coastal dwellers of the New World tended to view the interior Piedmont region to their immediate west as a "rude wilderness." The southernmost portion of the Piedmont frontier, or the "Southside" as it would eventually come to be known, remained an especially unsettled backcountry, encompassing some nine thousand square miles stretching between Fall Line of the James River and the base of the Blue Ridge Mountains. Although nearly a century had passed since the founding of Jamestown, the Southside's unique terrain—densely forested, hilly, and, most significantly, a river system full of shallow waterways that flowed not into the Chesapeake, but toward North Carolina's Albemarle Sound—meant that even the most intrepid settlers faced challenges that were "arduous in the extreme." By 1740, however, the region was finally beginning to attract a stream of settlers; most were poor Swiss, German, and Scotch-Irish immigrants who had been lured there by wealthy Tidewater land speculators. The entire Southside still encompassed just two counties, Prince George and Brunswick, but in 1746, the Virginia General Assembly carved out of the western side of Brunswick County a new entity they named Lunenburg County. Around this same year—and possibly occurring within the boundaries of this new county—a child named Zachariah Davis was born.[1]

Beyond a surviving family account that his father had worked as "a silversmith in Wales," almost nothing is known about Zachariah's parentage and formative years—including whether he was indeed born on the Virginia frontier or arrived there on his own as a young man. What can be confirmed is that a young Zachariah, in 1768, appeared as a witness for the routine surveying of land boundaries, or processioning, in Cumberland Parish, in the south-central section of Lunenburg County. Landless and still a bachelor, he lived on property owned by an older and much wealthier slaveholding tobacco planter named Charles Hamlin Jr. It was Hamlin who paid Zachariah's taxes, or tithes, at this stage. Though the exact connection between the two men is unclear, Zachariah most likely worked as an overseer on Hamlin's plantation.[2]

The relationships that Zachariah developed with Charles Hamlin Jr. and other nearby landowners seem to have played the single biggest role in his ability to begin making upward strides within his society. Around 1770, Zachariah married Diana Blackstone, one of the daughters of John Blackstone, a church sexton, landowner, and slaveholding neighbor of Hamlin's. Through this marriage, Zachariah acquired land from his new father-in-law. Although the size of the tract was not specified in records, the property was located very close to Hamlin's estate along a narrow waterway called Reedy Creek. Here, Zachariah and Diana began to establish their own family and farm. Their first child, Robert, was born in 1771; by 1776, two girls named Martha and Sarah had joined the household as well. Between those years, in 1773, Zachariah paid tithes for one enslaved individual over the age of sixteen. The following year he paid tithes for two bondspeople, both over sixteen. Extrapolating from later data, it is clear that these two individuals, named Peter and Brister, were the first people whom Zachariah enslaved. It is possible that Zachariah had gained enough of a financial foothold by this point that he managed to purchase Peter and Brister outright. Then again, just as Zachariah had acquired his first landholdings via a gift from his father-in-law, he may very well have come to enslave Peter and Brister in the same manner.[3]

Throughout the first half of the 1770s, as Zachariah transitioned from a landless, unmarried dependent into a slaveholding freeholder with a family of his own, British-America's troubled relationship with its mother country had passed the point of no return. The early events of the American Revolution were earth-shaking in their significance on a global scale. Yet the conflict at this stage existed on the periphery of the insular world inhabited by Zachariah and Diana Davis, their children, and the two men they enslaved. Though no longer a "rude wilderness," the Virginia Southside remained an isolated place where local concerns and day-to-day domestic issues took precedence over far-off political and military conflicts. To be sure, debates raged through the early 1770s in the Virginia colony's capital of Williamsburg. Very real tensions and occasional violence also emerged in remote interior areas as those who supported the cause of the "Patriots" clashed with British "Loyalists." Still, the shape and intensity of the turbulence in places like the Southside differed considerably from that which existed in the more settled and politically influential sections of Virginia.[4]

That all changed in 1776 when Thomas Jefferson and the Second Continental Congress drafted the Declaration of Independence. Afterward, even people from the most politically inactive and isolated counties began to "[come] to life." The men of Lunenburg County demonstrated a "quick and remarkable response." At least 61 percent of the 573 men eligible for military service volunteered in 1776 to fight the British. Some served as members of local militia companies that travelled great distances north to participate in the war. Others enlisted in one of the five companies from the county that became part of the regular Continental Army.[5]

It remains an open question whether Zachariah Davis was among the men from his county who fought in the American Revolution at one stage or another.* What is clear, according to records that do exist,

---

* Although Zachariah's great-great-granddaughter, Ellen Davies-Rodgers, would assert that he did serve in the conflict—and establish the Zachariah Davies Chapter of the Daughters of the American Revolution based upon that claim—the evidence supporting that assertion is circumspect since nowhere in Lunenburg County's surviving muster or payrolls does his name appear. Furthermore, the most up-to-date research has been unable to confirm that the "Zach Davis" referenced in Ellen Davies-Rodgers's original DAR chapter application (her source was a document from the Virginia State Library showing a "Zachary Davis" paid for wartime service) was one and the same with her great-great-grandfather. Regarding this open question, a number of points are worth noting: First, Davies-Rodgers was never aware that Zachariah had married Diana Blackstone; instead, she incorrectly identified her great-great-grandmother as one Diana Abernathy. Second, it is worth noting that nowhere in William Little Davies's surviving writings is it mentioned that Zachariah fought in the American Revolution. Third, Zachariah's wife gave birth to multiple children during the war years, and Zachariah himself made a number of land purchases at the time as well. On the other hand, it is also possible that Zachariah did in fact serve in the war and is simply not listed in the Lunenburg County muster rolls

is that Zachariah continued growing his family and making considerable investments in land throughout the Revolutionary War period. In 1779, the same year that Diana gave birth to the couple's fourth child, a son named William Early Davis, Zachariah purchased 565 acres on the south side of the Meherrin River. The tract was roughly ten miles south of his existing property along Reedy Creek, and marked his most aggressive land acquisition to date. Two years later, as the fighting front moved fully into Virginia, Zachariah was among the Lunenburg County freeholders recorded as furnishing supplies to support the Continental Army. In his case, he provided a beef cow "supposed to weigh four hundred pounds."[6]

In 1783, after eight long years, the Revolutionary War officially ended with the signing of the Treaty of Paris. Far away from those negotiations, on their estate along Reedy Creek, Zachariah and Diana had expanded their household to include a total of seven children. Peter and Brister (both of whom were definitively named for the first time in that year's tax records) remained enslaved on the farm as well. Though still a relatively modest-sized estate, it seems to have become a successful one, and Zachariah, assuming he was the sort to occasionally step back and take stock of his life, must have recognized that he had made significant strides since his bachelor days when he had depended upon Charles Hamlin Jr. for his livelihood. Now, having reached his late thirties, he could look toward the future knowing he was in prime position to capitalize on the thrilling opportunities available to white men of his station in life in the brand-new American republic.[7]

The American colonists' victory in the Revolutionary War produced breathtaking schisms in the social, political, and economic systems that had defined the rigid order of the monarchical-based world up to that point in history. For white, upwardly mobile, slaveholding freeholders like Zachariah Davis (and even for poorer classes of white men with-

---

due to the fact some of those records have been lost. For more on the county's incomplete Revolutionary War records, see John H. Wells, *Lunenburg's Unsung Heroes of the American Revolution: "A Peek Through a Door Barely Left Ajar!"* in the Ripberger Public Library local history room, Lunenburg County Public Library System, and "The Revolution" in Landon C. Bell's *The Old Free State*.

out land or slaves), the Declaration of Independence's assertions about equality and "unalienable rights" rang true in soul-stirring ways. Meanwhile, for Black people in America (as well as for women and Native American people), the core philosophical ideas underlying the new nation expressly did *not* apply. For Black people, of course, it was by no means "self-evident" that they possessed the "right to pursue life, liberty and happiness." Most of the leading founders were keenly aware that slavery represented an "embarrassing contradiction that violated all the principles the American Revolution claimed to stand for." However much the founders were trapped in the deeply racist assumptions of their era, most had also understood that they were making an enormous compromise by allowing the continuation of human bondage.[8]

Slavery's persistence through the nation's first years allowed the institution to thrive and expand in importance south of the Potomac River; and from here, seeping out of this southern portion of the infant republic, the reliance on forced human labor would spread west, metastasize, and corrode the moral underpinnings of the American experiment. In this sense then, the Revolution can be interpreted as an "extraordinary tale of monumental achievement" and "a tragedy of monumental proportions." It is a tale, in the words of the historian Joseph J. Ellis, that constitutes an "epic historical narrative that defies all moralist categories, a story line rooted in the coexistence of grace and sin, grandeur and failure, brilliance and blindness."[9]

Zachariah Davis's actions in the years following the Revolution poignantly illustrate how the core contradiction behind America's founding could manifest itself—and then pass down through the generations—as one single man, one single enslaver, pursued his own understanding of his natural rights through an ever-increasing acquisition of land, livestock, and bondspeople. The year 1785 was an important one in that respect as an enslaved woman named Nelly (who was at least sixteen) and a girl named Dilcey (under the age of sixteen) joined Peter and Brister at the Reedy Creek estate. Next, in 1788, Zachariah significantly increased his landholdings when he purchased 850 acres adjacent to his existing property from one of the sons of the now deceased Charles Hamlin Jr. A short time later, Zachariah sold for a profit the Meherrin River acreage that he had purchased a decade earlier. A few years after these moves, in 1792, he obtained additional acreage totaling nearly 1,500 acres in an area of the county further east of his primary Reedy Creek holdings. All the while, the community of people he enslaved had continued to grow. Childbirth on his estate (and possibly his inheritance of people) constituted the primary means that the enslaved population increased; but Zachariah may also have purchased and/or sold one or more people during this period. By 1794, what is certain is that Zachariah enslaved at least nine people and owned approximately 2,270 acres that he described then as his "mannor plantation."[10]

It is at this juncture that the names of these nine men, women, and children appear in a record. The "deed of trust" document that listed these people's identities was penned by Zachariah on February 13, 1794, after he had become concerned about his "health and constitution declining" and his "age advancing on." Rather than writing a final will with specific instructions for his children's inheritance, Zachariah had executed a deed that appointed two local men to act as trustees of his estate in the event both he and Diana died. The trustees' task, under such as scenario, would be to value and distribute to Zachariah's children his land, livestock, and tools, as well as "all the slaves" and "all their future increase."[11]

The individuals named in the trust were as follows: two men, Brister and Sampson; three women, Nelly, Dilcey, and Grace; and four children, Tom, Tabb, Hannah, and Nancy. As for Peter (the man who, along with Brister, had been enslaved by Zachariah since before the Revolution), his absence in the trust document indicates that he either died, escaped, or was sold prior to 1794. By examining the basic identities and age categories of these above nine people alongside data that emerges in later legal and estate records, it becomes possible to begin drawing ideas about their connections. For example, it as a good possibility that Sampson had entered the enslaved community at Reedy Creek in the late 1780s or early 1790s, perhaps through a purchase by Zachariah, and formed a union with Nelly. In subsequent years, Nelly would give birth to a daughter named Jinny (and almost certainly other children as well). Future estate and legal records also confirm that the four children mentioned in the 1794 trust had all been birthed by either Nelly or Dilcey or Grace (or a combination of the women). Such evidence, however sparse it might be, at least makes it possible to form speculative pictures about these people's family relationships. What we can know with certainty is that the enslaved population at Zachariah's estate had evolved from two people (Peter and Brister) in 1774, to four (Peter, Brister, Nelly and Dilcey) in 1785, to nine (Brister, Nelly, Dilcey, Sampson, Grace, Tom, Tabb, Hannah, and Nancy) in 1794.[12]

From a legal standpoint, the deed of trust that Zachariah executed in February 1794 was not an uncommon way to handle estate matters. But what was notable about Zachariah's trust was the degree of vagueness it allowed when it came to the subject of how the enslaved community on his estate should be treated upon his death. Leaving all the particulars in the hands of the trustees, the document simply stated that each of Zachariah's three daughters should be allowed to "have a choice negro each to be taken in rotation according to age." The document went on to say that the rest of the slaves, along with their children, or "increase" (both living children and those that had yet to be born), should be "equally divided" among the rest of Zachariah's offspring.[13]

Though he could not have anticipated it then, Zachariah's hands-off approach in 1794 would cause him a great deal of trouble decades later when a man by the name of Joel Neal married into the family. Neal, it turned out, had his own ideas about the people he believed he should rightfully inherit through his father-in-law. Eventually, in an effort to diffuse the threat this wayward son-in-law posed, Zachariah would pen a final will intended to nullify the earlier deed of trust, and, at least in theory, clarify the "personal property" that he wanted his children to inherit. By doing so, he hoped to ward off estate disputes breaking out after his death. What neither the trust nor the final will ever took into account, however, was any consideration of the enslaved community's most fundamental concern: that even within the parameters of bondage, they might somehow keep their family units intact.[14]

CHAPTER 2

God, Grace and Child, and Wonder

Judging by the surviving evidence, scant indications exist that Zachariah Davies harbored notions about enslaved people, or the institution of slavery, that would have been considered out of step from those of his Southside contemporaries. On the contrary, all signs point toward him understanding his relationship to the people he enslaved in ways that were entirely in line with the legal system, economy, and dominant social norms of his time and place. Like so many slaveholders, in other words, he seems to have viewed his human "property" primarily, if not exclusively, through a matter-of-fact commercial lens. His disregard for the separation of enslaved families is a key indication of his lack of attention to Black people's humanity. It wasn't only that he failed to consider the *future* separations that were inherent in the terms of both his 1794 deed of trust and, later, his final will; Zachariah, in the years *between* his execution of those legal instruments, explicitly and repeatedly caused separations. He did so, time and again, by "advancing" bondspeople—children in most cases—to his adult sons and daughters. For example, in two separate instances, when his daughters married, Zachariah contributed a young enslaved girl as a wedding gift. In four additional instances, he advanced a young bondsperson (and in one case, a woman and her child) to each of his sons who were in the process of migrating out of Virginia. Regardless of the context and circumstances behind these decisions, each one would have resulted in wrenching sorrow for the enslaved individuals and families affected.[1]

Given Zachariah's track record in this regard, it is natural to wonder how his own life path—in particular, his ambitious nature and ability to rise in relatively rapid fashion from a dependent to a wealthy freeholder—may have influenced his convictions about enslaved people or the institution of slavery more generally. In his younger days, working for Charles Hamlin Jr., he would have had the responsibility of managing and disciplining the community of approximately twenty people whom Hamlin enslaved. As Zachariah observed Hamlin and learned from the older man, he probably took for granted the idea that he would have to become a slaveholder himself to achieve his goals. Once Zachariah married into the well-to-do Blackstone family and successfully made that transition, he spent the rest of his adult life pursuing an expansion of his capital through both land acquisitions and slaveholdings. For Zachariah, in other words, the parameters of his own freedom (a concept of freedom that rested in every way on his *not* being dependent) increased proportionally according to the extent to which he denied others their freedom.

The day-to-day realities of running a thriving tobacco, cattle, and wheat farm would have exposed Zachariah to plenty of human suffering, and it is not hard to imagine him being a hardened or emotionally removed sort of man. In a backwater region like Lunenburg County, in an age of primitive medicine, heads of households like Zachariah were often expected to deal dispassionately with the business of death. In one case in 1809, for example, Zachariah was one of twelve men summoned by the county coroner "to say how" an enslaved woman named Cloe had come to be found "lying dead at the house of Henry Astrop," a neighbor of the Davis family. Zachariah and his fellow witnesses, being "good and honest men," made the determination that Cloe had died "by an accident in an affray" with another enslaved woman at Astrop's estate.[2]

Familiarity with death is revealed also in a letter that Zachariah wrote in 1821 to his oldest son Robert, who by that point had moved to Middle Tennessee and become a well-known Methodist minister. In his letter, as he mentioned a bout of illness that had ravaged his Reedy Creek estate the previous fall, Zachariah broke the news that Diana had died. "I had a very sick family last year and lost your mother," he told

Robert matter-of-factly. Then Zachariah continued, writing, "I lost five Negroes, Brister, Richard, Vilet, Charles, Rody, the hole family was sick but we have all got about again, thanks be to the Almighty God for the Blessing."[3]

The letter's brevity and absence of emotion offer clues about Zachariah's personality. Most significantly, though, the letter provides the approximate death dates of five enslaved people—biographical data points that in each instance would otherwise be lost. Beyond the appearance of their names in this one letter, nothing at all can be confirmed about Richard, Vilet, Charles, or Rody. As has already been discussed, however, we do know that Brister (along with Peter) was one of the two original members of the Black community at the Reedy Creek estate, going back to 1774, when he was at least sixteen years old. Likewise, even if it is not possible to remap with certainty Brister's family tree (the strongest likelihood is that he married or formed a child-bearing union with either Dilcy or Grace), we can know that his death in 1820, when he was probably in his late sixties, must have devastated the larger Black community at Zachariah's plantation. And of course, it would have especially impacted those who were related to Brister by blood. Reading between the lines of Zachariah's letter,* it is certainly possible that Richard, Vilet, Charles, and Rody were among Brister's children or grandchildren.[4]

There is also the complicated matter of the relationships and feelings that existed between Brister and Zachariah, and the other members of the Davis family. Despite the emotional neutrality in Zachariah's letter, we have to wonder how and to what extent Brister's death impacted the larger Davis household. Did the family genuinely mourn this man who they had held in bondage for the better part of five decades? Or might Brister's death have been viewed more in terms of simply being an unfortunate event? Or, further along that spectrum, is it possible that Zachariah shrugged off the loss of Brister in the same way that he seems to have casually disregarded the trauma he wrought

---

* On the one hand, Zachariah's use of "hole family" in his 1821 letter seems to refer to Brister, Vilet, Charles, and Rody as being a family unit. However, due to the fact Zachariah mentioned his wife's death in the same letter and also used "we," it is possible to interpret his use of "hole family" as being a broader reference to his estate's community as a whole.

by repeatedly forcing family separations? Such questions, even if they could be researched, would probably not lead to dichotomous answers. Slavery, after all, was nothing if not an "exceedingly complicated web of relationships" where "violence and oppression ran parallel to affection and dependency."[5]

Finally, there are questions that emerge related to the all-encompassing role that Christianity played within the Davis family. Similarly, we should consider the fundamental role that the divergent understandings of Protestant Christianity played in the structure and shape of Virginia society more broadly. By following threads related to the leading theological conflicts of Zachariah's day—and just as importantly, the interplay between those conflicts and Lunenburg County's economic, social, and political realities—additional possibilities emerge about the atmosphere that Brister, Richard, Vilet, Charles, Rody and the rest of the enslaved community living along Reedy Creek experienced as they moved through their days.

Between the mid-1700s and the outbreak of the Revolutionary War, a distinct split had opened in Virginia between the traditional Anglican church and emerging evangelical denominations. The Anglicans, who embodied the gentry culture (such as it was in Lunenburg County) and dominated the ranks of local government, espoused a society where church and government were fundamentally linked. Continuing traditions born of the Church of England, the Anglicans based their religious practices and day-to-day lives around formal hierarchies of vestryman, churchwardens, and sextons—all of whom were viewed as being crucial conduits to a higher authority. The evangelical denominations, on the other hand (with varying degrees of conviction), explicitly rejected those same hierarchies and accompanying religious styles and value-systems. Instead, they were motivated by "a leveling spirit" that emphasized the "self-abasement of clergy and congregants alike," and the pursuit of unfiltered relationships between God and man. What this often meant, in the practical context of business and social relations, was intense mutual disdain between Anglicans and the anti-establishment evangelical "dissenters" who believed governmental authorities had no business meddling in their worship practices.[6]

The Davis family, evidence shows, were firmly in the latter camp. To be more specific, the family (or initially, at least Diana) are believed to have been members of a distinctive community of Separate Baptists. It is significant that in 1774 a "Dianna Davis" appears in the baptism records for the Meherrin Baptist Church. This church, founded in 1771, constituted the first Baptist congregation in Lunenburg County. To the county's Anglican establishment, Meherrin's members were considered radical evangelicals who "threaten[ed] the subversion of True Religion." Later, Meherrin would be recognized in a wider context by religious historians as having played a "significant role in one of the great episodes of Baptist history in young America—the rise of the Separate Baptists and their influence in Virginia."[7]

In 1775, with its membership growing, Meherrin served as the mother church for a breakaway congregation named Reedy Creek Baptist Church. This latter congregation met in a building near the waterway for which it was named—and in close proximity to Zachariah and Diana's estate, situated a few miles south of the recently relocated county seat. Indeed, a separate record from Meherrin confirms that the same Dianna Davis baptized in 1774 was among the twenty-one female members given permission to form the breakaway "distinct church" a year later. Unfortunately, the Reedy Creek records have mostly disappeared, making it difficult to confirm with certainty the Davis family's membership. It is also true that Zachariah's name does not appear in the Meherrin records, leaving it something of an open question if the "Dianna Davis" listed was one and the same with his wife. One explanation, however, is that Diana had joined the mother church independently of her husband—and prior to his conversion or decision to officially become a member of the splinter congregation. This possibility is supported by the fact that Meherrin Baptist Church, like Reedy Creek, embraced a radically inclusive atmosphere relative to the time: in addition to allowing women to become full-fledged members, both congregations accepted enslaved men and women into their ranks. Indeed, on the same day that Dianna Davis was baptized, two enslaved people also received their rites of baptism. Their names, Sarah and Reubin, were listed in the Meherrin records as "Patterson's Sarah" and "Neal's Reubin."[8]

Much of the antipathy that developed between the Anglican gentry and Lunenburg County evangelicals stemmed directly from these interracial gatherings that the Meherrin and Reedy Creek Baptists encouraged—gatherings that would have been impossible to conceive under different contexts. Assuming Zachariah and Diana Davis were indeed members of these sister congregations, they would have regularly joined Black people in worship, baptism, and the confession of sins. To be sure, Separate Baptists were by no means social reformers committed to abolition or anything approaching general equality for the enslaved. Yet the relative openness of Lunenburg's Separate Baptists to fostering a biracial religious community was not insignificant. Within the Southside, a society where "masters were free to mete out punishment to slaves or break up slave families without interference from others in the community," the presence of the Meherrin and Reedy Creek churches would have provided enslaved people with a heightened ability to find through religion some relief from their conditions on earth.[9]

As leading scholars of African American religious history like Albert Raboteau have emphasized in their writings, the experiences stemming from religious worship and conversion provided many bondspeople "with a sense of individual value and personal vocation which contradicted the devaluing and dehumanizing forces of slavery." According to Raboteau, "That some slaves maintained their identity as persons, despite a system bent on reducing them to a subhuman level, was certainly due in part to their religious life. In the midst of slavery, religion was for slaves a space of meaning, freedom and transcendence." To continue this thread, we might also return to the scholarship of Daina Ramey Berry, who has charted in harrowing detail the chasm that so often existed between enslaved people's *internal* values—or their "soul values" as she has termed bondspeople's conceptions of their own self-worth and spiritual lives—and the *external*, commodified values that enslavers placed on their bodies at every moment between the womb and the grave. According to Berry, Black people's soul values were "enriched through an inner spiritual centering that facilitated survival." This centering, she goes on to say, might be facilitated through a variety of mediums, including "a spirit, a voice, a vision, a premonition, a sermon, an ancestor, (a) God. It came in public and private settings and was occasionally described as a personal message from a higher being, a heaviness in the core of their bodies. . . . This telling, this uplifting, this singing of a 'fearful trill, of things unknown but longed for still' made the enslaved feel free during captivity."[10]

Additional evidence that the Davis family were committed evangelicals emerges in different contexts in the post-Revolutionary years. For instance, in 1785, Zachariah joined seventy-five men from Lunenburg County who signed a petition to the Virginia General Assembly seeking to reaffirm the separateness of religious and earthly concerns. The petition campaign, which was spearheaded by Lunenburg's Separate Baptists, came in the middle of bitter debates throughout Virginia over the question of "disestablishing" Anglicanism from the state government. The following year, the legislature finally took action that aligned with the wishes of Zachariah and his fellow petitioners, formally passing "The Virginia Statute for Religious Freedom." Drafted by Thomas Jefferson, the bill paved the way for the widespread acceptance of religious pluralism in Virginia and the nation more broadly.[11]

The year 1785 also marked a notable moment in the debates over slavery that were then raging through Virginia. To the horror of many slaveholders, a segment of the newest evangelical denomination, the Methodists, were going even further than the Separate Baptists and issuing outright condemnations of slavery. So too were Quakers increasingly attacking the institution. Given Zachariah's stated support for disestablishment, he probably followed, and may have directly participated in, the related debates about evangelicals' role in a slaveholding society. In Lunenburg and surrounding Southside counties, particularly impassioned defenses of slavery emerged in reaction to the anti-slavery campaign being waged by the Quakers and leading Methodist preachers like Thomas Coke and Francis Asbury. Slaveholders felt outraged that prominent Methodists like Asbury were supporting gradual emancipation efforts, as well as the liberalization of Virginia's manumission laws. In November, seeking to take the teeth out of the anti-slavery campaign, 161 men from Lunenburg County—Zachariah's wealthy neighbor and original employer, Charles Hamlin, Jr. among them—signed a petition that made their position clear to the General Assembly. The petition stated that Methodists' support for emancipation represented a "flagrant Contempt of the constitutional powers of the Commonwealth." The petitioners declared that they had "seald with our Blood, a Title to the full, free, and absolute Enjoyment of every species of our Property, whensoever, or however legally acquired." Then, in fever-pitched rhetoric, they predicted that emancipation would lead to "Want, Poverty, Distress & Ruin" as well as "the Horrors of all the Rapes, Robberies, Murders, and Outrages, which an innumerable Host of unprincipled, unpropertied, vindictive, and remorseless Banditti are capable of perpetrating."[12]

It is notable that Zachariah's name does not appear on this petition alongside so many men that he knew. Yet the absence of his signature by no means indicates that he supported anti-slavery sentiments. It is intriguing to wonder then how exactly Zachariah and his family understood their evangelical beliefs—and along with those beliefs, the anti-slavery positions of evangelical leaders like Asbury—in juxtaposition to the staunchly pro-slavery proclamations that Charles Hamlin Jr. and his fellow petitioners signed. One possible clue can be glimpsed in a high-profile visit Zachariah received some years later from Asbury himself.[13]

Francis Asbury, known as the "Father of American Methodism," relentlessly travelled eastern America during the late eighteenth and early nineteenth centuries. Preaching anywhere he could reach a crowd—courthouses, tobacco houses, fields, private homes, and public squares—he gained fame for giving more than ten thousand sermons and ordaining some seven hundred clergy. Under his leadership, the Methodist presence in America grew from fewer than one thousand members in 1771 to more than two hundred thousand in 1816.[14]

On Friday, November 23, 1804, as Asbury was heading south through Lunenburg County toward the Carolinas, he stopped and stayed the night in Zachariah's home. As Asbury himself briefly recorded in his journal, "We came to Zachariah Davis's, near Lunenburg Courthouse. On Saturday, we crossed the Meherrin at Saffold's bridge." Though no other context is provided, leaving the particulars of the encounter unclear, there is a likely explanation as to why Asbury spent the night at the Davis family's Reedy Creek estate. By 1804, Zachariah's eldest son Robert was making a name for himself as a circuit riding Methodist preacher near Nashville. Zachariah's second eldest son, William

Early Davis, had also become a Methodist preacher. Though William had preached in an unofficial capacity since at least 1801, he received his ministerial license from the Methodist Episcopal Church in September 1803—just a year before Asbury's visit—and embarked on a circuit-riding ministry in the counties west of Lunenburg. It is quite possible then that Asbury, having become aware of the young Davis brothers and their ministries, decided he would pay a friendly visit to their father as he travelled through the area. (It is also possible that William himself was present for the meeting and went unmentioned by Asbury). Drawing any sort of a conclusive takeaway about Zachariah or the Davis family more broadly based on this one event is difficult. But at the very least we can assume that Zachariah—and most certainly his two sons who had become Methodist ministers—would have been exposed to, and probably interacted closely with, the leading religious figures of their day who harbored no love for slavery.[15]

Wherever his views may have fallen between the spectrum of vocal anti-slavery critics like Asbury on the one hand, and the staunchly pro-slavery Lunenburg petitioners on the other, Zachariah was clearly a man who placed his faith in God at the very center of his worldview. The most explicit proof of his evangelical faith emerges in the letters that he penned to both Robert and William after they had begun their ministries. Writing in 1804 to William, who was then preaching in Amelia County, Virginia, Zachariah opened with the news that despite some sickness in the family, they were enjoying a "tolerable state of health." For this, he "returned God thanks for his unspeakable favours and blessings that we daily enjoy while we remain in the land among the living." He then told William, "Go on my son and discharge your duty to God and man, labour faithfully in god's vinyard and you will wear a Crown, a Starry Crown of Glory—Oh that you may be wise to win souls to Jesus Christ Our Savior."* Almost two decades later, in another letter laced with fervent religious language, Zachariah would relay to William (who by this point had joined Robert in Tennessee) his disappointment that in Lunenburg County "religion is very idle." Still, he was pleased to hear of "very considerable revivals in various directions." He continued,

---

* Historical documents frequently contain variant or outdated spellings; I will be quoting them exactly as written, including reproducing those variant spellings.

writing, "I hope they will spread till we come under their influence. Different denominations appear more friendly toward each other than common."[16]

The Davises were undoubtedly deeply influenced by the "extraordinary religious phenomenon" sweeping the country through the early nineteenth century—the Second Great Awakening. Similarly, the forces of evangelism must have influenced life within the enslaved community at the Reedy Creek estate. How exactly that community reconciled the juxtaposition between their earthly plight and the spiritual tenets that Zachariah, Diana, and their two preacher sons espoused is unclear. So also is the extent to which the enslaved community may have worked to reconcile African-based religious traditions and beliefs with those of their enslavers' evangelical Protestantism.[17]

In October 1801, when Zachariah's eldest son Robert set out for Tennessee with his wife Eleanor and their two young children (although Robert did enslave people in Tennessee, it is not clear that he took bondspeople with him on this initial journey west), he did so at a time when the exodus of Anglo-Americans out of Virginia and other Seaboard states had reached a "stunning magnitude." The forces driving the tide of settlers into the Trans-Appalachian Southwestern frontier were numerous, having multiplied with each passing year since the Revolutionary War's conclusion. Ongoing ambiguities about jurisdiction in western lands was one factor that created openings for many people to migrate. With the British gone from the continent, and America's southern and western boundaries up for grabs, the fledgling federal government had found itself jockeying with the newly established states of North Carolina and Georgia over land claims in the sprawling territories of Tennessee, Kentucky, and eventually, Mississippi. Meanwhile, most of the land remained occupied by Indian nations—in particular, the Creek, Cherokee, Chickasaw, and Choctaws. Likewise, many of the white settlers and squatters who poured into the Southwest did so not despite, but *because* of, the frontier's chaotic and wide-open atmosphere. Forming a backdrop to this situation, the invention of the cotton gin and its increasing popularization had intersected with the problem of worn-out tobacco lands in Virginia and the Carolinas.

As a result, short-staple cotton production saw a "phenomenal expansion" through the 1790s—a development that sealed the link between slave labor and planters' economic interests and sowed the seeds for the emergence of a Deep South Cotton Kingdom. In the decades to come, the insatiable hunger for bodies to work the farms and plantations of this new cotton region would result in millions of enslaved people being forcibly transported from the Upper to the Lower South. Working hand in hand with all of these forces was the intense evangelical fervor spawned by the Second Great Awakening revival movement—"one of the most dynamic and important cultural forces in American life."[18]

In the case of Robert Davis, it seems to have been evangelism, rather than commercial ambitions, that drove him to leave Lunenburg County behind for a fresh start in the west. Having entered the ministry around 1795, the same year that he married Eleanor, Robert initially preached on circuits in and around the Virginia Southside. Even here, on the margins of the frontier, the work would have been dangerous. Described by one modern historian as the "Christian Lone Rangers" of their day, evangelical circuit-riders like Robert typically travelled alone, and endured great personal risks as they distributed bibles and preached in isolated settlements to audiences that were oftentimes hostile. Exactly when Robert began to consider taking his ministry beyond Virginia is unclear. However, circumstantial evidence suggests that he may have been directly inspired by a series of evangelical revivals, or "camp meetings," that were taking place around the turn of the century near the border of Kentucky and Tennessee. The Red River Revival, as these meetings became known, represented a pivotal moment in the Second Great Awakening, and launched what has been called "the most intense religious excitement ever known in America." The "climactic event" came in August 1801, when a crowd perhaps as large as twenty thousand people gathered for six days at Cane Ridge, in Bourbon County, Kentucky, to hear a mixture of Presbyterian, Baptist and Methodist ministers.[19]

Robert Davis and his family began their trip into the Trans-Appalachian West roughly two months after Cane Ridge. He clearly felt a great deal of anxiety about what lay before him. Writing his brother William shortly after leaving Virginia, Robert described the "hurt feelings of my heart" caused by "parting with . . . dear friends." He told William about travel hardships, reiterated his commitment to his calling, and, in quite fatalistic language, discussed the possibility that he and his brother would never again reunite. "I have made a start toward my long journey," Robert wrote, "but my horses does not work true, and I expect to go through a bundance of fatigue, but let that as it may, I shall not forget my public and private duties to my God and my fellow mortals." He went on:

> I return God thanks for his wonderful mercies to me and my family that we are spared in the land of the living. Blessed be the lord for his great patience and goodness. Dear William, I do not expect I shall ever see you in the friendly world again. O what I would give to see you once more, but alas I cannot enjoy the sight of you. Lord be merciful unto us both and guide our feet on the right way, faithful in our private duties to our God and if we never see each other in this life I hope we shall meet in a better world where we shall part no more.[20]

Whatever further trials Robert and his family may have experienced on that initial journey to Tennessee, they successfully arrived in Williamson County late that year or in early 1802. Settling in the town of Franklin, Robert established himself as a minister and school teacher. An account left behind by one of his former students described Davis as a "quiet, affectionate and retiring" person who was "as pious as any man I ever knew" and "remarkably patient under the trials and ills of life." Robert preached through the subsequent decades on the Nashville Circuit and interacted with many of the leading figures in the Methodist Church. A brief account in *Methodism in Tennessee* describes Robert as a "most exemplary Christian and devoted minister of the gospel" who was "known to all the preachers" on the Nashville Circuit. Eleanor, meanwhile, had become well known in her own right for both her religious zeal and her knowledge of diseases common on the Southwestern frontier. Described as a "real mother in isreal," Eleanor worked as a nurse out of the modest home that she and Robert occupied with their children, and as many as four enslaved people. She catered especially to the "sick preachers, who . . . had to travel in the lower parts of Mississippi and when taken sick, came up to Tennessee for their health."[21]

Considering the timing and nature of Robert's career in the Methodist Church, he must have thought long and hard about "the slavery question," as the Church put it. When he attended or preached at the revivals that were booming in popularity across his region, he would have encountered diverse crowds of white and enslaved congregants worshipping together in highly emotive fashion. When Methodist leaders debated the Church's official stances on questions connected to slavery and race, Robert would have followed along closely. Perhaps he even modified his own thinking as Methodists' attitudes gradually hardened.[22]

On the one hand, it was certainly true that a "notable shift" had occurred in the Church's anti-slavery advocacy since the 1780s when leaders like Asbury forcefully called for the liberalization of manumission laws and advocated emancipation. By the second decade of the nineteenth century (partly in response to violence against Methodists who supported abolition or preached to racially mixed crowds), ministers were increasingly finding ways to rationalize slavery so long as it conformed to their conceptions of biblical commands. For example, Methodists might believe in the spiritual equality of the enslaved at the same that they argued religion helped bondspeople work harder in the fields and accept their lot in life. Those of this mindset could simultaneously view slavery as a righteous and beneficial institution even as they departed with typical Southern ideas about the nature of the slave as purely property. Still, despite the equivocations and hardening attitudes within the Church, there were certainly Methodists of Robert's time who continued to forcefully preach the sinfulness of holding human beings in bondage.[23]

Robert Davis was not a preacher who fell in this latter category. Instead, he appears to have been among those ministers and people of faith who found ways to rationalize the ownership of bondspeople. Judging by what is known of his life, it seems possible he was the sort of Methodist who drew moral distinctions between engaging in the buying and selling of people and inheriting them.

Although much about Robert's life has been lost, it can be confirmed that he obtained an enslaved person in 1816 through an "advancement" from his father. That year, it turns out, was an important one in the Davis family. Writing from Virginia, Zachariah had summoned all his children to return home and discuss matters related his estate. When Robert made the trip to Lunenburg County, he did so with his youngest brother Sterling, who, eight years earlier, had also moved to Franklin. Once Robert and Sterling arrived, they learned that their father had decided to loan enslaved children to each of them, as well as to their three brothers—William, Baxter, and Paschal. Importantly, Zachariah made sure to emphasize that these people were not outright gifts, but advancements whose values would later be deducted from the larger inheritances he bequeathed. William received from his father a four-year-old girl named Vincy. Paschal (who, like William, continued to live in Lunenburg County at this stage) received a boy named Lewis. Baxter, who at this point resided near Chapel Hill, North Carolina, was advanced a girl named Judy.[24]

As for Robert, he returned to Tennessee having acquired Grace—one of the three women whom Zachariah had listed in his 1794 trust. Included also in the advancement was Grace's "youngest child," along with a "stud horse named Wonder." Sterling, meanwhile, left Virginia with a young woman named Amy. Significantly, Zachariah's decision to advance Grace and Amy resulted in both of those women being separated from their children. Amy "left two children" a later estate inventory document reveals; and compounding the tragedy, both those children of Amy ended up being sold after their mother's departure under circumstances that no one even bothered to record. The sole line of text in Zachariah's estate records that confirms the existence of Amy's children simply states, "not recollected when carried away." Even less of a narrative can be reconstructed about the traumatic situation that Grace must have faced. But based upon the fact that "youngest" was used to describe the child who Robert took back to Tennessee, it is apparent that Grace had at least one other child who she would have been forced to leave behind at the Reedy Creek estate.[25]

The heartbreaking scenario that Grace and Amy faced was one that Black women like them had become all too familiar with through centuries of enslavement in America. As scholars like Annette Gordon-Reed have emphasized, "overwhelming evidence" testifies to the "extreme sorrow" that enslaved parents and their children endured as they were forcibly ripped away from each other in all manner of ways by the whims of their enslavers. Yet despite the trauma of separations that they had to internalize time and again, enslaved people unquestionably persevered and built families bound together by love and affection. The emotional ties that they forged were born of myriad and untold intimacies, including the "mundane interactions that families engage in on a daily basis." However tragic and varied enslaved people's experiences could be, in other words, they never stopped working to hold and in some cases rebuild the family ties that *could* be preserved.[26]

If we evaluate Zachariah Davis based upon the decisions that he made in 1816 regarding the advancements of bondspeople to his children (and the key estate decisions that he made at other points in his life as well), we must arrive at one overriding conclusion: For all his evangelical faith—and however much that faith may or may not have affected his relationships with those he enslaved—Zachariah was a man who did not concern himself at all with the sanctity of bondspeople's families.

CHAPTER 3

Laborers in God's Vineyard

From the perspective of the enslaved community at Zachariah and Diana Davis's Reedy Creek "mannor plantation," the 1816 Davis family reunion had resulted in immense heartache and loss. The Davises, by contrast, must have viewed the chance to reunite as a blessing. Robert and William especially would have had much to catch up on now that they were reunited in the flesh. In the fifteen years since Robert's move to Tennessee, the brothers had remained in touch through correspondence. Sometimes, they sent each other their own works of poetry. If the poems were lacking in literary merit, they did succeed in conveying the depths of the brothers' evangelical convictions. One surviving example from William, penned in May 1803, reads as follows:

> Be hold the war like trumpet blow
> And force of arms appear
> To let the sons of freedom know
> The day of battle is near
> Our glorious Captain Jesus stands
> And hearts with all his might
> To search . . . his friends
> And who will list to fight.

A few months later, responding with his own tract dealing with the crucifixion, Robert wrote of the "groans of Jesus" that "pierced the sky" before closing with a brief personal note: "When this you see remember me."[1]

But despite Robert and William sharing a close emotional bond, and as much as their respective ministries and faith united them in common purpose, the brothers lived quite different lives in other respects. Once Robert returned to Tennessee with Grace and her child, his attention remained focused on his ministry rather than on expanding his wealth. The 1820 census shows Robert's household consisting of himself, Eleanor, their three children, and four enslaved people. One of these bondspeople, a woman between the ages of twenty-six and forty-five, was almost certainly Grace. The youngest, a fourteen-year-old boy, was probably Grace's child. The other two enslaved individuals included a young man between the ages of fourteen and twenty-six, and another man between the ages of twenty-six and forty-five. Extrapolating from what is known about Grace and her child's forced relocation from Virginia in 1816, it is unlikely that the two enslaved men in Robert's household were related to Grace and her child by blood. Due to the disappearance of 1810 census data, it is also an open question whether Robert enslaved the two men prior to his 1816 trip to Virginia, or acquired them after his return. One possibility is that Robert purchased them outright during his initial years in Franklin, either to engage in small-scale farming, or to perform a more specific skilled task around his approximately eighty-acre estate.[2]

Regardless of how Robert came to enslave the two men in question, he did not expand his slaveholdings in the years to come. By 1830, the number of bondspeople in his household had dropped by two. Extrapolating once again from limited data (the census that year listed one enslaved woman between thirty-six and fifty-five, and a young man between ten and twenty-four), these two individuals were probably Grace and her son. Assuming this was the case, it is an open question what became of the two other two individuals whom Robert had enslaved in 1820. Moving forward in time to 1838, two bondspeople (their ages are unknown but once again, they were probably Grace and her son) appear in Robert's tax records. However, from this point forward, Robert largely disappears from the historical record. (It is not clear why he does not appear in 1840 census records.) Likewise, so also do Grace and her child disappear. All that is known is that at some point in the mid-1840s—roughly a decade after Eleanor's death—Robert went to live in the home of a fellow minister named Mark L. Andrews. And there Robert stayed until his death in March 1857 at the age of eighty-six. The brief biographical sketch of Robert that appeared in a book about prominent Tennessee Methodists described him as a "good man, who lived eighty-six years, and was a preacher for nearly or quite fifty years. . . . But the righteous shall be in everlasting remembrance."[3]

The overall picture that forms of the Reverend Robert Davis, limited as it might be, is one of a passionately committed evangelical who, despite being able to reconcile his faith with his status as a small slaveholder, never placed much priority on commercial ambitions or upward social mobility outside the framework of the Church. His younger brother William, by contrast, took a different approach to his life and work. Though he certainly followed Robert's lead in his evangelical convictions, William, in a vein akin to their father, Zachariah, seems to have felt little conflict balancing his evangelism with a more secular-oriented mission to aggressively pursue profit. The wealth William obtained would be built in a literal sense by the blood and sweat of enslaved people's labors. But it was also wealth based in every way upon what those people's bodies and beings represented—specifically, the valuations of their future "increase." As this narrative will soon explore in more depth, William Davis, like his father, was unquestionably an enslaver who remained highly attuned throughout his life to the relationship between his own financial worth and the value of enslaved women on his estate giving birth. As for these women and girls whom the Davies men enslaved, they certainly would have moved through their lives constantly aware, at the deepest levels of their souls, that they were being valued for their "potential and projected procreation."[4]

Born on December 5, 1779, in the middle of the Revolutionary War, William Early Davis spent his formative early years observing his parents' generation emerge as the inheritors of America's new egalitarian opportunities. By the time William reached his teens, his family had made their entrance into an above-average category of landholdings and wealth. In terms of their values and general worldview, the Davises probably saw themselves as being the opposite of the establishment Episcopalian gentry. Yet the family still enjoyed a quite affluent existence by the standards of the Virginia Southside. At the Reedy Creek estate, William grew up surrounded by the sights, sounds, and smells of tobacco, cattle, and wheat production. He also must have interacted daily and in intimate ways with the people his parents enslaved, from the women who cared for him and his siblings, to the men, women, and children who performed the agricultural labor. One of the most important labor tasks would have involved transporting harvested tobacco to inspection warehouses. These were grueling trips that required painstakingly rolling hogsheads full of the valuable product down rough country roads. Perhaps William assisted his father and enslaved workers with such trips. Certainly, he frequently visited the small community and market emerging around the Lunenburg County Courthouse, a few miles north of his family's estate. There, he would have been exposed to a diverse cross-section of the county's white and Black inhabitants. William may also have made occasional trips to Petersburg, the nearest city of note, roughly sixty miles northeast. If so, he would have witnessed there the bustling commercial and social activity of a major regional market.[5]

But the single most important influence through William's impressionable youth seems to have been his family's evangelical faith. Reedy Creek Baptist Church was likely the setting for some of his earliest memories and community-oriented experiences, and as he grew older, he probably observed his parents engage in the impassioned debates over disestablishment. His brother Robert's decision to enter the Methodist ministry clearly had a major impact also, helping inspire William to follow a similar path. By at least 1801, when Robert left Virginia to preach in Tennessee, William had already begun to minister himself. We know this based on a letter the twenty-two-year-old William received in November of that year from his sister Ann. Writing as Robert was enroute to Franklin, Ann congratulated William for overcoming a recent bout of illness, then encouraged him to persist in his calling. "I hope the Lord will be pleased to raise you again and give you fresh strength both of soul and body and so that you may be able to call sinners to repentance and be the instrument in the hands of the Lord of turning many hundred from the evil of their ways to serve the true and the living God," she wrote.[6]

In 1802, the Methodist Episcopal Church recognized William as a Deacon—a title that allowed him to administer baptisms, marriages, and burials in the absence of an Elder. The following year, he received his official license to preach. Not long afterward, in October 1804, William married Joanna "Anna" Burnett, the daughter of a well-to-do local planter and slaveholder named Jeremiah Burnett. The marriage resulted in William receiving five enslaved people from his new father-in-law. The names and birthdates of three of those people—Patta, Anthona, and Fanna, respectively born in 1792, 1795, and 1798—were recorded by William in a ledger that he began to keep the same year of his marriage titled "1804, The ages of the Blacks." The names and birthdates of the two other people he received, Abraham, and Frankey, went unrecorded in the ledger (or do not survive) for reasons unknown. From Zachariah, around the same time, William also received the generous gift of roughly five hundred acres of the Reedy Creek estate. Additionally, Zachariah agreed to go into business with William and establish a mercantile store, the profits of which were to be "divided equally . . . after stock costs and all expenses were paid."[7]

However actively William may or may not have preached through the subsequent years, he managed to devote a great deal of attention to his commercial interests, combining the mercantile business with tobacco farming and other agricultural pursuits. Meanwhile, he and Joanna began their family. Between 1806 and 1811, Joanna bore three children—Mariah, Eliza Ann, and William Wesley. Shortly after the latter child was born, Joanna's father died. In his final will, Jeremiah Burnett made it clear that the five people he had given to his daughter and son-in-law at the time of their marriage were now officially theirs.[8]

Although much seemed to be going well for William, financial disputes involving the mercantile business had also emerged. In 1810, those disputes led him to file a lawsuit against his own father. The suit stemmed in part from disagreements about a lengthy trip William had made to obtain goods for the business. There were also allegations about a storehouse of tainted tobacco and William mismanaging a debt. To what extent the litigation resulted in personal acrimony between father and son is unknown. Judging by the depositions they gave in one another's company, William and Zachariah seem to have handled the affair in a relatively civil manner, even as the case dragged on for years afterward. Eventually, in 1816, a settlement was reached. That same year, probably not coincidentally, is when Zachariah summoned his children to return home to discuss his estate—and, in the case of his sons, advance them bondspeople. The fact that Zachariah advanced William the young girl Vincy at this point suggests that the litigation, rather than constituting a deep family breach, may have been viewed in more practical terms.

Regardless of the circumstances surrounding the lawsuit, events were about to unfold that would forever change the destiny of William Davis and his family, as well as the destinies of the people the Davises enslaved.[9]

At some point in 1817, Joanna Davis died. Perhaps it was his wife's death alone that made William decide the time had come to move to Tennessee. Or perhaps the 1816 reunion had resulted in persuasive conversations with his brothers Robert and Sterling about the advantages of life in the west. Or perhaps William had simply decided by this point that he was ready to get out of the declining tobacco market and cash in on the cotton boom. Whatever the case, William shortly thereafter sold back to Zachariah, for two thousand dollars, his Lunenburg County land. He and his children, as well as a sizable group of enslaved people, then struck out for Middle Tennessee. Instead of joining Robert and Sterling in Williamson County, William would establish his new estate in neighboring Maury County, near the town of Columbia.[10]

Along with Patta, Anthona, and Fanna (ages twenty-five, twenty-two, and nineteen respectively in 1817) and Abraham and Frankey (ages unknown but born prior to 1804, meaning they were both at least thirteen at the time of the trip), William is believed to have taken at least twelve other bondspeople with him to Tennessee. The oldest individual in the caravan was a man named Lewis. Born circa 1781, likely into the ownership of a different family than the Davises, Lewis had come to be enslaved by Zachariah (perhaps through a purchase) at some point after 1794, and in 1808, had been gifted to William. The remaining members of the caravan (other than those already named) were all young children who'd been born between 1811 and 1816. Among these children, the girl Vincy, advanced to William in 1816 by Zachariah, was probably descended directly from two of the nine people named in the 1794 deed of trust. (Given this likelihood, it is also reasonable to speculate that Vincy was separated from her family as a result of the migration.) The remaining ten children* taken to Tennessee had all been born into

---

* Not including Vincy, the ten children believed to have been brought to Tennessee by William were Elva, Zinna, Rachel, Jordin, Ivey, Lucy, Burrell, Bozwell, Chonna, and Nelson Harrison. See the appendix for more detailed biographical sketches of each of these people.

the ownership of William; based on inferences drawn from the birth ledgers that William kept between 1804 and his leaving Virginia, it is reasonable to speculate that some, if not all, of these ten children were blood related (by some combination) to Patta, Anthona, Fanna, Lewis, Abraham, and Frankey. Without knowing the particulars of the caravan's circumstances, or familial lines (or the family and kinship separations that they suffered as a result of the migration), we must surmise that intense emotions would have been coursing through the group as they embarked on the journey to a foreign environment far away from all they had ever known.[11]

The approximately three-hundred-acre farm that William Davis and his children and this larger group of enslaved people established in Maury County was situated along Rutherford Creek, a small tributary of the Duck River. The estate's proximity to Columbia provided easy access to a thriving market. So too could Nashville be reached within a day's travel. Given the demands of managing a new farm and raising young children himself, it is not surprising that the recently widowed William did not delay long in finding a new wife. In 1819, he married a twenty-five-year-old local woman named Sarah Hadley. As the couple settled and improved their estate, the enslaved community there also continued to grow, reaching twenty-two people by 1820. This labor force produced cotton, corn, wheat, and assorted livestock products. A flour mill that William owned added yet another dynamic to the operation. Still, as much as he strove for a diverse agricultural schedule—and as much as he would continue to do so in the decades to come—he prioritized cotton from the beginning. One of the few surviving business notes from this period shows that William was selling at least four thousand pounds of cotton annually by the mid-1820s, if not sooner. Meanwhile, as the letters addressed to "Parson William Davis" confirm, he continued to preach in Tennessee, although probably in a more localized manner than he had done in his younger years travelling the circuits of southwestern Virginia.[12]

Taken as a whole, the picture that emerges of William in Tennessee, in contrast to his brother Robert, is that of a man defined in no small measure by his commercial ambitions. However pious he may have been, however much he may have identified as a laborer "in god's vinyard" devoted to a higher power, the Reverend William Early Davis had ventured west driven by the very earth-bound ambitions and profits that came with being a successful slaveholding planter.[13]

Back in the Virginia Southside, Zachariah had continued to increase his property holdings and social standing while his sons were establishing themselves in Tennessee. By 1820, he owned approximately 3,500 acres of land and at least twenty enslaved people—figures that placed him in the upper third of Lunenburg County's wealthiest men. William, providing one of the few surviving third-party accounts of Zachariah, described his father around this time as a "very industrious and skillful farmer and an excellent economist" who had "acquired much property." A biographical sketch of Zachariah published many years after his death recalled him as a "wealthy land owner" who had left his children substantial property. The available evidence, in summary, supports a straightforward conclusion: Zachariah was a man who cared a great deal about creating generational wealth through landholdings, and enslaved people, that he could pass down to his descendants.[14]

Despite his commercial success, however, all was not well for Zachariah on the home front. In the fall of 1820, illness decimated the Reedy Creek estate. As the previous Chapter recounted, the wave of illness that claimed the life of Diana Davis that October also felled Brister and four other members of the enslaved community—Richard, Vilet, Charles, and Rody. Compounding these losses, larger forces having to do with weather and dire economic realities were placing strains on Zachariah's agricultural interests. Writing to his sons in Tennessee in June of 1821, Zachariah told them that even with a "wet spring," the Southside was seeing "middling promising crops at present." He admitted that "times is hard in this part of the world." In another letter from the early 1820s, Zachariah told his sons that "money appears to have fled from the country. Tobacco sells very low. Cotton is rising from 16 to 20 cents per pound but that don't bring much money to this part of the country."[15]

Still another development had occurred within the family that forebode trouble. A few weeks before Christmas 1821, Zachariah's forty-three-year-old daughter, Henrietta, married one Joel Neal. Joel, who was a few years older than Henrietta, knew the Davis family well. Joel's brother, John Neal, owned a sizable estate not far from Zachariah's. Joel himself did not own land and seems to have cobbled together a living as a yeoman farmer among other miscellaneous tasks. Evidence suggests that the Davis family and others in the community considered him an untrustworthy character who had married Henrietta in order to access Zachariah's wealth. As for Henrietta, records suggest that she possessed a frail temperament. Up until the time of her marriage, she lived at home and depended on Zachariah entirely for financial support.[16]

However deeply Zachariah may have harbored misgivings about the match at the time of the wedding, it did not stop him from providing financial assistance to Henrietta and Joel. The chief way he did so was by advancing them an enslaved girl. The girl, Jinny, was the daughter of Nelly (and possibly Sampson)—two of the nine people named in Zachariah's 1794 trust. Little is known about the Neals' activities over the next few years, but in 1826, Joel suddenly took Jinny and "carried [her] away to the west." His destination turned out to be Hickman County, Tennessee, where he sold Jinny for three hundred dollars.[17]

Joel's rationale for leaving Virginia can be interpreted in different ways. In one account of the situation (written years later by one of William Davis's brothers-in-law), Joel was described as having "desert[ed] his wife." Yet it is also true that he and Henrietta were living together in Hickman County by the end of 1826. It is possible then that Joel had initially headed to Tennessee to establish a homestead—and make a profit by selling Jinny—before bringing out his wife. Regardless, Joel's actions illustrate the wrenching pain that bondspeople at the Reedy Creek estate continually endured as a result of Zachariah's propensity to give their enslaved children away to his own offspring. In this particular case, Nelly—a woman who had been a part of the Black community at Zachariah's estate for forty years running—would have been helpless to prevent her daughter from first being loaned to Joel and Henrietta Neal, then seized and taken away by Joel to a far-off region. Sampson and Nelly and the rest of the Black community no doubt learned that Jinny had been sold to a stranger and probably had little hope they would ever see her again. As for Jinny herself, she had to endure the psychological trauma of being "carried away" to Tennessee and permanently separated from the familiar Southside community she had always known.[18]

In June of 1827, in direct response to Joel Neal's seizure and sale of Jinny, Zachariah made the decision to draft a final will that would take precedence over the trust he had established back in 1794. Zachariah spent the bulk of the will clarifying the names of bondspeople that he had already advanced to his children. He noted that in 1807, he had advanced his daughter Dianna a girl named Nancy as a wedding gift. Another daughter, Sarah, had received as a wedding gift a woman also named Sarah. Zachariah went into detail about the various individuals whom he had advanced to each of his five sons during the 1816 reunion. With respect to Henrietta, however, things were more complicated. Zachariah conveniently made no mention of Jinny in his final will—almost implying, through omission, that Henrietta had yet to receive any property. Furthermore, the will stipulated that upon Zachariah's death, Henrietta would not directly receive any enslaved people. Instead, a trust would be established for her benefit; that trust consisted of a man named Booker, and a woman named Dolly.* Zachariah's executors would be responsible for "hiring out" Booker, Dolly (and the couple's future children), then sending Henrietta the revenue earned off their labor. (In addition to Henrietta's trust, Zachariah also set up a similar arrangement for his daughter Martha that included "three slaves, Hall, Lucy and Lucky and their increase.") It would later come to light that the whole arrangement for Henrietta—and indeed the larger rationale behind the will itself—had been put into place "chiefly to prevent [Henrietta's] property from being squandered . . . by Neal."[19]

In contrast to the 1794 deed of trust, which named the full enslaved community at Zachariah's estate (nine people at that point), what should be emphasized about Zachariah's 1827 final will is that it named only a *portion* of the Black community he enslaved at that late stage of his life. The main purpose of the document was to clarify the property that he had *already* advanced to each of his children. Including the bondspeople

---

* The records that name Booker and Dolly through the years strongly indicate that they were a married couple.

whom Zachariah assigned to the trusts for Henrietta and Martha, the will referenced or directly named a total of sixteen men, women, and children. Based on later records, it can be determined that at least seventeen *additional* people whom Zachariah enslaved in 1827 went unmentioned in the will. With respect to the fates of these seventeen individuals, Zachariah simply stipulated that after his death they should be "sold by my executors" on "credit of 12 months." The "money arising from said sales" would then be "equally" divided among his children. (Notably, Zachariah did not include Robert, Martha, and Henrietta among the children who would receive money from the sales of the bondspeople.) Zachariah's will reveals clearly his indifference to the looming family separations that would come about after he died. Even the trusts that he established for his two daughters would later cause separations for Dolly and Booker and their children, and "Hall, Lucy, Lucky and their increase" as these individuals were "hired out" on year-long contracts to a changing roster of different estates.[20]

Along with documenting the names of human beings whose existences might otherwise have vanished entirely from the written record, Zachariah Davis's final will is notable for the insight it offers into the author's state of mind toward the conclusion of his long life. A close reading reveals a man doing his best to treat his children equitably. More to the point, Zachariah expressly sought to prevent future family squabbles over his estate. Evidence of this desire can be seen in the will's scrupulous accounting of money that certain children—namely Robert—still owed him for previous loans. But most revealing of all is the language that Zachariah inserted at the conclusion of the document: "It is my will and desire," he wrote, "that should any of my children be so undutiful as to contest this my last will and testament, should they oppose its admission to probate, or should they institute a suit or lawsuits to rescind and annul it afterward, then I do solemnly revoke every provision of this will which is in his, her or their favour and direct that they receive nothing of my estate." As Zachariah approached his deathbed, he harbored genuine fears about the impact his own death would have on his family. Soon, events would transpire that proved those fears were entirely justified.[21]

CHAPTER 4

A Mother and Grandmother of All the Others

At the same time that Zachariah was attempting to mitigate the threats posed by Joel Neal, William Davis found himself dealing with a conflict of his own in Tennessee that happened to be evolving along uncannily similar lines as the one playing out back in Virginia. Like his father, William had an unscrupulous son-in-law who'd entered the family. Also like his father, he had been unable to prevent the son-in-law from selling an enslaved person who was not legally theirs to sell. Ultimately, the actions taken by William's son-in-law, in a similar fashion to the actions taken by Joel Neal, would set in motion a chain of events with disturbing and far-ranging implications for the enslaved people involved.

The saga had begun in July 1827 in Maury County when William's sixteen-year-old daughter, Eliza, married a recently arrived schoolmaster from Alabama named William D. Mitchell. One afternoon shortly after the marriage, William summoned his daughter and her new beau to a backyard meeting. There, in the presence of witnesses, he informed the couple that he wanted to give them a young enslaved woman named Elcey as a wedding gift. Though Mitchell welcomed the news, the teenage Eliza expressed the opposite sentiment. Before she "got mad and walked into the house," Eliza told William that she "would not have" Elcey. If he insisted on the gift, Eliza went on, Elcey "would be sold." Later that same afternoon, after a period of reflection had left her feeling "pacified," Eliza informed her father that she would accept Elcey after all. However, by this point William had reflected more on the matter and changed his mind: instead of the original plan, he told his daughter, he would give her and her husband a nine-year-old boy named Willshire, along with a six-year-old boy named Washington, or Wash.[1]

The decision to give Willshire to Eliza and William D. Mitchell is one that William seems to have felt conflicted about to an unusual degree. The reason probably involved the nature of Willshire's and William's connection. More to the point, there is cause to wonder if Willshire was William's son. The timing of Willshire's birth is one clue: According to "The ages of the Blacks" birth ledgers that William kept, Willshire had been born on "Sunday 4 of January 1818 in Mury County." Notably, January 1818 was a point in time when the recently widowed William had just arrived in Maury County from Virginia; his second marriage to Sarah Hadley was still more than a year away. With this in mind, related clues can be found in later legal records involving Willshire: Along with Willshire being called a "mulatto boy" of "great value," he was described as having been "raised" by William. No other surviving account of any other person William enslaved includes language that implies such a close relationship. The clues, along with others from subsequent decades, point toward the possibility that William had sired Willshire by one of the women he enslaved.[2]

Whether that scenario was indeed the case or not—and regardless of what drove him to reverse himself in order to appease his daughter's tantrum—William's choice turned out to be disastrous for Willshire. (Similarly, as this narrative will later explore, the decision also led to disaster for Washington.) Almost immediately after Willshire went to live with the couple, Mitchell began to "abuse the boy" to such an extent that Mitchell was "willing to kill him." When William discovered the abuse and attempted to "buy [Willshire] back" from Mitchell, he was rebuffed. Part of the reason was Eliza. Just as she resented Elcey, Eliza apparently also held a grudge against Willshire, and expressed during this period that she "never wanted her father to have him." In late August 1827, acting with Eliza's approval, Mitchell sold Willshire for 275 dollars to a neighbor named Hardy Sellars.[3]

The ordeal took an even more unseemly turn a few weeks later. Sellar's brother had done some digging into Mitchell's background and discovered that the schoolmaster was not who he had claimed to be when he married Eliza Davis. In addition to being broke, it turned out Mitchell was still married to a woman back in Alabama. Moreover, allegations emerged that Mitchell was a professional grifter who "in all likelihood . . . had a plenty of wives" in "some of the upper counties." In late September—around the same time that he apparently impregnated Eliza—Mitchell was arrested for bigamy and sent to debtor's prison. He was later convicted on charges of bigamy and spent a full year in prison, a development that allowed Eliza to obtain a divorce. William, meanwhile, filed a lawsuit against Hardy Sellars in Maury County Circuit Court seeking to reclaim ownership of Willshire and obtain monetary damages.[4]

The suit asserted that because Mitchell had wed Eliza under false pretenses, the marriage was never legally valid; thus, Mitchell had never possessed the right to legally convey title of Willshire to Hardy Sellars in the first place. In 1828, even as the litigation continued over the monetary damages, Willshire, per the ruling of the court, returned to William's control. William subsequently travelled as far as Kentucky and Alabama to collect depositions from witnesses. His efforts angered the Sellars family. Other local families turned on William as well. In one instance, a wealthy neighbor of William's named Dickey Chappell gave testimony on behalf of Hardy Sellars. That testimony, it seems, contributed to a rift emerging between the Chappell and Davis families—a rift that would soon widen to a violent and very public feud.[5]

In 1830, the court ruled in William's favor, awarding him five hundred dollars in damages plus the costs of litigation. Though Sellars appealed to the Tennessee Supreme Court, in 1833 the state's highest court affirmed the lower court's ruling. No record exists of William or Eliza Davis commenting about either the Tennessee Supreme Court's ruling or Willshire himself. But once again, what *is* evident, reading between the lines of the court records, is that a unique relationship existed between William and Willshire. That relationship would persist through subsequent decades as Willshire came of age, migrated again with the Davis family, and started a family of his own alongside his enslavers.[6]

In the fall of 1828, while William was embroiled in the first phase of litigation over Willshire, Zachariah Davis died in Lunenburg County at the Reedy Creek estate. According to one account passed down through the family, Zachariah had died "suddenly" while "on his knees at family prayers." That December, just as Zachariah had requested in his final will, all the enslaved people whom he had yet to advance to his children or place in a trust were sold in an estate sale. Most of the buyers of these seventeen people ended up being Zachariah's immediate or extended family members. Zachariah's son Paschal, who still lived in Lunenburg County, purchased a girl named Rebecca and a young boy named Mike. Another son, Baxter, who resided in North Carolina, bought a man named John and two girls, Fanny and Patience. One of Zachariah's sons-in-law, Jeremiah Burnett, purchased Sampson and Nelly, along with Dilcy, Tom, and two boys named Peter and Sam. Finally, a cousin of Zachariah's purchased Hannah and her two children. According to the estate sale's records, two separate buyers, unrelated to the Davis family, respectively purchased a girl, Mary, and a boy named Abraham. Though it is impossible to parse out the exact relationships between the individuals named in the estate sale, it is known, based on cross referencing assorted records, that most were either people whom Zachariah had named in his 1794 deed of trust, or those people's children and grandchildren.[7]

Zachariah's two executors must have felt relieved in the wake of the estate sale that they did not immediately encounter legal challenges from the Neals or other disgruntled children. That changed a few years later, however. In 1832, just as Zachariah had feared, Joel and Henrietta defied the will's warning against litigation and filed suit in Lunenburg County Superior Court of Law and Chancery. The Neals' case argued that because Zachariah had either advanced or sold away enslaved people who had originally been named in the 1794 trust, he had violated, early on, the terms of that legal instrument. Likewise, they asked the court to reinstate the trust according to its original terms and negate the final will. Such an action, if approved by the court, would in theory have allowed the Neals to directly inherit bondspeople and do with them what they wanted. As it stood—and as Zachariah had expressly desired—the Neals were bound to abide by the executors' management of Booker and Dolly and the couple's now two children, Jeremiah and Amy.[8]

The litigation that dragged on for the next four years involved a great deal of wrangling over technicalities and court proceedings. For all of the legalese, however, the depositions proved revealing on numerous fronts. For instance, damning testimony emerged about the Neals' living conditions in Tennessee in the years after Joel had sold Jinny. In one deposition given by William Davis, Joel was described as having lived "in the most miserable and abject poverty" in Hickman County. William provided a grim account of Henrietta's condition there, writing that his sister had been "reduced to a child" and forced to suffer under a husband who was "not only poor and dissipated but exceedingly cruel." To prove his point, William stated that Joel had "sold [Henrietta's] last bed" and possessed no property of his own save "one horse, which has been levied on and which he was concealing from the constables." William's youngest brother Sterling, though more measured, offered a similar take: Joel, he wrote, "is without property, credit, or good habits, is utterly insolvent . . . and living with his said wife in great poverty and obscurity."[9]

Not surprisingly, Joel Neal harbored plenty of his own opinions about his wife's family. The Davises, he wrote in one letter, were "inhumane blood suckers," whose "conduct was a disgrace without exception." Referencing his feelings for Zachariah, Joel wrote that he had "formed a very contemptible opinion of the father and have no cause to think better of most of his children." Among the claims made by Joel was that two of Zachariah's sons, Sterling and Baxter, had fathered children by enslaved women that ended up being sold. According to Joel, "Sterling's son [William] is conveyed off and sold ab[out] 3 or 350 dollars. The woman with Baxter no doubt has several children. Being at a distance . . . [Sterling and Baxter] deny it." Joel went on to urge the court to contact Robert Davis in Franklin, Tennessee, to get "all the information in his possession" about Sterling's alleged sale of another enslaved child, a "boy Frank." Joel's apparent point, in making the allegations, was that he and Henrietta should have received portions of the proceeds from those sales and others made out of Zachariah's estate. Without any sense of irony, he wrote that Henrietta had been "kept from the use of her slaves and compelled to suffer every privation until worn out by hardship."[10]

Joel's claims about various men in the Davis family fathering children with enslaved women—children that they allegedly then sold—does not seem far-fetched. The possible blood relationship between William and Willshire adds another element of credibility to those claims. Still, it soon became clear that the Neals' lawsuit was headed for defeat. As their prospects to prevail in court diminished, Joel veered into self-pity, bemoaning physical ailments that prevented him from earning a steady income. He also conflated the wrongs purportedly done to him and Henrietta with his own opinions about larger societal ills. "When I take a view of things in our political cabinet and the church," he wrote, "I do not wonder at the prevailing plague and if this does not stop wickedness and spiritual wickedness in high places. Famine and the sword will follow for God is not asleep but will govern his universe and humble the prick of man."[11]

It is safe to assume that Joel Neal felt distraught when the court finally ruled for the defendants in 1836. Joel and Henrietta, the judge determined, would remain bound by Zachariah's will. The ruling vaguely addressed the possibility that the Neals should receive nothing since they had defied Zachariah's provision against bringing litigation but such was not enforced. Instead, the court determined that Dolly and Booker, and the couple's children (at least three by this point) would continue to be held in the trust intended for Henrietta's benefit.[12]

The court's ruling, it turned out, only marked the end of the dispute's first chapter. A full nine years later, the Neals once again filed a suit in Lunenburg County against Zachariah's estate. This time, they alleged that Zachariah's trustees had mismanaged the income generated off Dolly and Booker and the couple's (now seven) children. The trustees made it clear in their defense that they believed Joel, rather than Henrietta, was the driving force behind the second case. Holding nothing back, they alternately described him as "partially deranged," a "notorious prodigal," and "incompetent to transact business of any kind." In 1847, the court dismissed the suit and finally brought an end to the Neals' efforts.[13]

These two lawsuits bring to light vital data about specific enslaved people and their families. In the case of Dolly and Booker, for example, the court documents, in combination with Lunenburg County's fiduciary book records, show how the couple's family grew over time as trustees, on behalf of Zachariah's estate, persisted for decades in hiring out Dolly and Booker, their children, and their grandchildren as well. Although Joel Neal disappeared from the historical record in the 1850s, Henrietta continued until her death in 1864 to earn income off the labor of Dolly and Booker's family; by this point, that family consisted of two generations comprising at least fourteen people who were the couple's direct descendants. Booker (born to one of the three women—Nelly, Dilcey, or Grace—named in the 1794 trust) would appear in records as late as 1863 as being hired out to a man named David B. Bragg. What became of Booker after this point is unclear. Yet Dolly lived on through the final stretch of the Civil War, and perhaps well beyond. In early 1865, with the South's defeat almost certain and the trust that Zachariah had established nearly four decades earlier moving toward being dissolved, Lunenburg County officials made it clear in records that the "old woman Dolly" was the "mother and grandmother of all the others."[14]

CHAPTER 5

Blood on the Fence, Blood on the Ground

Despite his daughter's disastrous marriage to William D. Mitchell and the years of litigation over Willshire that followed, William Davis's troubles on these fronts by no means inhibited his ability to live the lifestyle of an upper-middle class Maury County planter. By 1830, William's combined land and slaveholdings totaled approximately four hundred acres and twenty-three people. The Davis family's place within the local planter-based society certainly was not analogous to that enjoyed by Middle Tennessee's "elite" class of citizenry. Yet neither was it dramatically removed from it either.[1]

By 1833, William and Sarah Davis had added six children to the household in the years since they'd married. Two girls, Mary Asbury and Sally Jane, arrived respectively in 1820 and 1822. Two boys, Logan Early and James Baxter, came in 1824 and 1826. Another girl, Elizabeth, was born in 1828. Henry Newton, born five years later, was the last of William's and Sarah's children. The presence of these six young people, combined with the four children from William's first marriage to Joanna (all had migrated from Virginia with their father) would have meant that the Davises' Rutherford Creek household remained a busy place. In terms of the overall ratio of white to Black people, William's estate also resembled the atmosphere in which he had been born and raised.[2]

Yet antebellum Maury County was a quite different place from the Virginia Southside of the late eighteenth and early nineteenth centuries. Here, in Middle Tennessee, the land was less worn out and more suitable for diverse crop schedules. Competition for the best parcels could also be fierce. Even if it was not positioned in the heart of the Deep South's cotton region, Maury County still offered a highly desirable location within Tennessee's emerging cotton belt. As such, it attracted no shortage of successful and aspiring planters, offering them a good location to grow cotton while also raising livestock and an array of less risky and labor-intensive crops. Located some fifty miles south of Nashville on the banks of the Duck River, the county seat of Columbia constituted an important regional market, and became especially renowned as a center of mule and livestock trading.[3]

Columbia also boasted connections to the highest levels of American political power. Tennessee's most famous public figure, Andrew Jackson, occupied the White House through most of the 1830s and maintained deep ties to Maury County's Democratic Party leaders. Jackson's protégé, James K. Polk, a member of one of Columbia's oldest and most powerful families, had risen to Speaker of the US House of Representatives by 1835. Like his mentor, Polk would eventually assume the highest office in the land. Another local figure on the rise, Gideon Johnson Pillow, was an ambitious planter-lawyer and close friend of Polk's, who would go on to earn fame—and ridicule—in a controversial military career. Although there is no direct evidence that the Davis family interacted with future president James K. Polk and his family, it is certainly possible since William did live in close proximity to one of Polk's cousins, Dr. William Julius Polk. As for Pillow, William and the planter-lawyer came to know each other well. Before long, in fact, William would hire Pillow to represent him in yet another acrimonious lawsuit that consumed a great deal of time, money, and emotional energy. This particular suit centered on fencing and a land boundary dispute. More so than the earlier litigation against Hardy Sellars, it would also bring about lasting consequences for William and his family, and the Black families they enslaved.[4]

In the absence of diaries or detailed correspondence left behind by William Davis, it is impossible to fully interpret his character or personality. But judging by the pattern he exhibited of becoming embroiled in financial disputes and contentious litigation, it is evident that he was a man accustomed to confrontation. Whatever satisfaction and meaning he may have found in his commercial success, whatever habits and dispositions characterized his roles as a husband, father, preacher, farmer, and enslaver, he unquestionably displayed a pattern of clashing publicly with

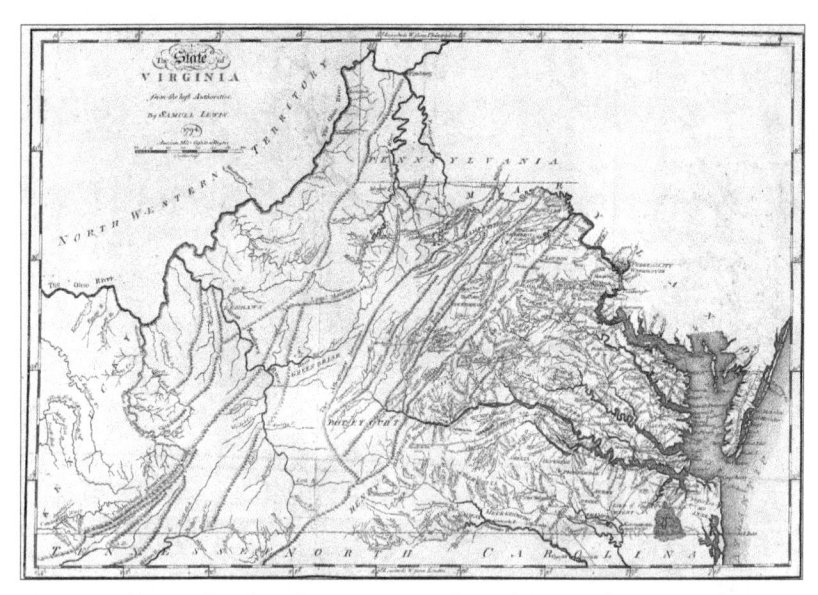

The sparsely populated Piedmont region of southern Virginia was considered a "rude wilderness" through the first half of the eighteenth century. By the 1770s, the "Southside" had seen considerable investment and population growth. Yet it was still a backwater place compared to the long-settled Chesapeake. The highlighted section of this 1794 state map depicts the approximate area of Lunenburg County, where Zachariah established his "manor plantation" along a small waterway named Reedy Creek. David Ramsey Map Center

In 1804, during his travels through southern Virginia, Francis Asbury, "the father of American Methodism," stayed an evening at the home of Zachariah and Diana Davis. His visit may have been prompted by his familiarity with Robert and Willam Davis, both of whom had become circuit-riding Methodist ministers. The Davis family's reconciliation of their devout evangelical faith with an entrenched commitment to slaveholding is one of the defining themes of their early story. Courtesy of National Portrait Gallery

This Indenture, made this Thirteenth day of February 1794 Between Zachariah Davis of the County of Lunenburg, of the first part, James Gee jr. and Daniel Williams of the Second part, and Martha Davis, Diana Davis, Henrietta Davis, William Davis, Paschal Davis, Sterling Davis, and Baptist Davis Children of the said Zachariah Davis and Diana Davis his wife of the third parts.

Whereas the said Zachariah Davis finding his health and constitution declining, and age drawing on, and desiring to settle and direct the distribution of his estate, subject only to support and maintenance of himself and his present wife Diana Davis during their Joint Lives and the life of the Survivor of them. Now this Indenture witnesseth that the said Zachariah Davis for and in consideration of the natural love and affection he hath and beareth to the Children aforesaid, and for the farther consideration of one Shilling current money to him in hand paid by the said James Gee jr. and Daniel Williams, the receipt whereof he doth hereby acknowledge, Hath given Granted, bargained, and sold and by these presents doth fully and absolutely, Grant, bargain, and sell deliver and confirm unto them the said James Gee jr. and Daniel Williams and to their heirs and assigns all the Lands tenements and hereditaments whereof he the said Zachariah Davis is at this time seized and possessed, Situate in the said County, and being on both sides of Reedy Creek and Brass Element containing by estimation about one Thousand Five hundred acres be the same more or Less, with all the rights, privileges and appurtenances to the same and any parts thereof, appending or appertaining;

Together with all the Slaves and personal Estate of him the said Zachariah Davis, consisting of the following nine Slaves by name Bristol, Sampson, Dilsy, Nely, Tom, Toll, Grace, Hannah and Nancy, with all their future increase Six head of Horses, Thirty head of Cattle, Sixty head of hogs and forty sheep being now in the possession of the said Zachariah Davis as also all the household furniture, and plantation utensils howsoever

used, Singularly and individually as if the same were here demised by particular Inventory, To have and to hold the same with all Singular the rights & appurtenances unto them the said James Gee jr. and Daniel Williams, and their heirs and assigns forever, UPON TRUST, Nevertheless that they the said James Gee jr and Daniel Williams shall stand seized and possessed of and in all and singular the Lands tenements and hereditaments with the appurtenances and appendages, and also all and singular the Slaves and personal estate herein before mentioned bargained sold and Delivered to and for the following uses and Trusts and no other, that is to say to the use of the said Zachariah Davis and Diana his wife for and during their Joint Lives and the Life of the Survivor, to be kept together for the Support and maintenance of them and the Survivor of them as aforesaid, and such Child or Children as may remain with them or the Survivor, and the four Sons above mentioned to have good education at the discretion of the said Trustees, but no more than the Clear nett profits of the said estate to be laid out or applied to the above uses or any or either of them on any Score or pretence whatever. And with power also in case of the marriage or other settlement of either the above mentioned Children, whereby such Child or Children will one

In the decade following the American Revolution, Zachariah Davis dramatically increased his wealth through tobacco and wheat farming, cattle raising, and land investment ventures, all of which was undergirded by the people he enslaved. In 1794, Zachariah executed a "deed of trust" legal arrangement that named the nine people he enslaved at that time: two men named Brister and Sampson, three women named Nelly, Dilcey, and Grace, and four children, Tom, Tabb, Hannah, and Nancy. Lunenburg County, Virginia Circuit Court Archives, photo by Andrew C. Ross

The decades between the late eighteenth and early nineteenth centuries witnessed a massive population shift of families from Virginia and other Eastern Seaboard states into the new states and territories west of the Appalachians. Traversing the Cumberland Gap was a key part of that journey for many settlers heading into Tennessee and Kentucky, and that route may have been used by Robert, William, and Sterling Davis, and the families they enslaved, during their relocations to Middle Tennessee. Steel engraving of the Cumberland Gap by S. V. Hunt after a painting by Harry Fenn, illustration from *Picturesque America* by William Cullen Bryant, ca. 1872. Courtesy of the Library of Congress, Prints and Photographs Division

The phenomenon of evangelical religious revivals, or camp meetings, was a driving force behind the Second Great Awakening, and directly influenced Robert Davis's decision to migrate to Middle Tennessee in October 1801. Camp meeting of the Methodists in N. America; hand-colored aquatint, Jacques Milbert, artist; M. Dubourg, engraver. Courtesy of the Library of Congress, Prints and Photographs Division

A single line in this 1865 Lunenburg County fiduciary book record confirms that Dolly was the "mother and grandmother" of two generations of people who had remained controlled, for almost forty years, by the trust that Zachariah Davis established shortly before his 1828 death for the benefit of his daughter, Henrietta Davis Neal. Lunenburg County, Virginia Circuit Court Archives, photo by Andrew C. Ross

> 1804, The ages of the Blacks
>
> Patta was Born February The 10 — 1792
>
> Anthona was born September The 15 — 1795
>
> Fanna was Born November the 17 — 1798
>
> Elvaa Was Born January the 12 in the year, 1811 on Saturday
>
> Rachel Was Born April The 10 in the year 1811
>
> Jordin was Born the 11 of November 1812

In 1804, the same year that William Davis married Joanna "Anna" Burnett and acquired five enslaved people through his new father-in-law, he began to record those people's names and birth dates. Between 1804 and 1860, when William recorded his final entry, his ledger documented fifty-eight people's names. Not all of the people who William enslaved throughout his life appear in the surviving ledger pages. DMA Archives

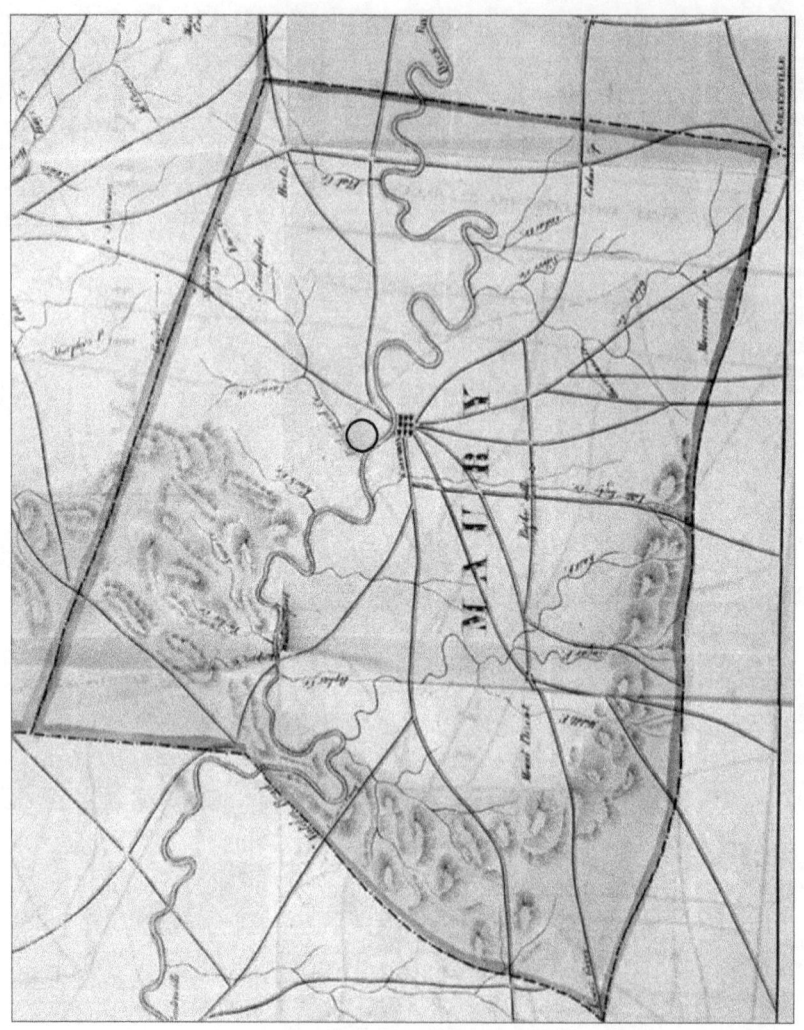

After the death of Joanna Burnett in 1817, William Davis migrated with his children and a group of people he enslaved to Maury County, in Middle Tennessee. The circled section of this 1843 Maury County map shows the approximate location of William's estate, a short distance north of Columbia, near Rutherford Creek's intersection with the Duck River. Courtesy of the Tennessee State Library & Archives others over money. Furthermore, almost all of his financial disputes had something key in common: They centered around enslaved people—the type of "property" that William would have valued most.

One afternoon in February or early March 1836, an envelope addressed to "Parson Davis in the Neighborhood of Columbia" arrived in William's hands. As William picked up the envelope on this late winter day and studied the postmark address from Nacogdoches, Texas, he would have immediately known the contents involved his daughter Eliza. In the aftermath of her divorce from the bigamous William D. Mitchell, Eliza Davis had married a man named Elijah Hanks. When the couple moved to Nacogdoches in 1835, they took with them Eliza's seven-year-old son, Robert, whom she had conceived with Mitchell shortly before his imprisonment. They also took three bondspeople whom William Davis had given the couple prior to their move. William, despite the litany of troubles that had occurred eight years prior when he'd given Willshire to Eliza, had made a similar move in this instance. Moreover, one of the enslaved individuals William gave to his daughter was Elcey, now age twenty-seven—the same young woman whom Eliza had once told her father she "would not have." William also included Elcey's two-year-old son, Samuel, in the arrangement. The third enslaved individual the Hankses took to Texas was Washington, or Wash—now fourteen—whom William had given to Eliza back in 1827 alongside Willshire. Although the relationship between Elcey and Wash cannot be determined with certainty, Wash may very well have been another of Elcey's children. Regardless, as they travelled the long route to Texas, Elcey, Samuel, and Wash shared in the grief of leaving behind immediate family members and/or extended kin from the enslaved community at William's Rutherford Creek estate.[5]

The transfer of Wash, Elcey, and Samuel to Eliza and Elijah Hanks marked yet another instance of William casually inflicting trauma upon the community of people he enslaved by giving members of that community away to his own children in order to support their marriages and migrations to faraway regions. Once again, there is no evidence that he recognized or wrestled with the implications of his decisions. And yet, perhaps William did experience something akin to guilt or remorse once he opened the envelope sent from Nacogdoches and read the contents inside.

The letter, dated January 27, 1836, had been penned by an anonymous informant. It opened with the news that "your daughter that married Elijah Hankes is no more. She disseat some time in August . . ." As William absorbed the news of his daughter's death, he would have read on to discover that he once again had an unscrupulous son-in-law on his hands. Elijah Hanks, the anonymous informant explained, had sold Elcey and Wash in Louisiana before moving to St. Augustine, Texas, and opening a grocery store. If that wasn't bad enough, William learned that his grandson, Robert, had been abandoned in Nacogdoches "without any relations in this country." Almost as an afterthought, the writer included the news that Elcey's son Samuel "was dead." The informant then closed with an explanation about why exactly he had decided to write to William and remain anonymous:

> Your informant thinks Robert will be badly raised, his property wasted. Your informant was well acquainted with your daughter in this country and from the respect he has for her and a true regard for the fatherless child he has made free to write you these lines but shall for-bare sining his name as he is living in the neighborhood of the Hankses and might in ker there displeasure.[6]

Not long after William received this letter, his oldest son, William Wesley, known as W. W., moved to Rapides Parish, Louisiana, near the border with the recently established Republic of Texas. Nacogdoches was roughly fifty miles from W. W.'s new home, suggesting that W. W's motivations may have been connected in part to Eliza's death—in particular, a need to attend to the business that the informant had described. Then again, W. W., like his late sister and Elijah Hanks, may have gone to Texas motivated more by the siren call of the times: With the Texas Revolution in full swing through the mid-1830s, tens of thousands of people from Tennessee and other Southern states were flocking to America's newest frontier to take advantage of cheap and abundant land. Whatever inspired the move, W. W. would have needed capital to fund the trip. In February of 1837, he obtained an unknown but probably substantial portion of that capital by selling to his father three enslaved people—Joshoway, age twelve,

Anderson, also twelve, and Alsa, a young woman, age unknown. The most telling aspect of the sale is that William had previously given to W. W. these same three individuals. Thus, the whole transaction probably constituted a financial favor between father and son just prior to W. W.'s move. Furthermore, that favor seems to have been tied to a request that W. W. investigate what exactly had happened to Elcey, Wash, Samuel, and Eliza.[7]

By October 1838, W. W. had managed to locate Elcey and Wash. Writing from Negreet, Louisiana, some ninety miles south of Shreveport, he informed his father about the troubling sequence of events that he had pieced together. Elijah Hanks, he'd discovered, had initially sold Elcey and Wash to a man named Isles (Samuel presumably died before the sale). This man Isles, once he learned about the circumstances behind the sale, decided that he had purchased "bad property" and demanded a refund. Hanks had provided the refund and regained control of Elcey and Wash, only to resell them a short time later to a man named Smith in Avoyelles Parish. Having at last pinpointed Elcey's and Wash's location, W. W. asked his father to "write . . . immediately how to proceed against the present owner."[8]

Since no record of William's response survives, and neither Elcey nor Wash reappear in any known historical records, it is unknown whether Elcey and Wash were somehow reacquired from Smith and returned to Tennessee, or if they remained in Louisiana. It is also an open question to what extent William and W. W.'s efforts to investigate the situation went beyond purely financial concerns. What is certain, though, is that Elcey and Wash would have suffered greatly as a result of William's decisions. In the span of less than three years, Elcey and Wash had changed hands between at least three different enslavers. Worst of all, Elcey's son (and possibly Wash's younger brother) Samuel had died. Here then, as was the case with Willshire—and as was also the case with Jinny, Amy, and so many other people whom Zachariah had enslaved back in Virginia—Elcey and Wash, due to circumstances entirely beyond their control, had found themselves haphazardly shuffled between different locations and a rapidly changing roster of enslavers, each of whom were motivated by little else beyond their bottom-line economic interests.

If William expended substantial resources tracking down Elcey and Wash in Louisiana, it did not impact his ability to make a major investment in his slaveholdings around the same point in time. The bill of sale from the transaction, signed on November 13, 1838, is one of the few surviving records that shows William directly buying an enslaved person from a third party. In this instance, he acquired a twenty-one-year-old man named London at a cost of 850 dollars. Given the dollar amount, London's age, and language confirming that he was "sound and free from any disease," it is evident that London was in the prime of his life and purchased to perform intensive field work for William.[9]

A few other clues can be gleaned based on the individuals named in the document. London's seller, one John W. Younger, was the son of a wealthy planter from Hopkins County, Kentucky. Though the bill of sale does not specify the location where the transaction took place, it may very well have occurred in Hopkins County, or another nearby county adjacent to the Kentucky-Tennessee line. Tennessee, beginning in 1826, had banned the importation of enslaved people into the state for the express purpose of sales. Yet the law was full of loopholes and by no means prevented planters from acquiring slaves. (The law also had nothing to do with humanitarian concerns and everything to do with stemming the growth of the state's Black population.) Thus, a common strategy—and one that William possibly employed in this instance—involved travelling a short distance across state lines to purchase people and legally transport them back.[10]

London's presence on William's estate cannot be tracked beyond the date of his purchase. But he was probably among the eighteen enslaved people enumerated at William's estate in the 1840 population census. If so, he may also have been present a few years later in 1842 when the long-running feud between William and his neighbor Dickey Chappell came to a dramatic head. That feud, as noted previously, seems to have begun back in the late 1820s during the litigation over Willshire that William filed against Chappell's ally, Hardy Sellars. From there, the conflict between the two planters devolved further over a land boundary dispute. Eventually, both Chappell and William would sue and countersue one another. They would also both be indicted and convicted on state charges of assault and battery, inciting a riot, and unlawful assembly. Yet Chappell, the wealthier of the two men, seems to have somehow weathered the ordeal in better shape. After paying a fine and court costs, he would go back to his interests on his plantation and carry on much as he had before. In William's case, both in terms of his finances and general reputation, the whole ordeal appears to have hit him harder. Despite hiring one of Columbia's best-known lawyers in Gideon Johnson Pillow, William, along with his sons James and Logan, would be found equally liable for the fracas. And shortly afterward, the entire Davis family would leave Maury County behind for good.[11]

In February 1832, the already-existing animosity between Dickey Chappell and William Davis had escalated to new heights one morning when three enslaved men from Chappell's plantation, acting upon Chappell's instruction, "came through [William's] plantation" and attempted to mark a boundary line on land that the Davis family claimed as their own. Naturally, William objected. According to the deposition that Davis would later give, Chappell's slaves proceeded to use "insulting language," calling William a "mean old rascal," threatening to "kill all [his] stock," and stating that "they would go through [William's] plantation when they pleased." One of the enslaved men named Albert even threw a rock at William that would have connected had the intended target not "jumped behind a tree." The following day, when William encountered the same three individuals working in the same spot, the tensions resumed once again and concluded with a more explicit exchange of words. According to William's account, Albert "came near me and stuck a stick at me . . . and said you can come in reach of this if you will for if any white man puts his hands on me I will kill him but Dick Chappell." William responded by telling Albert, "I wish I was able to buy you I would send you to New Orleans." Albert then "went off a pease" but not before daring William "to come to him" and declaring that he would "take 39 lashes" if it meant he could "get his hands on [William]."[12]

It is tempting to imagine the events that may have immediately followed this vitriolic exchange between William and three Black men enslaved by his neighbor. Based on what occurred years later, we can assume that the animosity between the Chappell and Davis families, along with the people that each family enslaved, only grew more intense after 1832. Relying on the available evidence, it is necessary to jump forward a decade to the culminating chapter of the feud in 1842. That June, a heavy rainstorm washed away William's fence that ran through the land that he and Chappell had continued to dispute. In response, William directed two young men whom he enslaved to make repairs. One of the men was Willshire. The other was Joshua (believed to be the "Joshoway" whom William had purchased back from his oldest son W. W. in 1837). As Willshire and Joshua started to repair the fence, they were confronted by two enslaved men from Chappell's plantation named Coll and Park. According to William's account, Coll and Park proceeded to "beat Wilshire and Joshua" and threatened to "beat Wilshire to death." Once William learned of the altercation, he armed himself and immediately went to the scene with his son Logan (and probably James as well). Chaos ensued. William's description, jumbled as it reads in the subsequent deposition he gave recounting the event, reveals the intensity of the fight that unfolded.

> I took my gun in hand and went there . . . Logan struck Coll and his stick flew out of his hand and the negro struck him 2 or 3 times and then Coll went to Chappell and Chappell came up to Logan cursing him and said to Logan what the hell are you beating my negro for and Logan replied why don't you make him behave better and Chappell came up to Logan with his crutches and shook them over his head and swore he could whip your father and you both and I and my [negroes] did whip your side and then Chappells negroes commenst throwing rocks at us and I asked him to make his negrows quit throwing and Chappell threatened us with a pine house he would have us in.[13]

As chaotic and violent as the scene sounds through William's words, the brawl is characterized even more vividly from Chappell's perspective. His deposition stated that he had arrived on the scene to witness Logan "throw the first lick." Meanwhile, William was "sitting upon his mule with his gun, bellowing out 'knock um down in their tracks where I can see them.'" As he raised his gun repeatedly, William threated to shoot Coll and Park, then bluntly told Chappell, "I can whip you." By the time the fighting concluded, the ground surrounding the scene, in Chappell's words, was "so stirred up that it looked like a slaughter pen or a place where they had been killing hogs . . . there was blood on the fence and blood on the ground."[14]

The surviving court records from the Davis-Chappell feud, despite containing detailed descriptions of violence, and surprising exchanges between enslavers and the enslaved, are unfortunately incomplete and paint a rather muddled picture of the confrontation. What comes across undeniably, though, is the striking degree of agency that individuals enslaved at both plantations exhibited throughout the feud. Far from being peripheral actors or indifferent bystanders to the drama, these Black men played front-and-center roles, passionately expressing their desires and anger and resentments right alongside the planters who held them in bondage. The image of Coll and Logan striking one another and drawing blood, for example, is a powerful and unexpected one. So too is the image of Albert and William engaging in such a uniquely personal back and forth. That Albert told William he would accept lashes if it meant he could fight him—and similarly, that William told Albert he wished he could buy him and send him to New Orleans, the nation's most brutal slave market—speaks volumes about the emotional intensity at play in the feud.

Perhaps then the ultimate significance of this obscure and long-forgotten family feud is the degree to which it deepens opportunities to reimagine the everyday dynamics that existed between white enslavers and the Black people they enslaved. For starters, this feud drives home just how much importance white and Black people alike placed on plantation boundaries and fences. Delineated spaces and property lines, and the control of movement through those defined spaces, were paramount concerns in the antebellum South.[15]

Looking beyond the specific issue of plantation boundaries, however, the feud more generally offers a reminder that the experiences of Black people during slavery times should not be reduced to themes of passive endurance or blind acquiescence. Instead, enslaved people, despite the litany of horrors they endured, worked throughout their lives to create and leverage whatever agency they could within the parameters of their oppression. Along the way, in acts both large and small, they constantly made decisions and took actions that were guided by their own self-interest, desires, and dreams. Sometimes, whether it happened through acts of sabotage, subterfuge, or truancy, agency could take the form of resistance to their owners and the institution of slavery. Escape (and in rare cases, rebellion) were the most obvious and direct ways to fight back. Sometimes, bondspeople took agency by working in much more subtle ways to maximize opportunities for short- and long-term personal gain.

74   THE REALMS OF OBLIVION

Still other times—and returning once more to the Davies-Chappell feud as an example—bondspeople took agency, albeit of a different kind, when they participated fully in the events and dramas around them that were spawned by their enslavers. However varied and unknowable their true motivations may have been, Coll, Park, Albert, Joshua, and Willshire all embroiled themselves so fundamentally in the Davis-Chappell feud that the normal boundaries between enslavers and the enslaved temporarily broke down. At least in the heat of the moment during that violent brawl in the summer of 1842, there seems to have been little distinction between the white and Black hands responsible for spilling all that "blood on the fence and blood on the ground."[16]

Finally, attempts to reimagine this bloody scene from the perspectives of the involved Black men should drive home just how skilled enslaved people had to be at navigating the shifting power dynamics that were constantly happening around them on their own plantations, and between planters in their communities. As scholars like Stephanie M. H. Camp have argued, the lived experiences of enslaved people were infused from birth to death by "contradictory and paradoxical qualities" whose complexities we can today barely imagine. Bondspeople, Camp points out, were "both agents and subjects, persons and property, and people who resisted and who accommodated—sometimes in one and the same act." Camp continues: "Enslaved people were many things at once, and they were many things at different moments and in various places. They lived multiple lives, some visible to their owners and to the archival record, some less visible. Side by side, public and hidden worlds coexisted in the plantation South; their black and white inhabitants shared space, agreed on its importance, and clashed over its uses."[17]

Beyond the scattered depositions found in surviving legal records, the Davis-Chappell feud is briefly addressed in a few other sources, one being a series of letters exchanged between William and his attorney Gideon Pillow. In late 1842, just after the litigation concluded, Pillow began to discuss a land swap with William. As the arrangement was presented, William would give up his Maury County land in exchange for property that Pillow owned in Fayette County, some two hundred miles to the west. Furthermore, William would be able to continue farming a portion of his Middle Tennessee land in absentee until he paid off the difference between that property and Pillow's more valuable land in the heart of Southwest Tennessee's cotton-growing region. Given the timing and context behind this arrangement, it is reasonable to speculate that the dispute with Chappell had left William in a diminished position (probably more reputationally than financially*) and triggered his decision to leave Maury County behind.[18]

By early spring 1843, William had settled on the 507-acre Fayette County estate. Joining him were his immediate family members and a portion of the community he enslaved. The remaining people William enslaved had stayed behind in Maury County to plant a crop that season. William's son-in-law, Robert Walker—married to William's daughter Elizabeth—was left in charge of the Rutherford Creek operation, along with an overseer named Mills. On numerous occasions that spring and summer, Robert Walker wrote to his father-in-law with updates. In one March letter, he brought the unwelcome news of yet another conflict with Dickey Chappell. This time, the disagreement surrounded the burial of a two-year-old enslaved child named John. The boy, Robert explained, had recently died a terrible death due to fever. Afterward, in defiance of Robert's explicit instructions, the overseer Mills had tried to bury John on land that Chappell claimed to be his own. "I told Mills not to ask Chappell to let him bury John on his land but he done so and Chappell refused," Robert wrote. "[Mills] had to bury him on your land."[19]

The scenario provides another indicator that Chappell had emerged from the lawsuit in a more favorable position than William, and had probably regained control of that portion of disputed property that drove

---

* Beyond the lawsuits and indictments that resulted from the feud with Dickey Chappell, William filed at least two other lawsuits during his time living in Maury County. In 1833, he obtained a favorable ruling in a lawsuit that he filed against one Robert McDaniel stemming from a financial dispute over bacon. In early 1843, on the immediate heels of the Chappell case, he received an unfavorable ruling stemming from a lawsuit that he had brought the year prior against two owners of a local cotton gin whom William claimed had "craftily and subtlety deceiveed" him by damaging bales he'd brought to the gin. When viewed in their entirety, the Maury County lawsuits in which William became embroiled paint the picture of a man who had made no shortage of enemies by the early 1840s when he decided to leave Middle Tennessee.

the feud from the beginning.* Robert's account also provides a grim picture about the primitive medical treatments of the time. The child, John, he told William, had suffered for more than three weeks before his head "broak out in a gore of matter." In response, "a tar cap was put on" John's head. This did not help and soon led to "swelling . . . all under the jaw." More attempts were made to save John's life through doses of calomel but "all availed to nothing," leading Robert to acknowledge, "I am at a loss to know what to do for little children."[20]

The illness that claimed John's life had occurred during a particularly harsh cold snap. Robert himself had come down with a "desperate sore throat and severe cole" and reported to William that the snowfall had reached twenty inches on the farm. "I never experienced such a winter in all my life before in no part of the world," he wrote. Meanwhile, a twelve-year-old enslaved boy named Yeatman ("Yateman" in William's ledgers) and an older woman named "Aunt Pat" (believed to be the "Patta" in William's ledgers) had also fallen ill. Yeatman managed to recover after a castor oil treatment and bloodletting. Aunt Pat fared worse and barely survived. At one point, she had become so sick that she "could not go from the fire to the bed," and "would have died but thank the Lord by good attention she still recovers." What bothered Robert especially about Aunt Pat's plight was the direct role that Mills had played in her falling ill. The overseer had forced the older woman to work "in the snow and rain up to her knees," a frustrated Robert explained to William. "I talked to [Mills] about it and told him never to expose Pat in rain that she was subject to be sick."[21]

The problems with Mills were by no means limited to the poor treatment of Aunt Pat. Three months later, in June, Robert wrote to William to excoriate the overseer for his decisions on both livestock and cotton production. Calling Mills a "hog-headed fool," Robert reported that "Your overseer knows little about the management of business. Everybody is talking about the way that cotton was killed. If [Mills] had scraped it, it would have been a live at this time." With respect to the livestock, Mills had made an equally grievous error when he hired a dubious local

---

* Robert Walker's letter opens the possibility that the boundary dispute between William and Dickey Chappell may have involved a Black cemetery. If so, this would help explain the passionate involvement of enslaved men from both plantations.

character named "Old Mack Mitchell" to spay William's hogs. Of the thirty hogs that Mitchell spayed, twenty-five died. "The woods stunk with dead hogs," Robert wrote. If all these mistakes weren't bad enough, Mills had allowed a store of meat to spoil, and neglected to feed and care for a horse that belonged to Logan. He was also lazy, and, attempting to compensate for that laziness, abused bondspeople. "Mills needs watching," Robert wrote. "He has never done 10 minutes of work this year and he generally will lash the negroes and never goes where they are more than 2 or 3 time a day."[22]

Taking into account the entirety of Robert Walker's criticisms, Mills emerges as a cruel man whose abuse of enslaved people probably extended well beyond the whippings and mistreatment of Aunt Pat—two events that just so happened to get recorded. We can only imagine what that abuse looked like, since nowhere else in the chain of correspondence is the overseer mentioned. Regardless, the decision to hire Mills was one that rested with William. Just as William, like his father before him, had shown carelessness and disregard for enslaved people's deepest desires when he haphazardly split apart families, so too did he show a similar lack of regard when he hired an overseer as incompetent and mean-spirited as Mills.

PART II
1843-1860

Earliest known image (ca. 1871) of Morning Sun Cumberland Presbyterian Church (constructed ca. 1852), Shelby County, Tennessee. Courtesy of Special Collections Department, University of Memphis

CHAPTER 6

Garden Spot of the World

If William Davis and his family regretted leaving Maury County behind under the cloud of the Chappell feud, they likely also felt a sense of promise about the chance to make a fresh start. Their new home, after all, happened to be in the most productive agricultural corner of the state. For the enslaved community brought west by William, on the other hand, the move would have presented new realities that were hardly promising. Situated on the Mississippi border, along the northern rim of the Deep South's Cotton Kingdom, Fayette County possessed a litany of natural features that made it ideal for the type of large-scale commercial cotton cultivation that ambitious planters loved and bondspeople dreaded. The nutrient-rich soil, which consisted of brown loam and alluvial compositions, resembled that found in the most productive plantation regions of Mississippi and Louisiana. Furthermore, the two waterways of note that crisscrossed the county—the Wolf River in the south section and the Loosahatchie in the middle—both flowed directly through neighboring Shelby County and into the nation's most vital commercial artery, the Mississippi River. The proximity by road travel to the rapidly growing city of Memphis added yet another advantage for planters seeking access to a market with both national and international connections.[1]

For planters then, Fayette County's lure was of a piece with the attractiveness presented by West Tennessee more generally. Encompassing some eleven thousand square miles between the Mississippi and Tennessee Rivers, the region had come relatively late to cotton cultivation and plantation culture. Even in the early 1840s, when the Davis family arrived there, West Tennessee continued to offer large swaths of virgin land. The reason had to do with its unique geopolitical history: For most of the first two decades of the nineteenth century, the Western District of Tennessee, as it was then known, was part of the Chickasaw nation, and, at least officially, closed to settlement. Although white settlers illegally squatted on Western District lands during this period, the landscape had remained in a state of primitive wilderness much longer than Tennessee's Eastern and Middle Grand Divisions. From the perspective of the Chickasaws, the region provided sacred hunting grounds that teemed with natural bounties and game. Theirs was a world where birds shrieked from jungle-like canopies of enormous oaks, hickory, and bald cypress; where bears, panthers, and wolves roamed the immense bottomlands and primeval forests; where the rivers, uncorrupted by deforestation and agricultural runoff, ran "pure silvery" and full of fish.[2]

However, in 1818, when Andrew Jackson coerced the Chickasaws into ceding claims to their ancestral West Tennessee lands, that world began to give way to the axe and plow. White settlers poured into Tennessee's "final frontier" through the coming decades as if a dam had lifted. They brought with them livestock and their most essential tools and belongings. Many also brought enslaved people to assume the backbreaking work of building homes, draining swamplands, and clearing and cultivating the land. By 1820, the total human population in West Tennessee, free and enslaved combined, amounted to some 2,500 people. Among them were hundreds of land-crazy surveyors and speculators who helped create an atmosphere where "the stakes were great and the pace hot for choice locations." By 1830, the population, free and enslaved combined, had skyrocketed to 120,000. A decade later that figure reached 200,000 people—a level of growth that amounted to a "meteoric ascent."[3]

As enticing as settlers found West Tennessee as a whole, many viewed the extreme southwestern corner—Fayette County especially—as being in a class all its own. With short-staple cotton yields often promising upward of nine hundred dollars per acre, the county, at least initially, attracted an egalitarian mix of people. Yeoman farmers, small slaveholders, and wealthy commercial cotton planters all came to get in on the action. One man who relocated to Fayette County from Virginia in the 1830s wrote home to his friends and family saying, "This is the most bountiful country I ever saw." Another woman, shortly before leaving North

Carolina, wrote that she was ready to say goodbye to the "old ... red hills for I am going to Fayette County Tennessee, the Garden Spot of the World." Joseph S. Williams, author of the 1873 history, *Old Times in West Tennessee*, summarized these sorts of boosterish sentiments when he wrote, "No county in West Tennessee was more inviting ... or could boast of richer virgin lands, peculiarly adapted to Southern agriculture, and capable of sustaining a large population." Williams continued by adding, "[Fayette County] took a stand among the most favored counties in the district, noted for the refined, cultivated taste and good morals of its citizens."[4]

As the historian's words about "cultivated" citizens suggests, Fayette County, despite attracting varied classes of people through its earliest years, increasingly became a local economy and culture more conducive to commercial cotton planters with large land and slaveholdings rather than yeoman or non-slaveholding farmers. Gideon Pillow's sizable investments in Fayette County illustrate how attractive the county was to men of his class as the antebellum years progressed. Along with the 507 acres that he conveyed to William Davis via their land swap, Pillow continued to own and invest in additional Fayette County property that he farmed in absentee through paid overseers and enslaved laborers. So too did Pillow's friend, James K. Polk, and other men who were considered among Tennessee's "elite of comfortable slaveholders."[5]

Data showing the dramatic growth of the enslaved population in Fayette County mirrors data revealing the steadily increasing presence of planters whose combined landholdings (at least three hundred acres) and slaveholdings (at least twenty people) placed them firmly outside the yeomanry class. By 1840, the county's enslaved population exceeded its white population—a trend that only continued in the years to come. Ten years later, 15,264 bondspeople were living in the county compared to 11,416 whites. In 1850, Fayette County would possess the highest concentration of enslaved people in all of Tennessee. No other county by that point had as many planters (103) who enslaved at least twenty people. Nor did any other Tennessee county have as many planters (50) who enslaved at least thirty people. Furthermore, a total of 27 planters in the county enslaved between fifty and seventy-four people (another state-leading statistic). At the very top of this list was the single Fayette County planter, one John W. Jones, who enslaved 235 human beings.[6]

While it cannot be determined exactly how many people William Davis enslaved in 1843 when he and his family arrived in Fayette County,* the number was probably in the low twenties. What *can* be confirmed is that between the year of the Davis family's arrival and the end of the decade, seven children were recorded in William's ledgers as being born into bondage on his new plantation. Furthermore, in 1850, the first year that the federal government published slave schedules alongside the general population census, enumerators recorded William owning a total of thirty people.† Out of the 835 landowning slaveholders in Fayette County that year, William was among the 103 heads of household who enslaved at least thirty people. Judging by these figures then, William would have certainly been among those planters who were viewed by nineteenth-century commentators like Joseph S. Williams as constituting the vanguard of the county's planter society.[7]

For somewhere approaching a third of the people whom William Davies enslaved in 1843, the move from Middle to West Tennessee marked the second time they had been forced to make a long-distance migration to an entirely new region. Patta, or "Aunt Pat," and Frankey—believed to be the two oldest members of the Black community (and also the rare examples of individuals whose presence can be definitively traced in the Davies family's records between the late eighteenth and mid-nineteenth centuries)—were among the handful of people who had reached adulthood back in Virginia before William's first move in 1817 to Maury County. Likewise, at the time of that initial westward migration, they would have been plenty old enough to feel the full emotional brunt of the uprooting. The process of coming to terms with the permanent nature of their separation from Lunenburg County would have been central to that experi-

---

* A group of enslaved people had remained behind in Maury County that season. It should also be recalled that eighteen bondspeople were enumerated at William's Maury County estate in 1840.

† This number should not be interpreted as definitive. For reasons that are not clear, for example, two of the oldest people enslaved by William Davis in 1850 were not listed in that year's slave schedule as being present at his estate. Later records from the early 1860s confirm that these two individuals (Patta and Frankey) were indeed still living and enslaved by William.

ence. Not only would Patta and Frankey have had to leave behind loved ones, but also specific places and natural landscapes that constituted their notions of family and home. Even a few of the children who had been born into William's ownership in Lunenburg County (very possibly by Patta and/or Frankey) would have been old enough by 1817 to make formative memories of life at the Reedy Creek estate.[8]

By the time they arrived in Fayette County then, these people who had been born and raised in Virginia (and survived to tell of it decades later in West Tennessee) had learned not once but twice over what exactly it meant to be forcibly removed—almost certainly forever—from a specific geographical place and the myriad associations that imbued that place with meaning. Moreover, in enduring the general experience of being transported from the older states of the South Atlantic to newer states and territories of the Lower South, these people joined more than a million other enslaved people in America whose lives and bodies were exploited in order to fuel "the plantation system's explosive expansion from the early 1800s to the 1860s."[9]

As the historian Edward E. Baptist has made clear in his studies of how formerly enslaved people looked back on their lives in bondage, the "experience of devastating separation" due to long-distance migrations occupied a central place in their memories. Those who endured uprooting and relocation at the hands of their enslavers "spoke a history that marked the move from the Upper to the Lower South as the truest measure of what slavery meant, a process that belied any myths about paternalistic planters and kindly masters, a history both stolen and of being stole."[10]

Patta and Frankey and numerous other individuals must have spoken this type of history during those years of the early 1840s as they and the rest of the community of bondspeople taken from Maury to Fayette County were adjusting to their new existence. Without knowing what exactly the move entailed, nor the particulars of the new trials that these people faced upon their arrival, we can easily imagine that memories connecting them all the way back to Lunenburg County, the Reedy Creek estate, and the initial 1817 move to Tennessee were shared as a means of coping with and better understanding the most recent uprooting from Maury County. Surely the oldest members of the group told the youngest members "who they were and from where and whom they hailed," in the process, acting as "interpreters and synthesizers of individual and collective pasts."[11]

For reasons that were never articulated in surviving records (but may have had something to do with the Chappell feud), the move to Fayette County seems to have loosely coincided with members of the Davis family modifying their surname to Davies.* In April 1843, addressing his recipient as "Rev. Davies," Gideon Pillow wrote to William to make it clear that he believed the tract he was conveying in the land swap constituted "one of the very best in [Fayette] County." Before signing off as "Your friend," Pillow stated his belief that "The section of county is remarkably healthy" and "convenient to markets," and the "society very fine." He continued, writing, "[Fayette County] is greatly more productive than Maury County in the growth of cotton. If you ever want to get a choice tract of land in a good neighborhood and a healthy section of county for your family hands, I would suppose you could not do as well again and you would be settling it without any responsibility which could embarrass you."[12]

The reference in Pillow's letter to bondspeople—that is, "your family hands"—affirms once again that William depended on a sizable enslaved labor force as he made the transition into ownership of a new plantation in West Tennessee. Subsequent communications from Pillow reveal that he and William considered temporarily swapping bondspeople—and may even have done so—as part of the land deal. Pillow's comment that William would not be "embarrass[ed]" by taking on the risk of settling the new estate is also notable. This had to do with the fact that Pillow had given William a degree of flexibility in paying off the difference between the value of his new and former property. Indeed, late that summer, around the same time that Robert Walker was writing about the trouble with the overseer Mills, eighteen-year-old Logan Davies travelled to Maury County and personally delivered to Pillow a

---

* It is difficult to pinpoint the exact point in time when the family made the decision to modify their surname. In at least one document that predated the 1843 move, Davies was used. Furthermore, although some records after the early 1840s continue to employ Davis, this narrative, for purposes of consistency and clarity, will use Davies from this point forward.

wagonload of corn that constituted a portion of his father's final payment for the land. Shortly afterward, in October, Pillow and William formally wrapped up the deal. The successful completion of the land swap with Pillow indicates that William managed to rebound relatively quickly from whatever losses he may have sustained in leaving Maury County. Similarly, the Davies family's routine business transactions during their first decade in West Tennessee suggest that they did not want for much in the way of material comforts.[13]

In December 1843, on the heels of his inaugural Fayette County harvest, William travelled to Memphis and consigned a portion of his cotton crop to the Mosby and Hunt firm of commission merchants. Located in the heart of Front Street's bustling cotton district, Mosby and Hunt, from this point forward, would handle a regular stream of William's business. In some cases, the cotton that William consigned to the firm ended up being sold in farther-off markets like Cincinnati and New Orleans. The details of such sales in surviving cotton receipts illustrate that William's economic interests by this stage had become directly linked to the wider currents of the national cotton market.[14]

A sense of the family's everyday needs and priorities are revealed in receipts from other transactions that William and his sons completed during their trips to Memphis to consign their cotton. Commonly purchased food items included cheese, sugar, molasses, coarse salt, imperial tea, coffee, and Irish potatoes. Perhaps indicating that William evolved in a more secular direction later in life, he bought whisky in large quantities—just one example being the forty-two gallons purchased on an 1848 trip. Along with the food and alcohol, the family's wagon typically returned to Fayette County carrying an array of farm equipment, household goods, and clothes. William bought rope, bagging, axes, saddles, shovels, and candles. He purchased brogans, buttons, cashmere, calico, spinning wheels, and spools of thread. The "ladies shoes" and bonnets he acquired must have pleased Sarah Davies and the other young women in the household, while the spelling books show that educational needs were at least nominally addressed.[15]

Selling cotton and acquiring domestic goods, vital as such business was, constituted only the most obvious reasons for travelling back and forth to Memphis. Trips to the city also helped facilitate and strengthen important commercial and personal relationships. Meanwhile, the enslaved people tasked with accompanying the Davieses would have formed contacts and relationships all their own. Constituting a roughly eighty-mile roundtrip journey by wagon, the excursion would have taken the better part of a week and involved multiple stops, some overnight, with friends and acquaintances. To reach the Memphis to Somerville Road, the main thoroughfare out of Fayette County, the Davies family and bondspeople who accompanied them would have had to first pass through Fisherville, a community that straddled the Fayette and Shelby County line. Here, as well as in the nearby Shelby County communities of Gray's Creek and Morning Sun, the Davieses came to know members of the Little, Thurman, Webber, Williams, and Crenshaw families. They also interacted with the Leake and Royster families. Each of these clans and their extended network of kin shared deep-seated commonalities with the Davieses. Most traced their roots to southern Virginia. Most were devout evangelical Christians. All of them were slaveholding cotton planters who had acquired substantial wealth upon migrating to West Tennessee. Before long, James and Henry Davies would respectively marry into the Little and Webber clans, further deepening their ties to the Fisherville community. As the Davies family formed these new bonds and connections across northeast Shelby County, so too were new networks forged among the Black people those same families enslaved.

The early months of 1847 constituted one period when William Davies and his sons stayed especially busy making sure the cotton grown in their fields found its way to market in Memphis. Between January and April, in three separate shipments, William consigned a total of twenty-six bales to Mosby and Hunt. An April 1 delivery of six bales arrived at the firm in "good order" by William's "own wagon," suggesting that even at the age of sixty-seven, Davies could make the trip. Receipts from the other two transactions are not denoted with similar details, leaving it unclear if William delivered the cotton himself or delegated the task to someone else. Perhaps Logan or James transported the cotton. Or perhaps they did so with the assistance of an enslaved person or persons.

The latter choice would not have been terribly unusual. Planters often tasked trusted bondspeople to either deliver or help deliver crops to market. So also did enslaved people—usually men—frequently take on other official tasks like delivering correspondence or retrieving purchases of goods. For Black people who travelled alone on such assignments, trips through the rural countryside presented no shortage of dangers, and would have required written passes from their enslavers that could be checked at any time by slave patrols or other curious whites. In this sense, enslaved people in the antebellum South suffered constantly under a system that sought to restrict, closely monitor, and criminalize unauthorized forms of movement. Illicit movement, especially escape, brought with it the gravest risks of punishment, including death. Yet even in this world where their enslavers made "tremendous efforts" to control Black mobility, bondspeople *did* travel beyond the boundaries of their farms and plantations and, despite the associated hazards, often welcomed opportunities to do so as a means of temporarily escaping the oppression of their owners' households, developing new relationships, or acquiring news about friends, family, and larger events.[16]

Whoever made each of these three business trips to Memphis in early 1847 on behalf of William Davies, they would have moved through a city that had changed dramatically from its earliest days. Established in 1819 atop a commanding line of river bluffs, Memphis had always possessed the natural advantages to become a major commercial center. The name itself, taken from the famous ancient Egyptian capital, spoke to the heady sense of promise that infused the city's beginnings. In reality though, Memphis remained little more than a rough-and-tumble frontier town through its first two decades of existence. One early visitor who briefly considered, then quickly abandoned the idea of settling down in Memphis, described a "squalid village" that was "ugly, dirty, and sickly, with miserable streets." Other early travelers to Memphis echoed these views, commenting with especially strong disdain about rampant disease and lawlessness.[17]

During the 1840s, however, the atmosphere began to shift markedly in a more commercial direction due to cotton. Earning monikers like "Manchester of the South" and the "Metropolis of the American Nile," Memphis had finally started to capitalize on its potential and emerge as a truly important center of commerce that connected Northern and Southern merchants. The changing population figures testify as much: Between 1820 and 1840 the number of Memphians grew from a grand total of 53 to approximately 1,799. Over the next five years, the population doubled to 3,400. Soon, it more than doubled again, reaching 8,841 by 1850. The city, defying so many early predictions, was at last making a clear break from its founding days as "just another raw" frontier town and developing into a place where "the spirit of progress began to take hold."[18]

In the late winter and early spring of 1847, as William Davies's cotton made its way through the streets of Memphis to Mosby and Hunt, the signs of this progress would have been unmistakable. With more and more cotton factors opening shop on Front Street, increasing numbers of small business were emerging to support the industry. These businesses sold everything from dry goods and groceries to mules and essential tools like cotton hooks and scales. Lodging houses like the Central Hotel and The Exchange Hotel offered both rooms and livery stables that catered to the needs and budgets of traveling planters. Taking advantage of the abundant timber from surrounding forests, small manufacturers like R. L. Cochran and Company sold lumber supplies, while a prominent craftsman named William Strebbling offered "first-rate carriages." Just a block to the west of Front Street, at the base of the river landing, "fast-running" steamboats such as the *Viola* and the *Sultana* docked on their regular routes between New Orleans and Cincinnati. A short distance north of the landing was the Navy Yard, a massive federal facility that manufactured the cordage, cables, and anchors used by the nation's growing fleet of steamers.[19]

Mirroring the rise of local industry and commerce, even the city's cultural sector appeared to be waking up to its long-standing deficiencies. One April 24 editorial in the *Appeal* lambasted the absence of a public library "or any thing resembling one," where "stores of knowledge and information" could be accessed without spending "thousands of dollars." The author felt especially aggrieved by the fact that public libraries existed in "other towns with half our population." The call to arms concluded by asking "Why should not Memphis also have her literary association and library! A small concerned effort and a trifling contribution on the part of our citizens would procure it." Still, for those who did have money to spend in bookstores, the city at least had options like CC Cleaves Southern Literary Emporium. Here, customers could purchase the most popular titles of the day—books like Alexander Dumas's *The Count of Monte Cristo* and *Christmas Stories Together with Pictures from Italy* by Charles Dickens.[20]

Whether it manifested in an emerging literary scene, or the opening of new hotels, or the city's ability to land a federal manufacturing facility like the Navy Yard, the "spirit of progress" that defined life in Memphis by the late 1840s circled back at all points to the cotton boom. Also tied to the cotton boom, of course, was another major sector of the city's economy—the slave trade. Although slave trading in Memphis existed in the city's earliest years, it took time for the industry to gain a prominent foothold. By the 1840s, the visibility of slave trading activity in Memphis would have been inescapable for anyone moving through the city's streets or reading a newspaper. Transactions and negotiations took place in taverns, hotels, and private homes, on street corners, and in public auctions. Yet it was Adams Street that eventually became the hub for the firms that specialized in the buying and selling of human beings.[21]

The most successful of Memphis's early slave trading firms was the Bolton and Dickens Negro Mart. The business had been established by two brothers, Isaac and Wade H. Bolton, who later partnered with one Washington Bolton (apparently unrelated to the brothers) and another man named Thomas Dickens. In 1847, the firm offered "all descriptions of Negroes. . . . From the best of house servants down to any kind wanted." That February, anticipating the upcoming planting season, the firm placed a typical advertisement in *The Daily Enquirer* urging planters not to miss out on the "last show" before spring. Headlined "NEGROES! NEGROES!," the ad stated that "by the 10th of March we will have in this market for sale, between 30 and 50 effective hands, cautiously selected to suit the spring market, which we are determined to sell low." The ad continued by telling interested buyers to "call if they wish to purchase for the right price, for we are determined to sell." In an apparent effort to undercut Bolton and Dickens, an auction firm called Moran and Company promoted in the same newspaper their ability to sell people at prices "cheaper than at regular stores." Although Moran and Company sold all manner of goods, they made it clear that their "attention will be given particularly to sales of real estate and negroes."[22]

William Davies and others from his Fayette County plantation would have regularly encountered firms like Bolton and Dickens as they travelled through Memphis's streets. There is no surviving evidence that

William or any of his sons ever returned to their plantation with people they purchased from Bolton and Dickens or another Memphis firm. Clearly, the increase in William's slaveholdings over the course of his lifetime occurred primarily through enslaved women on his plantation giving birth. Still, whether he did so through a dedicated slave-trading firm, or through transactions conducted in more informal settings, William *did* make outright purchases of people. The acquisition of twenty-one-year-old London back in 1838 is one such example. The other major purchase—that survives in writing—took place in 1850 when William paid $2,175 for four people.[23]

Only a portion of the bill of sale for this transaction has survived, leaving some questions about the particulars. Enough text exists, however, to reveal the basic details, as well as clues about the circumstances that may have been at play. For instance, it is notable that twenty-four-year-old James Davies cosigned the bill of sale with his father. James's involvement, and subsequent relocation to Shelby County, suggests that the purchase may have been made primarily for his benefit. The document also lists the names of the sellers, Milton Draper and Ridley Roberts. Both men, who hailed from Jackson County, Tennessee, had "conveyed and delivered" to William the people in question. Whether that delivery was completed in Fayette County or another location is unknown. Finally, with respect to the four people whom William purchased, the bill of sale's text reveals their names and basic identifying information: they were Ben, listed as "less than thirty-five"; Mary, "not exceeding twenty-six"; Amanda, "about fourteen"; and a child "about twelve years of age" whose name has been lost. Given the way these individuals are listed, it is possible that all four were members of a single family whom William bought as a unit. It is also quite likely that Ben, Mary, Amanda, and the unidentified twelve-year-old all were taken, shortly after this purchase, to the new plantation in Shelby County being launched by Logan and James Davies.[24]

CHAPTER 7

Storm Clouds

When William Davies purchased Ben, Mary, Amanda, and the twelve-year-old in April of 1850, Logan and James were already well underway with establishing their own independent estate. Logan had made the first definitive move toward that end the year prior when he purchased a two-hundred-acre tract in the Morning Sun community, roughly twenty miles northeast of the Fayette County plantation.* In 1851, after improving this initial tract, Logan and James jointly purchased from one Joel W. Royster an adjacent four-hundred-acre parcel. The Davies brothers' new land was situated a short distance north of the Memphis to Somerville Road, roughly halfway between their father's estate and Memphis. Along with easier access to market, the property the brothers purchased included a modest but comfortable two-story log cabin that Royster, probably through enslaved labor, had constructed and then gradually expanded in the decades after he had first moved to Shelby County (around 1830) from Goochland County, Virginia. Now, with a residence of their own, and plenty of prime farmland at their disposal, twenty-seven-year-old Logan and twenty-five-year-old James focused on securing the equipment, supplies, and labor force necessary to reap the sizable crop yields and profits that were suddenly within their reach.[1]

---

* Circumstantial evidence surrounding this transaction suggests that Logan (and possibly James and/or enslaved people) may have already been improving this tract—and temporarily staying there in a dwelling while they did so—earlier in the 1840s, while they were still a part of William Davies's household in Fayette County. See *Davies Manor Plantation Historic Structure Report* for the most up-to-date analysis of the early ownership of the land that became the Davies brothers' Shelby County plantation.

The brothers did so, at least in part, by taking advantage of financial assistance from their father. Receipts show that William picked up Logan's and James's tabs for sundry supplies purchased in Memphis during the period they were making a transition to running their own plantation. William also advanced his sons enslaved people in the same way that he had once received bondspeople from Zachariah. The already-mentioned 1850 purchase of Ben, Mary, Amanda, and the twelve-year-old—a transaction that James co-signed—is one piece of that evidence. So also is a note confirming that in 1849, William advanced James twenty-five-year-old Joshua, nineteen-year-old Yateman, and Mize, age twenty-two. The fact that William's total slaveholdings would drop by ten, from thirty to twenty people between 1850 and 1860, is yet another good indicator that William sent enslaved people from his estate to work his sons' land. All the while, William continued to manage a quite productive and diversified agricultural operation. According to the 1850 agricultural census, enslaved workers at the Fayette County plantation produced a total of fifty-six ginned cotton bales (400 pounds each, for 22,400 pounds total), 1,500 bushels of corn, and 100 bushels of wheat. Also recorded on the schedule that year were one hundred swine, thirty-five sheep, ten cattle, eight oxen, five milk cows, ten mules, and two horses.[2]

Willshire, now age thirty-two, was one of those individuals living and laboring on William's plantation in 1850. Since arriving in Fayette County with the Davies family, Willshire—or "Wilcher" as his name would be spelled in post-Civil War records*—is believed to have married an enslaved woman named Mary. Born in South Carolina in 1826, Mary does not appear in William's birth ledgers for bondspeople, leaving it unclear when exactly she and Wilcher connected. One good possibility, however, is that this Mary was the same Mary whom William purchased in 1850 from Milton Draper and Ridley Roberts. Still, other evidence raises questions about that likelihood. For example, in 1848 a young girl named Sarah Jane (who, according to later records, was the oldest child of Wilcher and Mary) was born. The girl was likely named after William's own daughter, Sarah Jane

---

* Because post-Civil War US census records (and an 1862 record from Fayette County related to William E. Davies's estate) refer to Willshire as "Wilcher," this narrative will also transition to using the latter spelling from this point forward. In *Along the Old Stage-Coach Road*, in her sole reference to Wilcher, Ellen Davies-Rodgers spells his name as "Wilkes."

(Davies) Walker, who had died just the year prior of illness. Assuming this was the case, here again was another example of an unusually close connection that existed between William and Wilcher.[3]

There at the Fayette County planation, enslaved in 1850 alongside Wilcher, Mary, and Sarah Jane, were thirteen other boys and men spanning the ages between one and thirty-seven, and at least fourteen girls and women between the ages of one and thirty-nine. One of those girls was Sisy (exact age unknown). G[e]orge, age two, is among the children whose identity can be recovered by cross-referencing records. The now fifty-eight-year-old Patta, or "Aunt Pat," and Frankey (age unknown but likely just a few years younger than Patta) also continued to be enslaved by William. (For reasons that are not clear, however, neither woman was enumerated at William's estate in the 1850 slave schedule.) These two women, as previously recounted, were among the group of five people whom William had originally acquired from his father-in-law, Jeremiah Burnett, in 1804. By 1850 then, it is almost certain that they were the two senior members of the Black community. Without knowing anything definitive about their blood ties to other people William enslaved, it is still reasonable to speculate that Patta and Frankey both occupied revered places within the larger Black community, and were very likely that community's matriarchs.[4]

As Patta, Frankey, Wilcher, Mary, and the rest of the enslaved community went about their day-to-day lives in 1850, they must have remained keenly aware of the latest developments happening within the Davies family. The frequent movement that James and Logan made between the Fayette and Shelby County estates almost certainly resulted in the brothers bringing enslaved people back and forth. More specifically, the emergence of the brothers' new plantation, coupled with William's advancing age, would have caused members of the enslaved community to once again consider the looming prospect of forced relocations and family separations.

As a case in point, in 1851 William decided to sell Sisy. In the January 14 note recording the transaction, William wrote, "I do deliver M. L. Williams a Negro girl name Sisy to sell for me he binding himself to sell said girl or Deliver her back to me provided she lives . . . I . . . do bind my self to satisfy ML Williams for his trouble." Nothing is known about the rationale behind the sale, nor about Sisy herself beyond the fact that she was young enough to be described as a "girl." However, quite a bit is known about M. L. Williams, the Fisherville man whom Davies tasked with carrying out the sale. Along with being an intimate acquaintance of the Davies family, M. L., whose first name was Markum, worked as a "Negro Trader," according to the 1850 census.* Though it's unclear if Markum Williams took Sisy to the Memphis slave market in order to carry out William's wishes, it seems likely, given the note's wording ("deliver her back to me provided she lives"; "for his trouble"), that the slave trader transported Sisy to a location beyond Fayette County.[5]

Since arriving in West Tennessee, the Davies brothers had forged especially close connections with families from Fisherville like the Williamses. Markum, who lived with his mother, was just a few years older than Logan and James and may have helped them purchase enslaved people during the initial years they were setting up their plantation. Along with his two older brothers, Charles and Robert Williams, Markum would continue to intersect closely with the Davies family going forward. The Webber and Little families were two other clans from Fisherville whom the Davies family had befriended shortly after their arrival in West Tennessee. With respect to the Webbers, one branch of this sprawling family was headed by Matthew W. Webber, a slaveholding Baptist preacher and planter originally from Virginia whose life course shared parallels with William's. The plantations run by the Leake, Royster, Crenshaw, Feild, and Ecklin families—all four of whom had become an integral part of Logan and James's network in Shelby County—were located further northwest from Fisherville toward the adjacent communities of Morning Sun and Gray's Creek. Dr. Virginius Leake was a young doctor and planter who treated the Davies family and people they enslaved. Virginius's younger brother, Edward Curd Leake, developed into a close contact. The Leake brothers' father, Samuel Leake, had migrated to Shelby County from Goochland County, Virginia in the mid-1830s along with his brother, Richard, and established adjacent plantations just east of the land Logan and James would later purchase.[6]

---

* Among the more than two hundred heads of household listed in Civil Districts Eight and Nine (the roughly fifteen square mile area of northeast Shelby County that constituted the primary boundaries of the Davies family's local world), Markum Williams is the only individual whose occupation was recorded as "Negro Trader."

Various members of the Royster family, also natives of Goochland County, had arrived in Shelby County around the same time as the Leakes and quickly established themselves in the upper echelon of local planter society. Joel W. Royster, before he sold the Davies brothers their log-home and four hundred acres in 1851, had acquired well over a thousand acres near the Fayette County line. Joel's son, David Richard Royster, formed a personal friendship with Logan and James, as well as their youngest brother Henry Davies. In one form or another, the relationships that Logan and James nurtured with these families all became key to the brothers' ability to quickly advance their business and personal interests within their new community of Morning Sun, Shelby County. Those interests, of course, were rooted in the exploitation of enslaved people's lives and labor.[7]

Attempts to remap in detail the social contours and landholdings of this one particular rural community can only go so far. However, what a close reading of surviving records does make clear is that Morning Sun, like so many other rural locales across the South, was a place controlled from top to bottom by a tightly linked network of white slaveholding families. In this antebellum Southern society, so far removed from notions about governmental authority that would emerge in the wake of the Civil War, real power and economic control stemmed from private property ownership rather than from the authority of local and state government—and certainly the federal government. Likewise, personal relationships between the men and women who headed these white planter families mattered immensely. And nowhere were relationships leveraged harder than when it came to decisions about how the system of slavery should operate at the ground-level *between* families.

Antebellum Morning Sun, whatever else it may have been, was at bottom a community that revolved around matters of agricultural labor, production, and profit. It was, first and foremost, a community whose cotton-based economy centered upon the "commodification and suffering and forced labor of African Americans." It was a community, in other words, that was "about making black people work for white people, and the whites had all the guns," to borrow a phrase from the historian Dylan C. Penningroth.[8]

Of course, the Black people enslaved by the Davies brothers and other surrounding planter families would have remained highly attuned to these "raw realities" of their local world. Central to that process, moreover, they would have developed intimate understandings about the social networks that their enslavers cultivated, and how those same networks could impact their own lives and families in the gravest terms imaginable.[9]

As Logan and James Davies rode their horses on inspections across their burgeoning plantation during the early 1850s, to what extent they were inclined to reflect upon the historical forces that had enabled their success? They were now part of the third consecutive generation of their family to benefit from the financial and social privileges that came with being upper-middle-class slaveholding planters. Their inheritance of those privileges could be traced directly to their grandfather Zachariah, who, beginning roughly seventy-five years earlier, had harnessed the wide-open opportunities available to ambitious white men in the Virginia Southside's burgeoning tobacco economy. Zachariah's relationship with Charles Hamlin Jr. and his subsequent marriage into the Blackstone family were the most critical early steps in his class transition from a dependent overseer into a wealthy slaveholding freeholder. But from that point forward, the wealth that Zachariah generated had at root been based upon two things: the buying and selling of large tracts of cheap land; and the steady growth of his slaveholdings as the Black women he enslaved bore children. Those enslaved offspring had only continued to add to Zachariah's wealth as they came of age and bore children of their own—children who were either put to work, sold, or "advanced" as gifts. The wealth that Zachariah generated through his sizable holdings in land and human capital had provided him with the chief means for supporting his own children as they married, migrated, and began careers of their own as slaveholding planters. It must have seemed natural then when William Davies followed the same pattern, often giving away enslaved people as a means of supporting his own children's marriages, migrations, and planting careers.

Likewise, Logan and James, as they gazed out across their sprawling estate, would have had every reason to feel optimistic about the future. They owned a large estate comprised of rich farmland. They enslaved enough people to grow large quantities of cotton across that land. And within a day's travel, their cotton could reach a major American market. Furthermore, the brothers were cultivating crucial relationships, both commercial and personal, with a growing network of wealthy and politically influential planters and their children.

Thus, having reached a place that allowed them to consider starting families of their own, Logan and James must have felt confident that the class privileges inherited from their grandfather and father could be passed on beyond them to yet another generation. But whether the Davies brothers could sense it or not, storm clouds were hovering over the slavery-based society that they depended upon for their livelihoods. It was still a ways out before those clouds would burst. But burst they eventually would, bringing war, cataclysmic suffering, and societal transformations more radical than anything the brothers or their network of friends ever could have imagined.

CHAPTER 8

Morning Sun

For all the radical upheavals that they were destined to experience in the coming Civil War, Logan and James Davies had already lived through a cascading series of monumental events that threatened to cleave the America they knew in two. They had been children when the South Carolina politician John C. Calhoun and his political acolytes first thrust the nullification crisis onto the country. In a debate that began over tariffs but quickly laid bare fundamental divisions between pro-slavery and anti-slavery forces, the seeds were sown for new levels of disunionism that would haunt the country for decades to come. The ideas embodied by the "spirit of Calhounism" would metastasize within that segment of the Davies brothers' generation who defined themselves as "unswervingly pro-slavery Deep South Democrats." Meanwhile, the Mexican-American War brought the debate over slavery's expansion into western territories to a head, leading to fierce debates over the Wilmot Proviso, and, eventually, passage of the law known as the Compromise of 1850. Yet that political act—more "evasive truce" than genuine compromise—would gradually be undone as the nation witnessed one "spectacular episode" after another involving resistance to the Fugitive Slave Act.[1]

As they came of age absorbing such dramatic events, the Davies brothers were also forced to adapt to revolutionary technological changes. With improvements to steamboat travel, the spread of railroad lines, and the increasing popularization of telegraph communications, Americans' notions about time, distance, and geographic space had once again been utterly transformed. Logan and James, more so than their father—and especially their grandfather—would have emerged into their adulthood enjoying far more opportunities for exposure to the ideas and debates emanating from the wider world. By the mid-1850s, when James made the first in a series of train trips to Texas to visit his sister Mary—trips that he used to explore the possibility of moving to that state himself—the ability to travel across such vast distances had become normalized in ways that would have been inconceivable to both his father and his uncle Robert during those early years of the nineteenth century when they had embarked on their careers as circuit-riding preachers.[2]

Yet the specific world that the Davies brothers inhabited through the final decade of the antebellum period still remained a hyperlocal one. It was a world that revolved around local land boundaries, local religious worship, local politics, and the minutia of conducting ordinary local business. The concerns that proliferated in this world dealt with field conditions, equipment inventories, the logistics of short-range travel, and shifts in the weather. People fretted about the conditions of local roads and bridges, the prices of cotton and feed, the health of livestock, and the myriad domestic responsibilities related to managing households, raising children, and attending to educational needs.[3]

The business of slavery undergirded and connected with all these things. Along with navigating the buying and selling of enslaved people, litigation involving bondspeople, and countless other financial matters related to the "peculiar institution," planters in need of labor routinely paid their slaveholding neighbors for the temporary "hire" of those neighbors' slaves. Similarly, planters in need of extra revenue routinely accepted payment to "hire out" people they owned. Enslaved people, meanwhile, had to navigate the traumas and complex interpersonal negotiations that resulted from being forcibly shuttled back and forth between local plantations and farms on temporary contracts and financial promissory arrangements. At the same time, bondspeople also forged their own networks, aspirations, and unique skills as a result of their movement between estates. Sometimes, especially in urban areas, enslaved people earned the ability to hire themselves out for skilled and semi-skilled jobs. As they did these things, the new relationships that they formed with other bondspeople often led to marriages, children, and vital kinship networks that would survive for generations to come.[4]

Yet another fundamental element of this world was the sexual exploitation of enslaved women by enslavers—and, likewise, the networks of offspring that were sired out of those relationships. Sexual encounters between white slaveholders and Black women in the antebellum South took shape in a wide variety of forms, and attempts to interpret the subject, according to Annette Gordon-Reed, should resist "bright-line rules." But as the historian makes clear, there is no question that the "rape of black women was endemic to slavery," and that sexual relations between white enslavers and enslaved Black women were imbued at every level with the extreme power differential inherent to the institution of slavery itself. For countless numbers of enslaved women, the psychological trauma born of rape and sexual abuse would also survive for generations to come.[5]

Like Logan and James Davies themselves, most of the planter families whom they befriended and did business with in northeast Shelby County were not comprised of people who made lasting marks on history. Still, within their place and time, they possessed real power and influence, and lived out their days guided by the assumptions and privileges inherent to their station in life. (These were the "aristocratic families in this locality" that Dr. William Little Davies would write about almost a century later.) First and foremost, the men who headed these families were agriculturists, land speculators, and enslavers. But along with these baseline identities, their ranks were quite diverse. As we will see, they included a preacher, a doctor, a politically connected tax collector and postmaster, a violin-playing innkeeper, and a Princeton-educated veteran of the California Gold Rush. Most stayed perpetually active in local politics, although a few eschewed that arena. Most were Presbyterians but some were Baptists. With the exception of one Thomas B. Crenshaw, a long-serving county court judge aligned with the last vestiges of Whiggery, they were all committed Democrats. Whatever their political differences, however, the wealthiest white men of antebellum Morning Sun were at their core slaveholding cotton planters who would have derived their power through "a paternalistic combination of hegemonic cultural control and violent discipline."[6] At the most basic level, they were men who saw themselves as possessing absolute control over the labor force they enslaved, as well as the financial well-being of their own families. Similarly, they were people who tended to see themselves as the natural inheritors of a biblically inspired Manifest Destiny—a charge that empowered them to carry out their own ideas about civilizing and cultivating the land. As Robert Ecklin, owner of Woodlawn Plantation near Fisherville put it to his young daughter, Sallie, in one 1850 exchange, "The people of our country are obeying a command given long since to multiply and replenish the earth." What Robert Ecklin did not mention, but what was implicitly understood, is that the system of slavery went hand in hand with his command to "multiply and replenish."[7]

When the Davies brothers arrived on the scene in Morning Sun and purchased from Joel Royster the largest portion of their new estate, they took over a piece of property that was already well known. The residence that Royster sold to the brothers was probably among the oldest in that area of the county, having originally been constructed circa 1830 as a humble, one-room cabin before later being expanded into the two-story dog trot form that the Davies brothers acquired. Royster himself was regarded as a leader within the community. Along with his extensive land and slaveholdings, he possessed strong Democratic Party connections that had helped earn him lucrative appointments as a tax collector and postmaster for Morning Sun during the Jackson administration. The appointments seem to have come about more through his siblings' marriage ties than anything else: Two of Joel's sisters, Kate and Jane Royster, had respectively married brothers Alex and Samuel Donelson—nephews of President Andrew Jackson's wife, Rachel Donelson Jackson. Alex Donelson's plantation, Orion Hill, was situated on a "magnificently located" tract a few miles northeast of Morning Sun near the Haysville community, and had been constructed as a replica of Jackson's famous Nashville estate, The Hermitage.[8]

The Royster family apparently influenced much of the larger settlement pattern in Morning Sun and surrounding communities. Along with Joel, and his two earlier-mentioned sisters who had married into the Donelson family, at least half a dozen other Roysters had migrated from Goochland County, Virginia to Shelby County between the late 1820s and mid-1830s. Other families they had known back in Virginia like the Webbers and the Leakes came also. Samuel Leake, better known as "Colonel Leake," became something of a local celebrity in the years after he arrived in Morning Sun. A tall and slender man, Samuel was regarded for his "tireless good humor," love of "storytelling," and talent as an "excellent violinist." In 1850, capitalizing on his reputation, Samuel established an inn on his plantation that catered to the circuit-riding lawyers moving back and forth between Memphis and Nashville on the Memphis to Somerville Road. The inn also attracted young people from surrounding plantations who came to "dance . . . as the colonel played." It is likely that Logan and James Davies, both still single when they established their plantation, would have been among the young men and women who congregated at Leake's inn.[9]

Whether they danced to the sounds of Colonel Leake's violin or not, there is no doubt that the Davies brothers successfully cultivated mutually beneficial relationships from the time they first arrived in the community. In addition to the Leake, Royster, and Webber families, they came to know and do business with Roscoe Feild, owner of Mt. Airy plantation, and Feild's older relative through marriage, the Whig-aligned judge Thomas B. Crenshaw. Roscoe Feild had grown up in Shelby County before heading off to Princeton and the California Gold Rush. His adventures earned him a degree of renown upon his return: The community of Cordova, which would later emerge just south of Morning Sun, was said to be named after the Cordova Mine in Calaveras County, where Roscoe had prospected. As for Crenshaw, he happened to be one of the largest slaveowners in the county; in 1850, at least eighty enslaved people were working the fields of his plantation known as Lone Hill. Two others who moved within Logan's and James's orbits were William Wash and Washington Bolton. The former owned a popular general store (simply called Wash's Store) that doubled as Morning Sun's political gathering place and a Masonic meeting hall; Bolton, who came to own an estate adjacent to the Davies brothers, was part-owner of Memphis's largest slave-trading firm, Bolton and Dickens.[10]

Each of these connections that the Davies brothers forged were of course different in nature. Some were short-lived. Others would last for decades. Some were casual, or purely commercial, while others evolved in more personal directions, or even led to marriage. To one degree or another though, they all influenced the brothers' lives in ways that were very real and unique to the time and place that was late antebellum rural Shelby County. By extension, those same relationships shaped and influenced the lives and destinies of the Black families whom the Davieses and their network of friends and extended relatives enslaved.

The intertwined forces of slavery and white supremacy undergirded the rhythms of life in northeast Shelby County, Tennessee. Yet even within such a place and time, distinct Black communities certainly existed—however low-profile they were forced to remain. These communities were based in deeply rooted kinship networks, blood ties, geographic histories, and emotional bonds forged through generations of shared knowledge and collective experiences grounded in resilience and survival. Black communities obviously formed within the boundaries of plantations and farms. But communities of color also sometimes emerged in unlikely shared spaces *between* the boundaries set by enslavers. The community that took shape within and around a particular church a few miles east of the Davies brothers' Morning Sun plantation is one such example.[11]

The church that would come to be known as Gray's Creek Baptist Church had formed in the early 1840s through the combined efforts of two free men of color, and a cross-section of enslaved people from surrounding farms and plantations. One of the church's founders, a biracial farmer and preacher named Joseph Harris, had migrated to Shelby County from Goochland County, Virginia, alongside Samuel Leake's family. Joseph Harris had made this decision for reasons that illustrate the casual barbarity of slavery: Although Joseph himself had been emancipated back in Virginia in 1832 by his original enslaver, one John Harris, Joseph's wife and children continued to be held in bondage by Samuel Leake. Thus, Joseph, despite being a free man, had joined the Leakes in order to remain with his enslaved family. Joseph Harris's close associate (and possible relative) Simon Price was the other biracial free man who co-founded the church and served as its inaugural preacher. Although less is known about Simon Price's life, including the circumstances behind his emancipation, the record suggests that he endured a similar situation to Harris's. In Simon's case, the ownership of his enslaved wife Kitty had passed in 1843 from the late David Royster (Joel Royster's father, who had migrated from Goochland County to Shelby County after his children) into the possession of Joel's sister, Ann, and her husband Fendal Carr Thurman. Simon, who was listed in census records as a shoemaker, lived as a free man alongside Kitty and their children on the estate of Fendall and Ann (Royster) Thurman. Despite the questions that remain about Simon and Kitty, and, likewise, the family unit that they formed on the Thurman's estate, three of their children—each of whom will later reenter this narrative in different ways—are believed to have been named Royal, Jim, and Young.[12]

The building that Joseph Harris and Simon Price used to establish their church had originally housed a white congregation jointly founded by the Leake and Royster families. Sometime around 1840, however, the two families had abandoned the building to join a new church in Morning Sun. In the wake of that decision, Joseph Harris, Simon Price, and their enslaved congregation moved into the building. Not long afterward, the church adopted the name taken after the surrounding community that had come to be called Gray's Creek.*[13]

During slavery, it was common for enslaved people or their enslavers to construct places of worship on plantations. These "praise houses," as they were often known, varied widely in form but typically consisted of a rudimentary frame structure capable of housing informal music, dancing, and preaching from one or more of the enslaved community's members. Gray's Creek Baptist Church, in contrast, constituted what some Memphis-area historians say was the first formal Black congregation in Shelby County. Here, a sizable community of enslaved people, led by two free men of color, had managed to bring to fruition, some two and half decades before Emancipation would arrive, a formal place of worship and fellowship in the rural hinterlands of the county. The roles that Joseph Harris and Simon Price played in the endeavor—and indeed, the unique circumstances surrounding each man's life and family—speak to the complex racial dynamics that existed within the overlapping communities of Morning Sun and Gray's Creek.[14]

West Tennessee was not a region that attracted many free people of color through the antebellum period, and when Joseph Harris and Simon Price arrived in Shelby County in the early 1830s, they were in extremely rare company. In 1830, only sixty-two of Shelby County's 5,648

---

* The name Gray's Creek probably came about to describe the area surrounding the estates owned by brothers John and Jim Gray, two of the more prominent land and slaveholders in northeast Shelby County.

total residents were free Blacks. Furthermore, most of that population lived in Memphis, or within the semi-urban environs immediately surrounding the city. Out in the rural sections of the county around Gray's Creek, Harris and Price would have garnered considerable attention from both the white and Black communities they moved within during the years that they established themselves and their congregation.[15]

In Joseph Harris's case, the financial independence that he acquired made him even more of a unique figure relative to his time. Beginning in 1834, immediately after he had arrived in the county from Virginia, he put down 150 dollars toward the mortgage on a farm adjacent to Samuel Leake's estate. Harris also paid Leake three hundred dollars for the freedom of his wife Fanny and daughter Virginia. Joseph purchased another of his daughters from Leake six years later. Then, in 1855, at a cost of nine hundred dollars, Joseph bought yet another of his daughters out of slavery who had been inherited by one of Samuel's children. During all this time, as Fanny Harris birthed more children into freedom, Joseph increased his personal wealth by simultaneously running a successful farm, purchasing land from various members of the Royster family, and, taking advantage of his location, operating a way station frequented by the stage coaches travelling the increasingly busy Memphis to Somerville Road.[16]

By 1860, at the age of sixty-two, Joseph Harris had become one of the wealthiest free men of color in the county, owning personal property and some four hundred acres whose combined valued was placed at $6,335. Unlike Simon Price and his family, whose vague legacies would barely survive the tests of time, Harris's story, just like the story of the church he helped found, continued to take shape and reverberate through the years of the Civil War and well beyond; eventually, narratives of his life would be rediscovered by Harris's distant twentieth-century descendants—one of whom came to popularize his intrepid forebear in a novel titled *Free Joe: A Story of Faith, Love and Perseverance*.[17]

The intertwined histories of Joseph "Free Joe" Harris, Simon Price, and Gray's Creek Baptist Church illustrate a sometimes-overlooked truth about life in small rural communities of the antebellum South: Even in places imbued at every level with the forces of slavery and white supremacy, Black people, whether through good fortune, or sheer willpower, or a combination of those and other things, oftentimes seized opportunities to transcend the limitations placed on them and establish spaces in which they could express themselves creatively, participate in the joys of community, and resist the dominion of their enslavers. Harris's and Price's experiences as biracial free men were by no means typical, of course. Their status would have given them distinct advantages over their enslaved peers and family members—the vast majority of whom moved through their days and weeks and months and years having little expectation that their plight would ever change. Indeed, for the enslaved congregants of Gray's Creek Baptist Church, the moment their church services ended, they would have stepped back into the outside world fully aware—and aware in ways that must have been all-consuming and lodged deep within their beings—that their bondage was "for life," as the standard language of slavery-related legal documents and bills of sale made clear.[18]

When it came to the task of building and maintaining an enslaved labor force large enough to meet their production goals, Logan and James Davies employed a multi-pronged approach throughout the 1850s. It is evident (based upon the overall size and median age of their plantation's enslaved population by the end of that decade) that the brothers purchased adult men and women outright at various points in time; they probably did so by either going through a local trader like Markum Williams, or by visiting one of the established firms in Memphis like Bolton and Dickens. As has already been mentioned, the brothers also received bondspeople as advancements from their father. The children born to enslaved women on the plantation would have gradually increased the overall labor pool as well. The names of enslaved children that can be confirmed as being born on the Davies brothers' Morning Sun estate between 1852 and 1862 are as follows: Amos, Elias, Young, Madison, Polly, Martha, Jacob, Emily, Harry, Archa, Arominta, and Mat. Finally, Logan and James also engaged in the common practice of temporarily hiring—in effect, leasing—enslaved people from other surrounding planters.[19]

In March of 1855, just as that year's planting season commenced, Logan paid Robert Williams (Markum's older brother) twelve dollars for the hire of four women—Mary, Molly, Elizabeth, and Dianna. Judging by the dollar amount of the transaction, these women (their ages were not listed in the surviving receipt) were probably hired for no more than a month or two, after which they would have returned to Robert William's estate. Another temporary hire occurred in December 1859. In a note issued on Christmas Day, Logan promised to pay the Fisherville preacher-planter Matthew W. Webber $126 for the year-long hire of a man named George. Notably, the document specifies that Webber had by this point become guardian to one of the daughters of the recently deceased Ann (Royster) Thurman and the late Fendall Thurman. Following Ann's death, her orphaned daughter had inherited George. Likewise, Webber was taking it upon himself to generate revenue off George's labor—revenue that would have presumably supported his ability to raise Ann Thurman's daughter—by hiring George out to Logan.[20]

Reading between the lines of the situation, it is evident that George, prior to moving to Webber's estate, had lived and labored on the same plantation where Simon and Kitty Price and their children resided. Yet another interpretive thread that can be followed has to do with the promissory note's final two lines: "He [George] is to have two suits of summer clothing and one of winter, two pairs of shoes, one pair of socks, one Hat and Blanket," the document reads. "He is to be returned as above death excepted." Such details about George's meager clothing provisions, meant to last him all of 1860, reveal just how much attention enslavers paid to cost cutting measures as they attempted to squeeze every bit of profit they could from the labor that they exploited. These two instances of Logan and James hiring bondspeople from surrounding planters are merely the only such transactions with a surviving paper trail. The Davies brothers undoubtedly engaged in similar business on other occasions. Later, when money would become tighter during the Civil War, records show that Logan and James frequently earned revenue themselves by hiring out people they enslaved to other local planters.[21]

Planters engaged in these sorts of short-term transactions for a variety of reasons. Earning revenue for a dependent (as Webber did with George on behalf of Ann Thurman's daughter) was common. So too was it common for slaveholders to hire out bondspeople to the county for labor on road and bridge projects. Maintenance on the Memphis to Somerville Road, for example, relied in large part on enslaved labor. In other cases, a planter might determine that their crop production for a given year did not demand intensive labor beyond a specified period. Thus, short-term hires could make more financial sense. Similarly, some planters might decide that they simply could not afford to purchase people outright and engaged in the next best thing. Finally, there were those owners of smaller farms who preferred to temporarily hire bondspeople rather than become known as permanent slaveholders.[22]

Beyond the business notes that pertain to slave hiring, some of the most illuminating records the Davies brothers left behind have to do with the subject of enslaved people escaping. Although these records are nothing more than brief receipt notations, with limited contextual information, a close reading confirms that Logan, on multiple occasions, accepted jobs to "hunt" escapees with dogs. For example, on August 12, 1858, a notation was made in the Davies brothers' books that Logan had been paid ten dollars by a man named Burrell Keynes for "ketching Negro Orange with Dogs." Two weeks later, Logan was paid five dollars by a man named D. H. Branch "for hunting." The following year, in June, Logan was paid five dollars by a man named John Farabee for "hunting Negro by Request of Edward." The final surviving entry dealing with a similar situation was recorded a few years later, on January 11, 1862. That receipt shows Logan receiving five dollars from Thomas B. Crenshaw, the wealthy county court judge and owner of Lone Hill Plantation, for "hunting Simon."[23]

Extrapolating from these records, it evident that Logan Davies was not only well known within northeast Shelby County for his skills catching escaped slaves, but also for raising dogs that were specifically trained to track people through the surrounding forests and bottomlands. How often Logan (and possibly James) carried out this sort of work beyond the instances that got recorded is an open question. But it is not hard to imagine that "hunting" enslaved people who had taken flight from local farms and plantations was a regular sideline business activity. Similarly, it is probable that Logan (and James) played prominent roles leading and/or participating in the regular slave patrols that would have kept a vigilant watch over the roadways crisscrossing northeast Shelby County.

From the perspective of enslaved people in Morning Sun, especially those living in bondage at the Davies brothers' plantation, Logan's reputation as a local slave catcher must have resonated ominously. Each and every day, for instance, the men, women, and children enslaved at the brothers' estate would have encountered the sights and sounds of the dogs that Logan trained. Perhaps some in the enslaved community were even tasked with caring for those same dogs—animals that they would have known, at all times, had the potential to be unleashed upon them if they ever dared to act upon their impulses to escape. As for Orange and Simon, the two individuals who *did* make the decisions to flee from their enslavers, we can only speculate about what became of them as a result. In Orange's case, is notable that "ketching" was recorded in the receipt, a detail that strongly suggests he was captured by Logan and returned to Burrell Keynes. With respect to Simon, there is also some circumstantial evidence (which this narrative will later touch on) that he was caught. That being said, however, the possibility should not be entirely ruled out that one or both of these men, against overwhelming odds, did actually manage to make their way out of Shelby County and reach a place of freedom beyond.

CHAPTER 9

The Time for Moderation Has Passed

When it came to high-stakes decisions about labor—specifically, the "hiring" and "hiring out" of enslaved people—it is not surprising that planters in a community like Morning Sun preferred to deal with their established network of extended family and friends. The Davies brothers' plantation records make clear the extent to which they conducted such business with their closest circle of intimates. More to the point, the local families with whom the Davieses most frequently swapped bondspeople also happened to be families whom they were connected to through marriage.

The circumstances surrounding James Davies's personal life speak to the interrelated dynamics between marriage ties and the business of slavery. In December 1854, thirty-year-old James wed sixteen-year-old Almeda Little of Fisherville. Orphaned since the death of her parents a few years earlier, Almeda, at the time of the union, was the legal dependent of James and Logan's close friend, the slave-trader Markum Williams. Taking into account Almeda's age, it is seems likely that Markum, in an effort to secure Almeda's future, played an active role in facilitating the marriage.[1]

The connections between the Davieses and Fisherville-area families deepened further in 1857 when James and Logan's youngest brother, Henry, wed Mary A. Webber—a young cousin of the Baptist preacher-planter (and close associate of William Davies) Matthew W. Webber. Edward Curd Leake, one of the sons of the late violin-playing innkeeper and planter Samuel Leake, served as the witness to Henry and Mary's union. That same year, Matthew W. Webber officiated the marriage of Almeda (Little) Davies's youngest sister, Polly Little, to Edward. The ceremony took place at the home of Matthew W. Webber's neighbor, Mary Octavious (Little) Williams. The latter was the oldest sister of Polly and Almeda—and, by this stage, the widow of Charles Williams, the deceased oldest brother of Robert and Markum Williams.[2]

These byzantine familial connections reveal the degrees to which families could become intertwined and mutually dependent upon one another within a specific rural area like northeast Shelby County—referred to from this point forward as the Northeast Shelby Triangle.* Furthermore, as these interconnected planter families went about doing all those things that defined their lived experiences—as they married and had children; as their children married and had children; as they died; as they bequeathed and inherited estates; as they migrated elsewhere (sometimes returning but oftentimes not); as they assumed guardianship for minors; as they bought and sold land and homes; as they went into and out of business with one another; as they feuded and sued one another; as they reconciled; as they worshipped together; as they socialized together at picnics and dances and political barbecues; as they formed political alliances and rivalries with one another; and, yes, as they bought, sold, hired, and hired out enslaved people among each other—the decisions that they made did not occur in vacuums. Instead, their choices rippled outward, impacting in profound ways the enslaved people trapped within the confines of their enslavers' whims, desires, and ambitions.

When James Davies and Almeda Little married in 1854, people enslaved by both families were certainly affected. One of those individuals was a young man named Richmond. Born in 1833, Richmond, by the

---

* This term refers to the roughly fifteen-square-mile geographic area surrounding the Davies brothers' Morning Sun plantation. The term is the author's and has been conceived as a variation of "The Crescent," a term that some local historians have used to refer to a particular swath of eastern Shelby and western Fayette Counties. Usage of the "Northeast Shelby Triangle" in this text refers to the historical terrain of Shelby County that existed between Fisherville on the extreme southeastern end, Haysville/Wythe Depot (later called Arlington) on the extreme northeastern end, and Bartlett/Union Depot on the extreme southwestern end. Located in between these points were the communities that function as the key settings for the remainder of this book: Gray's Creek (later alternately called Sewardsville and Eads), Morning Sun, Shelby Depot (later called Brunswick), and Bonds Station (later called Ellendale).

time he was a teenager (if not from the time of his birth) was enslaved on the Fishverville plantation owned by Almeda's father, William Little. When William Little died intestate in 1851, Richmond was listed in a property inventory along with thirty-two other enslaved men, women, and children. Some of these individuals were subsequently sold off to pay Little's debts while others were bequeathed to various siblings of Almeda's. In late 1854, when one of her siblings died, Almeda inherited Richmond through a process of drawing lots. Just three weeks later, she married James and brought twenty-one-year-old Richmond with her to her new husband's plantation.[3]

Despite the relatively short distance between Fisherville and the Davies brothers' Morning Sun estate, the move would have constituted a disruptive, and probably painful experience for Richmond. More likely than not, Richmond had been surrounded by blood relatives on the Little family's plantation—relatives whom he would have become separated from once Almeda inherited him and took him to Morning Sun. Then again, Richmond had probably *already* been separated from family members since the earlier-mentioned estate sale in 1851. Even in the off chance that he did not lose ties with blood relatives, Richmond would have certainly been impacted by the dissolution of the larger enslaved community that was at least thirty-two people strong at the time of William Little's death. Though the particulars that Richmond endured up to this point are impossible to reconstruct, his move to the Davies brothers' plantation marked a distinct turning point in his life with far-reaching consequences. Soon, once the nation descended into civil war, Richmond's enslavement would force him to experience the vortex of that conflict.[4]

Of course, Richmond was not the only enslaved person buffeted by Almeda's marriage to James. Almeda, despite her young age, would have immediately assumed the role of mistress at the Davies brothers' plantation, and, accordingly, would have been in a position of authority over the enslaved workforce—in particular, the women and girls. Attempts to reimagine Almeda in this capacity raise a host of speculative questions. Though she left nothing behind in her writings about anything so specific as slavery or individual bondspeople, she was raised on an estate surrounded by a sizable enslaved labor force. After her parents' death, she became the dependent of a well-known slave trader in the community—an experience that surely influenced her perceptions about the institution. Once she wed James and settled into the log house in Morning Sun, how and to what extent did Almeda wield power, influence, or control in her interactions with bondspeople? Did James encourage his wife to play an active role in plantation affairs? Or conversely, might he have tried to prevent Almeda from asserting her will and desires and expectations over the enslaved workforce?

The historian Thavolia Glymph, who has studied the power dynamics of gender within antebellum plantation households, reminds us that although the power wielded on plantations by white male heads of household like James and Logan was overtly visible and "unquestionably formidable," the agency and authority held by white women like Almeda has been "profoundly underestimated" by most scholars. Similarly, Glymph asserts, historians have tended to give short shrift to the agency that enslaved women possessed as they navigated the high-wire balancing act of keeping plantation mistresses appeased. "Domestic slaves have come down in history to us as fairly uncomplicated people who did their job, knew their place, and, after slavery, remembered the plantation mistress and her household fondly," Glymph writes. The reality, however, is that enslaved women who worked in the domestic sphere remained attuned at all times to the "complex politics" of "language, posture, and subordination" that was required of them to survive. Similarly, enslaved women, even within the limits of their bondage, worked constantly to "act on their desires for freedom, privacy, mobility, and respect."[5]

When it came to the personal lives of Logan and James Davies, as well as their younger brother Henry, the second half of the 1850s was a period when joy tended to overlap with sorrow. There would have been reason to celebrate in 1855 when Almeda gave birth to her and James's first child, a boy named Julius Augustus, or Gus, as they called him. A second son arrived in 1857. This child, William Little, or Will, derived his name from Almeda's father (and Richmond's original enslaver). Meanwhile, Henry, newly married to Mary A. Webber, had decided it was time to leave his father's Fayette County plantation and join his brothers in Shelby County. At some point in 1857, Henry established a farm of his own on land directly adjacent to his two older siblings. Later, in 1860, Logan would

Gideon J. Pillow, the prominent Columbia, Tennessee, lawyer and planter, shown here in the 1850s. Earlier, in 1842, Pillow had defended William E. Davies against state charges and related litigation stemming from a violent altercation with a neighboring planter, Dickey Chappell, and a group of men whom Chappell enslaved. William subsequently completed a land swap with Pillow that resulted in the Davis family relocating to Fayette County in West Tennessee. Courtesy Tennessee State Library & Archives

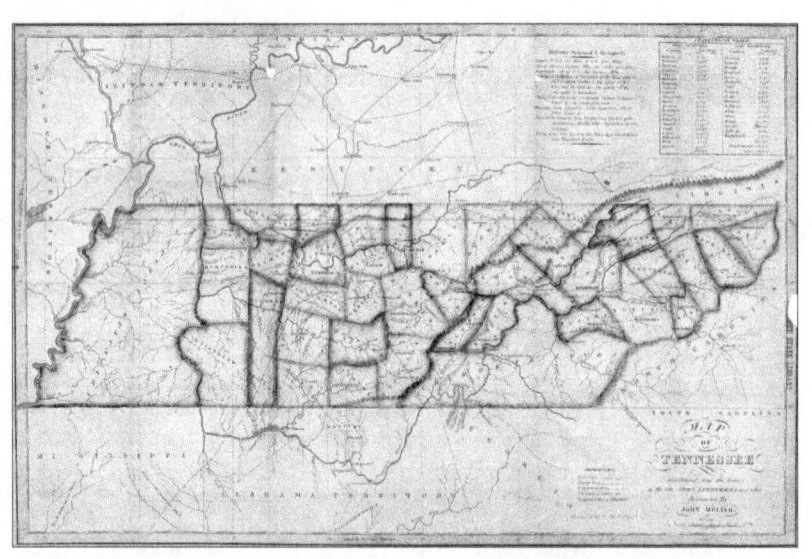

This 1818 map reveals how unsettled West Tennessee remained well into the nineteenth century when the Chickasaws signed a treaty with the US government that forced the tribe to concede their ancestral lands between the Mississippi and Tennessee Rivers. By 1843, when William Davies's family and the community of people they enslaved migrated to Fayette County, West Tennessee's population had witnessed a "meteoric ascent" due to the scramble to cultivate cotton in the region's rich soil. Courtesy of Tennessee State Library & Archives

1847 newspaper advertisement for the Bolton Dickens & Co. "Negro Mart." Until a bloody business feud in the late 1850s ended the firm's financial fortunes, Bolton & Dickens was the largest and most successful slave-trading business in Memphis, with agents operating offices in Richmond, Vicksburg, Mobile, and other Southern cities. Washington Bolton, one of the firm's partners, owned an estate in northeast Shelby County adjacent to the Davies brothers' plantation. *Memphis Daily Eagle*, September 25, 1849, Memphis and Shelby County Room, Memphis Public Library

James Davies, photographed here at an unknown date, probably in the late 1850s. By the late 1840s, when he was in his early twenties, James and his older brother Logan had begun taking steps toward establishing a plantation of their own in the Morning Sun community of Shelby County, roughly halfway between their father's Fayette County estate and Memphis. DMA Archives

Almeda Penelope Little, pictured here in the late 1850s. She was sixteen years old, recently orphaned, and the dependent of a local slave trader and close friend of the Davies family when she married James Davies in 1854. Prior to her death in 1859, Almeda gave birth to two sons, Julius Augustus "Gus" Davies and William Little Davies. DMA Archives

Charcoal portrait of Logan Davies completed by an unknown artist circa 1861. DMA Archives

Portrait of Logan's wife, Frances Anna Vaughn Davies, believed to have been completed at the same time as her husband's. DMA Archives

Amos was born
November 9th 1858

Elias was born the
31 of October 1859

Young was born the
27th July 1860

Madison was born
20 December 1861

Polly was born the
13 January 1862

Martha was born
February 14th 1852

Jacob was born Sept
1st 1855

Emily was born
March 19, (10) 1856

Harry was born
July 18 1857
Died 1858

Archa was born
March 27 1858

Arominta was born
February 1852
Died April 4 1858

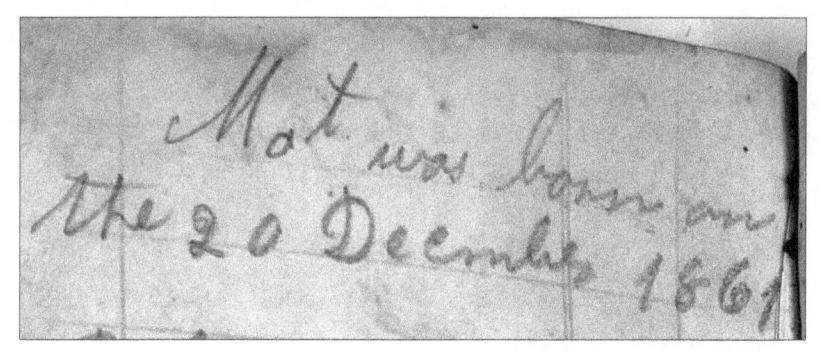

Most of the birth ledgers that survive in the DMA Archives pertain to people whom William Davis/Davies enslaved in Virginia, and later, on his Tennessee plantations in Maury and Fayette counties. The exceptions are these twelve individuals whose births (and in a few cases deaths) were recorded at Logan and James Davies's Shelby County plantation between 1852 and 1862. DMA Archives

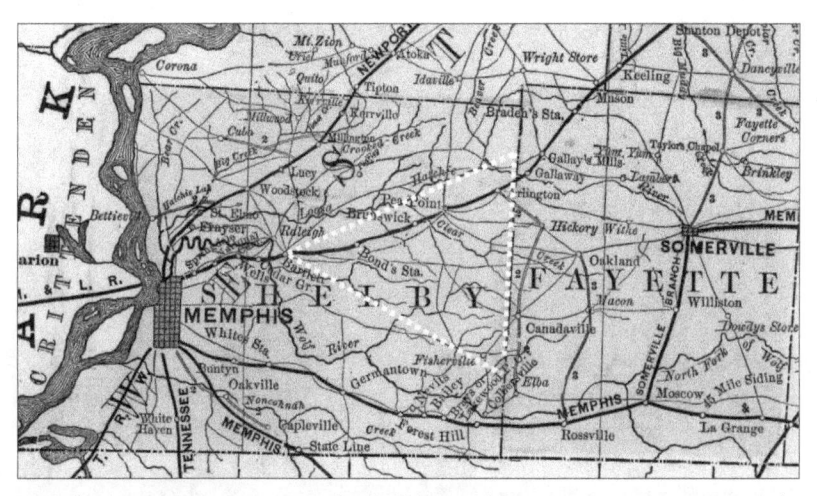

Map depicting the approximate boundaries and communities that composed the "Northeast Shelby Triangle." Highlighted dots indicate the approximate location of Logan and James Davies's estate and their father's estate in Fayette County. Courtesy of Shelby County Archives

For commercial cotton producers, it was crucial to establish trusted relationships with the firms of agents, or factors, who negotiated sales of their consigned cotton to the wider market. The Fowlkes & Co. factorage firm in Memphis was one of the most important for William Davies. *Weekly Bulletin*, October 26, 1860, Memphis and Shelby County Room, Memphis Public Library

This undated photo from the 1860s, believed to be among the earliest images of downtown Memphis, gives a sense for what a bustling street scene in the city might have looked like prior to the Civil War. Courtesy of Shelby County Archives

become a family man also through his marriage to an eighteen-year-old neighbor named Frances Anna Vaughn.[6]

Yet these happy developments were tempered by losses. The Davies brothers' mother, Sarah Hadley Davies, died in 1855. Beyond a vague reference to Sarah being buried on the family's Fayette County land, nothing else was recorded for posterity about her final resting place, nor her cause of death. Most impactful of all, Almeda died suddenly in September 1859 of an undetermined illness. Only twenty-one years old at the time, she was laid to rest in the Little family's cemetery in Fisherville.[7]

Almeda Little Davies's brief life underscores the precariousness of life for women in rural antebellum communities. By the time that she married James at the tender age of sixteen, Almeda had already endured the deaths of both of her parents, three of her brothers, and her initial guardian, Charles Williams. Given the condensed timeline of these fatalities, combined with evidence showing that quinine treatments were administered, yellow fever was the likely culprit. Almeda would have developed her own unique understandings of mortality and human suffering as she witnessed all that death occur around her through her formative years. Judging by her surviving writings, she seems to have become quite aware that her options in life were limited. When she was sent by her second guardian, Markum Williams, to attend the Macon Female Institute boarding school in Fayette County, she penned essays that spoke to a sense of yearning for grander adventures than the life in front of her. In one example, she spoke of her desire to experience the "lofty grandeur" of mountains. "Mountain scenery I have never witnessed," she wrote, "though my idea of it is peculiarly grand and beautiful. I have often pictured to myself the . . . long range of elevated earth, studded with every variety of shrubbery. Here and there . . . the blue sky, then a precipice so sudden as to give one a sensation of dizziness, with large jutting rocks overgrown with long flowering moss like beautiful velvet." Almeda struck a notably different tone in another essay she penned a few years later, just before her marriage to James. This time, while reflecting on nature and the beauty of singing birds, she admitted that "man is truly . . . a cipher in comparison."[8]

In the wake of Almeda's death, James made sure to record in his ledger the date of his wife's passing, along with an accompanying note that read "Rest sweet spirit Rest." Whatever grief he continued to endure, however, he did not let it influence his and Logan's planting schedule.

The following year, the brothers' plantation recorded a real estate value of $15,840—more than triple the value of their father's operation at that point. Furthermore, their personal estate—a figure that was largely based on the twenty-two bondspeople enumerated in the brothers' 1860 slave schedule—had climbed to $27,800.[9]

The Davies brothers' rather rapid rise into a new wealth class had been built almost exclusively on cotton. Following the 1859 planting season, for instance, their plantation recorded a total of eighty-five ginned cotton bales. This figure placed the brothers firmly in the upper echelon of Shelby County's most productive cotton growers. In fact, out of the 269 heads of household who appear in the 1860 census for Civil Districts Eight and Nine (an area that encompassed the bulk of the Northeast Shelby Triangle), only six are listed as growing more cotton than Logan and James. To be sure, it wasn't solely cotton that enslaved workers produced at the brothers' estate. They also raised a large contingent of livestock, especially sheep and swine. Other commodities included corn, butter, and sweet potatoes. Still, judging by the agricultural census data for the brothers' operation, there is one glaring takeaway: Having reached the very climax of the antebellum cotton boom, Logan and James had made the decision to throw themselves fully—and by extension, the enslaved people they forced to work their fields—upon the fortunes of King Cotton.[10]

By taking a deeper look at the demographics of the enslaved community* at Logan and James's plantation—and then comparing that

---

* The (at least) twenty-two men, women, and children who were enslaved at the Davies brothers' plantation in 1860 resided in five houses on the plantation, according to data from the 1860 Slave Schedule. The Davies Manor Historic Site has not been able to determine the location of these dwellings. Extrapolating from Ellen Davies-Rodgers's accounts, however, it is possible they were located along a narrow road that ran south from the brothers' log house for roughly a mile before intersecting with the Memphis to Somerville Road, a.k.a., the Old Stage Road (today's US 64). Davies-Rodgers claimed that this road had originally been a Chickasaw trail. She also stated in her books that the road had been called "Smokey Road" before the Civil War as a result of the home fires built by enslaved people. As she writes in *Along the Old-Stage-Coach Road*, "Along this part of the old road (ca. 1850) were located a number of log cabins in which the workers on the plantation lived. When the families came from the fields and built fires in their cabins with which to cook suppers and smoke encircled the area that part of the Trail became known as "Smokey Road."

picture to similar data about the estates run by Henry and their father—additional insights are revealed about the Davies family's entrenched position within the commercial cotton economy on the eve of the Civil War. Of the thirteen men and boys whom Logan and James enslaved in 1860, two were in their early thirties; four were in their twenties; four were between the ages of ten and nineteen; and three were less than ten. Of the nine women and girls they enslaved, one was in her early thirties; three were in their twenties; three were between ten and nineteen; and two were under ten. The Davies brothers, in short, placed top priority on enslaving young people who were capable of performing the intensive field work inherent to high-yield cotton production.[11]

Adjacent to Logan and James's plantation, Henry's two-hundred-acre farm held an even younger enslaved community. Of the ten people whom Henry enslaved, the oldest was a thirty-year-old man, followed by two women in their early twenties, an eleven-year-old girl, a ten-year-old boy, and five children under the age of six. These figures are contrasted somewhat by the demographics of the enslaved population at William Davies's Fayette County plantation. There, a seventy-year-old woman (probably Patta, or "Aunt Pat") and another woman, age sixty (possibly Frankey), constituted the two oldest members.* A forty-five-year-old man and a forty-year-old woman were the next two oldest people. Beyond these individuals, the remaining people were quite young: Two were in their early thirties; four were in their twenties; six were between the ages of ten and nineteen; and four were less than ten.[12]

When considered together, these three Davies family estates enslaved a total of (at least) fifty-two people in 1860 whose combined labor yielded 139 cotton bales. As a result, the combined real estate and personal estate values for the three operations had reached a figure of $85,619—or approximately $3.2 million adjusted to 2024. Although it is true that cotton production had undergirded the Davies family's livelihood since the 1820s, when William first established himself in Tennessee, the degree to which the family had leaned into large-scale cultivation of the cash crop had

---

* Patta's age, based on her birth ledger entry, would have been sixty-eight rather than seventy. However, it should be noted just how frequently mistakes were made in slave schedules that listed the ages (not names) of people enslaved on estates. Similarly, enslaved people themselves oftentimes did not possess clear understandings about their own birthdates.

reached new heights by the eve of the Civil War. Success in cotton was relative though; even when grouped together into the above-mentioned figure, the crop yields, slaveholdings, and overall wealth of the Davies family still paled in comparison to those planters who existed at the pinnacle of the late antebellum socioeconomic hierarchy.

Within the Northeast Shelby Triangle, there were two planters who most conspicuously fit such a description. The first was a man named Samuel Jackson Hayes. A nephew of Andrew Jackson, Hayes had served in the Jackson White House as a young man before returning to West Tennessee and establishing himself as a prominent planter and political figure. Although Hayes's primary residence was on his massive Madison County plantation, he owned a separate 4,500-acre estate roughly four miles northeast of the Davies brothers that he ran in absentee through family members and overseers. In 1860, the seventy-eight enslaved workers on Hayes's Shelby County plantation produced a staggering five hundred bales of cotton, helping bring his combined real and personal estate value—again, in just Shelby County—to $216,662, or approximately $8 million adjusted to 2024. The other extremely wealthy figure in the Davies brothers' community was Thomas B. Crenshaw. The planter and Whig-affiliated county court judge enslaved eighty-one people across his 2,300-acre Lone Hill plantation just north of Fisherville. Whereas Hayes's plantation focused almost exclusively on cotton, the enslaved community at Lone Hill produced a more diverse crop schedule. Yet they still managed to produce 130 bales of cotton in 1860, in the process helping bring Crenshaw's combined real and personal estate value that year to $141,00, or approximately $5.2 million today.[13]

The broader economic, political, and social forces that enabled planters like Crenshaw and Hayes to garner such enormous personal wealth had been coalescing and intensifying for decades. By 1860 though, the South's cotton and slave-based economy functioned as the single-most important driver of an internationally linked web of capitalistic commerce and industrial-style production. An "insatiable demand" existed for the "practically imperishable" commodity that was raw cotton—a commodity that "possessed more of the attributes of a legal tender than anything produced by human labor except gold." US export figures testified to the seemingly bottomless global demand: The American South in 1860 produced two-thirds of all commercially grown cotton in the world, and four-fifths of all the cotton that ended up in Britain's "mammoth" textile industry. Not surprisingly, the twelve wealthiest counties in America, per capita, were all located in the South. The South's enslaved population by this point had reached approximately four million people; these four million human beings were collectively valued at some three billion dollars, an amount that exceeded the value of all the South's farmland.[14]

Within the cotton-growing counties of West Tennessee, slaveholding planters, whether they were considered upper-class status (Logan and James), or members of an "elite" class (Thomas B. Crenshaw and Samuel Hayes), enjoyed the advantages that came with being located near a major market whose conditions could not have been more ideal. Memphis, due to its unique geographic location and strong economic ties to the industrializing North, had transformed itself into the nation's largest inland port by 1860. The Memphis slave market was also "by far the largest" in the central South, providing "the best readily accessible market for slaves from the upper Carolinas, upper Georgia and most of Tennessee." Testament to Memphis's attractiveness is data on the growth of cotton shipments through the antebellum years: Between the mid-1820s and 1860, the amount of cotton being shipped out of Memphis skyrocketed from a mere three hundred bales per year to an astounding four hundred thousand bales a year. The explosion of railroad lines in the 1850s—none being more important than the Memphis to Charleston line—further solidified the city's preeminent position in the nation's cotton economy.[15]

Not surprisingly, as these developments took place, Memphis's population had continued to skyrocket, reaching 22,623—17 percent of whom were Black—by 1860. Simultaneously, the taxable wealth rose from $679,000 in 1840 to $18.2 million twenty years later. Recognizing the boom times for what they were, entrepreneurs from near and far had flocked to the city known as the "Child of Cotton." Some were Northerners who had originally made their fortunes manufacturing high-end cotton goods before moving south and establishing brokerage firms that bought and sold the raw commodity in bulk. Others were natives of the Southern Atlantic Seaboard states who had come west to Memphis to carve out their niches in the factorage industry. Hundreds of others came to open the lodging houses, grocery stores, and artisan businesses that supported the cotton economy. And then there were those like the Davies brothers' neighbor, Washington Bolton, whose place in the cotton economy centered on the highly lucrative profession of slave trading.[16]

Despite the drought conditions that plagued West Tennessee during the summer and early fall of 1860, the Davies family's fields had managed to remain at least moderately productive. Throughout October, the peak month of the cotton harvest, Logan and James, as well as their now eighty-one-year-old father, all stayed active transporting their cotton to market in Memphis. On some occasions they shipped cotton by rail on the Memphis to Charleston line. Other times they used wagons. Receipts issued during the first two weeks of October show the Jones Brown & Co. factorage firm selling eleven bales on behalf of James, netting him a combined profit of $658.50 after charges for freight, drayage, fire insurance, and commission. On October 30, Jones Brown sold seven bales for Logan, earning him $402.43 after charges. The receipt for Logan's sale that day mentions a "Bob Davis" being present—perhaps indicating that Bob was an enslaved man who had either handled or assisted with the trip to market. William, meanwhile, continued to consign his cotton to the Fowlkes & Co. firm. On the same day that Logan's cotton was sold, the Fowlkes & Co. netted William $987.74 through the sale of seventeen bales. The fact that William did not pay freight or drayage on this particular occasion suggests that he either assigned someone else to transport his cotton (probably Logan and Bob Davis) or (less likely) continued to make trips to Memphis himself at his advanced age.[17]

That October, as the cotton produced on the Davies family's land wound its way into and out of the Memphis market, the looming presidential election gripped the nation's attention. With the Democratic Party split between Stephen A. Douglas and John C. Breckenridge, and the Kentuckian Abraham Lincoln having emerged as the Republican Party's nominee, the contest for America's next chief executive had evolved into a fever-pitched battle between forces pushing fundamentally different visions of the nation's future. For the time being, the winds of disunion blew more moderately in Shelby County and the rest of Tennessee than they did in places like South Carolina and the Deep South cotton states. Tennesseans' widespread support for the third-party Constitutional Unionist candidate, John C. Bell, was one sign of that relative moderation. Still though, for the vast majority of Southerners, Tennesseans included, the election had essentially developed into a referendum on way of life—one that was built upon the economic realities of race-based slavery, and, more generally, varying degrees of white supremacy embedded into the body politic.[18]

Stark divisions over questions of states' rights and slavery's role in national expansion had been building since the earliest days of the Republic. Yet throughout the 1850s those divisions had become amplified to previously unimaginable levels as a series of "spectacular episodes"—the Fugitive Slave Act, the publication of *Uncle Tom's Cabin*, the events at Bleeding Kansas, and John Brown's failed raid at Harper's Ferry to name just a few—rocked the national consciousness. Against this backdrop, the stakes of the 1860 presidential race came to be viewed by many in apocalyptic terms.[19]

In Memphis and Shelby County, when Abraham Lincoln won the election, newspapers described a "gloom of despair" that settled over the populace as they absorbed the "sad intelligence." Shelby County voters had overwhelmingly supported Douglas and the Unionist Bell over the secessionist candidate, Breckenridge. Their reasons were largely economic: With Memphis's strong commercial links to the North, the city had little to gain and much to lose if the nation turned on itself in a fratricidal conflict. Still, few could bring themselves to see Lincoln's election as anything other than a harbinger of war. Gradually, even in the relatively moderate political climate of Memphis, the voices of the fire eaters began to sound less and less extreme. With the reality of war looking more and more certain, many began to feel that it would be impossible for Tennessee to remain neutral. If war arrived, the editor of the *Memphis Appeal* wrote in late November, "Tennessee, being a Southern State–Southern in sympathy–Southern in interest–Southern in susceptibility–stands in no position to wage a fruitless war upon her Sister States."[20]

By the middle of December, a definite change was in the air. The *Daily Memphis Avalanche* urged the recently formed Minute Men group to continue their "noble work" of pressuring all locals, especially Northerners and foreigners, to support the push for secession. The paper even endorsed violence committed against locals who expressed hostility to "healthy Southern sentiments." Though the newspaper had always been hardline, its editorials now veered into new rhetorical territory, telling the

Minute Men they should "Hunt up the cowardly ingrates, and if necessary nail their vile carcasses to their own doors or hang them upon the public lamppost." The time for moderation had clearly passed. Now, in order to rid Memphis of the "blighting stain of abolitionism," it was necessary to take drastic action. "When you find a traitor," the editorial continued, "consign him to a dishonored grave, with no monument to mark the accursed spot save a rough stake driven through the body of the miserable ingrate."[21]

PART III
1861–1865

Federal troops entering Memphis, June 6, 1862. Courtesy of Shelby County Archives

CHAPTER 10

Goodbye Pa

Throughout the morning and early afternoon of April 1, 1861, people from all corners of Shelby County streamed into the county seat of Raleigh to attend a series of political meetings at the courthouse. The men who led the competing factions of this crowd sought consensus within their respective political camps about how to respond to larger events that had occurred since President Lincoln's November election. With the formal secession of South Carolina and six other Deep South slaveholding states, Tennesseans across the political spectrum were now facing a watershed decision: they could either follow the breakaway states into the new Southern Confederacy, or they could push their state leaders to somehow find a way to remain with the Union.[1]

Although Unionist sentiments in Shelby County had deteriorated dramatically, plenty of people still believed alternatives to secession were possible. Those who held out faith in compromise—men like Thomas B. Crenshaw—had convened in Raleigh under the banner of the Union Convention of Shelby County. By the time that Crenshaw and the unionists had concluded their portion of the day's events, they had appointed local delegates for the upcoming congressional and gubernatorial elections. They had also adopted a resolution supporting a proposed convention of eight Upper South states that would seek a response to the "political troubles growing out of the slavery question."[2]

On the opposite end of the ideological spectrum, the States Rights Secession Party of Shelby County emerged from the gathering in Raleigh with their own list of resolutions and election delegates. Appointees from the Davies brothers' social circle included Joel Royster, Roscoe Feild, Alex Donelson, Dr. Virginius Leake, and Robert Williams. The platforms that these Shelby County secessionists drafted were every bit as fervent as the Unionists' platforms were tepid. Along with denouncing anyone who continued to support the "northern Black republican confederacy," they agreed to "accept the Constitution of the Southern Confederacy as furnishing a platform of sound principles, upon which good and true men can safely stand." Likewise, they would "vote for no man for any political position who is not in favor of immediate and unconditional secession of the state." The speeches that accompanied the resolutions denounced "with unmerciful severity" anyone who continued to show "hostility to the South." An older man in the crowd, Col. R. G. Payne, gave an especially rousing performance, according to news accounts. Employing his "ready oratorial charge," Payne argued for the "impossibility of ever effecting any settlement of the slavery question, inasmuch as the North would never acknowledge the right of property in man, and the South never could be satisfied without it." This hard truth, Payne said, "settled" the matter of secession as "the only remedy."[3]

Eleven days later, Confederate artillery fired on federal troops stationed at Fort Sumter in Charleston harbor. When Lincoln responded by calling for state militias—including two from the Volunteer State—to put down the rebellion, Tennessee Governor Isham Harris declared that his state "will not furnish a single man for coercion, but fifty thousand if necessary for the defense of our rights, and those of our Southern Brethren." Now, many Tennessee Unionists, Thomas B. Crenshaw among them, found themselves converting to the once unthinkable position of secession. Fort Sumter, virtually overnight, had changed everything.[4]

Crenshaw's sudden transformation into a secessionist illustrates the enormous social and political pressures facing Unionists in West Tennessee: On April 20, just three weeks after he had helped lead the Unionist convention at Raleigh, Crenshaw joined Robert Ecklin and Roscoe Feild to organize a meeting at Wash's Store in Morning Sun. The purpose of this meeting was to form "a military company to protect home interest, as well as to rally the young men for the purpose of volunteering . . . service to the Southern confederacy." By the time that Crenshaw, Ecklin, and Feild adjourned the gathering, seventy-three men, including James Davies, had joined the "Morning Sun Home Guards," and pledged themselves to "repel aggression from the North and to assist our fellow citizens of the Southern Confederacy with all the means in our power."

Joining Davies in the home guard were his friends and close acquaintances Edward Curd Leake and Markum Williams, along with Joshua B. Ecklin (Robert Ecklin's son) and Florian and Merritt Crenshaw (Thomas B. Crenshaw's sons).[5]

In the days and weeks that followed, similar meetings to form local home guard companies and prepare for war occurred in communities across Tennessee. In Somerville, Fayette County, near William Davies's plantation, a public gathering at the county courthouse raised two thousand dollars to support a local military company. The citizens there also approved a resolution demanding that Tennessee "secede as soon as practicable . . . and connect herself for weal or for woe with the destiny of the Confederate States."[6]

Although William was ill and bedridden by this point in his old age, he still probably followed these developments closely. To what extent he supported or did not support his community's embrace of secession is impossible to say for certain. One takeaway, though, is certain: from his birth in the middle of the American Revolution, to his preaching through the Second Great Awakening, to his ambitious commercial pursuits on the expanding slave-powered cotton frontier, to his observations of his country splitting apart, Davies had managed to participate in and bear witness to a spectacularly dramatic stretch of the American experiment. Now, as he neared the end of his life, he was witnessing in the Southern reaction to Lincoln's election the beginnings of a "momentous shift in American politics." Soon, politicians like Thomas B. Crenshaw who descended from the "hierarchical conservatism of Federalism and old-line Whiggery" would be all but extinct. In their place, a new brand of Southern conservatism would emerge—one that was based on the "presumptions of white supremacy, the supreme power of local elites, and the proclaimed virtues of 'small government.'" The long-term shift in that direction would take some time yet to fully coalesce. In the short term, fundamental existential questions about America's fate would have to be decided.[7]

Taken as a whole, Tennessee had gone through a "quantum leap in attitude," shifting in less than half a year's time from a majority Unionist state that was deeply skeptical of disunion to one firmly aligned with its fire-eating Deep South neighbors. When the General Assembly voted on June 8 to leave the Union, Tennessee became the last of the eleven states to join the Confederate States. Military preparations had already commenced in the Volunteer State well before legislators made secession official, however. William Davies's former lawyer, Gideon Johnson Pillow (by this point he had become famous for his actions in the Mexican American War), was tapped by Gov. Harris in April as the senior major general in the Tennessee Militia and commander of the Provisional Army of Tennessee. Pillow focused on construction of fortifications along the Mississippi River north of Memphis. By early June, the largest fort, named in Pillow's honor, had emerged on the northernmost of the Chickasaw Bluffs overlooking the river. Simultaneously, Pillow led the early recruitment efforts in Tennessee for volunteer soldiers. Twenty-year-old Beverly Thurman (youngest son of the late Fendal and Ann (Royster) Thurman and nephew to Joel Royster) was among the eager young men from the Northeast Shelby Triangle who immediately answered the call to arms. On May 15, Thurman enlisted in Company A of the Fourth Tennessee Infantry, or the "Shelby Greys," and reported to duty at Fort Pillow. Following Thurman's lead—and, in effect, directly responding to the calls for soldiers made by their own fathers back in April—eighteen-year-old Joshua B. Ecklin and twenty-five-year-old David "Dick" Royster (Beverly's first cousin) enlisted on June 4 in Company H of the Thirteenth Tennessee Infantry.[8]

As they committed themselves to the destiny of the new Confederacy, each of these young men grappled with their own distinct emotions. In the case of Beverly Thurman and Joshua B. Ecklin, whatever fears they harbored would have at least been mitigated by the fact that neither ventured into the war alone; instead, each took an enslaved "body servant" with him. Young Price, the enslaved teenager who accompanied Beverly Thurman, and Arthur, brought to war by Joshua B. Ecklin, were forced to act as personal camp servants.* Histories of the Civil War frequently

---

* Young is believed to have been one of at least five children born to Simon Price (the shoemaker, free man of color, and co-founder with Joseph "Free Joe" Harris of Gray's Creek Baptist Church) and Simon's enslaved wife Kitty. As this narrative has already discussed, the Price family (all of whom, other than Simon, remained enslaved) lived on the estate of Fendall and Ann (Royster) Thurman between the early 1840s and early 1850s. In 1852, when the widowed

note that enslaved men were attached to higher-ranking Confederate officers and generals. Yet plenty of low-ranking soldiers like Thurman and Ecklin entered the army accompanied by body servants. With respect to David Royster, there is no record of him enlisting with an enslaved man. What is known about Royster is that he joined the Confederate army with his eyes wide open to the mortal dangers he was about to face. Just two days before he enlisted, commenting upon the "uncertainty of human life," he penned a final will that named his three sisters and a niece as the beneficiaries of his estate. Notably, the property that David Royster concerned himself with in this final document consisted exclusively of nine enslaved people.[9]

Just a few months earlier, at the Shelby County Courthouse meeting in Raleigh, the popular speaker Col. R. G. Payne had bluntly addressed the South's intractable reliance on slavery. Southerners, he declared, would "never be satisfied without [slavery]." The actual task of putting such rhetoric to the ultimate test had now fallen to novice soldiers from Payne's community like David Royster, Joshua B. Ecklin, and Beverly Thurman. James and Henry Davies, along with most of the other men of fighting age from the Northeast Shelby Triangle, would soon be enlisting as well. That so many of these young Confederates entered the war with enslaved men at their sides illustrates yet another facet of white Southerners' addiction to the forced labor—not to mention the emotional support—of bondspeople.[10]

At some point in late 1861 or early 1862, in the midst of the secession crisis, James Davies had travelled to Central Texas to visit his recently widowed sister, Mary (Davies) Scantlin, and her two young boys. Although

---

Ann Thurman died, the Price's children—Young, Royal, Jim, Eliza, and Louisa—along with Kitty herself, were inherited by Fendall and Ann's then eleven-year-old son, Beverly. (Simon Price is believed to have died prior to 1852.) Beverly Thurman, along with the Prices, then relocated to the plantation located just over the Fayette County line owned by Beverly's oldest brother, J. P. Thurman, and J. P.'s wife, Sallie (Ecklin) Thurman. (Kitty Price is believed to have died in 1854.) Because Simon Price's unique background and status allowed his family's surname to appear in pre-Civil War estate and census records, subsequent references in this narrative to Young, Jim, and Royal will use their surname also.

nine years Mary's junior, James shared a close bond with his sister and seems to have made this trip to help her navigate the aftermath of her husband J. D.'s death in 1859. Mary and J. D. Scantlin had left Tennessee for Texas around 1856. They took with them three enslaved people—a woman named Alee and two girls, Frank and Lece—whom they had acquired via advancements from William Davies. Settling in the community of Clifton, on the banks of the Bosque River, they established a small farm on what was then the newest edge of America's expanding frontier. Initially, Mary seems to have handled the move to Texas well. But after J. D.'s death she became increasingly lonely and anxiety ridden. In a letter that she penned to James in the spring of 1862, shortly after he had returned home from the visit, Mary explained that she was "so nervous . . . I can't hardly write."[11]

Compounding her emotional struggles, Mary worried constantly about the theft of her livestock. Similarly, she fretted about unwittingly doing business with one of the untrustworthy "rogues" that were "many and hard to find out." According to Mary, a chaotic atmosphere of violence and mistrust, intensified by the coming war, permeated her community. She told James that shortly after he had left Clifton, a mob of some one hundred men hung three teenage boys from the limb of a live oak as punishment for stealing cows. Another man connected to the theft had been shot dead outside his home. Fears of attacks from Indians persisted also. "I expect there to be a great deal of trouble here this fall with the indians abolitionists and cow thieves," Mary told James. "We watching every one now that comes in here." Adding yet another layer to Mary's troubled mind was her awareness that she would probably never see her father alive again. "Tell Pa I want to see him worse than anybody on earth," she wrote of William. "I want to be with him and wait on him in his old age. I think I could help him if I could do nothing more than hand him his crutches and hand him a drink of water and fix around about him and fix the pillows under it sometimes. . . . Goodby Pa."[12]

Despite her trials, Mary tried to put on a brave face, informing her brother about the healthy hogs that she owned and her plans to acquire more. She told James that he should consider moving to Clifton and starting fresh. "You could enjoy yourself. You could look round and see what would be best. You could enjoy yourself so much more than I do." James does seem to have given a move to Texas real thought. Recently widowered himself, he may have considered it an ideal time to make a new start with his two young sons. During his stay with his sister, he had told her he "wasn't going to farm" with Logan for the coming planting season. Given the events playing out around him, however, his comments may have had more to do with the secession crisis than anything else: If war came, the likelihood that he would be able to focus on a normal planting season probably seemed doubtful. Soon, of course, the war did come. And with it went any dreams James may have had about "enjoy[ing] himself" in Texas.[13]

The American Civil War erupted throughout the summer and fall of 1861 on battlefields in Virginia, Kentucky, and Missouri. Beverly Thurman, stationed at Fort de Russey in Columbus, Kentucky, was in high spirits in June as his regiment prepared for an assault by the Union forces gathered upriver at Cairo, Illinois. Writing his sister-in-law Sallie Ecklin Thurman, Beverly predicted that the Yankees would be "whipped whenever the Bloody 4th [Infantry Regiment] gets after them." He went on to write of his body servant that "Young is doing very well. I have had no trouble from him."[14]

The following month, on July 25, Confederate forces decisively defeated the Federals at Manassas, Virginia, in the war's first major engagement. Though sobered by the horrifying casualty counts, Southerners steeled themselves for what lay ahead with displays of bravado and self-assurance that their cause was heroic. In Memphis, *The Avalanche* virtually rejoiced that the South's "christening of Blood" had at long last arrived. "Most nations have received the baptism of blood," the editorial proclaimed. "They have had their birth stand the convulsions of Revolution and the fiery tempests of war. . . . They have had to establish their claim to nationality with the sword, and write out the charter of their existence in characters of blood. Our own young nation of the South, the latest born of earth, forms no exception to this great historic law."[15]

Perhaps James Davies encountered this very same editorial as he followed the war's early progress in local newspapers. As a member of his local home guard unit, chances are also good that he encountered firsthand reports of fighting through letters written home by his friends and acquaintances like Beverly Thurman, David Royster, and Joshua B. Ecklin. Though no record of James's specific activities in the home guard survives, we can assume that his Morning Sun unit did what most Confederate home guard companies did: encourage enlistments, patrol for runaway slaves, and harass those Unionists too principled to have made their conversion to the Confederacy's cause. Meanwhile, Logan Davies, on the verge of his thirty-seventh birthday, stayed busy managing the plantation's affairs with his young wife Frances. Though he would have been on the older end of the spectrum, Logan was still young enough to enlist. Nevertheless, an agreement seems to have been reached early on that he would assume primary responsibility for running the plantation while James went to war. In the short term though, it would be James who took the lead managing a financial matter that had nothing to do with soldiering.

In late September or early October of 1861, William Davies died at the age of eighty-one. Given his poor heath and advanced age, his death would not have surprised his children. But what may very well *have* surprised them, especially given William's long track record of business acumen, is that he died intestate. As a result, James assumed the task of settling the estate.

In October, when he wrote to Texas with news of their father's death, James asked his sister Mary to either travel to Tennessee to sort out the details, or send a full accounting of the property she had received over the course of her lifetime. Mary replied that it would be impossible for her to visit. She doubted her ability to endure such a long trip. She also had no one she could trust to "attend to the hire of my negroes." Mary promised that she would mail James the information he needed in a subsequent letter. For the moment though, she simply wanted to process the "source of grief" caused by the "sad intelligence of our dear father's death." Mary admitted to James that she felt "so lonely and disconsolate," then added, "You say you have hard times there but I know you can't have half so hard as we have. . . . You don't know how low down I get sometimes."[16]

Mary sounded in slightly better spirits in the follow-up letter she sent a month later. She reported that her sons were doing well in school under the instruction of a new teacher. This was rather surprising, she wrote, given that the teacher had come to Clifton from the North. "He is a Yankee but he knows how to advance the children," Mary admitted. Relaying war news, she described the anxiety among Texans about a probable

Federal attack on Galveston. Referencing the Union blockade of that city, she told her brother that she had recently learned about a Confederate acquaintance stationed on the coast who "could see the rascals with his naked eye." As usual, she also feared attacks by Comanches given how many local men were being recruited into Confederate companies bound for out-of-state action. "I don't think they ought to take any more men off the frontier but they keep going," Mary reported. "Some to VA some to KY and some to MO. I think we will need all on our own borders." Finally, getting to the business of her family's estate, Mary included a list of all that her father had given her dating back to 1841.[17]

Unwittingly reinforcing the degree to which the recordkeeping of American slavery reflected the dehumanization of Black people by their enslavers, Mary's inventory, signed by the local justice of the peace, listed "a mare and cow and calf" directly beside "one negro woman named Alee," "one girl named Frank," and "one girl named Lece." Mary also included a summary of the cash her father had given her over the years. Though she wasn't entirely sure, she placed the figure at three hundred dollars. In a note below the list, she made sure to add one last bit of clarification: "I have forgotten the exact date that I got the money but I am sure I got the negroes the date that I have got set down. I guess you all recollect as well as I do. If there is anything else that you recollect just name it and it will be all right. I didn't get any hogs or sheep either."[18]

CHAPTER 11

Disposed of as Follows

As James Davies took charge of communicating with Mary and his other siblings about their late father's estate, he must have taken comfort in the fact that the Civil War's fighting front had yet to reach Tennessee. Such would not be the case for long. On February 6, 1862, Union General Ulysses S. Grant captured Fort Henry on the Tennessee River. A week later the Federals sacked nearby Fort Donelson on the Cumberland River north of Nashville. The prolonged campaign that Grant subsequently launched through Middle and West Tennessee's river and rail systems served as the staging ground for the larger effort to gain control of the entire Lower Mississippi River Valley.[1]

James and his peers in the Morning Sun home guard no doubt understood that the Confederate losses at Forts Henry and Donelson bore major implications for the Southern cause. James would have also grasped by this point in the war that he and Logan could not escape disruptions to their personal financial interests: On February 8, James received a note from one of their factors in Memphis who reported the extreme difficulty of selling cotton due to the Union blockade in the Gulf of Mexico.[2]

In the midst of these foreboding developments, James turned his attention to the most important aspect of the estate situation: the distribution plan to his siblings of the people his father had enslaved at the time of his death. In keeping with state law in cases of intestate death, the task of valuing and "allot[ing] off the negroes belonging to William E. Davies" had been handed to four commissioners appointed by the county court of Fayette County. It would then be up to James to make sure the court's determinations were carried out. On February 7, the commissioners gave their signatures to the details of their allocation plan. The document the commissioners left behind—when cross referenced with other records—offers crucial insights into the fates of twenty-eight men, women, and children who were enslaved by William Davies in the fall of 1861.[3]

Between 1804, when he began keeping his "The ages of the Blacks" ledger, and November 1860, when he made the final entry in that ledger for a girl named Rachel, William Davies documented a total of fifty-eight people's names. Beyond these individuals, William, in at least two documented instances (the purchase of London in 1838, and of Ben, Mary, Amanda, and the unidentified twelve-year-old in 1850) bought additional bondspeople whose names he did not record in his ledgers. We also know there were other people (Abraham and Frankey, who were inherited by William through his father-in-law Jeremiah Burnett, and Sisy, the girl sold by William in 1851 via the local slave trader Markum Williams) whose names appear in outside records but are not included in William's surviving birth ledger pages. Likewise, an approximate (if probably quite conservative) figure for the total number of people William enslaved throughout his lifetime can be placed at about sixty-five. By juxtaposing this approximate figure against the twenty-eight individuals recorded by the Fayette County commissioners in 1862, it can be surmised that William probably enslaved somewhere approaching forty people who, over the course of his long lifetime, either died, escaped, or were sold or given away as advancements or outright gifts.[4]

Because Logan and James had already received from their father significant assistance in the form of direct cash and the advancements of enslaved people*—and then used that assistance to establish a thriving plantation that left them in better financial shape than their siblings—the brothers did not receive any of the individuals allocated off by the commissioners. (Curiously, their youngest brother Henry was also left out of the commissioners' allocation plan.) However, even though they were not named as direct recipients of bondspeople by the commissioners, Logan and James still took charge over many of their father's former

---

* Logan and James had received approximately $7,800 in combined cash advancements from their father, according to probate records from William's estate.

slaves. In numerous cases, the brothers became the de-facto owners of additional people as they assumed the task of hiring out enslaved individuals that their siblings had inherited through the commissioners—and then distributing to those same siblings the revenue earned. The allotments to Mary Scantlin of a fourteen-year-old teenager named Thomas and a three-year-old boy named Green offer a case in point: Neither Thomas nor Green were ever taken to Mary's home in Clifton, Texas. Instead, on March 6, Thomas, or "Thom" as he was referred to in the promissory note, was hired out for the rest of that year to Gabe Finney, one of James and Logan's brothers-in-law who ran a nearby farm. The one hundred dollars that Finney promised to pay James for Thom's hire would eventually be sent to Mary. Green, on the other hand (at least for the time being), was too young to be hired out, a situation that likely resulted in him staying at the Davies brothers' plantation, perhaps under the care of one of the enslaved families there.[5]

A somewhat similar arrangement occurred in the case of four people—Ben, Mary, Sealy, and Harriet—allotted to the "heirs of Nancy Davidson." Nancy was one of the Davies brothers' half-sisters who had died in Maury County in 1859 of typhoid fever. Nancy's children continued to live in Middle Tennessee. Thus, they were scheduled to receive the revenue earned when James and Logan reached an agreement to hire out Ben and Mary to two local planters—one of whom was Edward Curd Leake. (It is quite possible that this Ben and Mary were one and the same with the Ben and Mary purchased by William back in 1850.) As for Sealy and Harriet, it is not clear if they remained in Shelby County or were taken to Maury County after the commissioners' decision. Nor is it clear if Sealy and Harriet were related to Ben and Mary by blood.[6]

More evidence of James managing the hiring out of bondspeople in the wake of his father's death becomes evident by tracing the people allotted by the commissioners to the heirs of another deceased sibling, Sarah Jane (Davies) Walker. The three Walker children had become orphans back in 1847 when both Sarah Jane and her husband Robert Walker died. William had subsequently assumed guardianship of the Walker children. That role then passed to James and Logan when William died. The Walker heirs, once they moved into their uncles' log home in Morning Sun, received from the commissioners legal title to five people: a woman named Hannah, a woman named Emily, a man named Burrell, and two children named Coleman and Linda. Emily is believed to have been the mother of Coleman and Linda. As for Burrell and Hannah, they may have been a couple. Evidence supporting that possibility includes a promissory note issued to James by W. L. Daley, a white yeoman farmer who rented land from the Davies brothers in Fayette County on their recently deceased father's estate. Daly's note, dated February 13, 1862, reads as follows: "On or before the 25th Dec. next I promise to pay Jas. B. Davi[es] Guardian for the heirs of Sarah J. Walker Two Hundred & Eighty Dollars, for the hire of two negroes—Burrell and Hannah and am to furnish said negroes with the usual clothing." Promissory notes that would be written as late as 1865 continued to list Burrell and Hannah together as a pair.[7]

Still other clues about the fates of individual people—insights that would otherwise be lost—are contained within this single estate document. For example, Logan and James's oldest half-brother, W. W. Davies, who was still living in Texas, received through the commissioners a man named George, a woman named Adaline, and Adaline's child. Based on inferences drawn from postwar correspondence between James, W. W. Davies, and W. W.'s sons (the letters centered on money that James apparently still owed them), it is a good possibility that George, Adeline, and Adaline's child remained in Morning Sun so they could be hired out rather than being taken to Texas.[8]

The Davies brothers' oldest half-sister, Mariah Lockridge, received five people—Daniel, Ann, Vina, Enoch, and Emeline. No records exist showing any of the five being hired out. Furthermore, Mariah Lockridge was alive and still residing in Maury County in 1862—a location far easier to reach than Texas. Therefore, in this instance, all five individuals may have been relocated to the sizable Maury County farm that the widowed Mariah ran with her sons. Turning once more to William's ledger as a point of cross reference, the entry for Enoch shows a birthdate of June 30, 1854, making him seven years old at the time he was allocated to the Lockridge family. Emeline was recorded in William's ledger as "Emeline Pettilar," born on September 6, 1851. Both Enoch and Emeline were respectively valued by the commissioners at 400 dollars and 550 dollars. As for Daniel, Ann, and Vina, nothing else about their existence is known beyond the valuation amounts that the commissioners assigned them. The 800-dollar figure for Daniel indicates that he was in his late teens or twenties and considered a prime age for field work. Vina's valuation of 325 dollars suggests she was either a young girl or an older woman; Ann's assigned value of 675 dollars suggests she was closer to Daniel's age. These five individuals may have been a family unit that the commissioners decided to keep together even as they were (possibly) forced to move across the state.[9]

Ultimately, speculation is the key word that must be emphasized when attempting to map out and reimagine these obscure histories and familial connections. Perhaps somewhere—in the dusty pages of unexamined courthouse records, or in long-forgotten trunks of personal papers, or, much more likely, in the faint traces of oral stories passed down through the generations and preserved by nothing more than the fundamentally human yearning for a past—there exists more evidence that would allow the descendants of these particular people to definitively trace their ancestors' historical footprints. Until such evidence comes to light, however, the tragic fact remains that for Daniel, Ann, Vina, and untold numbers of people like them, virtually every trace of their time walking this earth has vanished save for documents penned by enslavers that place dollar figures beside their names. Of course, these "external values" are not what truly defined them as human beings. Instead, and returning once more to Daina Ramey Berry, it was bondspeople's "internal values"— their "soul values"—that ultimately sustained them, sometimes taking shape through religion, other times through more earthly mediums, yet always playing a key role in their ability to survive and retain their own sense of humanity.[10]

And yet, in some cases, more definitive pictures of people's lives in bondage *can* be rediscovered in the records. Some of the most revealing data gleaned from the allocation documents pertains to the seven individuals allotted to William's youngest daughter, Elizabeth, and her husband, Gabe Finney. Cross referencing those details with a range of other records clearly shows that the seven people in question—Wilcher, Lucious, Margrett, Amos, Anthony, Pricilla and Mary—were indeed all members of a family unit.

Wilcher (the father of the other six individuals listed in the document) appears more prominently and consistently in surviving records than any other person William Davies enslaved. Wilcher was listed by the Fayette County commissioners alongside six children he is believed to have sired with Mary since 1850. (It might be recalled that Sarah Jane, also believed to have been a child of Wilcher's, was born in 1848.) Notably, it is believed to be Wilcher's *daughter* Mary, not his wife by the same name, who appears in the commissioners' document (which does not list Sarah Jane either). The absence in the document of the elder Mary and Sarah Jane raises questions about their circumstances and location at the time of William's death. A likely explanation is that both women had already been transferred elsewhere by 1862—probably to Logan and James's plantation. Postwar records showing Wilcher, Mary, and their children (by this point having adopted the surname Tucker) continuing to stay connected to the Davies brothers' after Emancipation further support the likelihood that Mary and Sarah Jane were already living at the Morning Sun plantation when William died.[11]

Wilcher and the six children listed in the commissioners' document were presumably taken after William's death to the farm that Gabe and Elizabeth Finney owned a short distance south of Logan and James's estate. Gabe Finney was a man of modest means who had started off his career as a Fayette County merchant. He had married Elizabeth relatively late in life, at the age of forty-eight, and only then did he turn to farming. Judging by his absence in the 1860 slave schedule, Gabe does not appear to have enslaved people prior to his inheritance of Wilcher and the six children. Likewise, at the Finneys' farm, Wilcher and his children probably found themselves in a much more isolated environment than on William's plantation, where they'd been surrounded by a community of people they'd known most all their lives. On the other hand, at least Wilcher and his children had remained together. And furthermore, assuming Mary and Sarah Jane were indeed living nearby at the Davies brothers' estate, perhaps the changes resulted in the full family being able to reunite on a more regular basis than they had in the past.[12]

What is clear, however, is that Wilcher, now age forty-three, had once again been roiled by events utterly beyond his control. Taking into account what is known about the trauma he endured in his youth in Maury County, we have to wonder how he perceived the death of his long-time enslaver (and possible father). Did he grieve William's passing? Or by contrast, might he have welcomed, even celebrated, the chance for a new beginning? Or perhaps Wilcher did neither. Perhaps he simply confronted the newest round of disruptions to his and his family's world with a sense of stoicism and resignation, tapping into an ability learned from a young age to compartmentalize his complex emotions and experiences in the interest of survival.

The final clues found in (and between) the lines of this one single document are revealed in a brief note the commissioners included just above their signature. After stating that they had provided each of William's heirs with an equitable distribution of property, the commissioners wrote: "Omitted in the proper place that two of the Negroes Frankey and Patty being of no value was dispose of as follows: We allowed Mrs. [Elizabeth Blanche] Finney one hundred dollars for taking Frankey and [Henry Newton] Davies fifty dollars for taking cear of Patty and desire the Heirs to pay the same."

As noted earlier, both Frankey and Patty were among the first five people whom William had inherited in 1804 through his marriage to Joanna Burnett. Although Frankey's exact birth date is unknown, Patty, known alternately through the years as "Patta," and "Aunt Pat," was the first person William recorded ("Patta was Born February the 10, 1792") in his ledger. Through all the subsequent years—through William's circuit-riding ministries; through his days planting tobacco and opening a store with his father in Lunenburg County; through his migration to Middle Tennessee; through his planting pursuits and personal feud with Dickey Chappell in Maury County; through his second major migration in 1843 (a development that almost resulted in Patty being worked to death by the overseer Mills); and through the subsequent decades in Fayette County, until William's death—Patty and Frankey would have been a constant presence in the Davies family's life.[13]

Most importantly, Patty and Frankey had no doubt achieved prominent status within their *own* community. To what degree, and how exactly, each woman played matriarchal roles for the larger group of people William enslaved is impossible to say for certain. Given their ages in 1862, these two women were very likely mothers and grandmothers (and possibly great-grandmothers) to other members of the Black community—perhaps even many members. What is certain, though, is that Patty and Frankey would have possessed fountains of knowledge about the extended network of people who had migrated with William and his various siblings through the first half of the nineteenth century between Virginia and multiple locations in Tennessee. Likewise, they would have been in a unique position to link their historical knowledge with stories about the earlier generations of people whom Zachariah Davis had enslaved at the Reedy Creek plantation. In the specific memories that Patty and Frankey preserved and passed down about ancestors, origins, and migrations, and in the hard-earned wisdom that they imparted through their actions, words, beliefs, and survival—and surely also in the practical influence they carried when it came to negotiations, large and small alike, between members of the Davies family and the larger community that the Davieses enslaved—these two women must have carried enormous weight and importance. The Fayette County commissioners, basing their decision upon the crass economic system of slavery, may have deemed Patty and Frankey to have "no value." In reality, nothing could have been further from the truth.[14]

CHAPTER 12

His Erring Children

James Davies's efforts to hire out enslaved people in rapid succession through February and early March of 1862 suggest that he worked quickly to settle his late father's financial affairs in anticipation of joining the war effort. For Shelby Countians like James, the Civil War had morphed rapidly from a distant conflict to one that posed an immediate and visceral threat. As a result of the defeats at Forts Henry and Donelson, Nashville surrendered to Union forces on February 25. This loss—the first instance of a Confederate state capital falling into enemy hands—shocked the larger South and resulted in Tennessee Gov. Isham G. Harris and the entire state legislature fleeing to Memphis to set up a makeshift capital. Shortly afterward, President Lincoln appointed the former Tennessee governor and Unionist US senator, Andrew Johnson, as military governor of Tennessee. Meanwhile, Federal forces began a siege seeking control of Island No. 10, the Confederate stronghold that guarded the Kentucky Bend of the Mississippi River—and, by extension, all points on the river south toward Memphis.[1]

By early March, James and numerous other men from the Morning Sun home guard had decided to enlist. On March 5 (just a day before he would sign the promissory note with his brother-in-law, Gabe Finny about hiring out Thomas and Green), James joined Company L (soon to become Company I) of the Thirty-Eighth Tennessee Infantry. Following the lead of Beverly Thurman, Joshua B. Ecklin, and other young, well-to-do planters from his community, James entered the war accompanied by an enslaved body servant, Richmond, age twenty-nine. Why James took Richmond to the war instead of another man is an open question. Perhaps Richmond had developed a unique personal rapport with James in the years after Almeda's death. Or perhaps something about Richmond's health or talents gave James the impression that he would be well suited for such a dangerous and demanding role. Also, Richmond, by this point, had formed a union with Sarah Jane, believed to be the oldest daughter of Wilcher. Though it is not clear if they were officially married—as they would be after the Civil War—their first child, a girl named Hattie, was born in January 1862, just a few months before James's enlistment. Whatever the contours of James and Richmond's relationship, the decision to take Richmond to war is one that would have been grounded first and foremost in James's self-interest.[2]

The recently converted secessionist, Thomas B. Crenshaw, although far too old to enter the fray himself, performed the role of enlisting officer for the Thirty-Eighth. In addition to signing James's muster rolls, Crenshaw enlisted his own two sons, Florian and Merritt, on the very same day. The former, age twenty-three, entered the army at the rank of sergeant. Florian's younger brother, Merritt, just seventeen, joined as a private, and brought with him an enslaved man named Simon.* Enlisting alongside Florian and Merritt was their older half-cousin, thirty-nine-year-old Roscoe Feild. The local planter, Princeton graduate, and veteran of the California Gold Rush had joined as a corporal and brought with him an enslaved man named Randle. Yet another of the Morning Sun men to enlist on March 5 was James's nephew, seventeen-year-old Watt Little. Watt (the youngest brother of Almeda) entered the war accompanied by a body servant named Gabe.[3]

These Black men no doubt experienced a range of complex emotions as they were forced to join a war effort that sought to perpetuate the slave system that held them in bondage.† Their Confederate enslavers, on

---

* As recounted in Chapter 7, Logan Davies, in January 1862, received a five dollar payment from Thomas B. Crenshaw for the purpose of "hunting Simon." Although it is by no means clear that the Simon being referred to in the note as having escaped Crenshaw's plantation in January was the same Simon who Merritt Crenshaw took with him to war a few months later (in fact, logically, it seems problematic: why would Merritt risk bringing a man to war who was prone to escape?), that possibility must be considered.

† Historical notes left behind by Dr. William Little Davies in the early twentieth century are the primary—and often-times exclusive—source that has been used to determine the names of the enslaved men who were brought to war as body servants by Confederates from Morning Sun.

the other hand, would have been prone to celebrate enlistment. James, the Crenshaw brothers, Roscoe Feild, and Watt Little had spent most of the war's first year watching from the sidelines. Now, as members of a society that held vaunted ideas about manhood and valor, they would finally get their chance to prove their mettle in combat.

James Davies, for his part, left behind only the scantest evidence relating to his enlistment and the experiences that he and Richmond went through over the next three-plus years. In fact, James developed a reputation for refusing to speak at all about the war: "With him the war was over and he did not love to dwell upon its scenes," one family friend reflected many years later. Still, even if James himself did not record for posterity what he and Richmond endured, it *is* possible to obtain a ground-level glimpse of the Thirty-Eighth Regiment through other sources. Chief among those sources are the war-time letters exchanged between Beverly Thurman, his older brother J. P. Thurman, and J. P.'s wife, Sallie Ecklin Thurman. The Thurman family's letters, which directly reference Roscoe Feild and other men who knew and intersected with James and Richmond, provide a unique window into the perspectives of Confederate soldiers from Morning Sun as the war evolved. The letters also open up revealing insights about the shifting perspectives of those soldiers' loved ones on the home front as the war increasingly headed toward a Southern defeat.[4]

By the end of March 1862, Beverly Thurman and his body servant Young Price were encamped with the rest of their infantry regiment in the extreme northeastern corner of Mississippi, in the railroad town of Corinth. Approaching Corinth at the same time was J. P. Thurman, attached to the Third Tennessee Cavalry. The men of the Thirty-Eighth Tennessee—among them James Davies and Richmond, Roscoe Feild and Randle, the Crenshaw brothers and Simon, and Watt Little and Gabe—had arrived in Corinth days earlier. Corinth had also become the destination for David Royster, Joshua B. Ecklin, Joshua's body servant Arthur, and the rest of the Thirteenth Tennessee. All of these men from the Northeast Shelby Triangle were part of the larger forty-five-thousand-man army that had concentrated in the critically important railroad town upon the orders of Confederate General Albert Sidney Johnston, head of the newly formed Army of Mississippi.

Beverly Thurman, like so many others, projected an attitude of fearlessness as he waited to prove himself in the major conflict that he (correctly) suspected was at hand. He also brimmed with confidence about his own army's apparent superiority. Writing his sister-in-law on March 30, Beverly stated that he felt "certain" the Confederates would hold Island No. 10 on the Mississippi River and defeat the Federals' protracted siege. "The Yanks have come as far as they can," he told Sallie, and if they attempted to move any further south, they would "be shot from every door and window." Beverly then stated matter-of-factly, "I wish they would meet us here for I am anxious to be in a big Battle. I don't like these little skirmishes." A few days later, in his camp nearby, Beverly's brother J. P. was feeling more circumspect, penning a letter of his own to Sallie that predicted, "You may rest assured there will be some bodily hurt."[5]

The sheer mass of humanity gathered in Corinth had created an incredibly charged atmosphere. One soldier described the place as follows: "Imagine you are in the streets of New York or not quite so much crowded, and you have a pretty good notion of the amount of soldiers about here, carts mules but instead of pavement, mud about ankle deep." Along with Confederate soldiers, and the regular townspeople who had been unable to flee, thousands of enslaved people moved through the muddy streets of Corinth in these final days that preceded the Battle of Shiloh. The contingent of body servants from Morning Sun—among them, Richmond, Arthur, Randle, Gabe, Simon, and Young Price— constituted just one category of the Black population attached to Johnston's army. There were also a great many enslaved men from the surrounding region who had found themselves impressed by their owners into the general service of the Confederate army rather than on behalf of any individual soldier. For these men, army life translated into serving as cooks, teamsters, and hospital attendants. They dug trenches, mended clothing, and hauled ammunition, among other supporting roles. Significantly though, what enslaved men attached to the Army of the Mississippi were *not* doing was preparing to venture into the heat of battle themselves.[6]

Contrary to the distortions that would later be perpetuated by Confederate veterans and their descendants ("the Civil War's most persistent myth," in the words of one historian) enslaved people, with the rarest of exceptions, did not fight alongside the South's soldiers in the field. The reason is rather straightforward: For the vast majority of white Southerners, the mere thought of Black men taking up arms amounted to an anathema that directly contradicted their deeply held conceptions about the supposed supremacy of their own race. The debates that would erupt in the Confederate Congress late in the war over the issue of enslaved people taking up arms—a time when the South was utterly desperate for new manpower—epitomizes the degree to which Southerners remained opposed to Black soldiers in their ranks until the very end. As the Confederate leader Howell Cobb of Georgia stated during those debates, "The day you make a soldier of them is the beginning of the end of the Revolution. If slaves will make good soldiers our whole theory of slavery is wrong."[7]

With the exception of Richmond (whose role would be discussed and memorialized by James's son, Dr. William Little Davies, as well as Logan's granddaughter, Ellen Davies-Rodgers) and Young Price (who would be discussed in the published writings of a former Confederate general and who also appears in letters penned by various members of the Thurman family), virtually nothing has been discovered about the war-time experiences of the enslaved men from the Morning Sun area who appear in this narrative. Attempts to follow their movements and actions alongside their enslavers can likewise only go so far. Still, Richmond, Arthur, Randle, Gabe, Simon, and Young Price would have endured a litany of hardships and horrors at various points during the war. Even if they did not participate on the front lines of combat, Black men forced into the Confederate Army's service bled and died as they were caught up in peripheral fighting and stray artillery. Like the Confederates they accompanied, enslaved men endured grueling marches along terrible roads. They suffered weather extremes, sweating beneath their woolen clothing in summer, battling endless mud in the spring, and shivering through the bitter cold of long winter nights. So also would enslaved men have lived and died through the stretches of malnutrition and disease that decimated Confederate camps. In stark contrast to the romanticized historical manipulations that have so often been used to characterize enslaved men in the Confederate army as "loyal" soldiers dedicated to the Southern cause, any authentic war-time examination of James Davies and his Morning Sun contemporaries must contend with the reality that enslaved men like Richmond and his peers were there as well.[8]

Late on the afternoon of April 9, 1862, roughly forty-eight hours after the final shots rang out over the battle-scarred forests and fields of Shiloh, an exhausted, rain-soaked J. P. Thurman and his fellow survivors in the Third Tennessee Cavalry stopped in the hamlet of Monteray, Tennessee, as they retreated back to Corinth. J. P. could hardly believe he had escaped the two-day battle in one piece. Dashing off a hurried letter to his wife Sallie, he described enduring a constant "rain of shell" from a "merciless foe," and marveled, "I am without a scratch which would seem almost a miracle." Even though news about casualties remained murky, J. P. had learned that James Davies and the men of the Thirty-Eighth endured some of the worst fighting. Referring to the Thirty-Eighth's commander, Col. Robert Looney, J. P. wrote, "Looney's Regiment suffered extremely." Moving on to his concern for his brother Beverly, his brother-in-law Joshua B. Ecklin, and his cousin David Royster, J. P. added, "I can't hear anything from Bro. Josh or Dick Royster. And we are not permitted to drop our arms a moment. My horse was unsaddled last night the first time in 2 days and nights and all that time without food for him or myself.... I stand it better than I thought I could."[9]

A week later, back inside the fortifications surrounding Corinth, J. P. sent his wife two follow-up letters that contained more details. He had recently "camped near Roscoe" and visited with the men of the Thirty-Eighth, he told her, and found them "nearly all sick." Acknowledging that he was "in one of [his] moods," J. P. seemed to be processing in a more complete way the "awful and harrowing incidents of which it would take a book to write." One of those incidents, he reported, was the death of David Royster, killed during the first day's fighting. "The loss of such a child as he is a great loss indeed," he wrote. Compounding this blow, J. P. had begun to comprehend the full extent of the Confederate defeat at Shiloh and what that might mean for the larger war.[10]

Now, as J. P. assessed the totality of the situation, he could not shake a foreboding sense of gloom. Further to the west—and despite his younger brother Beverly's predictions to the contrary—Island No. 10 had fallen into the Federals' hands on the same day that the Battle of Shiloh ended.

Furthermore, a crisis of allegiance had erupted in response to the decision in Richmond to authorize the Confederacy's first conscription act. The law required all white males in the South between the ages of eighteen and thirty-five to serve a three-year enlistment. J. P. felt none too optimistic about any of it. "The Confederate army here is in the most imaginable disorder," he told his wife, "and if it is to be taken as a sample of our ability to win independence, it is exceedingly doubtful I assure you. I could tell you things that I saw upon the battlefield that I consider a burning shame to honorable Southerners." Understanding the gravity of what he was admitting, J. P. made sure to add, "The above is for you alone."[11]

Although J. P. Thurman did not name in his letters any of the "sick" men from the Thirty-Eighth other than Roscoe Feild, James Davies and Richmond were probably among those he encountered amid the post-Shiloh chaos of Corinth. Indeed, James would be listed in his muster rolls as "absent sick" for the period between May and June 1862. Whatever the particulars of James's difficulties—and however Richmond's responsibilities or health may have been impacted as a result—the conditions in Corinth were quickly becoming untenable for the entire army as the month of May wore on. Disease ran rampant due to filthy drinking water and a shortage of food supplies, leading some men to seek refuge in the hills southeast of town. A putrid smell of death permeated everything as caskets piled up on the railroad platform and the wounded and dying were crammed into the makeshift hospital at the Tishamingo Hotel. All the while, a combined Union force estimated at ninety thousand men inched ever-closer toward Corinth, threatening the complete destruction of the roughly thirty-five thousand Confederates who remained there.[12]

Back in Morning Sun, families with loved ones at Corinth desperately sought information on casualties. Rumors swirled of another major battle that would soon be at hand. Pleasant Hill Church, located in Shelby Depot a short distance north of the Davies brothers' plantation, was converted into a hospital. Two local doctors, Snowden Craven Maddux, and Abel Beaty—both of whom were close acquaintances of Logan and James—volunteered to help at the hospital along with "upwards of one hundred ladies of the vicinity." Others from the community did their best to put on a brave face. The *Memphis Daily Avalanche*, reporting on Pleasant Hill Church's transformation, predicted that the wounded men received there would be restored to "health, strength and happiness" just as soon as they got back to the simple comforts of home. Those comforts included things like "country air, quiet nights, cool butter milk, hoe cake, ash cake, chickens, squirrels, and, last but not least, woman's gentle, soothing attentions."[13]

For all their attempts at optimism, however, a great many Southerners in communities like Morning Sun felt despondent as a direct result of what had transpired at Shiloh. Citizens across the North were also horrified at the battle's body count. As for the soldiers themselves who had gone through the bloodbath and lived to tell of it, they could now dispel once and for all any remaining hopes that the war might somehow be a quick and easy affair.

Sallie Ecklin Thurman's response to the collective trauma rendered by the Confederate defeat at Shiloh illustrates how one Tennessee woman attempted to make sense of the realities that the Southern experiment in secession had begun to bring about just a year into the war. On May 18, after attending service at Morning Sun Cumberland Presbyterian Church—a day she described as a "lonely quiet sabbath" in which "all nature wears a tranquil solemn air"—Sallie wrote J. P. to update him on matters at home. She informed her husband that because of the precarious conditions surrounding the cotton market, their overseer had made the decision not to plant their leading cash crop. Otherwise, she found "everything moving on very well." The overseer was "conscientiously doing his duty" and the prospects for wheat and corn looked promising. With respect to the slaves working their plantation, she admitted that "Some of the negroes are rather refractory, but I talked to them yesterday. Hope they will do better in the future."[14]

Although Sallie did not specify who she found being "refractory," circumstantial evidence strongly suggests that one of the people she had in mind was Young Price's brother, Royal.* In contrast, however, an enslaved man named Jim—believed to be Young and Royal's other brother, Jim Price—was supposedly proving to be an exemplar of obedience.

---

* The following year, Royal Price would escape from the Thurman family's estate and enlist in the US Colored Troops (USCT).

Referencing this particular man, Sallie told her husband, "Jim told me to tell you howdy and say to you that he feels like a house without a top—says when he saw you walking about the yard he always felt easy but is now lost he wants to be in the army with you. What a faithful servant."*15

But more so than practical matters related to the plantation's crops, or the attitudes of certain slaves, what Sallie seems to have really wanted to communicate were matters of the heart. She told J. P. about the tears which "ran down my cheek" due to the "emotions which ever crowd my mind and occupy my heart." What she feared most, she went on, was the notion that their "happy days" might be "buried" in a "deep dark oblivion" that "can never be resurrected." "Oh, harrowing thought," she added, before offering a tentative disclaimer of hope: "It has been said," Sallie wrote, "that every cloud has a surface lining and through the vista of the future I catch glimpses of summer hours. God will not always be angry, he will not always chastise us, we will get down in the very dust of humility, acknowledge our iniquities and as a tender parent he will have mercy and forgive his erring children."16

---

* Contrary to Sallie's assertion that Jim Price was "a faithful servant" pining to join the Confederate army alongside J. P., evidence suggests that Jim had other ideas in mind. Unlike his brother Royal, who seems to have already begun to resist his enslavement in direct ways, Jim was probably simply performing the role of a "faithful servant" until the opportunity for escape presented itself. Indeed, in 1863, Jim, like Royal, would also escape the Thurman estate and join the US Colored Troops.

CHAPTER 13

No-Man's-Land

The events that took place in Corinth in the final days of May 1862 may have provided Sallie Ecklin Thurman with a sign, however fleeting, that God had indeed listened to her prayers for mercy. On May 29, in a "masterfully executed" strategy of deception, Confederate General P. G. T. Beauregard ordered cheers and whistles and the music of regimental bands to accompany the arrival of empty train cars at the Corinth depot. The move tricked the Federals encamped around the town into believing reinforcements had arrived and bought the Confederates enough time to board the trains and slip away in the dead of night to the safety of Tupelo, fifty miles to the south. The Army of Mississippi would live to fight another day.[1]

Successful as the Confederate retreat may have been, however, it was just that. By abandoning Corinth, the Rebels had given up control of one of the most strategically vital rail junctions in the entire South. The retreat also compelled Confederate forces further to the west to evacuate their last remaining Mississippi River defenses above Memphis—a development that left the city virtually defenseless against the "overwhelming Union naval superiority." On June 6, in a river battle beneath the Memphis bluffs that lasted a grand total of ninety minutes, Federal gunboats decimated the small fleet of steamers that the Rebels had converted into their own "ragtag" version of a navy. Memphis, for the duration of the war, would stay firmly in the Federals' hands.[2]

The ramifications of the Confederacy's loss of Memphis immediately rippled through the larger region. For enslaved people living in Memphis and on surrounding Shelby County farms and plantations, the arrival of Federal troops provided cause for celebration. Many bondspeople subsequently escaped and sought shelter behind Federal lines. Those who could not manage to escape still felt newly emboldened to resist their enslavers' control. For white Southerners like Logan and Frances Davies, on the other hand, the war's latest development brought on a host of frightening new realities and disruptions to their day-to-day lives. Travelling to Memphis suddenly became a complex affair as Union forces gained control of all railroad lines and major roadways leading into and out of the city. Planters who depended on the Memphis factorage market were forced to request official permission from the occupying Federals in order to merely step foot in Memphis. Loyalty oaths to the Union also became a prerequisite for participating in any commercial activity of substance.[3]

But just because Federal troops had established dominance over Memphis proper and its surrounding transportation infrastructure, the Federals by no means controlled all of Shelby County's countryside. In the vast rural areas of the county beyond Federal picket lines—places like the Northeast Shelby Triangle—Confederate guerrillas and partisan groups continued to operate with "near impunity." This meant, in effect, that most of Shelby County constituted what the Civil War historian Stephen V. Ash has classified as a "no-man's-land" zone. This status applied to those geographic areas of the occupied South that were just beyond the largest garrisoned cities like Memphis. Here, in these zones, the Northern occupiers technically claimed dominion and certainly attempted to project their will whenever they ventured outside picket lines on patrols, military maneuvers, or foraging excursions. And yet, because the Federals could not be everywhere at once, their reach and power was limited. As a result, residents of no-man's land zones existed in a "kind of vacuum of authority, a twilight zone neither Union nor Confederate that seethed with violence."[4]

Surviving accounts of war-time confrontations between Federals and Morning Sun residents provide a localized glimpse of the extreme hostilities that became a part of everyday life in rural Shelby County as the war dragged on. How those confrontations were remembered also speaks to the war's ability to shape and define the generational legacies of individual families. With respect to the Feild and Ecklin families, for example, family narratives passed down through the generations recounted an instance in 1862 when the Federals burned the wheat fields of Mt. Airy, owned by Roscoe Feild and his wife, Emily Ecklin Feild (sister of Sallie Ecklin Thurman).* According to one version of the story, Emily Feild's father, Robert Ecklin, "saw the flames and rode through the burning wheat fields on a horse covered with wet blankets to see about his daughter and her young son . . . thinking her home was being destroyed."[5]

Another oft-told narrative centered on a young woman named Jennie Gardiner. Jennie, who lived with her sister and brother-in-law a short distance from Logan and James's estate, was said to have shot and killed a Federal intruder through the door as he was attempting to break into the home one night when she was there alone. Epitomizing the fluid nature of such histories, another version of the same story would claim that Jennie, rather than shooting the intruder through the door, had done so as the man was choking her brother-in-law and demanding to know where money was hidden.[6]

In a somewhat similar vein to the account of Jennie Gardiner's heroics, another story emerged from Morning Sun that detailed a local woman getting the better of a Union forager. The setting in this case was Logan and James's plantation, and the protagonist, Logan's wife Frances. The account of Frances Davies and the Federal forager would be told and retold frequently by Davies family descendants and acquaintances. Eventually, the story would appear in summarized form on a Tennessee Historical Commission marker placed at Davies Manor in 1953 by Ellen Davies-Rodgers. Later still, Davies-Rodgers penned and published a more detailed version. According to that account, the "dramatic episode" occurred one day when Frances, who was apparently at home without Logan, "looked out the front porch opening of the dog-trot and saw near the front gate a Union officer holding the bridle of her horse in readiness to take him from the premises." Davies-Rodgers continued:

> [Frances] thoughtfully surveyed the scene and knew that the situation demanded her courage and a usable weapon. Back to the kitchen she went and secured a well-sharpened butcher knife. Under the many folds

---

* Mt. Airy was not destroyed by the fire; the home, which rivals Davies Manor in age, would be placed on the National Register of Historic Places in 2002.

of her full skirt she held her weapon as she walked down the broad brick walk to encounter the intruder who held the reins of her horse. She approached the officer in the true style of a gracious southern lady. With words cushioned in courtesy and reason she asked the officer twice to please leave her horse. Each request was refused! She stepped by her horse, caught his bits and left the officer holding the ends of the reins. She drew the knife, previously unnoticed, and slashed the reins in two, leaving the officer holding the ends! She stood by her horse with her knife well poised and said to the officer, "Sir, I have my horse. You go!" He went![7]

Despite the dramatic flourishes (and apparent accidental error on at least one minor detail*) that are embedded in Davies-Rodgers's retelling of this family story, the underlying scenario of Frances thwarting an attempted horse theft is probably true. Horse and livestock thefts were rampant in the vicinity of the Davies family's plantation. Moreover, one piece of postwar correspondence between Logan and James confirms that the Federals did indeed steal property from the plantation on at least one occasion. The type of property that the Federals took is not made clear, nor is the timeframe it happened. But the brothers clearly placed substantial value on whatever had been taken—so much so that they later filed a claim against the federal government seeking compensation. Though the claim itself has not been located, the reference that James made to it can be seen in a September 1865 note to Logan in which he states that a formerly enslaved woman named Nice possessed firsthand knowledge of what had been stolen during the war. As a result, James told his brother, he and Nice would be travelling together to Memphis in order to "prove the claim against the government for property taken by the Federals."[8]

By the middle of 1862, the foraging and violence that permeated no-man's land zones like rural Shelby County were being driven by national policies. President Lincoln, having gone through a dramatic evolution in his

---

* The oldest surviving image of Davies Manor, from 1875, clearly shows that there was no "broad brick walk" leading to the home in the nineteenth century. Thus, it appears that Davies-Rodgers's retelling of the story of her grandmother and the Federal forager accidentally referred to the brick walkway that she herself installed in front of the house in the twentieth century.

war strategy, had become convinced that the backbone of the South's economy—that is, its plantation system—would have to be destroyed. Along with giving Union generals more freedom to pillage plantations and survive off the land, the president took deliberate aim at slavery, declaring that he intended to execute a war of "subjugation" in which the "Old South is to be destroyed and replaced by new propositions and ideas." The passage of the Second Confiscation Act in July 1862 marked a major step in this new direction. The act declared "forever free of servitude" those slaves who escaped from disloyal masters and reached Union lines. Importantly, the act also expressly forbade the Federal army from returning escaped slaves to their former owners. A few months later, in September, Lincoln went further with his issuance of the preliminary Emancipation Proclamation. Beginning January 1, 1863, the proclamation declared, all slaves in those states still in rebellion would be declared "forever free."[9]

However radical the president's proclamation may have seemed to Southerners, the motivating force behind it lay in military strategy rather than abolition. Furthermore, the proclamation contained explicit concessions to slaveholders. The freedom that it promised, after all, did not apply to the roughly 500,000 enslaved people living in the four Border South slave states (Kentucky, Maryland, Delaware, and Missouri) that had remained with the Union. Neither did the proclamation apply to the approximately 275,000 enslaved people living in Tennessee. Lincoln's rationale for excluding Tennessee centered on the fact that most of the state was occupied by Federal troops, and, thus, technically not in rebellion. And yet, regardless of this omission—and regardless of the larger weaknesses of the preliminary Emancipation Proclamation—Black people in Tennessee still rejoiced upon its announcement. From the perspective of the enslaved, Lincoln's action, combined with the on-the-ground reality of an occupying Federal army, provided the most definitive evidence yet that their days living in bondage were numbered.[10]

Runaway slaves had been seeking protection behind Union lines ever since Grant's army first pushed into the state. Now, though, enslaved people began to flee farms and plantations in droves. For those bondspeople who were unable or unwilling to flee, many found new and increasingly bold ways to subvert the institution they despised. They did so by refusing to obey their enslavers' commands or trying to resist punishment. Sometimes, they quit working entirely. In other cases, they undermined their enslavers by providing valuable information or direct assistance to Federal troops. Plenty of bondspeople in Tennessee did none of these things, of course. The dangers of resistance were very real, and for many, the risks simply were not tenable with the demands of short-term survival. Taken as a whole, however, the institution of slavery in Tennessee had begun to break down in dramatic fashion by the late summer of 1862.[11]

The most visceral evidence of the slave system's weakening foundations could be seen in the sheer numbers of shoddily clothed and famished Black people who desperately sought out the Federal Army's protection in West Tennessee. On the one hand, the Federals celebrated the blow against the South's slaveholding power that these people represented. Some men in the Union Army were also genuinely moved by humanitarian feelings and moral disgust over slavery. Yet the dominant feeling among the Federal troops was one of alarm about the seemingly never-ending tide of refugees in their midst.[12]

The logistics of managing the population of escaped slaves became one of Ulysses S. Grant's chief concerns in the summer of 1862. In August, Grant established the Union Army's first refugee camp for runaways at Grand Junction, Tennessee, on the border of Fayette and Hardeman counties. Since runaways were considered "contraband" property under the terms of the Confiscation Act, the term "contraband camp" came into being for the refugee center in Grand Junction. Grant tapped a chaplain from Ohio named John Eaton to gather the necessary shelter, clothing, and food supplies and oversee operations. Despite enormous challenges, Eaton proved an able leader. Grant soon placed the chaplain in charge of additional contraband camps built in Memphis and other locations in West Tennessee. The perilous circumstances facing the runaway population truly shocked Eaton. "Imagine if you will," Eaton wrote, "a slave population coming garbed in rags or in silks, with feet shod or bleeding, individually, or in families and larger groups. . . . The arrival among us of these hordes was like the oncoming of cities. . . . There were men, women, and children in every stage of disease or decrepitude, often nearly naked, with flesh torn by the terrible experiences of their escapes."[13]

By November, approximately 150,000 Black refugees across the Mississippi Valley region were living behind Federal lines in contraband camps, forts, and garrisoned towns and cities. Such a massive population shift would have undoubtedly impacted the people who continued to be enslaved on farms and plantations in the Northeast Shelby Triangle. News about the nearby contraband camps at Grand Junction, La Grange, and Memphis would have gripped their attention especially, and further heightened their motivations to escape. At least four enslaved women and girls from Thomas B. Crenshaw's Lone Hill plantation successfully escaped to Memphis at some point circa 1864. (Recall that Crenshaw, in January 1862, had paid Logan Davies five dollars for the express purpose of "hunting" a man name Simon who had escaped from Lone Hill.) Their names and ages—Mincy, age twenty-four; Rachel, eleven; Mima, three; and Frances, two—survive alongside Crenshaw's name in the registers that that Federals kept at Camp Shiloh, which had emerged on the southernmost bluff of Memphis near Fort Pickering. The successful flight in late 1863 of Royal and Jim Price from J. P. and Sallie Thurman's plantation is yet another example of confirmed escape. These two Price brothers, as we have already seen, are believed to be the same individuals who Sallie mentioned in one of her 1862 letters to J. P. Royal and Jim Price, shortly after their escape, made the decision to join the Federal Army as members of the newly formed US Colored Troops.[14]

As for the enslaved people living at the Davies brothers' plantation, no records have been located definitively confirming instances of escape. What does survive instead is evidence showing that the brothers continued to rely on enslaved labor through the entirety of the war—even when the Confederacy's defeat became imminent. Along with scattered business receipts and promissory notes showing bondspeople being hired out for full year contracts as late as January 1865, three births of enslaved children—Mat in December 1861, Madison the same month, and Polly in January 1862—were recorded in Logan and James's daybooks during the war. Other records from the immediate postwar months reveal two individuals—Joshua and Nice—whose presence on the Davies brothers' land can be tracked prior to and just beyond the end of slavery. Ultimately, though, there are far more questions than answers when it comes to discovering how the enslaved community at the Davies brothers' plantation may have reacted in real time to the war's progression—and, more to the point, the increasing prospect that they would, at long last, finally be free.[15]

CHAPTER 14

Honorable Mention

For the circle of men from the Northeast Shelby Triangle attached to Company I of the Thirty-Eighth Tennessee Infantry, the time between the Battle of Shiloh and the end of 1862 continued to drive home the brutal realities of war. The soldier's life had proven too much for Florian Crenshaw and James Davies's nephew Watt Little. In early May, Watt had been discharged without pay and sent home to Morning Sun. Presumably, Watt's body servant, Gabe, would have accompanied him back to Shelby County. Twenty-three-year-old Florian, on the other hand, hired a substitute to serve in his place—an option only available to planters who owned twenty or more slaves—and returned to the relative safety of the home front. Florian's situation illustrates why many rank-and-file Confederates came to believe that they had been duped into participating in a "rich man's war and poor man's fight."[1]

As for James Davies, Roscoe Feild, and Florian's younger brother, Merritt Crenshaw—as well as for the Black men forced to accompany them—the post-Shiloh campaign involved extensive movements that took their company on a meandering railroad journey to Chattanooga. From there, they marched north into Kentucky, and, on October 8, participated in the Battle of Perryville. The largest engagement of the war in Kentucky, the bloody battle ended with a strategic Union victory and a Confederate retreat back into Tennessee. By December, both Merritt Crenshaw and James were sent to hospitals in northwest Georgia along the Western & Atlantic Railroad. Presumably, they were accompanied by Simon and Richmond. Roscoe Feild, meanwhile, received a promotion to first sergeant, and probably continued to be accompanied by his body servant, Randle.[2]

James's admittance to St. Mary's Hospital in Dalton, Georgia (his muster rolls list rheumatism), arrived at a fortuitous time since it caused him to miss the Battle of Stones River. Fought near Murfreesboro between December 31 and January 2, 1863, the battle ended in yet another Federal victory. Once again, the fighting produced ghastly casualties on both sides. Joshua B. Ecklin of the Thirteenth Tennessee was among those captured at Stones River and sent to Camp Douglas military prison in Chicago, while Arthur, who had been Ecklin's body servant, likely returned to Shelby County in the battle's aftermath. Arthur's name and general role as a body servant for Joshua would appear in a memoir published more than three decades after the war by A. J. Vaughan, commander of the Thirteenth Tennessee. In a section of his book entitled "Faithful Colored Servants," Vaughn compiled a roster listing the names of Arthur and thirty-three other Black men who "followed us during the dark and bloody period."* Explaining that he wanted to "save from obscurity some of my old comrades," the ex-Confederate wrote, "I have endeavored to collect the names of these colored men—slaves then, but freemen at the end—and add them here to this roster, believing as I do that their personal loyalty and faithful service entitle them to 'honorable mention.'"[3]

Joshua B. Ecklin, unlike the man he enslaved and took to war, did not make it home to Shelby County. A little over a month after he had been sent to Camp Douglas, Joshua died of pneumonia. Initially buried at Camp Douglas, his remains were later exhumed and reinterred alongside some four thousand other Confederates in a mass grave at Chicago's Oak Woods Cemetery.[4]

As James Davies and Richmond endured the Civil War's frontlines and hospitals, Logan and Frances Davies spent the year 1863 attempting to

---

* Along with Arthur, one of the thirty-three men Vaughan listed was Young Price, referred to by Vaughan as "Young Thurman." Young, in fact, was the only body servant Vaughan discussed in his book who had not been attached to the Thirteenth Tennessee. He was also one of the only body servants to receive an actual narrative. Vaughan, like so many other ex-Confederates in the late nineteenth century, filtered his account of the war through a lens of nostalgia and romanticization—something that certainly extended to his account of Young's "heroic devotion" to Beverly Thurman.

carry on affairs on the home front with whatever sense of normalcy they could muster. The log house would have been a busy place. Along with raising their infant son Gillie, Frances and Logan continued to serve as guardians for James's two young sons, Will and Gus. Furthermore, at least one (and possibly three) of the orphaned children of Logan's late sister, Sally Walker, had come to live at the plantation. As she managed such a bustling household, Frances undoubtedly relied upon enslaved women and girls to work in the home and tend to the estate's myriad other related jobs. Frances's needs would have become even more pronounced that summer and fall after she became pregnant; the following March, twenty-one-year-old Frances would give birth to her and Logan's second child, a girl they named Linnie Lee.[5]

The responsibility to financially support their children and dependents would have surely weighed on both Logan and his wife. Along with the general anxiety presented by the day-to-day realities of living through the war, they faced no shortage of economic threats: Inflation had soared to new heights, the cotton market remained precariously unstable, and thefts and pillaging by Federal soldiers continued. Still, Logan and Frances seem to have kept their financial house in relatively good order. The fact that Logan paid regular tuition bills to send Will and Gus and (at least) one of their orphaned nephews to private school is notable. So too are the business records and receipts that show Logan carrying on the business of the plantation much as he had before the war: namely, he regularly hired out enslaved people to neighboring estates, rented farmland to tenants, and, most importantly, continued to task bondspeople with growing large quantities of cotton.[6]

Logan had begun 1863 by hiring out two bondspeople, Ben and Mary, to Edward Curd Leake and Markum Williams for a total of two hundred dollars. Later, he hired out for an unknown sum three women—Sally, Harriet, and Emily—to persons unknown. All five of these individuals had come into the control of Logan and James after the death of their father. Once again, the revenue earned by hiring these people out to neighboring planters seems to have been distributed to various nieces and nephews. Outside of hiring out enslaved people, Logan generated income in 1863 by renting 230 acres of his family's Fayette County land to W. L. Daley—the same tenant farmer who continued to pay Logan and James annually for the hire of Burrell and Hannah.[7]

Yet cotton, then as always, provided the most vital revenue stream. Whereas many Shelby County farmers and planters had significantly decreased their cotton production during the war, or given up on the crop entirely, Logan remained committed to his plantation's leading cash crop. He made this choice despite the continuing breakdown of the slave system across the region, not to mention the logistical challenges associated with frequently transporting cotton to market in occupied Memphis.

The clearest picture of Logan's agricultural production during this period of the war comes into focus during the fall harvest season of 1863. On September 18, he received a note from his friend and nearby neighbor, Madison H. Chambers, asking for a loan of "8 or 10lbs" of "picked cotton" that Chambers had learned Logan "had on hand." Chambers (it had been at his residence where his sister-in-law, Jennie Gardiner, allegedly shot and killed the Federal forager) admitted in his note that he was "entirely out of spinning cotton" and promised to "return it as soon as we can have some picked out & ginned." At the very least, the request suggests that others in Morning Sun were aware that Logan had produced a successful cotton crop.[8]

Indeed, shortly after fielding the loan request from Chambers, Logan repeatedly travelled to Memphis to sell his cotton. On October 13, he consigned twelve bales to the factorage firm of Robert McGregor & Co. Logan's ability to enter Memphis means that he would have already taken a loyalty oath to the Federal government. So too would the Federals have required him to obtain a travel permit that granted permission to arrive on that particular date. One of the permits he obtained that fall does survive and confirms that Logan came to Memphis with an additional load of cotton in late October. The document, signed by Federal officials on October 21, granted Logan permission to enter the city six days later with six cotton bales. The permit affirmed that the cotton had been grown in Shelby County and nowhere else, and by Logan and no one else. It stipulated that Logan should report to the surveyor of customs, and it also made clear that "this permit is good for the twenty seventh day of Oct only." A week later, on November 5, with yet another permit presumably in hand, Logan consigned an additional eight bales to the McGregor firm. Notably, the receipt from this transaction reveals that the firm expected to sell the cotton at fifty-five cents a pound—an astounding rise from the average price of ten cents a pound seen in Memphis in 1860.[9]

As the enslaved community at the Davies brothers' plantation continued to perform the labor of large-scale cotton cultivation through the 1863 planting and harvest seasons, developments on battlefields far from Shelby County brought more blows to the system that bound them. Earlier that summer, Vicksburg, the "Gibraltar of the Confederacy," had finally succumbed to General Grant's protracted siege and given the Federals full control of the Mississippi River. "Slavery is dead," Grant would declare after the victory, "and cannot be resurrected." Meanwhile, in the east, at the small town of Gettysburg, Pennsylvania, Union forces decimated the Army of Northern Virginia, ending General Robert E. Lee's offensive movements into the North. Farther south, on Morris Island outside Charleston, South Carolina, a less strategic, but no less significant battle took place a few weeks later. The heroic beach assault led by the Fifty-Fourth Massachusetts Infantry Regiment may have failed to take Fort Wagner from the Confederates. But what the actions of the all African-American unit *did* do was reshape public opinion about Black men serving in combat, paving the way for tens of thousands of former and escaped slaves and other men of color to join the Union cause.[10]

In Tennessee, by the end of that summer, more than three thousand Black men, most of them escapees of plantation slavery, had joined US Colored Troop (USCT) units. When US Secretary of War Edward Stanton made it clear in September that "all Colored Troops will forever be free," thousands more Black men decided the risks of army life were well worth the rewards. The first engagement in Tennessee involving newly recruited Black soldiers occurred that December in Moscow, Fayette County, southeast of the Davies brothers' plantation. There, soldiers in the Sixty-First USCT, along with Black troops attached to the Second West Tennessee Infantry, encountered some three thousand Confederate cavalry at the Memphis and Charleston Railroad bridge spanning the Wolf River. Following a hard afternoon of fighting—one participant described the river as "running blood instead of water"—the Confederates retreated. The Black soldiers engaged in the battle received special notice for their bravery. "The recent affair . . . has demonstrated the fact that colored troops, properly trained and disciplined, can and will fight well," declared Union General Stephen Hurlbut.[11]

After Moscow, increasing numbers of Black men in Tennessee made the decision to take up arms in a bid to destroy the American slave system once and for all. Two of those men were brothers Royal and Jim Price from J. P. and Sallie Ecklin Thurman's plantation. Although so much about their stories remains obscure, Royal and Jim are believed to have taken flight from the Thurmans' estate in the late fall or early winter of 1863. Evidence supporting this assertion comes from a few different sources, one being an undated letter that Beverly Thurman sent home to Sallie. In his missive, probably written that November, Beverly asked his sister-in-law to send him money, then went on to state, "Never mind about sending Royal. I believe I will not want him." Continuing, Beverly wrote, "Give my Love to all the Darkies. Young sends his Love to All." Around the same time as this letter is believed to have been written, Jim Price enlisted as a corporal in Company B of the Fifty-Ninth USCT. Roughly a month later, on December 20, 1863, Royal Price, age nineteen, joined Company C of the Third USCT Heavy Artillery. By the end of the war, Jim and Royal Price would be serving alongside some twenty-four thousand other Black men who had been recruited into the twenty-two infantry units and eight artillery units that composed the Tennessee USCT.[12]

In many cases, as these Black soldiers enlisted, their wives, children, and other kin who had escaped slavery with them took refuge in Federal contraband camps. The populations of the camps continued to swell. Disease ran rampant and shelter was scare, sometimes nonexistent. Theft and assaults committed against the refugees by Union soldiers were also commonplace. Still, for most of these people, the dangers and indignities of life behind Federal lines remained preferable to what they had endured under slavery. Meanwhile, even those people who remained in bondage on farms and plantations would increasingly find ways to resist their enslavers, and claim new forms of autonomy over their lives.[13]

It's an open question to what extent enslaved people at the Davies brothers' plantation expressed resistance or changed their behaviors as the Civil War progressed and the institutional authority of slavery weakened. Similarly, it is not clear how Logan's behaviors as an enslaver may have evolved through the war's duration. But perhaps some insight can be gleaned from an unusual note written to Logan on Christmas Day, 1863.

The note's author, Thomas W. Coulter, worked as the overseer at Thomas B. Crenshaw's plantation. Coulter began by expressing his "wish" to hire an enslaved woman named Celia "again for the next year." He then told Logan:

> She says she is willing to live with me again and also she want me to hire her daddy & mother too which I have agreed to do if you have not hired them out yet. I want her mother to work in the house nearly all the time. I will come to your house in a few days to see you about hire them. Do not hire Celia before you see me to anyone else. I send this note by Celia this morning as she is coming home to day.[14]

Along with the rather insistent tone that Coulter takes toward Logan in his note, he also offers clues about Celia and the agency that she apparently possessed. Having spent the year 1863 living in Coulter's home, Celia had managed to gain a degree of leverage with the overseer—leverage that she was now using to not only secure an agreement to keep both her parents by her side for the following year, but also give her mother a more comfortable domestic position in the home. Coulter's statement that Celia "is willing to live with me again" also implies that she had some say in the matter. Reading between the lines, it is reasonable to wonder if a sexual dynamic may have been at play. Finally, it is revealing that Celia travelled independently with the note in hand between Lone Hill and the Davies brothers' plantation—a situation that suggests she had done so previously and probably possessed familiarity with Morning Sun's roadways.

The brief note reminds us that enslaved people like Celia were not always bound to their plantations; instead, even within the "geography of containment" that was inherent to their lived experiences, bondspeople did travel within their communities, and sometimes well beyond—all the while developing their own unique associations and emotional attachments connected to the landmarks, structures, and natural landscape features that defined the communities they called home. Furthermore, as Celia made that trip from Crenshaw's plantation to the Davies brothers' estate on Christmas morning 1863, she probably did so with a sense of optimism. Not only was she "coming home" to spend the holiday with her mother and father and friends, she also would have been moving through a countryside that contained physical evidence of the toll the war was taking on the Confederate side fighting for the right to enslave her.[15]

Although the city of Memphis would remain occupied by the Federals after June 1862, the rural countryside surrounding the Davies family's Morning Sun plantation remained a no-man's land zone that was rife with pillaging and guerilla activity. A family story about an encounter between Frances Anna Vaughn Davies (pictured here shortly before the Civil War) and a Union forager would become one of the defining narratives of the Davies family's war experience. DMA Archives.

Elizabeth (Davies) Finney and her husband Gabe ran a small farm a short distance south of Logan and James's estate. After William Davies's death, the Finneys were allotted Wilcher and his six children. It is likely that Wilcher's wife, Mary, and another daughter, Sarah Jane, were already enslaved by 1861 at the Davies brothers' plantation in Morning Sun. DMA Archives

As captured in this 1862 *Harper's Weekly* illustration, occupied Memphis was a city awash with smuggling activity during the Civil War. "The levee at Memphis, Tennessee.—Hauling sugar and cotton from their hiding-places for shipment North.—Sketched by Mr. Alex Simplot." Courtesy of Library of Congress, Prints and Photographs Division

James Davies enlisted in the Thirty-Eighth Tennessee Infantry Regiment in March 1862, shortly before the Battle of Shiloh, and took with him an enslaved man named Richmond Bennett as his personal "body servant." This May 31, 1862, notice in the *Memphis Daily Appeal* speaks to the loss of morale affecting troops in James's regiment in the wake of the Confederates' defeat at Shiloh. Newspapers.com

LATEST FROM HICKORY WYTHE.

CITIZENS FLEEING FROM THEIR HOMES.

RICHARDSON BACK AGAIN.

A MEMPHIS EDITOR CONSCRIPTED.

We learn from gentlemen who have just arrived from the neighborhood of Morning Sun and Hickory Wythe, that RICHARDSON, the notorious guerrilla, has returned to West Tennessee, and is now engaged in committing all sorts of outrages on the citizens in that part of the country. More than thirty persons have been forced to leave their homes, and arrived in this city during the past three days. The citizens are fleeing in every direction from the high-handed, petty despotism of this infamous banditti.

RICHARDSON has now a brigadier's commission, and has returned to conscript enough men to make up a brigade. He has already about two hundred men; with these he is doing a large business in conscripting, horse-thieving, and villainous outrages of every kind. The farmers are leaving their farms, the mechanic his work-bench, and the teacher his school room. Among those who have been favored with a notice to join his ranks within the next two days after the serving of the notice, is Mr. H. L. PRIDDY, late publisher of the *Argus*. The last heard from Mr. PRIDDY he was making tracks for Memphis, at what the soldiers call "double quick." We suppose that he did not fancy a ride through the country with a prospect of being captured, and getting lodging furnished gratis at the Irving Block.

A July 16, 1863, report in the *Memphis Bulletin* (a newspaper that favored the Union through the Civil War), revealing the extent of guerilla activity in the vicinity of the Davies brothers' Morning Sun plantation. Newspapers.com

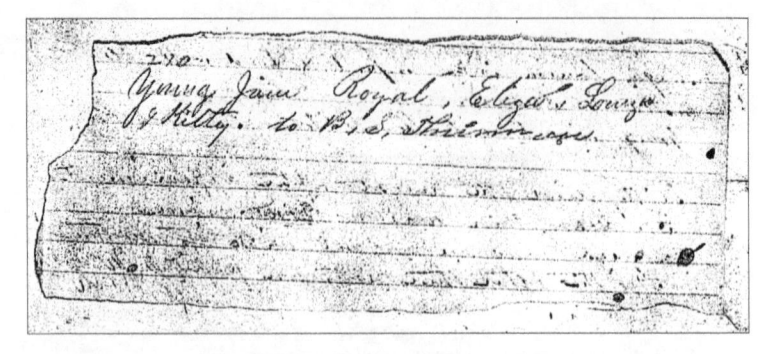

This scrap of paper from the probate records of Ann (Royster) Thurman, when cross referenced with a range of other records and correspondence, supports the assertion that Royal, Young, Jim, Eliza, and Loui[s]a Price were the children of the preacher, shoemaker, and free man of color Simon Price and his enslaved wife Kitty. Vague as their surviving historical traces remain, what is known about the wartime experiences of Royal, Young, and Jim Price illustrates a dramatic story of escape, survival, and resistance during slavery's final days. Courtesy of Shelby County Archives

As the authority of slaveholders broke down across Shelby County and West Tennessee, throngs of Black people escaped the farms and plantations where they had been enslaved to seek protection in the "contraband camps" established by the Union Army. This rare photograph, according to scholarship by Dr. Earnestine Jenkins at the University of Memphis, is believed to depict freedpeople at Camp Shiloh near Fort Pickering on Memphis's southern bluff. Courtesy of Beinecke Rare Book & Manuscript Library

Following the Battle of Stones River, and continuing through the first half of 1863, the Thirty-Eighth Tennessee, along with the bulk of General Braxton Bragg's Army of Tennessee, had assumed defensive positions south of Murfreesboro, Tennessee. By July, Federal advances had pushed Bragg's army into Northwestern Georgia. There, in late August, for reasons unknown, a surgeon ordered James Davies hospitalized. He shortly reentered the fighting ranks, however, and participated in the Confederates' costly but ultimately victorious stand at Chickamauga. Fought between September 18 and 20, the battle would go down as the single deadliest in the Western Theater, and second only to Gettysburg in the entire war. Exactly what happened to James at Chickamauga or in the battle's aftermath is unknown. But on the first of November he entered Bragg Hospital in Newnan, Georgia. Presumably still accompanied by Richmond, James spent the next sixty-one days in recovery. James's health during this period was good enough that he managed to work as a cook in the hospital, earning $15.25 in extra wages by the conclusion of his stay on New Year's Day, 1864.[16]

By May 1864, when General William T. Sherman launched his Atlanta Campaign, the circle of James's closest intimates from the Northeast Shelby Triangle who were still alive and participating in the war had been cut roughly in half. Within James's own regiment, Roscoe Field (and presumably his body servant Randle) remained. But Watt Little (along with Gabe) had left the army with a discharge; and Florian Crenshaw had escaped by hiring a substitute. Florian's younger brother, Merritt, after being captured and sent to a federal prison in Memphis, had been released (he had managed to pay a bond set at two thousand dollars—a reminder of his family's wealth), only to reenlist in a Confederate cavalry company that spent the remainder of the war in Alabama and West Tennessee. What became of Merritt's body servant Simon through these developments is unknown.

Outside of the Thirty-Eighth, Beverly Thurman and Young Price both remained with the Fourth Tennessee in Georgia near James and Richmond's position. Beverly's brother, J. P., attached to the Third Tennessee Cavalry, also continued to fight; like Merritt Crenshaw, J. P. would spend the rest of the war participating in cavalry raids further to the west of the Georgia Campaign. And then there were the casualties within the Morning Sun circle: David Royster (killed at Shiloh)

178   THE REALMS OF OBLIVION

and Joshua B. Ecklin (killed by pneumonia at Camp Chase) were just two of James's closest acquaintances who had perished. James's friend and neighbor Edward Curd Leake had also died in the war at some point in mid-1863. In the case of Leake (he had been married to Pauline "Polly" Little, a sister of Watt Little and James's late wife, Almeda Little), the circumstances of his death have been lost. Yet Leake's passing was notable enough to earn mention in one of Beverly's letters to Sallie: "And Ed Leake poor fellow is gone. How sad is death," Beverly wrote in July 1863.[17]

Thus, James Davies and Richmond, Roscoe Feild and Randle, and Beverly Thurman and Young Price found themselves immersed in the flurry of fighting that took place in central Georgia through the spring and summer of 1864 as Sherman pushed closer toward Atlanta. Following the campaign's major clashes at Resaca, New Hope Church, Pine Mountain, and Peach Tree Creek, the two armies met at the Battle of Atlanta on July 22. At some point that day, Roscoe Feild suffered an injury to his right arm. Doctors performed a field hospital amputation, leaving Feild with an arm that "is useless to him as a soldier." He subsequently received a medical discharge and returned home to Mt. Airy, presumably taking Randle with him.[18]

The fight for full control of Atlanta continued through August as Sherman's army surrounded the city for a siege. During this stretch, James and Richmond may very well have encountered the familiar faces of Beverly Thurman and Young, both of whom were camped in and around Atlanta. On August 16, writing his sister-in-law, Beverly reported his mixed feelings about the likelihood that the Confederates would hold the city. But the most important news he wanted to share involved his own newfound faith in a higher power. Just a few days earlier, he told Sallie, he had officially been confirmed as a believer in Christ. "Sister, I know you will be surprised when I tell you that I have been confirmed," he wrote. "But such is the truth. I have thrown aside all bad habits and absolved in future to be a better man.... I am delighted to see the spirit.... I am tired of wickedness and have humbled myself before him who has promised forgiveness of our sins." The letter turned out to be one of the final messages Beverly would write. On September 2, the same day that the defeated Army of Tennessee evacuated Atlanta, Beverly was killed in action.[19]

An unusually detailed account of Beverly's death and burial—one that centered around the actions taken by Young Price—would later emerge in the 1897 memoir published by A. J. Vaughan, the former commander of the Thirteenth Tennessee. For Vaughan, the story of Beverly Thurman and Young represented "proof" of a slave giving "heroic devotion to his master." According to the narrative Vaughan published, "Lieutenant Thurman was shot at Atlanta, and his body servant, Young, taking charge of him, through all sorts of hardships and deprivations, faithfully nursed him until he died." Vaughan continued, writing:

> Young then dug a grave with his own hands, buried his young master, and, making his way across two States, came back to Shelby County, where the stricken father and mother heard the pitiful story from his lips of how their boy had passed away. They told Young that they wanted their boy buried at their old home; so the negro, with a wagon and team, made his way back to the unmarked grave he had dug and brought the body all the way through a thousand difficulties and dangers to the old master and mistress.[20]

Vaughan's account of Young was part of a very specific brand of memorialization that emerged in the postwar years as ex-Confederates sought to harness for their own ends the narratives of enslaved men who were forced into the service of the Southern army. On the one hand, it is true that Vaughan felt a desire to recognize Young. Similarly, and assuming the overarching details of the story are true,* the journeys that Young made back and forth across the heart of the war-torn South would indeed have been extraordinary, and filled with "a thousand dangers." On the other hand, Vaughan's account was told through a paternalistic lens that reflected the romanticized "Lost Cause" narratives that had come to dominate ex-Confederates memories of the Civil War by the 1890s. Ultimately, what mattered most to Vaughan—what he found inspiring to the point of "tears"—was less about Young himself than the "personal loyalty" the Black man demonstrated toward his white owner. "I do not

---

* Vaughan was mistaken in referencing Beverly's "stricken father and mother"; Beverly's parents, Fendall and Ann Thurman, had died well before the Civil War, which resulted in Beverly being raised by J. P. and Sallie Ecklin Thurman. It is almost certain then that Vaughan was referring to J. P. and Sallie in his narrative.

know that this negro is now living," Vaughan wrote, as he closed the passage on Young, "but I mention his deed that those of this generation may know something of a faithfulness strong enough and great enough to command the admiration of the world."[21]

Stories uncannily similar to Vaughan's account of Young Price and Beverly Thurman permeated the histories and memoirs penned by ex-Confederates and their descendants in publications like the *Confederate Veteran* magazine. One reason, according to the historian Kevin Levin, was to "smooth over the rougher edges of the master-slave experience at war." Such stories could simultaneously "provide reassurance to readers of a unified white and Black population bravely resisting Yankee invaders both at home and in the army."[22]

A few clues about Young after he returned from Georgia emerged in Thurman family documents from 1865, but nothing about his postwar life and fate has been confirmed. As for Beverly, no official gravesite, either in Georgia or Tennessee, has been definitively located either. However, four decades later, in August 1905, just seven months before he himself would die, J. P. Thurman erected a stone in Morning Sun Cemetery in memory of his younger brother.[23]

CHAPTER 15

Oh for a Better State of Things!!!

The fall of Atlanta on September 2, 1864, could not have come a moment too soon for President Lincoln and the Northern cause. The war, for most of that year, had been an agonizing affair from the North's perspective and the public's mood heading into the fall elections placed Lincoln's reelection odds very much in doubt. In August, Lincoln himself had reportedly admitted to a White House visitor, "I am going to be beaten . . . and unless some great change takes place, beaten badly." Atlanta's capture constituted the "great change" that the president so desperately needed. The culminating battle of the Georgia Campaign not only struck a decisive blow to the already diminished Confederate Army, it played a pivotal role in Lincoln winning all but three states and 55 percent of the popular vote in November.[1]

In the wake of Atlanta's surrender, James Davies's regiment limped south with the rest of the Army of Tennessee before winding their way further west into North Alabama.

By the end of October, the recently installed head of the Army of Tennessee, General John Bell Hood, had hatched a bold new scheme that would take his army north into Tennessee and Kentucky before linking up with Robert E. Lee's Army. Though it may have sounded promising on paper, Hood's strategy was reckless in the extreme given the terrible condition of his troops.[2]

On November 21, after being joined by cavalry forces under General Nathan Bedford Forrest, Hood marched into Tennessee. J. P. Thurman was among the men riding with Forrest who joined Hood's army for the campaign north. So did James Davies's youngest brother Henry,* who by this point in the war had joined the Fourteenth Tennessee Cavalry.[3]

The combined Rebel forces initially clashed with Federal troops in small skirmishes and battles near James and Henry's birthplace of Columbia, then at Spring Hill. Next, late on the afternoon of November 30, Hood ordered a series of frontal assaults at Franklin. The Battle of Franklin ended in disaster for the Confederates, with Hood's army suffering more than six thousand men killed and wounded. After Franklin, instead of retreating and risking more desertions, Hood's decimated army, along with Forrest's cavalry, pressed on toward Nashville and a Federal force that now consisted of sixty thousand firmly entrenched troops. The Battle of Nashville, fought between December 15 and 16, resulted in a decisive Confederate defeat. Some thirteen thousand USCT soldiers, many of whom were seeing their first heavy combat experience, played a pivotal role in the fighting at Nashville even as they sustained significant casualties. Afterward, James and the surviving men in the Army of Tennessee retreated south to Corinth, then on to Tupelo. Hood's military career soon came to an end. And never again would the Army of Tennessee fight as an effective force.[4]

At some point in late December, surely reeling from his experiences that fall and winter, James made his way back to Morning Sun and would remain there until late January, when he resumed his service. Richmond's whereabouts during this period are less certain. According to one account, written decades after the war by James's son, Dr. William Little Davies, Richmond—probably between the Georgia Campaign and the Battle of Nashville—had been "captured by the Federals." Richmond then "escaped and returned home and to the army."[5]

Henry Davies, by contrast, did not return to Shelby County. Captured at Nashville on the second day of fighting, the youngest of the Davies brothers was sent in early January to Camp Chase military prison in Columbus, Ohio. There, two months later, on March 5, Henry died of pneumonia in the camp's military hospital at the age of thirty-two. Henry was buried in a mass grave before being exhumed a few years

---

* As with much else about Henry Davies's story, the details of his military career are murky. A single reference in a muster roll record does indicate that before he joined with the Fourteenth Tennessee Cavalry, Henry spent time in the Thirty-Eighth alongside his brother and the other men from Morning Sun.

after the war and reinterred in the Camp Chase Confederate Cemetery. It is not entirely clear if James or Logan, or Henry's own wife, Mary, ever learned the full story of what had happened to Henry following the Battle of Nashville. Almost forty years after the war, in one of the few known family accounts to even mention Henry, it was incorrectly stated that he had been "killed at Nashville on the Confederate line." Perhaps the family genuinely believed this to be true, or perhaps the obituary writer simply made a mistake. Or perhaps a narrative of death in combat was preferable to the reality of death by sickness in a prisoner-of-war camp in the victorious North.[6]

By New Year's Day 1865, James Davies was back with his family at the Morning Sun plantation. Two business records, both of which deal with the hiring out of enslaved people, help confirm James's presence at home. In one of those transactions, W. H. Webber (Henry's father-in-law) promised to pay James 150 dollars "in current paper money for the hire of Ben and Mary." In the other note, the tenant farmer W. L. Daley promised to pay James 250 dollars "in gold for the hire of Burrell and Hannah." The other piece of evidence confirming James's whereabouts in January 1865 involves his personal life: on the fourteenth of that month, James married Pauline "Polly" Little, the older sister of his late wife Almeda—as well as the widow of James's late friend Edward Curd Leake.[7]

After James's marriage, it is difficult to confirm his movements with certainty. The same goes for Richmond. James's muster rolls did not continue beyond 1864 and no other surviving records provide firsthand accounts of his experiences through the final three-month stretch of the war. Yet it is believed that sometime in late January or early February, James and Richmond both rejoined the skeletal remains of the Army of Tennessee, which had been ordered to head east into the Carolinas. The Carolinas Campaign would attempt to confront the vastly superior Federal forces under General Sherman. The Confederates, now under the command of reinstated General Joseph Johnston, hardly constituted a legitimate fighting force. Still, the shattered Army of Tennessee persisted in a last-ditch attempt to somehow turn the tide of the war back to their favor.[8]

Among the circle of Northeast Shelby Triangle men examined in this narrative, J. P. Thurman left behind the most revealing accounts of the period. Though he did not participate in the Carolinas Campaign with James and Richmond and the bulk of Johnston's army, J. P. did continue fighting under Nathan Bedford Forrest in North Mississippi and Alabama until the conclusion of the war. In mid-January, around the same time that James and Richmond rejoined the army, J. P. wrote Sallie from Verona, Mississippi, to report that "our command is in a very disorganized condition and the Lord only knows when it will be otherwise." Voicing his own desire to desert, J. P. said, "I am almost determined sometimes to quit and come home but I have gone too far now to quit in dishonor."[9]

A few months later, on March 6, Thurman wrote again to Sallie from his camp near Oxford, Mississippi. The men in his company, he told his wife, had gotten wind that General Sherman was continuing his march with "unbroken success." As a result, he wrote, "our ranks are depleted by desertion." In the meantime, J. P. had been reduced to living in an open-door shanty with nothing but an oil cloth to protect him from the spring rains. "I am perfectly disgusted, sullen, sick and worn out," he said. He went on, writing, "I begin to feel from the prospects around us that we had as well make up our minds to spend the balance of our lives slaves to the ambitions of aspiring men for I can't see for my life that there is any other result to be won." Two weeks later Sallie replied, telling her husband, "Times are getting awful here. Speculators alone seem to thrive. Oh for a better state of things!!!"[10]

Just as Sallie had been bothered earlier in the war by the "refractory" attitudes of her family's slaves, she once more reported to her husband similar problems. In particular, she had become troubled by Young Price. Since returning from his time as Beverly's body servant, Young had begun to display a disquieting spirit of independence. Specifically, he was negotiating with outside parties for paid work. In an undated response to his wife, probably written in April 1865, J. P. acknowledged he felt "surprised that Young should act as he has." He continued, writing, "I don't think it his fault so much as the parties contracting with him and I want you to tell the Gentleman the right to dispose of my property through my proper agents I still claim." Seeming to grow more and more indignant about his lack of control over Young, J. P. went on to say, "Young has no right to dispose of himself. By my sanction he is to solicit any plan . . . You tell him for me that he has done well and for it I am disposed to favor him but it is to be done so as not to create a dissatisfaction with the other negroes." Sounding more exhausted than ever, J. P. advised Sallie that they would have to resign themselves to "live without them as slaves." He added: "That matter I think is positively decided by the acts of our own Gov't so that leaves us poor indeed."[11]

At the root of J. P. and Sallie Ecklin Thurman's nervous exchanges through those final weeks of the Civil War was a gnawing awareness that their ingrained assumptions about Black people's inferiority were being utterly upended. Meanwhile, in the halls of the Confederate Congress in Richmond, the South's leaders were grappling with propositions that challenged the fundamental order of their society in similarly radical terms. Specifically, the Confederacy's legislators were confronting calls for what had once been unthinkable: the enlistment of slaves as fullfledged soldiers. Having suffered extraordinary losses in 1864, only to fall back into the trenches around Petersburg and Richmond for a protracted Union siege, Robert E. Lee's Army of Northern Virginia had become more desperate than ever for new manpower by the spring of 1865. As a result, Lee had reached the conclusion, however reluctantly, that the South's only hope for replenishing its ranks lay with arming Black men. Although similar plans had been proposed by a few Southern leaders a full year earlier, Lee's endorsement, combined with the dire on-the-ground realities, finally led the Confederate Congress, on March 13, 1865, to approve legislation authorizing President Jefferson Davis to raise three hundred thousand new troops "irrespective of color."[12]

The bitter debates that accompanied the legislation managed to poignantly reveal the warped underpinnings of the Southern cause. Robert Toombs, who had served as the Confederacy's first Secretary of State, captured the feelings of many when he argued that "the worst calamity that could befall us would be to gain our independence by the valor of our slaves instead of our own." For men like Toombs, in other words, just about anything, including military defeat, was preferable to the ignominy of living in a society of racial equality. For all the tortured debate that it generated, however, the plan to enlist and arm Black men turned out to have little practical impact. Jefferson Davis, never fully on board with the plan, dithered a full ten days after the bill's passage before formally issuing the order that made it official military policy. Even then, wording included in the order weakened the military's authority by declaring "that nothing in this act shall be construed to authorize a change in the relation which the said slaves shall bear toward their owner." Although a contingent of Black Confederates were seen conducting drills in the streets of Richmond on March 23, the new war policy had arrived too late to be put in motion.[13]

By this point, Lee's dramatically outnumbered army was on the verge of collapse. On April 2, the Federals finally broke the Rebel lines at Petersburg, resulting in the evacuation of that city and the Confederate capital of Richmond. Lee limped west with what remained of his army, his intention being to connect with Joseph Johnston's forces in North Carolina. Their rendezvous was not meant to be. On April 9, Lee surrendered to Ulysses S. Grant at Appomattox Courthouse. Johnston's troops—a force that is believed to have included James Davies and Richmond—surrendered a few weeks later on April 26, 1865, at Bennett Place in Durham, North Carolina. The terms of the treaty, which applied to some ninety thousand remaining Confederates spread through the Carolinas, Georgia, and Florida, constituted the largest single surrender of the entire war.[14]

The evidence that James and Richmond stayed with Johnston's army through the war's final days in North Carolina comes through narratives recorded by James's descendants and acquaintances. In the early 1900s, a minister close to the Davies family stated that James "enlisted in the Confederate army in 1862 and remained to the close of the war and surrendered in Charlotte, N.C." In another early twentieth-century account—this one made in the context of discussing Richmond—James's son, Dr. Will Davies, wrote that Richmond "was the body guard of James Baxter Davies during the Civil War and was in the war when the surrender occurred after a career of many battles." Later, Ellen Davies-Rodgers would also assert that James and Richmond had surrendered in North Carolina. Writing in 1992 in her book, *Turns Again Home*, Davies-Rodgers provided her version of James and Richmond's homecoming. According to Davies-Rodgers:

> On returning from the War, they, Uncle Jim and Richmond, left the stage-coach on the Old Stage-Coach Road, near Morning Sun, and entered Smokey Road leading home to the Plantation. As they trudged

along the narrow dirt road—quite foot-sore and weary—they were met by Uncle Jim's dog who had come to welcome his master home! How could the dog have known that his master and his faithful bodyguard would be coming home at that time? Of course the dog walked close by his master's side for the approximately one-half mile to Davies Manor![15]

What Davies-Rodgers did not mention in her book is that Richmond, upon returning to Shelby County and assuming the surname of Bennett, began a new life in freedom with his wife Sarah Jane—believed to be the eldest daughter of Wilcher.* In the years to come, as Richmond and Sarah Jane Bennett expanded their family to include a total of twelve children, they continued to live in close proximity to the Davies brothers and intersected in each other's lives in a range of ways. As for James, "who did not love to dwell upon the war's scenes," he would try to put the memories of all he had seen and done in combat behind him. With his new wife Polly, he returned to raising his two young sons. With his older brother Logan, he turned to the task of rebuilding their plantation using a labor system other than slavery. Judging by the actions that James was about to take, however, the Civil War was far from done with him.[16]

---

* Richmond's motivation for adopting the Bennett surname has not been able to be determined. Although certainly speculative, it is worth considering if there was some connection between Richmond's choice and his presumed presence at Bennett Place on April 26, 1865, when the last of the Confederate Army surrendered. Wilcher and Mary formally adopted the surname Tucker following the Civil War.

PART IV
1865-1893

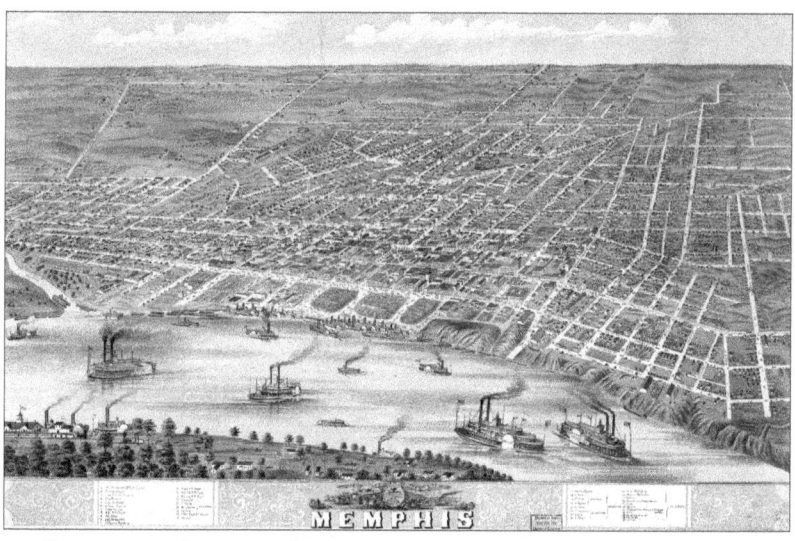

Bird's-eye view of the city of Memphis, Tennessee, 1870, by A. Ruger. Library of Congress, Geography and Map Division

CHAPTER 16

There Is Danger of Much Trouble

On the morning of Wednesday, May 24, 1865, hundreds of Black men, women, and children streamed out of the neighborhoods, contraband camps, and densely populated tenement settlements concentrated throughout South Memphis in order to join a celebratory parade being led by US Colored Troops regiments stationed at Fort Pickering. The plan for the day called for a march that would travel north along Main Street through the heart of the city's business district. The procession would then terminate with a "Negro Mass Meeting" at Pleasant Grove, a park near the Collins Chapel African Methodist Episcopal Church—the latter an important gathering place for Memphis's rapidly expanding postwar population of freed-people.[1]

That the event had been scheduled for this specific day was no accident: Some nine hundred miles to the east, in the nation's capital, an estimated sixty-five thousand Union soldiers, along with throngs of formerly enslaved people, were at that very moment leading an immense victory parade along Pennsylvania Avenue. The soldiers who marched in the Grand Review of the Armies were the very same men who had marched through Georgia with General Sherman, defeated John Bell Hood's army in Tennessee, and then finished off the Confederates in the Carolinas Campaign. The day prior to Sherman's army's celebratory jaunt through Washington, the Army of the Potomac's roughly eighty thousand men had marched the very same route to celebrate their role preserving the Union and ending slavery. All told, more than two hundred thousand Americans would either participate in or observe the two-day celebration in Washington that both signaled the formal end of the Civil War and provided a cathartic release for a populace still reeling from the assassination of Abraham Lincoln the month prior. One Memphis newspaper, reprinting the telegraphed reports from Washington, described the Grand Review of the Armies as "the grandest military spectacle ever seen in this country, and the preparations and crowd of spectators were on a corresponding scale."[2]

Although the Memphis version of the celebration constituted a small-scale affair compared to the scene unfolding in Washington, the event still shocked the local white population and drew intense interest. Memphis remained a city awash with Confederate sympathy and bitterness over the war's outcome, and for many, the sight of a Black-led celebratory parade horrified them to their core. As the morning wore on, a "very sensational" crowd full of "joyous black boys" began to line up in formation near the intersection of Beale and Main streets. A martial band from the Third Colored Heavy Artillery Regiment stood at the head of the procession. An estimated 250 colored soldiers from the Third and the Fifty-Ninth Heavy Artillery Regiments trailed the musicians. And bringing up the rear of the formation, organized into groups according to their genders and approximate ages, were some six hundred of those newly arrived Black Memphians—many of them the soldiers' own family members—who had made the decision that morning to participate in the festivities.

Around noon, the martial band launched into a rendition of "John Brown's Body" and began marching north. The rest of the crowd joined in behind them, belting out the lyrics that had become the anthem of Black Americans' battle for freedom. "Glory Glory Hallelujah! / His soul is marching on," the people sang. They also added a new stanza variation—"They will hang Jeff Davis to a sour apple tree"—that spoke to the plight of the Confederacy's recently captured former president.[3]

Among the uniformed men who had taken to the streets on this warm spring day, the most prominent contingent came from the Third Heavy Artillery Regiment. The Third's troops—one of whom was twenty-one-year-old Royal Price—had served continuously on garrison duty at Fort Pickering for the better part of two years. During that time, and "to an extent unusual for a military unit in the occupied South," the regiment had become deeply embedded into the social fabric of Black Memphis.

Most men in the Third had wives, children, or extended kinfolk who'd escaped to the city during the war from surrounding farms and plantations. These families depended on the military pay, along with the emotional support and physical protection, that the Federals' presence in Memphis provided. Virtually all of them, soldiers and civilians alike, now found themselves, in their own myriad and complex ways, confronting the simultaneously exhilarating and daunting realities brought about by the destruction of the South's slavery-based society.[4]

On this one Wednesday, however, as they participated in what was possibly the largest public gathering of Black people that Memphis had ever seen up to that point, the marchers remained intent on communicating the pure joyfulness of their emancipation. Some in the crowd carried backlit banners, or transparencies, that bore poignant messages of hope: LIBERTY, EDUCATION AND THE RIGHT OF FREE SUFFRAGE, read one of the more visible banners. Other banners proclaimed simple mantras like WILLING TO WORK. Still others were more pointed in their messaging: referring to the Emancipation Proclamation, which had gone into effect throughout most of the South (but not Tennessee) at the beginning of 1863, transparencies carried by groups of teenagers proclaimed, LIBERTY TWO YEARS OLD—WE ARE MARCHING ON.[5]

Roughly an hour after beginning the march, the martial band heading the procession reached the intersection of Main and Adams streets. Turning east onto Adams, the musicians led the crowd through the stretch of cityscape that not long before had been the heart of the Memphis slave market. Moving through this space, the marching freed-people must have felt an especially heightened sense of triumph. Still, they knew, their trials were far from over. Surrounding them on all sides were white onlookers, including throngs of recently paroled Confederates, who hurled out insults and demeaning jeers. A *Memphis Bulletin* correspondent on the scene reported overhearing a constant stream of vitriol from white bystanders. "A n***** has no right to vote," one man in the crowd exclaimed upon seeing the banners calling for Black suffrage. "It would not do to have so many ignorant people allowed to vote," railed another.[6]

More disconcerting than verbal attacks were the instances of outright violence. The night prior to the march, as the pastor of Collins Chapel left a planning meeting, assailants had stormed his carriage. The attackers' "bricks and other missiles" caused a carriage crash that the pastor barely escaped without serious injury. Another altercation had occurred in the opening hours of the march itself when a group of paroled Confederates confronted a man named Robert Waldron, the leader of the Third Heavy Artillery Regiment's cornet band. "I've come to kill every God damn n***** in uniform," one of the drunken parolees had yelled at Waldron. Waldron, backed up by a white Union officer, confronted the man, after which a gun battle broke out into the open. Alternately described as a "desperate fracas," and a "speck of a riot," the shootout only ended after the intoxicated ex-Confederate fled into a Main Street photo gallery—and then leapt off the roof in a futile attempt to escape. Upon landing, he was arrested and taken to the provost marshal's office.[7]

Such scenes were only a sampling of the racially fueled unrest that had already begun to plague postwar Memphis. Much worse was yet to come. In the meantime, though, on this spring day, there would be no stopping the freed-people's celebrations. Upon reaching Pleasant Grove, the jubilant marchers gathered around a bandstand that had been erected earlier that week. A large American flag decorated the front of the stage, along with a "beautiful picture of Lincoln." A reproduction of the Emancipation Proclamation hung from the rear of the bandstand. After a series of speeches from local leaders, the martial band once more launched into "John Brown's Body." The crowd "all joined in with one accord and sung with good effect." A "solemn prayer" commenced. Finally, the new attorney general for the western district of Tennessee—a man appointed by the new Unionist Governor, William "Parson" Brownlow—took the stage and promised to do all he could to keep law and order. The crowd responded with "lusty cheers" and "frequent applause." Afterward, a correspondent from the *Memphis Argus* attempted to make sense of all he had witnessed. In the article that appeared the following morning, the correspondent, sounding both confused and disturbed, reported that "The object of the meeting we presume can be inferred from their transparencies."[8]

On the very same day that Black Memphians and USCT veterans marched through the city's streets celebrating the end of the Civil War, Logan Davies and Roscoe Feild happened to be in Memphis for reasons all their own. More likely than not, the two men observed the procession of freed-people moving along Main Street, or perhaps even the mass meeting at Pleasant Grove. At the very least, they would have been aware of the festivities taking place all around them. Whatever the case, the scenes unfolding in Memphis no doubt affected them emotionally. Barely a month had passed since the surrender of the Confederacy's armies, and both Logan and Roscoe, well into that final stretch of the war, had legally owned people—"property" in their minds—on their respective plantations. Now, those same people, in effect, were proudly parading down the main thoroughfare of a major Southern city. In every banner they carried, in every joyous song they sang, they conveyed a powerful underlying message to former slaveholders: The old order of things would never be the same.

Along with scenes from the march itself, the business that had brought Logan and Roscoe into the city further reinforced the dramatically altered power dynamics of their society. Both men, at some point that afternoon, made their way together to the federal building housing the Supervising Agent of the Treasury Department. There, one after the other, they each signed a brief affidavit swearing that they would "henceforth faithfully support, protect, and defend the Constitution of the United States, and all laws made in pursuance thereto." Although occupying Federal forces had required certain Southerners like Logan Davies to swear their allegiance to the Union during the war, the postwar oaths took on new meaning and urgency as Lincoln's successor, Andrew Johnson, embarked on his Presidential Reconstruction plan aimed at speeding re-entry to the Union of seceded Southern states. The new president made the readmittance of his home state of Tennessee a top priority. Yet Johnson's approach to Reconstruction was proving difficult to decipher. Contrary to his earlier signals that he supported far-reaching changes in the defeated South, the president—"the great anomaly of the post-war United States," as he would be characterized by future historians—had thus far proved surprisingly lenient in his policies toward former Confederates.[9]

The ease with which so many Southerners were able to sign simple oaths of allegiance, also known as amnesty oaths, and return to relative normalcy, was a key part of that leniency. Around the same time that Logan and Roscoe travelled to Memphis to sign their oaths, for example, dozens of their friends and relatives from the Northeast Shelby Triangle did the same thing. A small sampling of Morning Sun-area residents who signed amnesty oaths in late May 1865 includes Dr. Virginius Leake, Joshua Ecklin (uncle to the late Joshua B. Ecklin), J. P. Thurman, Thomas W. Coulter (the overseer for Thomas B. Crenshaw's plantation who had negotiated with Logan for the 1864 hire of Celia and her parents), and Sarah Bolton (widow to the late slave trader Washington Bolton). Two other signers were James Davies's new wife, Polly, and Polly's sister, Mary Octavious Williams (wife of the former slave trader Markum Williams).[10]

As for James Davies, in late May he and Richmond Bennett were still traveling home from the Army of Tennessee's surrender in North Carolina. Even in subsequent months, however, there is no record to be found of James ever signing an oath of allegiance, an act he likely would have viewed as debasing. Given James's lowly rank in the army, neither would he have needed to apply for an individual presidential pardon—a requirement that Johnson placed (and granted with relative ease) on the Confederacy's high-ranking military officers, politicians, and wealthiest citizens.* Despite the oath being easy to complete from a practical perspective, many Southerners, especially returning soldiers like James, struggled emotionally with the implications of signing. The *Memphis Bulletin*, referring to the hundreds of former Rebel soldiers who were being paroled every day in Memphis, reported on May 25 that "many of them at first refuse to take the amnesty oath, but finding how things are going, they come back in an hour or two and very modestly ask to have the amnesty administered to them."[11]

The fate of Joel Royster, the prominent Morning Sun Democrat and original occupant of the Davies brothers' log home, illustrates just how troubling the amnesty oaths could be for those who had yet to fully accept that "the old arrangement of things is broken up." According to multiple accounts left in family histories from Morning Sun, Joel had continued to

---

* Johnson's Reconstruction plan spelled out fourteen classes of Southerners who were required to apply for individual presidential pardons. The most notable two classes were major Confederate officials and people who owned taxable property valued at more than twenty thousand dollars. Accounting for the fact that in 1860 Logan and James's real estate was valued at $15,850, and their personal property at $27,800 (the bulk of that figure equating to slaveholdings), it might seem that the brothers would have been required to apply for individual pardons. However, the brothers lost virtually all their personal property valuation due to the demise of slavery.

feel "saddened and bewildered" after the war by the loss of his son, David Royster, who had been killed at the Battle of Shiloh. He also felt disturbed about being shut out of politics by the Unionist officials who had come to power under the new administration of Gov. Brownlow. The tipping point came sometime in the fall or early winter of 1865 when Royster, in need of farming supplies, travelled to Memphis, swallowed his pride, and took the amnesty oath. Back in Morning Sun, though, he apparently became distraught. According to one account, he felt "sorrow and humiliation" over having to "bow to the carpet bagger after the war." Another account—this one from Ellen Davies-Rodgers—claimed that Royster felt "disturbed by a cause in which he was required to participate." Concluding that "life was worthless," he then "went out to the barn" and hung himself.[12]

The march and demonstrations led by Black Memphians on May 24, 1865, thrilling as they were for freed-people—and disturbing as they were for so many whites—were also simply part and parcel of a time period defined at every turn by momentous upheavals and drama. The radical societal transformations born of the Civil War—transformations that were just beginning to blossom that spring—had only happened as a result of a national trauma that was almost incomprehensible in its scope. After four-plus years of that trauma, Northerners and Southerners alike were emotionally and physically exhausted to the point of being shells of their former, pre-war selves. The conflict had claimed the lives of approximately 750,000 soldiers—a toll that equates in modern-day terms to roughly seven million people. Notably, Confederates who fought in the Civil War died at a rate three times higher than their Federal counterparts, meaning that one in five white Southern men of military age did not survive. These figures do not include the tens of thousands of civilians and enslaved people who died either as a direct (or indirect) result of battles and guerilla fighting, or through food shortages and disease. Death itself had become the war's most widely shared experience, and those who had managed to survive it developed phrases like "harvest of death" and "republic of suffering" as they attempted to convey the depths of such enormous collective pain.[13]

For a great many surviving Southerners, the world they gazed upon in May 1865 must have seemed apocalyptic. Towns and cities had been reduced to heaps of rubble. Railroad infrastructure had been decimated, and Confederate currency was worthless. Most dramatically, a way of life based upon legalized human bondage was no more. Although the Thirteenth Amendment would not be fully ratified by the states until December 1865, Congress had already passed in January the amendment that formally abolished slavery. The war and the destruction of the slave system had landed "like a massive earthquake, permanently alter[ing] the landscape of Southern life," and "exposing and widening fault lines that had lain barely visible just beneath the surface." As the military phase of the war now gave way to the beginnings of Reconstruction, bewildering new questions emerged about what the postwar order would look like. People did the best they could to get their minds around those questions. They also grappled with monumental political intrigues playing out daily in the pages of the country's newspapers.[14]

If Logan Davies had picked up any Memphis paper when he was in the city signing his amnesty oath, he would have encountered yet another day of staggering headlines. Correspondents covered every detail of Jefferson Davis's recent capture in Georgia and imprisonment at Fort Monroe in Virginia. Other leaders of the former Confederacy faced similarly dire straits. The governors of North Carolina, Georgia, and Virginia had all been arrested and imprisoned, while the governor of South Carolina remained on the run. Isham Harris, the former Tennessee governor who had so forcefully pushed his state's secession, was another figure on the lam, fleeing to Mexico alongside hundreds of other Confederates who hoped to rally support from Emperor Maximilian. The response to Harris's situation from the new Tennessee governor revealed as much about William "Parson" Brownlow's colorful personality as it did the fury that Brownlow and his fellow radical Tennessee Unionists felt toward the secessionists whom they blamed for dragging their state into the losing side of the war. As he issued a warrant for Harris's arrest that included a five-thousand-dollar bounty, Brownlow made sure to throw in a personal insult, describing the exiled Tennessee politician as possessing eyes that were "deep and penetrating—a perfect index to the heart of a traitor—with the scowl and frown of a demon resting upon his brow."[15]

Far from everyone in the General Assembly shared Brownlow's sentiments. In fact, the Tennessee legislature had entered the postwar period immersed in a political civil war of its own between radical Unionists of the governor's stripe, and conservative Unionists aligned with President Johnson. The warring factions had at least agreed on the fundamental desire to quickly see their state readmitted to the Union. In April, even before the war ended, the assembly had unanimously ratified the Thirteenth Amendment abolishing slavery; the following year, state leaders would ratify the Fourteenth Amendment—a move that resulted in Tennessee becoming the first former Confederate state to return to the Union. Still, the state's politicians clashed intensely over how—or even if—former Rebels should be allowed to participate in the restored civil government. Brownlow himself became convinced that such a move would lead to a new war and pushed forward bills to disenfranchise from voting or holding office those who had supported the Confederacy. The plight facing freed-people, meanwhile, remained of secondary concern. Even among the radicals, there were few who believed Black people should fully acquire the franchise. In postwar Tennessee, in other words, Unionism, at least among whites, did not necessarily indicate a willingness to extend civil and political equality to freed-people.[16]

Few places in the state saw the larger conflict between radical and conservative Unionists—not to mention those who still proclaimed the mantle of secession—play out with more intensity than West Tennessee. In May of 1865, Memphis newspaper readers encountered regular stories about the contentious public meetings being held in surrounding counties over questions of conciliation and governance. Oftentimes, warring words in courthouses spilled out into violence in the rural hinterlands. As reports increased of ambushes and robberies, Federal officials in Memphis made sure to publish daily reminders of General Orders No. 58, which required paroled Confederate soldiers to surrender their arms. Coverage of violence against freed-people, though typically limited in scope and whitewashed, received some attention. Much more frequent, though, were stories that hysterically reported on the "fiendish" behavior of liberated former slaves.[17]

Yet another local storyline reflective of the city's anxieties had to do with its rapidly changing demographics. Newspapers reported at length on the "rush of strangers" who had flocked into the city "looking for profitable investment." These newcomers included intrepid Northern planters and merchants hungry for new business opportunities, as well as native Southerners desperately searching for laborers to work their fallow fields. Thousands of paroled Confederates made their way through the streets, many of them physically disfigured, full of bitterness, and searching for a renewed sense of purpose in their lives. Not surprisingly, these former Rebels mixed uncomfortably, sometimes disastrously, with the ever-increasing population of freed-people, armed US Colored Troops, and white Federal soldiers. Rounding out the volatile mix of humanity was a large Irish population who had fully supported the Confederacy and now viewed the recently arrived freed-people as a direct economic threat. Postwar Memphis, in short, was a "highly distinctive" place inhabited by groups of people with diametrically opposed desires.[18]

Of all the debates happening in Shelby County, however, nothing stirred as much passion as the subjects of Black citizenship and suffrage. Mirroring the ideological divides at the state level, most local leaders, even those aligned with the radicals, believed that freed-people simply could not be trusted to vote, either due to their own "ignorance," or because they would be coerced into voting their former masters back into power. A debate that played out in the *Memphis Argus* on May 24 epitomized the local divisions over the question of Black suffrage. In the lead editorial that day, the editor, Brower Harnwell, declared that "Every thinking man knows that the negro is entitled to his freedom, but that he is entitled to vote is a matter of deep and grave consideration. . . . The Ballot is a Dangerous instrument in the hands of the ignorant." A lengthy letter to the editor that appeared adjacent to Harnwell's piece provided a competing view that made the former's seem almost progressive by contrast. The anonymous author (he signed as a "A Southerner, but Not less an American, and Henceforth as Before the war, opposed to all Geographical parties") made it clear in his letter that he had been a prominent "Old Line" Whig and slaveholder before the war. Now, though his "views of slavery had not changed as much as others," he was willing to acknowledge, being a "sensible" man, that the "institution is doomed" and "the negro must be set free." The difficulty lay in "how the thing is to be done." He continued, writing that "the peculiarities of the black race and the undeniable superiority of the whites" left no question about the "disastrous effects of immediate, unconditional emancipation." What was needed instead, he believed, was a gradual process of bestowing privileges of freedom on former slaves. Yet what that process should look like he could not say: "Indeed the negro question in its present phase perplexes all minds beyond any perplexity of the Past," he admitted. The writer then revealed his bottom-line conclusion: "One thing seems to be certain: The Negroes are going to be disappointed no matter what disposition is made of them and there is danger of much trouble."[19]

CHAPTER 17

A Relic of the Old Barbarism

In early November 1865, correspondents from *The Memphis Argus* decided to leave the "noise and confusion of the pent-up city" for a reporting excursion on the "newly repaired but important line" of the Memphis & Ohio railroad. After visiting stops between Memphis and western Fayette County, including Shelby Depot, near the Davies brothers' plantation, the correspondents reported that especially in cotton "there were not so many acres planted as usual, by a great deal." But overall, despite their being "some neglect to be sure," the "waste and desolation shown in many other places has not visited the farms and plantations along and in the vicinity of" the railroad line. Reporting specifically on Shelby Depot, the reporters noted that the "railroad buildings have all been destroyed" and the "village wears a dilapidated appearance." Still, they went on, "This station has not suffered greatly by the war. . . . The people are repairing the little damage sustained, and are returning to the same habits they used to have in the 'good old times' before the war."[1]

What exactly the correspondents meant by the "habits" of the "'good old times' before the war" is open to interpretation. But if they were referring to planters' dependence on exploiting impoverished Black laborers—in essence, a situation where "freedmen still farmed white man's land with a white man's plow drawn by a white man's mule"—such a situation certainly applied to Logan and James's estate. The Davies brothers' surviving plantation records show that they quickly transitioned to the postwar period in control of a sizable Black labor pool; by 1870, if not well before, that labor pool seems to have been larger than what had existed on the plantation under slavery.* The brothers, like so many other farmers and planters, secured their labor force by implementing various wage and crop share arrangements with freed-people—most of whom the brothers themselves had recently enslaved. In the earliest confirmed example, from December 1865, Joshua Davies agreed to accept two hundred dollars "for the services rendered . . . by my self and family up to this the 21st of Dec. 1865."[2]

This Joshua Davies is believed to be the same Joshua whom William Davies recorded in his ledger as born "Fryday the 31 about the brake of day December 1824." He is also believed to be the same "Joshoway" whom William's oldest son, W. W. Davies, acquired and then sold back to his father in 1837 before moving to Texas. Five years later, as discussed earlier, Joshua was one of two enslaved men (the other being Willshire/Wilcher) who was attacked by Black men from Dickey Chappell's plantation while repairing a fence—an incident that led to the bloody melee and contentious litigation that followed. Extrapolating from a range of other sources, a rough picture of Joshua's life can be reconstructed in the decades following the brawl in Maury County.

In the late 1840s, around the same time he was advanced by William to James and taken to the Davies brothers' new Shelby County plantation, Joshua is believed to have married a biracial woman named Mitzi, also known as Meize (who had likely been enslaved by the Hadley family before coming into William's control through his second marriage). Between 1849 and 1865, Joshua's wife is believed to have given birth to four children: Perry, Martha, Archie, and Joe. The family almost certainly remained enslaved at the Davies brothers' Morning Sun estate through the Civil War and probably resided in one of the five "slave houses" census enumerators documented in 1860. After the war, it is unknown whether Joshua and his family continued to reside in the same dwelling that they had occupied during slavery or if they moved into another structure. But what is clear, based on the 1865 note, is that the now forty-one-year-old Joshua, along with his family—all of them having assumed the

---

* An examination of 1870 census records in conjunction with the Davies brothers plantation ledgers indicate that somewhere approaching thirteen Black families, constituting approximately sixty people in total, resided on land owned by Logan and James.

surname of their former enslavers—were working for wages on Logan and James's land.

Five year later, Joshua, Mitzi, Perry, Martha, Archie, and Joe Davies occupied the household immediately adjacent to James and Logan's log house—a situation that reinforces the complexities of the relationship that existed between these white and Black families who shared a surname. In summary, the biographical sketch of Joshua and Mitzi Davies and their children, however fragmentary, is in truth a rather expansive one compared to the barely discernable shadows that constitute the known histories of most of the people the Davies family enslaved.[3]

Between the war's conclusion and the early 1870s, dozens of other individuals formerly enslaved by Logan and James were recorded in the brothers' commissary records as either farming for wages or, more commonly, entering into sharecropping contracts wherein they agreed to turn over a portion of their crop in exchange for living quarters and advancements of farm equipment and supplies. A sketch of these people and their families can be reconstructed by cross-referencing the commissary ledger books (and in some cases other Davies family sources) with US Census records. The postwar Black community living on Logan and James's estate in 1870 included Ben Gray, age forty-five, his wife Mariah, age thirty-eight, and their six children—Virginia, age seventeen; Joe, sixteen; Cora, fourteen; Sophia, twelve; Bennie, six; and Jim, five. The Gray residence in 1870 also included an unmarried thirty-five-year-old man named Lewis Gray, and Celia Gray, age eighty and blind. The closest household to the Grays was that occupied by Richmond and Sarah Jane (Tucker) Bennett, and their six-year-old son Steve. Not far away in the opposite direction, directly beside the log home occupied by Logan, James, Gus, Will, and Linnie Lee Davies, was the household occupied by Joshua and Mitzi Davies and their children. Adjacent to Joshua and Mitzi's family lived Tom and Susan Cartwright and their four children—ten-year-old Young, eight-year-old Polly, six-year-old Lucy, and Caroline, age two. With respect to Tom and Susan's family, all of them, with the exception of Caroline, born after emancipation, had formerly been enslaved by the Davies brothers.[4]

At least six additional Black families lived in close proximity to those already mentioned. They included Gordon Davis, his wife Delia, and their eight-month-old child named Baby. Enumerated in the same household as Gordon and Delia Davis and Baby was a young couple named William and Emily Cartwright, and their seven children—Elias, Linda, Green, Coleman, Will, Lucious, and Alich. (Although it is not clear how exactly William and Emily's family were related to Tom and Susan's, a blood connection between these two Cartwright clans can be presumed.) Next to the Davis-Cartwright household was the home occupied by Joe and Maria Davis, and their three children—Amos, age twelve; Mat, ten; and Wat, eight. Finally, there was thirty-year-old Bob Green, his twenty-four-year-old wife Fanny, and their three children, Lizzie, Elnora, and Geo.* Notably, Wilcher and Mary Tucker (Richmond Bennett's in-laws through his marriage to Sarah Jane), along with their seven children—Lucious, Mary, Amos, Pricilla, Amy, Noah, and Andy—lived a few miles away from the Davies brothers, where they sharecropped another wealthy planter's land.†[5]

With the exception of the Tuckers then, these families were core members of the Black community who lived on and worked the Davies brothers' estate through the immediate postwar years. The heads of each of these families had once been enslaved by Logan and James and/or their father William. Some families (those headed by Joshua and Gordon) had assumed the same (or approximate) surname of their former enslavers. Others (those headed by Tom, William, Ben, and Bob) adopted entirely new surnames. In the years to come, a select few (Lewis Gray and various members of the Tucker family) would come into possession of their own land and farms. Others would move short distances away to sharecrop different planters' land. Still others, through death or relocation, would disappear altogether from the historical record. Regardless, almost all of the individuals named here would remain bound to livelihoods based in sharecropping. Though they were done living in bondage, these freed-people, along with countless others like them across the postwar South, were now moving into a new chapter of a very old

---

* One possible scenario, extrapolating from the entirety of known sources, is that Bob Green was one and the same as the "Bob Davis" who appeared in Logan's transactions in October 1860 with the Jones Brown factorage firm.
† In 1872, Wilcher purchased land of his own adjacent to Logan and James. The Tucker family lived and farmed on this property in close proximity to the Davies brothers for years to come.

struggle—one that was at bottom rooted in the twin forces of racism and economic exploitation.

Leading historians of Reconstruction have stressed that "a new set of labor arrangements did not spring up overnight" in the South. Instead, planters and workers fumbled and groped their way through the confusing transition from a slavery-based economic system to one supposedly based in free-market labor. Initially, planters made payments to freed-people using a "welter of arrangements." Sometimes, as the contract for Joshua Davies reveals, the arrangement called for straight cash wages, paid monthly or at year's end. In this case, the Davies brothers provided the necessary materials; Joshua, Mitzi, and their children would have then turned over the crops that they grew for the agreed upon sum. In other cases, planters agreed to provide a share of a harvest season's revenue that would be divided equally between the entire labor force or smaller groups of laborers. Sometimes, combinations of wage and shared crop payments were agreed upon. In still other instances, freed-people who had managed to own small plots of land might agree to "time-sharing plans," whereby they would work part of each week for the planter, and part of the week on their own property. Finally, there were those freed-people who earned wages in kind or through performing specific skilled tasks. As time went on, though, the most common arrangement became a version of sharecropping where individual families (instead of large groups of unrelated laborers) entered into contracts with planters to farm dedicated pieces of land in exchange for crop percentages. Tenant farming arrangements, based in straightforward rent payments to a landowner, also became common for freed-people, as well as poor white farmers.[6]

Eventually, after the end of the Reconstruction era, the sum total of these economic transformations would result in what the historian Eric Foner has described as the "consolidation of a rural proletariat composed of the descendants of former slaves and white yeomen, and of a new owning class of planters and merchants, itself subordinate to Northern financiers and industrialists." Nothing about that future state-of-affairs was preordained in the summer of 1865, however. In that initial period following the end of slavery, the free labor situation remained fluid, and characterized by "endless confusion, and absurd contradictions." As both freed-people and former slaveholders attempted to navigate the confusion and ambiguities of free labor, they each, in very different ways, dealt with profound anxieties. Many freed-people had no interest in returning to the cotton fields and saw urban centers like Memphis as offering the best route to achieving their dreams of economic independence. In a sense they were right: Beginning in the summer of 1865, the presence in Memphis of the Freedmen's Bureau provided formerly enslaved people desperately needed protection and basic resources. The new educational opportunities that became available were also transformative for many freed-people and their children. Still, the Freedmen's Bureau was far from a perfect institution. And cities themselves brought their own forms of danger and struggle. In Memphis and plenty of other Southern cities with Freedmen's Bureau offices, Black people were not allowed to move about without employer passes or even be on the streets at night. Black Memphians found to be in violation of such restrictions were routinely rounded up as "vagrants" and forced into plantation labor contracts. Officials from the Freedmen's Bureau, at various points, also directly coerced freed-people against their wishes to return to plantations. At one point that summer, outraged by such actions, a contingent of Black Memphians declared, "It seems the great slave trade is revived again in our city."[7]

As external pressures mounted on freed-people to return to the "good old days" of rural field labor, many eventually gave in, or were forced to give in; thus, they returned to lifestyles that were not so different in practice from what they had endured under slavery. Although circumstances certainly varied from plantation to plantation and farm to farm, what was developing was a labor system fundamentally coercive in design. It wasn't slavery. But it wasn't free market labor either. Instead, for freed-people, the rural postwar South was fast becoming a world characterized by "tangled and desperate struggles that allowed no easy division to be made between dependence and independence."[8]

One poignant example of the complicated new reality that Black people faced in places like rural Shelby County can be seen in the actions taken in the community of Union Depot to enforce a uniform approach to hiring laborers. In November 1865, a group of Union Depot leaders met and drafted a series of resolutions supposedly intended to "harmonise the Blacks and whites of this district for the ensuing year." However, the spirit of the resolutions had little to do with harmony and everything to do with maintaining economic control. A key part of that control involved the establishment of a strict wage scale for Black field hands that topped out at two hundred dollars annually for "first class men." The scale bottomed out with a pledge to pay one hundred dollars to "third class women." Out of these wages, hired laborers would "clothe themselves" and "pay their Doctors Bill" and also have all lost time deducted from their wages. Included in the resolution's wording was a command that planters should not "pay more for servants than the price agreed upon" in order to avoid "disaffection" among the freed-people.[9]

Along with mandating paltry wages, and restricting employers from providing any extra benefits, the Union Depot citizens drafted another resolution demanding that "no citizen will employ a servant who has ever lived in this District without the recommendation of his former owner and employer." Yet another resolution declared that employers should not rent, lease, or sell any lands to freed-people, "nor suffer them to live on his or her Lands unless they are under their amediate Controll and responsible for their conduct." Finally, employing language with unmistakably menacing implications, the leading men of Union Depot resolved to "look upon any citizen who may violate any of these resolutions . . . as not willing to aid in harmonising the District. We will not look upon such as good citizens, but on the other hand regret that we have such in our District." Tellingly, a Freedmen's Bureau official who reviewed the resolutions coming out of Union Depot deemed them a "Relic of the OLD BARBARISM."[10]

The core desire to retain power and control over Black people drove the white citizens of Union Depot to take the actions that they did. Here, and in countless other communities around the South, planters who had lost their power as enslavers struggled mightily to accept the new order and adapt to any semblance of a normal give-and-take, employer-employee relationship. Instead, it was a time when the "ideas inherited from slavery displayed remarkable resiliency." Similarly, forces beyond pure economic control were also at work—namely, an unvarnished fear of emancipated people. Throughout the fall of 1865, persistent rumors swept throughout West Tennessee that a coordinated and violent Black uprising was imminent.[11]

In Shelby Depot (just one stop up the Memphis & Ohio railroad from Union Depot) that very fear was expressed in a letter written to the

Freedmen's Bureau by Snowden Craven Maddux, the local doctor and close acquaintance of the Davies family. The letter—written two days before the Union Depot citizens adopted their list of resolutions—was penned on behalf of a group of "White Tennesseans" who complained that armed freed-people were "behaving very badly." As he recounted a list of grievances about the "specimen of [freed-peoples] conduct," Maddux appeared incredulous that former slaves believed they "had just ground for the enmity existing between whites and blacks." The doctor went on to pen a summary of his community's feelings that conveyed a sense of bewilderment over Black people's discontentment with their wages and lack of opportunities to purchase land. Considered in its entirety, the letter encapsulates the yawning chasm that existed between the perceptions and desires of former enslavers and the perceptions and desires of the people that they had so recently enslaved. "They may not have any preconcerted plan of an insurrection," Maddux wrote at one point, "but we fear that harm will result from them to our families." Then, without any irony, he continued:

> We are friendly to the Freedmen and wish them well—We are willing to employ all of them that will work and give them good wages—we know that they are not to be blamed for the result of the rebellion. We know that they are much corrupted by unprincipled men—who are selling spirits and arms to them—Gen[tlemen] we are part and parcel of one great and united country. We are Loyal to the US government and wish to reap the benefit of its protection to our community and to our families—Gen[tlemen], we will be under lasting obligations to you for any aid you can render us in these distressing times.[12]

CHAPTER 18

A Terrible State of Frenzy

All surviving evidence shows that Logan and James Davies had managed to emerge from the Civil War in a fortunate financial position relative to many of their peers in the Northeast Shelby Triangle. For starters, the log home that centered the brothers' plantation had survived the war unscathed. Their agricultural operation had remained intact as well. Exactly how productive the brothers' plantation remained compared to earlier years is difficult to say. But letters and scattered business receipts do show that Logan and James moved directly into the postwar period earning substantial revenue through cotton sales completed by their trusted network of Memphis factors. Another financial boon came via the Fayette County land that the brothers had inherited from their father and continued to rent to tenant farmers like W. L. Daley. Finally—at least according to family lore that passed down through their descendants—Logan and James had retained a windfall of hard currency in the form of gold coins that they'd had the foresight to bury near their home early in the war and afterward recover.[1]

But perhaps the best glimpse of the brothers' postwar financial position can be seen in data from the 1870 census. That year, they were listed with real estate valued at fourteen thousand dollars and a personal estate valued at two thousand dollars. Out of the 165 total households enumerated that year in Civil District Eight (the area of Northeast Shelby County comprising Shelby Depot and the portion of Morning Sun where the brothers lived), only three households reported higher combined property values than Logan and James. The single wealthiest household in District Eight, far and away, was that of Robert Butler Hayes and his wife Josephine, who together reported a combined estate value of eighty-two thousand dollars.* Second to Robert and Josphine Hays was the household headed by Alexander Donelson (Alexander's wife Kate was one of Joel Royster's sisters), who reported a combined value of more than twenty-three thousand dollars. Just beneath the Donelsons was the estate headed by Sarah Bolton (widow of the late slave trader Washington Bolton). In summary, the Davies brothers' wealth in 1870 may have paled in comparison to that of Robert Hays. Yet Logan and James undoubtedly enjoyed a better financial position than the majority of their peers.[2]

Still though, the brothers' good fortune was relative. The Davieses certainly *did* suffer financially as a result of the war. The (unknown) property that Federal troops stole from the plantation represents one example. As we have already seen, the brothers deemed the theft worthy enough that they sought redress by filing a claim (one that relied on the firsthand testimony of the freedwoman Nice) with government officials in Memphis. But by far the largest monetary hit they took involved the drop in their personal property value as a result of emancipation. In 1860, the brothers' personal property was enumerated at $27,800—most of that reflective of the twenty-two people they enslaved that year. Ten years later, their personal property value had plummeted to $2,500. Additionally, business records show that as late as November 1865, the brothers continued to pay off debts that they owed for temporarily hiring enslaved people. Similarly, they themselves were still owed money from other planters for hiring out slaves. It is doubtful that all or even most of those debts were recovered by Logan and James. One acquaintance, writing about James many years later, made the assertion that "much money was lost in the payment of security debts" during the postwar years when the "ravages of war had wasted the country and freed his slaves."[3]

Putting aside their personal finances, however, there is no question that the Civil War left indelible emotional scars on the Davies brothers, their loved ones, and their wider community. Along with claiming the life of their brother Henry, the war had resulted in the death of some of their closest acquaintances—David "Dick" Royster, Joshua B. Ecklin,

---

* Robert was the son of the previously discussed General Samuel J. Hays. Samuel J. Hays's primary residence was in Madison County, but his extensive landholdings in Shelby County had formed the basis for the "Haysville" community, later called Withe Depot, directly east of Shelby Dept.

Edward Curd Leake, and Beverly Thurman among them. Others like Roscoe Feild had returned home alive but physically disfigured. All of these men's wives, sisters, daughters, and mothers had to sustain their households and deal with the repercussions of death and injury as best they could. The war's reverberations also diminished key figures in the older generation who moved within the brothers' orbit—Joel Royster and Thomas B. Crenshaw being two examples. Crenshaw died not long after Royster's suicide. The obituary for the long-time Whig judge, slave-holding planter, and once-stalwart Unionist described Crenshaw as "one of nature's noblemen," and alluded to the inner turmoil he had gone through in the course of being convinced to support secession and war. "He has passed into the 'better land,' where the demon of the Civil War will no more afflict his patriotic spirit, or sap, as here, the roots of life," the obituary read.[4]

Of all the deaths that Logan and James processed, though, surely their youngest brother's affected them most viscerally. Despite the fact that neither of the Davies brothers nor their descendants left behind much of anything about Henry, his death must have been a blow. It probably also resulted in Logan and James stepping in to help financially support Henry's widow, Mary, and their infant daughter, Mattie.

By late 1865, the possibility of another major loss in the family arose when Frances Davies fell ill. The nature of her condition went unrecorded in the cursory receipts issued by Dr. Maddux for the treatments he administered beginning that holiday season. The Shelby Depot doctor continued his medical visits through the opening weeks of 1866. His efforts turned out to be for naught; on February 8, Frances "Fanny" Anna Vaughn Davies died at the age of twenty-three. As was the case with her late sister-in-law, Almeda, Fanny's exact cause of death did not survive. What would survive, however, along with the story of her confrontation with a Union forager, was the headstone of Italian marble that Logan later ordered for her gravesite.[5]

Compounding the impact of Fanny's death on the family, a great deal of trouble was brewing with James. In the months since he and Richmond had returned home, James, along with Will and Gus, had moved out of the log house and onto an estate just south of Morning Sun owned by James's new wife Polly. (Polly is believed to have inherited the estate after the death of her first husband, Edward Curd Leake.) James's behavior toward his wife and family at this time was described as erratic and "tyrannical." Friends and family grew concerned as they observed James's "annoyances and jealousies." Sometimes James refused to speak to his wife. Other times he threatened her with physical harm and reportedly even accused her of being a Union spy. When Polly sought comfort from her sisters, James became angry. On one such occasion, he threatened to kill "every horse on the place" to prevent his wife from leaving their property.[6]

By early 1867, the behavior had become so disturbing that Polly stayed "in continual dread and alarm for fear of her life, or violence to her person." One evening, James's long-time friend (and Polly's brother-in-law) Markum Williams attempted to intervene during a disturbance. He described James being "in a terrible state of phrenzy endeavoring to fight every body and every thing, making it dangerous for any female to be near him." On another occasion, James threatened suicide "unless things were mended at home." Not long afterward, James snapped.

According to legal depositions recorded in the incident's aftermath, Polly had been sitting on their porch one August evening around dusk when her husband, "in a fit of excitement," approached her "with a gun in his hand loaded and cocked." Believing she was about to be shot, Polly called for help from her stepsons. Either Will or Gus (the records are not clear) successfully wrestled the gun away from their father. At some point during this scene, Polly's screams for help reached a neighbor named Redford Hall. About the time that Hall arrived, James retrieved another gun, walked into the yard, and attempted to shoot himself. The pistol failed to fire, however. Undeterred, James obtained a razor and "attempted the taking of his own life by cutting his own throat." Again, fate intervened, this time in the form of Hall who somehow prevented the suicide in progress and helped get a bleeding James under control.[7]

Six months later, Hall would testify in the divorce proceedings that Polly successfully brought against James. When the divorce was finalized, Hall married Polly and together the two began a new family. Though nowhere would it be stated explicitly, the trauma stemming from James's lengthy war experience surely contributed to his descent into domestic violence and self-harm.[8]

Family lore claimed that James wore a fur collar over his neck for the rest of his life to hide the scars. James, Will, and Gus returned to live in the log house with Logan and his two children, Gillie and Linnie Lee. There, the Davies brothers continued to "hold all property in common between them" and raise their children "together . . . as children of one man."[9]

During the same period that James was veering toward his breakdown, various siblings and half siblings living in Texas were going through ordeals of their own as they attempted to acclimate to the realities of postwar life. In April 1867, James's older sister Mary Scantlin wrote to Morning Sun with an update from Bosque County. Despite the bond that she shared with her younger brother, she and James had not been in communication since 1861—a fact that Mary made sure to emphasize in her letter. Explaining that she was "doing as well as could be expected under the circumstances," she told James that she had managed to "stay clear of debt" by renting out her farmland to tenants. She also felt pleased by the progress her two sons were making in school. "Not boasting but no woman ever raised better boys than they are," she wrote. Mary went on to express her feelings on emancipation: "I was not materially injured by the war further than the loss of my negroes," she told James. "They have all left. I am doing my own work entirely and have been for more than twelve months. They was not much account when slaves and a heep less now. They are doing no good in this country."[10]

When Mary wrote her brother two months later, she admitted more details about her financial difficulties. As she asked James to send her money, she referred to the rent she collected from a tenant farmer, and wrote, "That is all that we make and that is not much." Once more—and probably because she remained unaware of James's mental struggles—Mary expressed her disappointment with her brother's lack of communication: "I hardly know what to write for I have written three letters. . . . I can't think why I don't get any answers but I think the fault must be in the mails."[11]

In September, when Mary followed up, she reported that she and her two sons had recently gone through "a good deal of sickness" but managed to recover. Turning back to the subject of money, she encouraged James to send funds in the care of a local judge she called an "intimate friend." Again, she also noted the impact of emancipation on her own life, writing, "I am doing all of my own work and have been ever since I first turned the darkies off. I don't know but what I get along smoother and better than I did when they were slaves."[12]

By the end of that year—and echoing some of the ideas that he had once harbored prior to the war—James was expressing interest to Mary about relocating to Texas himself. In the responses she sent in early 1868, Mary stated, "You wrote that times was very hard. We have no great reason to complain. Money is very scare at this time but every thing else is plenty." She went on: "You spoke of moving to this country. We would be glad to see you and think you would do very well." Mary followed up afterward, adding, "I have a nice lot of bacon so come on. I would be so glad to have you come. Nothing would please us better. I do hope and trust you will come." However serious he may or may not have been about making the move to Texas in the wake of his assault on Polly and attempted suicide, James ultimately decided he could not leave his home in Morning Sun behind.[13]

During the final years of the 1860s and into the following decade, Will and Gus Davies both displayed similar academic inclinations and career interests as they came of age. On the heels of their initial schooling in Morning Sun, and at a private boarding school in Fayette County, the brothers attended Pleasant Hill School in Shelby Depot, where they studied under an instructor who "taught them the early rudiments of science." The brothers then spent their teenage years learning from Dr. Snowden Craven Maddux in the so-called "Academy of Medicine" that Maddux established in a room above his home office. Maddux at this same time was becoming increasingly politically connected. Those connections may have helped Will and Gus when they both enrolled in medical school at Vanderbilt. The brothers seem to have benefitted greatly from their time in Nashville, and graduated just a year apart, in 1878 and 1879 respectively.[14]

After Nashville, Will returned to the log house in Morning Sun while Gus went to work as a general physician in the nearby town of Raleigh. Gus also worked as the interim doctor for the Shelby County "poorhouse." In 1881, revealing a notable streak of independence, Gus headed to New York City and earned a postgraduate certificate studying surgery and bandaging at New York University. He returned to the South after his time in Manhattan but not to Shelby County. Instead, he settled in the small Mississippi Delta community of Alpika (later renamed Walls), just south of Memphis, where he set up a successful ophthalmology and dentistry practice. Through the subsequent years he would combine his medical career with planting pursuits, purchasing approximately one hundred acres of rich Mississippi Delta bottomland that he primarily farmed in cotton through sharecropping arrangements. Later still, Gus earned a degree of renown as an amateur archeologist. Utilizing a "field crew" that consisted of two local sharecroppers (one of whom, Mose Frazier, would later move to Davies Manor), Gus gradually unearthed a collection of Mississippian Period pottery from the "Walls Site,"* an ancient Indian burial ground located a short distance from his home near the banks of the Mississippi River.[15]

Meanwhile, back in Morning Sun, Will had immersed himself in building his medical practice out of the log house that he continued to share with his aging father and uncle. Whether Will had moved back into his childhood home eagerly, or more out of a sense of duty, is difficult to say. What is clear, though, is that the practice he established was a demanding and not especially lucrative one. Sometimes patients visited him. Other times he traveled to them by horseback. When he needed to perform surgeries, he often did so out of Dr. Maddux's office in Shelby Depot. Consistently collecting fees, he discovered, was challenging. Like Gus, Will did spend a brief stretch in the 1880s doing post-graduate work in New York City. He also gave real thought at various points to starting over somewhere new and more financially rewarding. Ultimately, though, like his father and uncle, Will was destined to remain attached to the same land and home that he had always known.[16]

By 1880, the Black community living on Logan and James's plantation had undergone many changes since the beginnings of emancipation.

---

* The collection Gus Davies and Mose Frazier unearthed from the Walls Site would later be donated to the University of Mississippi Anthropology Department. The Davies Collection, which is still housed at the university today, is recognized as one of the largest and most intact assemblages of Mississippian vessels ever found.

Though contours of that community are hard to trace with certainty, at least fifteen Black families lived on the brothers' land that year; most continued to carve out their livelihoods through sharecropping arrangements. Some of these families—Lem and Minnie Hunter and their six children; Jim and Rachel Bell and their daughter; Peter and Mollie Harris and their three children—had only moved to the brothers' estate after 1870 and probably did not have a direct connection to the Davies family that dated to antebellum times. In other cases, though, the families who remained on the plantation were comprised of people whom Logan and James had enslaved until the end of the Civil War. One example was Amos Davis, now age twenty-four, who lived with his wife Cora and their one-year-old daughter Carry a short distance from the brothers' log house.* Richmond and Sarah Jane Bennett and their now eight children lived next to Amos' family. Lewis Gray and his family, and Ben Gray and his, also still lived in the area, just a few households away from the Bennett residence.[17]

The now fifty-six-year-old Joshua Davies, his wife, Mitzi, and their three sons, Archie, Joe, and Josh, lived close to the Gray and Bennett families. Notably, Joshua and Mitzi, by this point, had decided to change their family's surname from Davies to Hadley. The name change (combined with evidence suggesting Mitzi's parents were originally enslaved by the Hadley family in Georgia before they came to Maury County) indicates that Joshua and Mitzi felt a closer affinity to the late Sarah (Hadley) Davies's side of the family than they did to William's. The fact that Joshua and Mitzi's youngest sons, Joe and Josh, were listed in 1880 as attending school also shows the Hadley family taking advantage of whatever educational opportunities had opened up for them at that point in time. The final traces of Joshua's story would emerge a few years later in a receipt showing Logan and James paying one J. R. Matthews ten dollars on January 22, 1882, for "1 coffin for Joshua Hadley."[18]

A few cases can be tracked of people formerly enslaved by the Davies brothers moving short distances away from the plantation to sharecrop or lease other planters' lands. One example is Tom and Susan Cartwright

---

* As we have already seen, Amos's parents, Joe and Maria Davis, had been enslaved by the Davies brothers; Joe and Maria's absence in census records in 1880 leaves it unclear what had become of them by this point.

and their growing family, all of whom had moved just south of the Memphis to Somerville Road by this point and were probably farming land owned by one George W. Davis (no related to the Davieses). For another branch of the Cartwrights, this one headed by William and Emily, the 1870s had brought life tragedies that resulted in their disappearance from the historical records. According to coffin receipts kept by Logan and James Davies, Emily and one of her sons had died in 1875, less than a month apart, probably of yellow fever. What became of William Cartwright and most of their other children by 1880 is unknown. However, by 1880 Elias Cartwright (William and Emily's oldest son) had acquired a 115-acre tract of his own land a short distance northeast of the Davieses' estate where he lived and farmed with his wife Mariah and their four children.[19]

Three households away from Elias in 1880—and located directly adjacent to the northeast corner of Logan and James's plantation boundary—was the 115-acre estate owned by Wilcher Tucker, now sixty-two, and his fifty-two-year-old wife Mary. In 1872, Wilcher had purchased this piece of property for 150 dollars from another Black landowner named George Cherry. Since then, Wilcher and his family had improved the value of the farm to 745 dollars. The Tucker family's livestock holdings included four cows, four sheep, more than thirty-five hogs, and two mules. Wilcher and Mary's children who still lived at home—Anthony, age twenty, Pricilla, nineteen, and Amy, fifteen—helped their parents and a small number of hired laborers farm a total of thirty-four improved acres—eighteen of which was planted with corn and eight with wheat. The remaining eight acres the Tuckers planted in cotton. Meanwhile, Wilcher and Mary's oldest son, Amos, lived either on or adjacent to the estate with his wife Pleasant and their daughter Maggie. Lucious Tucker, by contrast, did not live on or beside his parents' farm. Instead, he lived with his wife Alice and their three children on land owned by Gabe and Elizabeth (Davies) Finney a few miles away.

Lucious, more so than his father, would continue to appear in Logan and James's commissary ledgers in the years to come. The Tucker family's ability to acquire a sizable and successful farm of their own amounted to a major success relative to many of their peers.[20]

CHAPTER 19

Yearning for the "Days of Yore"

Fifteen years after achieving emancipation, most Black Southerners—especially landless Black Southerners who had been economically stifled year after year under exploitative sharecropping contracts—continued to claw their way toward securing the basic rights granted to them under the law as American citizens. From their perspective, it would have been bewildering to look back on the political and social changes wrought by Reconstruction. It had been nothing if not a paradoxical time. Beginning with the Thirteenth Amendment and the Civil Rights Act of 1866, Congressional Republicans had managed to pass a series of radically progressive measures that enshrined entirely new rights and federal protections for Black people. At the same time, state and local jurisdictions had done all they could to resist enforcement of those same rights and protections. A mixed record of success had characterized the Freedmen's Bureau as well. Though the federal agency had indeed helped countless freed-people transition out slavery, severe underfunding and internal administrative problems restricted the Bureau's effectiveness and far too often left its protections beyond the reach of those who needed them most.[1]

Broadly speaking, however, Reconstruction had created exhilarating new opportunities for Black engagement across the political spectrum. Harnessing those opportunities, Black voters helped elect some two thousand men of color to positions of public office between 1867 and 1877. Those positions ranged from local county and municipal offices, to seats in state legislatures, to seats in the halls of the US Congress. Still, Black political ascendency had proven ephemeral; by 1880, the gains made via the ballot box were in danger of being erased altogether by the "Redemption" movement led by conservative white Democrats horrified at the notion of rising Black political power. Decades later, from the vantage point of the 1930s, the scholar and historian W. E. B Du Bois would succinctly summarize the maddening plight that freed-people had endured under Reconstruction: "The slave went free," Du Bois wrote, "stood a brief moment in the sun; then moved back toward slavery."[2]

In Tennessee, Black people had gained access to the levers of power most explicitly during the brief window between 1865 and 1870. During these years, as Radical Republicans allied with Governor Brownlow took charge of county courthouses, newly enfranchised freed-people had flocked to polling places, leading to Republican sweeps of local elections. A glimpse of the political scene in Shelby County in 1867 provides just one illustration: That May, in the first election in which freed-people could cast their ballots, an astounding 4,652 Black voters registered in the county; a few months later the number climbed to more than seven thousand. Meanwhile, a new class of Black political leaders had emerged. None in Shelby County became as influential as one Ed Shaw. Born in Kentucky in the 1820s, Shaw had arrived in Memphis as a free Black man around 1852. He had gone on to operate a saloon and gambling house after the war, then leveraged his commercial success to enter the political arena. Along with playing key roles at the Tennessee Colored Political Conventions in Nashville, Shaw became Shelby County's "paramount" Black leader during the 1870s, serving as a county commissioner, a Memphis city council member, and, in 1874, the wharfmaster—a position that briefly made him the county's highest paid public official. Larger forces would eventually coalesce to end Shaw's reign. But in his rise and influence, he presented a new model for what could be achieved through local politics.[3]

Yet again though, it was a paradoxical time. Even as Reconstruction opened previously unimaginable opportunities for Black political participation, the furor that same participation ignited reinforced just how deeply and potently the currents of white supremacy ran. Acts of racially motivated violence and intimidation occurred throughout the Reconstruction South. In scale and intensity, however, few events rivaled the tragedy that unfolded in Memphis in 1866. That May, a mob led by policemen carried out a "massacre of historic proportions" that epitomized the depths white Memphians were willing to go to fight back against rising Black mobility. The conflict began with a shooting altercation between members of the mostly Irish Memphis police force and a group of US Colored Troop veterans who had recently mustered out of service at Fort Pickering.* Tensions quickly spiraled out of control and by the time the violence ended the mob had murdered at least forty-six Black Memphians and burned more than one hundred Black-owned structures to the ground. Later that same summer, in New Orleans, a mob of ex-Confederates in league with policeman carried out a massacre that killed at least thirty-four Black people—and according to some estimates, as many as two hundred.[4]

Of course, neither of these tragedies were the last acts of racially fueled mass violence to plague the Reconstruction South. But what the mob attacks in Memphis and New Orleans had done was horrify a great many people across the nation and help create the political will necessary for Congressional Republicans to fight back against President Andrew Johnson's lenient policies toward the defeated South. In June 1866, following an investigation into the events in Memphis, Congress passed the Fourteenth Amendment guaranteeing African Americans citizenship and equal protections under the law. Constitutional guarantees for Black voting rights would subsequently be addressed in the Fifteenth Amendment, formally adopted in 1870. The Thirteenth, Fourteenth, and Fifteenth Amendments, along with other key pieces of federal legislation born from Reconstruction, permanently altered the constitutional status of African Americans and forever changed the trajectory of the debates over the meanings of freedom and citizenship. In the years to come, and continuing well into the twentieth century, most white historians would malign the legacy of Reconstruction as little more than a period of corruption and failed governance. In actuality—and as leading historians of the period like Henry Louis Gates have so forcefully argued in more recent times—Reconstruction, for all its failures and missed opportunities—should be understood instead as "nothing less

---

* Royal Price very likely witnessed firsthand the Memphis massacre. A member of Company C of the Third Heavy Artillery Regiment—the same regiment that was at the center of the altercation with policemen on May 1, 1866—Royal's service records confirm that he had mustered out of duty at Fort Pickering just the day before.

than the monumental effort to create a biracial democracy out of the wreckage of the rebellion."[5]

Still, it had been a time of painful contradictions for African Americans. State and local-level resistance to federal protections had manifested in the birth of paramilitary groups like the White League and the Ku Klux Klan. Acting in the service of the Democratic party, the planter class, and all those who yearned for the full return of white supremacy, these groups carried out countless outrages. In Tennessee, the birthplace of the Klan, political assassinations and other forms of terror committed against African Americans and Republicans became commonplace in the late 1860s. Reports of murders and beatings saturated Memphis newspapers through these years. Northern papers covered the violence also. A Memphis-based correspondent for the *Chicago Tribune* reported in October 1868 that "West Tennessee, as is well known, is the scene of action of nine tenths of the lawless outrages that have made our state so notorious for a long time past. As West Tennessee is the field, so Memphis is the head and heart from which emanates the control and vitality of the Ku-Klux organizations, through which all this lawlessness arises." The attempted assassination of Ed Shaw during a November 1868 political meeting in Memphis was just one example of Klan violence. Although the attendees of that meeting had managed to successfully fight the Klan off, Shaw continued to face threats to his life going forward.[6]

An even more extreme instance of a "lawless outrage" had occurred in the Northeast Shelby Triangle in January 1869. The victim, one Wash Henley, was a Black army veteran and blacksmith who had served in the same USCT company as Royal Price's brother, Jim Price. The circumstances that led to the crime reportedly involved Henley running away and attempting to elope with the teenage daughter of his employer, a Union Depot-area farmer named Philip T. Jones. The next day, Jones located his daughter and Henley in a nearby town and returned her home. A handful of Jones's friends then apprehended Henley. A short time later, a group of "masked horseman, estimated at 25 in number" intercepted the group and took Henley into their possession. The following day, Henley's lifeless body was discovered near a local creek. According to one newspaper account, Henley had been hanged and set on fire, and his body riddled with bullets. Another account, this one published even before the body had been discovered, reported that "the negro we have not yet heard from, and hope when we do again that he may be hanging gracefully from the limb of a tree."[7]

The murder of Wash Henley typified the extreme brand of racially fueled terrorism that had become a fact of life for Black people in Shelby County. The ability of the masked killers to commit their act with total impunity also spoke volumes about the shifting political winds. The same year as Henley's lynching, Governor Brownlow made the decision to step down from office and accept a US Senate seat. Afterward, conservative Democrats, their ranks filled with ex-Confederates, retook control of the Tennessee General Assembly and did all they could to dismantle Black political ascendency. Republicans, particularly in East Tennessee, continued to win elections. And even in parts of West Tennessee, including Shelby County, Black politicians such as Ed Shaw maintained their influence well into the 1870s. Still, for all intents and purposes, the period of Republican dominance in Tennessee had proven to be remarkably brief.[8]

Within their local circles of influence in the Northeast Shelby Triangle, Logan and James Davies had worked throughout Reconstruction to champion the Democratic Party's goals to defeat Republicans and wipe away gains made by freed-people. James seems to have stayed more behind the scenes with his political involvement. By contrast, Logan played an active role, and by the mid-1870s, held leadership positions within the county's Democratic Party.

In May 1874, the Democratic Executive Committee of Shelby County appointed Logan to a subcommittee tasked with overseeing the election of delegates who would represent Morning Sun and Shelby Depot in the county's "Anti-Radical Convention," slated for later that summer. Logan himself was elected to attend the convention as a delegate. Another selection was Logan's friend, Dr. Snowden Craven Maddux. Yet another delegate chosen from the Eighth Civil District was John Park, a former mayor of Memphis who had moved to Shelby Depot after retiring from politics. It had been Park who had held the mayor's seat during the May 1866 massacre. His leadership during the violence had not exactly been inspiring: The Congressional committee that investigated the Memphis massacre found that an intoxicated Park had "lost control of his subordinates" and "completely failed to suppress the riot and preserve the peace of the city." Still, whatever reputational damage the ex-mayor had suffered for his handling of the massacre, it was not enough to prevent his selection as a delegate to the 1874 convention.[9]

That July, when Logan Davies, Maddux, and Park attended the anti-radicals' gathering, they helped choose a slate of local and state candidates who vowed to "place Memphis and Shelby County far out of the reach of the negroized Radical party." Describing the Republican party as an "ill-omened bird of night" which "sits and croaks upon the battlements presaging evil and misfortune," the anti-radicals' platform left little doubt about whose interests they represented: "The white people of Memphis and Shelby County are determined to give this ultra and vile party the coup de grace in August and November next," read one of the convention's advertisements.[10]

The Democrats ended up sweeping Shelby County's general election that November. Afterward, Logan, along with Maddux, Park, and a small circle of other Shelby Depot men (chief among them, a planter named William H. Bond and a grocery store owner turned wealthy landowner and timberman named Charles B. English) remained at the forefront of Democratic leadership within the vicinity of the Eighth Civil District. In June 1876, both Logan and Maddux were appointed to another subcommittee tasked with supervising the local election of delegates to the upcoming Shelby County Democratic-Conservative Convention. Maddux was nominated at the convention to run for a state senate seat; and a few months later, in the fiercely charged November 7 election, Shelby County voters elected Maddux to represent their interests in Nashville.[11]

Notably, the chairman of the Democratic Executive Committee through the election season of 1876 was Nathan Bedford Forrest. Since the end of the war, the former Memphis slave trader and Confederate general had helped found the Ku Klux Klan, becoming the organization's first Grand Dragon, and leading efforts in the late 1860s to direct the Klan's actions toward the interests of the national Democratic Party. Forrest had distanced himself from the Klan and national politics by the early 1870s. But he still stayed active within Shelby County, helping bring about the sweeping victories for local Democrats like Maddux in both the 1874 and 1876 contests.[12]

In the wake of the 1876 election season, the Democratic-controlled Memphis newspapers hailed the defeat of Republican candidates up and down the ballot. The lead editorial of the November 8 *Public Ledger* called the Republicans the "plundering party that has so long rioted in power and fancied security." The paper went on: "The day of reckoning finds them with unbalanced accounts and crimes upon their heads that no penance or deed of restitution can ever atone for. Deliverance is at hand and millions rejoice. We are about to be emancipated from a state of misrule which for several years has fast been verging into a fixed despotism."[13]

Not quite everything had gone in Democrats' favor. At the national level, a presidential election marred by widespread allegations of fraud had resulted in Republican Rutherford B. Hayes winning the White House. But Hayes's victory had come with a cost: In exchange for Democrats conceding the disputed electoral votes, Hayes and the Republicans agreed to withdraw the last federal troops from the South. With that agreement, Reconstruction—and any remaining semblance of federal protections for African Americans—officially came to an end. Even if Republicans had gained the presidency, the Democrats had unquestionably gained the upper hand when it came to their long-term goal to "redeem" the South by ensuring it remained firmly in control of white men.[14]

On Thursday, July 29, 1880, a business associate of the Davies brothers named James Herron sent Logan and James a letter about an event set to take place in Shelby Depot the following week. The owner of a successful factorage firm, who was also active in political circles, Herron had been working with Logan and James to plan a barbeque on behalf of the Shelby County Democratic Party. Referencing in his letter the ad he had placed for the event, Herron told the Davies brothers, "I send the circular and hope you will have a big crowd and enough to eat for all. Do all you can for the ticket. The speakers will be there. Have someone to meet them at the depot and take care of them. A good pull, a long pull and all pull together and we'll beat Ed Shaw."[15]

The barbeque being organized by Herron and the Davies brothers was part of the larger effort to defeat Ed Shaw in the upcoming August 5 sheriff's election. Though plenty of other races were on the ballot, the sheriff's race between Shaw, the Black Republican, and the white Democratic candidate, Phil R. Athy, had become the most high-profile contest of that year's election season. Described in newspapers as "the final struggle for the restoration of Radical Rule in Shelby County," the race was perceived in deeply symbolic terms. From the perspective of Democrats, it had been bad enough to witness Shaw win elections through the 1870s to the county commission and city council. Shaw's term as the well-paid wharf-master had been especially galling. So too had it irked Democrats to see Shaw escort Ulysses S. Grant through Memphis when the former president and Civil War icon had visited the city in April 1880. Still though, a Black man holding the top law enforcement position in the county was unconscionable to most whites. Furthermore, Democrats, despite their political dominance of late, had reason to be nervous about shifting demographics. In 1870, Shelby County's white residents had outnumbered African Americans roughly forty thousand to thirty-six thousand. Following a series of catastrophic Yellow Fever epidemics, however, much of the white population had permanently fled to safer climes; by 1880, Black residents in the county outnumbered whites forty-four thousand to thirty-five thousand.[16]

Against this backdrop, the racist rhetoric surrounding the sheriff's race reached a fever pitch in the weeks leading up to election day. In one lead editorial from the *Memphis Daily Appeal*, the editors urged readers to unite against Shaw, who was a "menace" to the white race. "It becomes the duty of every man in whose veins the warm blood of the Caucasian flows, and in whose heart throbs the genuine love for the great interest of the people, to exert himself" and defeat Shaw, the editors wrote. Other editorials and letters to the editor in the same paper described Shaw in near demonic terms, alternately calling him a "foul-mouthed salacious Blackguard," a "negro communist notorious for his ignorance and incompetency," and a "bold, bad man, notoriously unfit to be sheriff." Shaw, the paper went on, was "a disturber of the peace, an agitator, a howling ward bummer" who was "impudently aggressive upon all the decencies of life." The *Public Ledger*, meanwhile, published similar sentiments, including the following directive aimed at the military population working in Memphis: "Marines, look to your interest and defeat the 'n*****' Ed Shaw."[17]

On August 3, spurred on by the sensational press coverage of the sheriff's race, a "rousing gathering" of citizens estimated between five and eight hundred converged on Shelby Depot to hear Athy and other prominent Democrats speak. Logan and James Davies would have been in attendance. Presumably, Dr. Maddux, Charles B. English, William H. Bond, and the other leading white men of Shelby Depot attended as well. Notably, the event also drew a sizable crowd of Black attendees. According to one description of the barbeque, "about one-hundred colored men" had responded when one of the speakers asked if any Republicans were present in the crowd.[18]

These same Black citizens from Shelby Depot would enthusiastically head to the polls for Shaw two days later. Within the Eighth District, in fact, Shaw garnered 120 votes to Athy's 116, demonstrating that even within the repressive political climate of the day, Black men continued to resist intimidation from Democrats, exercise their constitutional right to vote, and wield a notable degree of power. Beyond the vicinity of Shelby Depot, however, the Democrats were able to overcome Shaw's appeal. Shaw ran credibly but ultimately lost the sheriff's election. Democrats, not surprisingly, were jubilant. "The Better elements of society were aroused as they had not been in many years before," the *Public Ledger*'s editors wrote after the election.[19]

Reflecting the feelings of those "Better elements," an aspiring local poet by the name of Petrowski even penned an ode that ran beneath the lead editorial. In its characterization of race relations, the poem spoke to the widespread nostalgia for the pre-war era when white people could legally own Black human beings. Petrowski wrote:

> On hist'ry page theirs' no record
> Like that was shown in the accord
> Between the then master and slave,
> Each to each was true—as the brave
> Whate'er their condition may be
> The black for home, the white to be free
> They're on the track!
> They're coming back!
> The negroes, as in days of yore
> Again will see
> Now all are free
> True friendship 'tween us as before.[20]

Republican political leaders alleged after the election that despite the turnout for Shaw, large numbers of Black voters had been intimidated and prevented from voting. Still, there was little recourse. According to the historian Roger L. Hart, who has studied the 1880 Shelby County sheriff's election in depth, "The defeat of Ed Shaw demonstrated that even with a strong candidate and a clear majority of the voters, black people had little hope for political power when white employers, landowners, public officials, newspapers, [and] ballot-counters united against them."[21]

Through the 1880s, Shaw would make unorthodox political shifts and concessions. For a time, he even aligned himself at the state level with Democrats. Overall, though, Shaw's influence steadily diminished. It was a fate that mirrored the wider decline of African American political participation. In 1891, the same year that Shaw died, a new poll-tax law went into effect in Tennessee that effectively put an end to whatever Black political aspirations remained. The era of Jim Crow segregation had officially begun.[22]

For decades afterward, and extending through the first half of the twentieth century, African Americans in the South would technically still hold the right to vote. Yet in practice, the combination of poll taxes, literacy tests, violent intimidation, and other forms of disenfranchisement effectively prevented them from exercising their constitutional right to participate in American democracy. The biracial republic that Black Americans had briefly glimpsed during Reconstruction—that "moment in the sun"—was now decidedly behind them.[23]

CHAPTER 20

A Promising and Pleasant Little Village

From the perspective of Logan and James Davies, the 1880s must have seemed a time defined by optimistic developments. From the shifting political climate that they had helped bring about, to the state-of-affairs on their plantation, to their own children's coming-of-age, the brothers had plenty of reasons to feel fortunate. Whatever mental struggles may have lingered for James, he still managed to successfully handle much of the estate's day-to-day business. Logan, for his part, had expanded the family's commercial interests beyond agriculture even as he deepened his involvement in local politics. Both brothers remained active members of the Morning Sun Masonic Lodge. As for their own fraternal relationship, the "long and lovingly associated" bond between them seems to have only strengthened as they entered their twilight years. In the evenings, according to one visitor to the log house in 1882, Logan and James loved nothing more than sitting "around their fireside in great mirth and pleasure."[1]

The rhythms of life and business at the brothers' plantation carried on in ways both familiar and quite new through these years. As was the case from the estate's beginnings, cotton continued to be the leading cash crop. Yet cotton production remained roughly half of what enslaved laborers had harvested prior to the war. To compensate, the Davies brothers had gradually diversified their agricultural schedule, purchased more land, and expanded their overall improved acreage. Along with the cotton yielded by sharecroppers, the brothers employed a labor force of African American farmhands who raised swine and sheep, and produced oats, wheat, corn, and cow peas. Peach and apple orchards emerged on portions of the plantation that had once been forested. To further supplement their income, Logan and James opened a grist mill and cotton gin, and launched a lucrative mule-breeding service using a stud they named Mammoth and promoted as "The Renowned Jack." In 1881, Logan also opened a dry goods store in Shelby Depot (by this point known as Brunswick) with a local businessman named Alfred Young. "Good Times are Coming," the Davies & Young establishment promised in one ad that featured a stagecoach, driven by a finely dressed white man, being guided by an angel-like figure defeating a demonic spirit labelled "Hard Times."[2]

As new offshoots of the brothers' business operations took root, Logan and James—both of whom had entered their sixties by the middle part of the decade—could take comfort in the knowledge that their children were making confident strides into adulthood in their own right. Will and Gus had both established successful medical practices that provided them social respectability and economic independence; James surely felt pride in his two sons' achievements. So also would Logan have had reason to feel pleased about developments with both of his children, Gillie and Linnie. The former had graduated from Bethel College in 1882 and returned home to help manage the plantation. As for Linnie, she married a well-to-do local man named William Bond Beaty in 1886.[3]

Linnie's husband, alternately known as "Bond," and "W. B." was a "highly respected farmer" who had also worked as an elected constable for Brunswick since the early 1880s. His family had deep roots in Shelby County. Bond's father, Dr. Abel Beaty, had moved to the Morning Sun community not long after Logan and James had arrived in 1851. The plantation that he established near the Davies brothers led to the two families becoming close. In 1861, Abel had joined the Morning Sun home guard alongside James before enlisting in a Confederate cavalry unit and serving out most of the remainder of the war. After the war, Abel had focused on his medical practice and became regarded as "one of the best-known practitioners in Shelby County." Bond Beaty's mother, Mary Lucinda Bond, also possessed a name that carried a great deal of weight locally. Various branches of Bonds had arrived in Northeast Shelby County in the 1840s by way of Virginia and Alabama. Eventually, so many came to reside in the community along the railroad just west of Brunswick that a depot emerged there named Bond's Station.[4]

The farm that Bond and Linnie (Davies) Beaty established was located between Brunswick and Bond's Station. The new couple almost immediately began to have children after their marriage. They also adopted (for reasons that are not clear) an orphaned teenager named Mollie McCadden. In the years to come, the Beaty's adopted daughter would find herself at the center of a high-profile incident that resulted in enormously tragic consequences. In the meantime, Linnie's marriage and relocation to Bond Beaty's estate meant that the Davies brothers' log house in Morning Sun had returned to being an entirely male-dominated household occupied by two widowered men and their young bachelor sons.[5]

Known as both an "excellent conversationalist" and a "skilled sheep shearer," Gillie Davies seems to have been the sort of man who could move easily between farm life and more refined social settings. After returning home from college, he took on more responsibilities managing the plantation's agricultural operations. Yet he also embraced leisurely pursuits in ways that his more conservative father and uncle did not. Gillie built a half-mile horse racing track on the estate, raised fighting cocks, and hosted popular croquet games. A "skilled marksman," he organized hunting excursions for wild turkey, squirrels, and quail. Fox hunts through the "deep woods to the north" of the log house became popular, attracting "many men" from Brunswick and Morning Sun who came to "share the chase." Taking full advantage of his status as an eligible young bachelor, he became a "favorite participant in the local square dances of the community." Still, Gillie balanced his pleasure-seeking with more traditional endeavors. Like his father, he took on leadership roles in local Democratic politics, accepting appointments as a delegate to county conventions, and to positions as an election judge and registrar for the Eighth Civil District. He also valued religious faith—albeit with a more liberal approach than his forebears. (A Universalist himself, Gillie alternated his attendance between the local Cumberland Presbyterian congregations in Morning Sun and Brunswick. He only did so, it was said, because "there was not an Episcopal Church in the area."[6])

In the sense that he seems to have been a man with a relatively free-spirited streak, Gillie shared much in common with his older first cousin, Dr. Will Davies. The latter, his own letters show, embraced a decidedly humanistic world view. Though he came from a long line of evangelicals, Will had grown into a man who expressed skepticism of traditional religious tenets. Furthermore, Will, like Gillie, took full advantage of being young and single. Throughout the 1880s, Will courted a number of "lovely ladies" and often spent time in Memphis. A favorite spot was Duffy's European Hotel. Located at the corner of Adams and Main Streets, the hotel had a first-class restaurant and a lively social scene that provided the young doctor a welcome respite from the isolation of rural Morning Sun. Will's lifestyle was unorthodox enough that it even drew some public attention. In 1886, a Morning Sun gossip correspondent reported to the *Memphis Avalanche* that "The neighborhood has assumed its wonted health and our doctor, W. L. Dav[ies], has little to do beside paying attention to the fair sex. 'Tis rumored the center of attraction for him is in your city."[7]

It is intriguing to wonder what exactly Logan and James thought about their bachelor sons' lifestyles at this time. It is also worth considering how Logan and James perceived their own place in the community as the generation behind them assumed more control of politics and business. The brothers' "little burg" of Morning Sun had seen significant changes since the Civil War as long-time residents relocated or died, and economic activity shifted in the direction of Brunswick. According to the same correspondent who teased Will about his romantic life, "Those who knew Morning Sun before the war and see it now would not recognize it as the same. There are but few of the old citizens here and the business part has moved hirer up."[8]

The Davies brothers must have felt a certain pride, however, that they were among the "old citizens" who *had* remained. Whereas so many other farms and plantations around them had come and gone through the years, their operation had proven to be a model of resilience. Furthermore, as they moved closer toward the dawn of a new century, Logan and James could rest easy knowing that their sons, despite their more free-wheeling lifestyles, were already on their way toward carrying the family business and name into the future. All things considered then, the four Davies men who occupied the log house through the 1880s seem to have enjoyed a rather charmed existence.

And yet, within this privileged world of square dances and fox hunts and evenings of fireside cheer, darker forces were also at work. These forces were not new, of course. Whether the Davies men recognized as much or not, the long shadows born of slavery and pervasive white supremacy had always been with them, infusing their commercial ambitions, shaping their worldviews and perceptions, and permeating the broader culture that had formed them. Now, though slavery was gone for good, the economic and political oppression of African Americans remained ingrained in Southern society. The manifestations of entrenched racism had also continued to evolve in places like rural Shelby County—most dramatically, in the widening embrace of mob violence and lynchings. Soon, two high-profile instances of this brand of violence would unfold that involved the collective participation of the Brunswick community—and, to varying degrees, members of the Davies family themselves. The first tragedy touched the Davieses in the sense that it was supported—and covered up by—men who moved within the family's social, political, and business circles. The second—spawned in the wake of an alleged assault on Bond and Linnie Beaty's adopted daughter, Mollie McCadden—connected more directly to the Davies family. Both of these lynching crimes would reveal just how brutal and dichotomous life could be in a post-Reconstruction community that had been fully "redeemed."[9]

During the same period that Morning Sun had witnessed its population and economic activity decline, Brunswick experienced the opposite. Regarded by the 1880s as a "promising and pleasant little village," Brunswick's most obvious advantage was its strategic location on the Louisville & Nashville Railroad. Along with a renovated railroad depot and the stately homes that had emerged nearby, Brunswick boasted a church, a school, and multiple dry goods stores and groceries. Like many small communities experiencing growth, it was a place where the most essential matters of business, land use, politics, and religion tended to be controlled by a tight-knit circle of local families. Logan and James Davies, along with their sons Will and Gillie, were certainly part of the network of prominent locals whose opinions, actions, and business interests carried weight. Bond and Linnie Beaty were also regarded as leading young members of local society. Along with serving as a constable, Bond Beaty, beginning in 1888, had joined his brother-in-law Gillie as a delegate to the Shelby County Democratic Party Convention. Bond Beaty's

KU-KLUX IN SHELBY COUNTY.

Colored Men Cause Them to Skedaddle.

We have repeatedly had occasion to refer to the fiendish outrages perpetrated by the Ku Klux in the northern part of this county. They have rode rough shod over a large section of country, and held inoffensive, hardworking colored citizens in mortal terror. For nearly six months they have run riot, several nights in every week, and perpetrated whatever outrages they listed. On Wednesday night week they attempted to take out and hang a colored man living on Person Brock's place, about a mile and a half this side of Shelby Depot. They were armed to the teeth, and dressed in full uniform of tall hats, masks and shrouds, and had succeed in breaking in the door of the cabin, when several colored men, wakened by their shooting a dog, rushed out of the adjoining houses, with arms, and incontinently skedaddled the cowardly assassins, who fled to the woods. The colored men deserve credit for their manly defense of their homes against such odds.

If reports that come to us are substantiated, there are some villains, not a thousand miles from Shelby Depot, whose hands are red with the blood of innocent citizens, who had better arrange their mortal affairs before the arrival of the militia.

While most Memphis newspapers downplayed or ignored violence committed against freedpeople across Shelby County in the years after the Civil War, some publications did report in detail on the outrages, as seen in this January 30, 1869, news item from the *Memphis Evening Post* about Black resistance to Ku Klux Klan activity near Shelby Depot. The paper was founded by John Eaton, who had left his position as assistant commissioner of the Freedmen's Bureau to launch the pro-Union newspaper. Newspapers.com

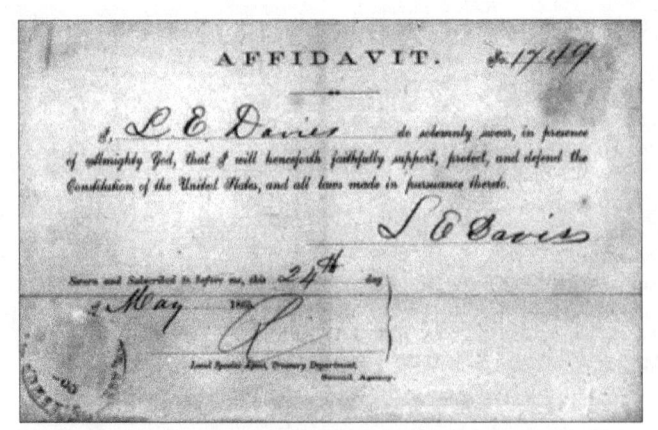

On May 24, 1865, the same day that US Colored Troops veterans led a march of freedpeople through downtown Memphis celebrating the end of slavery and the Civil War, Logan Davies was in the city signing his loyalty oath and promising to "faithfully support, protect, and defend the Constitution of the United States, and all laws made in pursuance thereto." No record has been found of James Davies signing a loyalty oath following his service in the Confederate Army. Microfilm, Memphis and Shelby County Room, Memphis Public Library

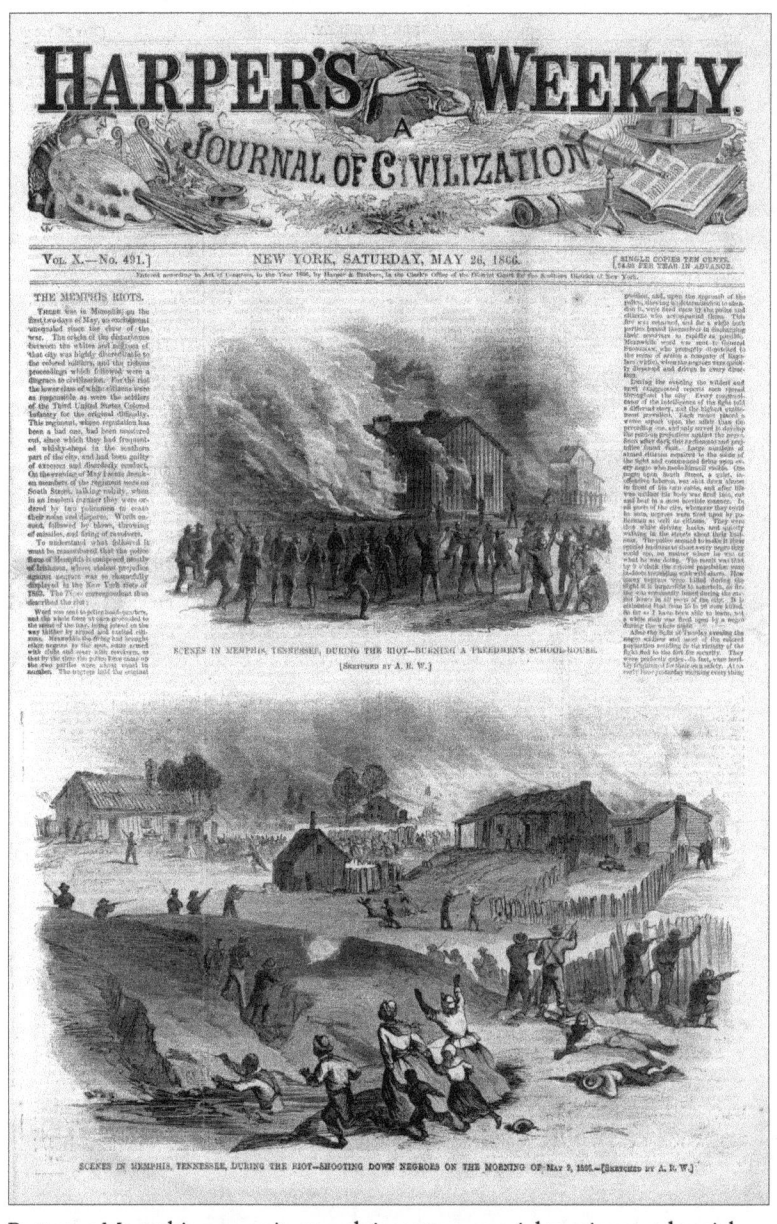

Post-war Memphis was a city awash in extreme racial tensions and social upheaval. In May 1866, a mob of policemen led a "massacre of historic proportions" that left at least forty-six Black Memphians dead and demonstrated the depths of white backlash against freedpeople's rising mobility. Royal Price was a member of the US Colored Troop company that clashed with police in the lead up to the massacre and probably witnessed the events firsthand. University of Memphis Digital Commons

Dr. Snowden Craven Maddux (front center) was a close friend of the Davies family and a political leader in the Shelby Depot/Brunswick community who mentored Will and Gus Davies prior to their enrollment in medical school at Vanderbilt. Here Maddux is seen posing with his former students, including Will (back right) and Gus (back left) while Maddux was in Nashville representing Brunswick in the Tennessee General Assembly. DMA Archives

The Renowned Jack,

MAMMOTH

Will stand the remaining part of the season, commencing APRIL 16th and ending JUNE 10th, 1883, at our stable, 7 miles east of Bartlett, 3½ miles south of Brunswick, 1½ miles northwest of Morning Sun, and will serve Mares at $10 by the insurance, $8 for the Season, and $6 for the leap. Money due when the fact is ascertained or property transferred, with a lien on the foal for service.

All care will be taken to prevent accidents, but will not be responsible for any that may occur.

DESCRIPTION and PEDIGREE

Mammoth is a dark iron gray, nearly black, fifteen hands high, Jack measure, and well formed, very heavy. He was sired by old Mammoth of Kentucky, his dam was a Jennet of the celebrated General Wool Stock.

L. E. & J. B. DAVIES.

By the 1880s, Logan and James Davies were increasingly diversifying their plantation's operations and business interests. This 1883 advertisement promoted a mule-breeding service that became quite lucrative for the brothers. DMA Archives

In 1886, in a ceremony that took place at the Davies brothers' Morning Sun estate, Logan's daughter, Linnie Lee, married a local constable and planter named William "Bond" Beaty. Seven years later, the Beaty's adopted daughter would make an allegation of attempted rape that led to one of the most vicious lynching crimes in the history of Shelby County. DMA Archives

Gillie Mertis Davies, the only son of Logan and Frances "Fanny" Anna (Vaughn) Davies, pictured here circa 1885, around the time he was beginning to assume a lead role managing his family's plantation. In 1891, Gillie married Frances Ina Stewart and in 1903 the couple gave birth to their only child, Frances "Ellen" Davies. DMA Archives

influence only continued to grow after 1890 when he won election as a deputy sheriff for Brunswick.[10]

Snowden Craven Maddux, the doctor, politician, and long-time friend of the Davies family, had continued to be a leading figure in the community until he relocated to Texas around 1888. Other prominent names and close acquaintances of the Davieses included Richard Inge, an "eccentric" self-ordained Presbyterian minister, and C. G. Hughes, who at various points occupied just about every local political office possible. Inge, who "loved to play croquet in the yard" of the Davies estate, was something of a controversial figure inclined to blend his politics with his work as an evangelical "exhorter."* As for C. G. Hughes, he alternately served through the 1880s and 1890s as an alderman, elections judge, deputy sheriff, and member of the county court. Hughes enjoyed recreational pursuits as well: In at least one instance, in 1888, he partnered with Gillie to raise a popular "Irish game" fighting cock named Cleveland "on behalf of the Democratic citizens of Brunswick."[11]

Along with C. G. Hughes, Bond Beaty, and Richard Inge, two of the other most influential men in Brunswick were William H. "W. H." Bond and Charles B. English. The former served subsequent terms alongside Bond Beaty as a constable and deputy sheriff. He also had a long history of gaining political appointments. As early as 1876, W. H. Bond had joined Logan Davies and Snowden Craven Maddux in serving on a subcommittee to appoint delegates to the Shelby County Democratic-Conservative Convention. In subsequent years—and often doing so alongside Gillie—W. H. Bond frequently served as an election judge and registrar for the Eighth Civil District. Newspaper readers came to know W. H. as a "a reputable, intelligent and wealthy representative of the rural elements around Memphis." However, this local lawman and politician also had a history of criminal activity. In 1884 (just two years before he was appointed to a position as an election judge) he had been convicted in federal court for stuffing ballot-boxes and "interfering with a supervisor of election." Years earlier, in the mid-1870s, W. H. had also been caught up in a sensational scandal that erupted when his younger

---

* In 1884 Inge had been indicted by the Shelby County Criminal Court for "desecrating a graveyard." Later, in 1893, he would be suspended from preaching by the Cumberland Presbytery for "having rendered himself obnoxious and objectionable . . . by his general conduct and peculiar mannerism."

brother, Golly Bond, murdered a man near Brunswick who had objected to Golly's efforts to marry his daughter.*[12]

As for Charles B. English, he had risen from his humble roots as wagonmaker before the Civil War to become one of the single wealthiest residents in the Northeast Shelby Triangle. He did so by opening a grocery store—"*one of* the most, if not *the most* mammoth country establishments in Shelby County," according to one description—and then parlaying that success into a series of expansive land purchases. He later won terms as schools commissioner for the Eighth Civil District and as Brunswick's mayor, bolstering his reputation as a "fearless advocate for the people," and a "veritable Davy Crockett." Eventually, English managed to acquire more than two thousand acres of old-growth bottomland surrounding the Loosahatchie River on the northern boundary of Brunswick. Here, he opened a booming lumber operation and stave mill that employed upward of a hundred employees.[13]

In the summer of 1887, one of English's employees at the stave mill was a Black teamster named Jim Eastman. Another employee, one William P. Coffman, was a white man from Illinois who had come to Brunswick to work as the mill's superintendent. Regarded as a "somewhat overbearing man," Coffman also reportedly moonlighted as "the leader of the Latter Day Kuklux" around Brunswick.[14]

On the afternoon of August 30, 1887, Jim Eastman was driving a wagon on the job when he accidently hit a stump and broke the tongue of a wheel. An angry Coffman censured Eastman, leading to a physical fight between the two men. Eastman, by all accounts, got the upper hand. The following day, a group of men impersonating law enforcement officers apprehended Eastman at gunpoint and brought him to Coffman's office at the stave mill. Binding Eastman's hands, they told him they were going to march him to Brunswick to be jailed. Eastman, understanding what he faced, told Coffman, "Captain, you are going to do me some dirt." Coffman denied it and told Eastman they were taking a shortcut to town. Then the superintendent and Klansman leader, along with three other

---

* Golly Bond, with W. H.'s help, had fled to Louisiana after the murder. He was later apprehended and returned to Tennessee, where he was placed in an asylum and "regarded as a dangerous lunatic . . . bent on self-destruction." The case received extensive media coverage with headlines such as "A Thrilling Narrative of Disappointed Love, Madness and Murder."

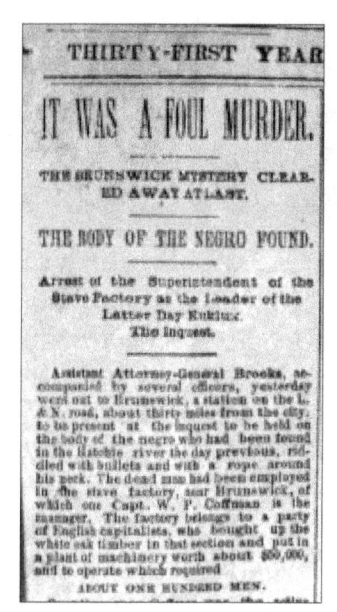

Memphis Avalanche, September 4, 1887, Memphis and Shelby County Room, Memphis Public Library

men, took Eastman to the banks of the Loosahatchie. There, they riddled him with bullets, "tied a sack of mud around his neck," and threw him into the river. Two days later, one of Eastman's friends discovered the badly decayed body. A high-profile investigation ensued. "Nothing has so excited the people in the Brunswick neighborhood for years as this high-handed Ku-Kluxism," reported the *Memphis Avalanche*.[15]

The events that followed constituted a convoluted tale of injustice and corruption that garnered intense media interest in Memphis and well beyond. Shortly after the coroner's report on Eastman's body, Coffman and three other men from the stave factory were arrested for the murder. Yet only Coffman remained in the hands of authorities. His three accomplices had managed to flee out of state after posting bonds paid for by English—and set at nominal rates by C. G. Hughes. In October, as Coffman awaited his trial, W. H. Bond curiously surfaced in Ord, Nebraska, where at least one of the murderers named Al McMahon had fled. Meanwhile, Shelby County authorities, carrying extradition orders from the Tennessee governor, arrived in Nebraska themselves to bring McMahon back for trial. Yet the Nebraska governor refused to comply with the extradition. Reporting on the case, a correspondent from the Memphis *Public Ledger* wrote, "The affair is a most mysterious one, and people are beginning to inquire into the motive of Bond in endeavoring to further the escape of one of Jim Eastman's murderers. Someone is evidently defraying his expenses in Nebraska. It is thought that Coffman is doing it, and if so it's a strong circumstance against him." Another newspaper reported that W. H. Bond had gone to Nebraska "in the service of English, a rich man at Brunswick."[16]

In November, as the case against Coffman headed toward trial, W. H. Bond was arrested for attempting to bribe a jury member. Again, English came to the rescue by helping secure his friend's bail. Public sentiment in Brunswick supported both W. H. Bond and Coffman. According to one article, "A majority of Brunswickians are in sympathy with Coffman." Furthermore, the community expressed "considerable indignation" with the deputy-sheriff who had first reported W. H. Bond's attempted bribe. Later, during the trial, the prosecution presented more than a dozen witnesses. The star witness told the jury that not only had he heard the murder take place, he had been asked by Coffman to participate in and cover up the killing. Despite the damning testimony, Coffman "sat unconcernedly . . . evidently feeling that he will be acquitted as without McMahon, the witness who rests under the sheltering wing of the governor of the state of Nebraska, the case is based on purely circumstantial evidence."[17]

Coffman's confidence turned out to be warranted. After returning a not guilty verdict, the jury "showered their congratulations on [Coffman] for having been acquitted of the heinous crime of murder." The *Chicago Tribune* reported on the case with an article headlined, "He killed a Negro. But the Jury led him go Because he was Rich and Influential." The article went on to report, "Coffman's acquittal has caused considerable comment and is generally attributed to the fact that it was only a Negro who was killed." Meanwhile, the *Weekly Public Ledger* reported that "The acquittal of W. P. Coffman . . . was no more than everybody who read the evidence expected."[18]

In the wake of Jim Eastman's murder and William P. Coffman's acquittal, life in the "pleasant little village" of Brunswick returned to relative normalcy. The following year, Charles B. English was described in the *Memphis Avalanche* as being Brunswick's "most highly esteemed citizen" who is "now having a beautiful residence constructed after the completion of his store-room." W. H. Bond earned praise for an incident in which he came to the aid of his "fellow townsmen" by shooting down a mad canine

> # HE KILLED A NEGRO.
>
> ### But the Jury Let Him Go Because He Was Rich and Influential.
>
> MEMPHIS, Tenn., Nov. 22.—[Special.]—After being out twenty-four hours the jury in the case of William P. Coffman returned a verdict today declaring the defendant not guilty. Coffman, McMahan, Webber, and Walker, all white, were indicted for the murder of Jim Eastman, a negro, committed near Brunswick, Tenn., last August. They bound their victim's hands behind him, led him into a cane-brake, and riddled him with bullets. After tying a sack of mud around his neck they threw the body into the Hatchie River, where it was found two days afterward. Walker, Webber, and McMahan fled, but Coffman, who is wealthy, remained and was arrested for complicity in the murder. He had two ribs broken in a fight with the negro the day before the murder was committed. According to the testimony of Charles Thorn, the principal witness for the State, Coffman was the ringleader in the tragedy. His acquittal has caused considerable comment and is generally attributed to the fact that it was only a negro who was killed. Coffman came from Illinois.

Chicago Tribune, November 23, 1887, newspapers.com

that "threw Brunswick into excitement." The two men continued to be leaders in local politics. In May 1890, both English and W. H. Bond, along with their younger friend, Gillie Davies, were appointed as the three election registrars for the Eighth Civil District. Despite Bond's previous conviction for stuffing ballots—not to mention his arrest on charges of bribing a jury in a murder trial—the Democratic-controlled Shelby County Commissioners of Registration had continued to place him in a position that allowed him to oversee his local community's elections.[19]

In 1891, Gillie, now age thirty, married "a very accomplished young lady" named Ina Stewart, the daughter of one of English's business partners, James Rufus Stewart. Gillie and Ina (Stewart) Davies spent the next few years living in the log house alongside Logan, James, and Will. The Davies estate, now more than ever, had become a hub of social activity. Will's medical practice had also stamped a new identity onto the estate. By the early 1890s, as he took over Dr. Maddux's former role as the community's leading doctor, the log house increasingly became known as the "Doctor's House."[20]

This community that the Davies family identified with so closely, and helped lead, was seen by many as epitomizing the qualities of an idyllic rural existence. Yet this same community was once again about to demonstrate just how swiftly it could collectively embrace mob violence as a means for carrying out "the unwritten but supreme law of the people."[21]

On the morning of Tuesday, July 18, 1893, nineteen-year-old Mollie McCadden set out on horseback from the Beaty family farm near Brunswick enroute for the railroad depot at Bonds Station. Joining Mollie was her eighteen-year-old sister, Katie, who was set to catch the train back to nearby Withe Depot, where she lived with an adopted family of her own. As the two young women moved along a secluded section of the road, they encountered a Black man. According to the testimony that Mollie later provided, the man proceeded to take the reins of her horse and say, "I want one of you women." He then allegedly pulled Mollie down from her horse, choked her, and began "dragging [her] to the side of the road." When Katie McCadden leapt down, grabbed a stick, and began to hit the man over his back, he released Mollie and ran away. Once the two women made it back to the Beatys' farm and reported what had occurred, groups of armed men immediately formed in Brunswick, Union Depot, and Bond's Station, and set out to track down the attacker. "A posse led by Bond Beatty [sic]" was among the groups who "scanned the highways, byways, the fields, and the coverts for the negro." According to the *Memphis Commercial*, "Nobody asked any questions about what would be done with him. Everybody knew that he would be hanged."[22]

News reports of the events that followed reveled in sensational descriptions of the perpetrator, alternately calling him a "fiend" and a "Black Brute," and alleging that in the course of escaping from Bond Beaty's posse, he had raped a Black woman at a mill near the Wolf River.

Newspapers also made sure to describe Mollie McCadden as "a petite and pretty girl of 19," with "brown hair blue-eyes and a slight but exquisitely molded figure." The incident, one reporter made clear, had set off the "wildest state of anger and excitement" among the white population of Northeast Shelby County.[23]

As Bond Beaty's group scoured the countryside, an eager constable in the nearby town of Raleigh arrested a Black man who seemed to fit the description that McCadden had provided. Doubt was soon cast on the man being the correct suspect, however. As the arresting constable debated how to proceed, the man managed to break away and flee. The constable fired shots at the man "but does not know whether he was hit or not," one newspaper reported. Later that same evening, a similar event described as a "sad episode" occurred near Withe Depot when a vigilante group stopped a twenty-two-year-old Black man named Charley Martin and "demanded he give an account." Terrified, Charley Martin fled, only to be "fired upon and hit in the back twice." Martin was later observed "spitting blood and lying upon the depot platform" even as it became clear that he was "guiltless" and had nothing to do with the assault in question. One correspondent reported, "It is thought that he will die . . . beyond a disposition to steal it is said he is not a bad negro."[24]

The next day, as the group of armed men continued their rampage, reports circulated that Bond Beaty's posse had at last apprehended the correct suspect. Rumors spread that the man was being brought back to Brunswick. In response, hundreds of people, some of whom took the train out from Memphis, began to congregate in Bond and Linnie Beaty's yard in anticipation of the lynching to come. A reporter on the scene described the crowd being comprised of "farmers in the majority, though there were two or three professional men, some merchants and clerks and—tell it not in Gath—a politician or so." All of them were said to be "anxious to help rid the earth of the black blot on humanity." Although the crowd waited until deep in the night, they were eventually informed that the suspect had once again evaded Bond Beaty and his men.[25]

In the midst of these developments, a constable from Brunswick, acting independently of Bond Beaty's group, had travelled to the town of Holly Springs in North Mississippi, where he'd received a tip that the suspect had fled. There, on the evening of Friday, July 21, the constable arrested a nineteen-year-old laborer named Lee Walker. Shortly after the arrest, Walker reportedly confessed to the assault on Mollie McCadden. Knowing full well what would occur to Walker in Brunswick if he was taken there to be identified, the constable instead turned the suspect over to the Shelby County sheriff, A. J. McClendon, who promptly placed Walker in the county jail in downtown Memphis.[26]

As soon as word got out that Lee Walker was incarcerated in Memphis, citizens from Brunswick and surrounding communities began to hatch a plan to break into the jail and seize him. Meanwhile, the *Public Ledger* published an astonishing telegram that the paper had sent to a Republican newspaper in Chicago: "Lee Walker, a colored man, accused of raping white women, in jail here, will be taken out and burned by whites to-night," the telegram read. The taunting question that concluded the telegram—"Can you send Miss Ida Wells to write it up?"—referred to the young investigative journalist (and one of the future founders of the NAACP) whose editorials on public lynchings in Memphis the year prior had so infuriated the local white population that they had threatened Wells with death, destroyed the newspaper she co-owned, and forced her to flee to safety in the North.[27]

Shortly before midnight on Saturday, July 22, a drunken mob said to be "howling like madmen" broke into the county jail in Memphis using a sledgehammer and iron battering rams, overpowering modest resistance put up by Sheriff McClendon and a small team of deputies. Included in the estimated one hundred men who composed this mob were an unknown number of "Brunswickians," most of whom had travelled to Memphis by train earlier that afternoon. The Brunswick contingent were furious that their constable had turned Lee Walker over to the sheriff instead of bringing him back to their own community for a hanging at the Beaty's farm. Referring to the constable, one correspondent reported, "His constituents do not appreciate the desire to abide by the law which prompted him to deliver the rapist to the sheriff and there are ominous rumors that he may not be reelected." Still, the decision to outright storm the jail had apparently not been the Brunswick contingent's desired means of obtaining Walker. According to one account, the "concocted scheme" they had hatched earlier in the day called for a small number of men gaining entry to the jail with the help of a friendly deputy sheriff. From there, they would obtain Walker and speed him back to the Beatys' farm where he would be "disposed of in a quiet and orderly manner." For whatever reason, however, that had not taken place. Instead, beginning around dusk, a crowd of increasingly belligerent citizens, many of them Memphians, had gathered at the jail. Charged up by the sensational press reports, they drank and fumed and worked themselves into a fury that culminated in the midnight charge.[28]

The extremes of lurid violence that this mob carried out against Lee Walker in the hours that followed almost defy description. Walker, for his part, had attempted to cut his own throat "with a glass bottle found in his cell" as he witnessed the mob move in toward him. Before he could do so, the mob gained entrance to his cell and seized him. Described in one account as fighting back like "a demon in desperation," Walker "scratched and bit" his attackers but soon fell limp as he was stabbed "again and again." The men proceeded to drag him out of the jail through a gauntlet of "yelling, cursing men and boys who beat, spat upon and slashed" him. Once outside, the mob stripped Walker of his clothes and obtained a rope. Fitting a noose over his neck, they threw the other end of the rope over a telegraph pole on Front Street, then lifted Walker until his feet "were three feet above the ground." A "big fellow who helped lead the mob" proceeded to yank on Walker's legs "until his neck cracked." Next, as Walker's body "hung to the telegraph pole, blood streaming down . . . from the knife wounds," the same man "mutilated the corpse"—a description that probably indicates castration. Still, Walker was not yet dead. "The neck was not broken, as the body was draw up without being given a fall, and death came by strangulation," one reporter wrote. "For fully ten minutes after he was strung up the chest heaved occasionally and there were convulsive movements of the limbs." Eventually, a policeman on the scene cut the rope, dropping Walker's body in a "ghastly heap" before a crowd who "laughed at the sound and crowded around the prostrate body . . . a few kicking the inanimate corpse." The *Public Ledger*—the same newspaper whose reporting had fanned the flames of public anger—wrote of the scene, "It was a spectacle the hideousness of which cannot be comprehended except by those who witnessed it."[29]

Yet even now the barbarity was not finished. Cries of "Burn him! Burn him!" echoed through the crowd. The same policeman who had

LYNCHED AND BURNED.

Such Was the Fate of Lee Walker, the Rapist.

Taken from Jail by an Unorganized Mob.

Prison Poorly Guarded---Resistance a Farce.

Doors Broken Down With Sledge Hammers and Rams.

The Mob Swarmed Into the Corridors and Among the Cells.

The Rapist Fought Like a Demon When Seized by the Crowd.

Cuffed and Stabbed as He Was Dragged Down Stairs.

Strung Up to a Telegraph Pole Just North of the Jail.

The Corpse Cut Down and Burned to Ashes in the Street.

Sheriff McLendon Badly Hurt by One of the Mob in the Attack on the Jail---Awful Scenes While Mob Wreaked Its Furious Vengeance.

Memphis Appeal-Avalanche, July 23, 1893, Memphis and Shelby County Room, Memphis Public Library

SCENE OF THE LYNCHING AND CREMATION.

Newspaper sketch of Lee Walker's lynching, the *Memphis Commercial*, July 24, 1893, Newspapers.com

cut down Walker's body "begged" the mob "not to bring disgrace on the city" through a public burning. The pleas fell on deaf ears. Upon gathering enough wood to light a bonfire in the middle of Front Street, the crowd cheered as "half a dozen men" seized Walker's corpse and "giving the body a swing," threw it in the "middle of the fire."[30]

The *Memphis Commercial* correspondent later reported that the ghastly sights and smells had "proved too much for a large part of the crowd" who left. Still, many stayed and were "not a bit set back by the sight of a human body being burned to ashes." Some even "laughed as the flesh cracked and blistered." In the final phase of the execution, the rope used to hang Walker was cut up and divided among the crowd as souvenirs. Another contingent of "relic hunters" waited until the "ashes cooled" so they could obtain the "teeth, nails and bits of charred skin of the immolated victim of his own lust." Summarizing the episode, the correspondent wrote,

"And so Lee Walker died, and his remains were scattered in ashes to the four winds of heaven, a horrible warning to those of his bestial kind."[31]

In the days immediately following the lynching and burning of Lee Walker, newspapers across the country ran stories detailing what had taken place in the streets of downtown Memphis. If Northern papers did not outright condemn the murder, most still reported on Walker's murder in a much more critical tone that papers in the South. In Memphis, the same newspapers that had stoked the worst passions of the public began to take a more measured tone as they seemed to pause and gauge which way public opinion would blow. Most surprising of all, on July 26, the Shelby County attorney general promised to investigate and bring charges against leaders of the mob, as well as the sheriff and his deputies for failing to defend the jail. The idea that local officials might pursue justice was said to cause many in Memphis to experience "a sort of 'where-am-I-at' air." Sheriff McClendon made the case that he had done all he could to defend the jail. "I did not want to hurt any citizens, and could not have prevented the negro from being lynched except by shooting the lynchers," the sheriff told reporters. "I am deeply regretful that it resulted as it did, but I acted in what I believed was the best manner."[32]

It soon became apparent that people from Brunswick and rural Shelby County fully supported the sheriff and viewed the investigation as a cynical political move by city politicians looking for press. If Brunswickians felt upset about anything, it was the fact that "their plans were spoiled" for bringing Walker back to Bond Beaty's farm and hanging him there. Public opinion among many Memphians seemed to fall along similar lines: "The respectable element of the community does not regret that Walker was killed, but it does not approve of the manner of the taking off," the *Memphis Commercial* told its readers. "It is safe to say that had the lynching taken place at Bond Beaty's house, or near the scene of the attempted assault, all such demonstrations as shocked decent citizens Saturday night would not have been tolerated for a moment," the *Appeal-Avalanche* added. Meanwhile, the *Public Ledger* announced that "the people of Brunswick and vicinity" would be holding an "indignation meeting" where they were expected to "pronounce it a righteous act as far as the hanging was concerned and heap condemnation upon the authorities who are moving to have the lynchers punished according to the letter of the law."³³

As consensus across Shelby County aligned in opposition to the investigation, a grand jury convened in Memphis and handed down an initial set of indictments. Four men—one Phil Bode; a cook named Jake Onetti; a lawyer named Dewitt Clinton; and Harry M. Frayser, the "railroad man" who had yanked on Walker's legs—were charged with murder or accessory to murder. Meanwhile, something of a split had emerged between local newspapers competing for readers. The *Memphis Commercial*, despite all its lurid coverage prior to the lynching, gradually moved toward the most critical assessment of the mob's actions. The paper assured its readers that "no paper in the South has stood more stoutly and resolutely for white supremacy than the *Commercial*." Yet the "barbarities" involved with Walker's lynching had caused "immense injury to the good name and material interests of Memphis." Warning against the "growing strength and licentiousness of the mob spirit," the paper argued that Walker should have been killed, only in a more orderly way that did less damage to the reputation of Memphis. The editors went on to attack their rival, the *Appeal-Avalanche*, as the "indorser, the champion and the defender of all the shameless and disgusting barbarities, which no self-respecting newspaper could print or describe."³⁴

In response to the indictments, large public meetings intended to solidify support for the sheriff and the lynchers were held in rural communities. In Rosemark, northwest of Brunswick, James Hill Barrett chaired a meeting that declared Walker had violated the "unwritten law of the land." The participants concluded by passing a resolution that expressed "our tender sympathies to the parties in confinement and accused of participating in the execution." In Union Depot, one John Priddy Bond led a gathering of more than one hundred people who approved their own set of resolutions. The Union Depot citizens declared that they were "sorry the crime was avenged by any other than ourselves," and went on to say that they approved of "all the officers of the law in not hurting anyone in the defense of the brutal fiend, who justly deserved all he receives." In the nearby community of Oak Grove, a ladies group led by a sister-in-law of Bond Beaty met and publicly endorsed the actions of the sheriff.³⁵

Perhaps not surprisingly, the most vehement support for the lynching of Lee Walker came from the mass meeting at Brunswick. Charles B.

English, once described as Brunswick's "veritable Davy Crocket," chaired the meeting. Richard Inge, the self-ordained minister who loved playing croquet with the Davies family, served as secretary. By the time the meeting concluded, the participants had approved ten resolutions that they submitted for publication. One of those resolutions declared, "We have no apology or excuse to make to anyone, but approve the death of Lee Walker, the negro rapist." Another resolution asserted that "No prison should ever be used to protect or shield a demon rapist from an outraged people." Yet another stated, "We heartily approve our brave sheriff and deputies in refusing to fire shots into the body of the people who dared to avenge the terrible crime the brute, Lee Walker, attempted to commit." Including Charles B. English and Richard Inge, a total of fifty leading men of the community gave their signatures to the resolutions. Among them was the county court judge and local cockfighting enthusiast, C. G. Hughes. Another signer was Brunswick's leading doctor, "W. L. Davies."[36]

In the weeks that followed, as the investigation continued, Sheriff McClendon and four other law enforcement officers were indicted on charges that they had failed to perform their official duty. Five additional members of the mob were also charged with murder and accessory to murder. Against all odds, it seemed, authorities might succeed in bringing accountability to the crime of a public lynching. "This case is one of the most interesting in the annals of criminal jurisprudence in Shelby County, or in fact, in the South," the *Commercial* declared in late October as plans for a jury trial commenced. "It is one of the few instances where the law has been brought to bear in cases of this sort."[37]

Yet it soon became evident that justice would not, in fact, be brought to bear. Out of five hundred individuals who were questioned for jury duty, a grand total of one single man was found acceptable. All 499 others were determined by prosecutors to have been influenced to an unfair degree by the sensational press coverage. Concluding it would be impossible to secure an impartial jury, the county court judge dismissed the case. Sheriff McLendon, Harry Frayser, and the rest of the mob members charged with murder were let go "scott free." In a remark that was representative of the prospective jurors' feelings, one man, after being dismissed by attorneys, stated that rather than being prosecuted, the sheriff should have actually received a "gold medal."[38]

EPILOGUE

You Can't Tell All the Good Parts Unless You Bring in Some of That Bad Part

In the final days of 1893, newspapers around America published "The Year's Record," a chronological summary of notable events, some from overseas, for each day of that year. The event listed for July 22 was the lynching of Lee Walker in Memphis. Walker's lynching was hardly the only one that appeared in that year's summary of news. July's list alone included Walker and two others—the "lynching and burning of S. J. Miller, a negro at Bardwell KY," and "Dan Arata, an Italian, lynched in Denver." Between August and the end of the year, an additional four lynching crimes were included in the list. Of course, these were merely a fraction of the total number of lynchings from that particular year. And 1893 was just one year within the longer period that scholars have described as the "nadir" of race relations in America.[1]

As Dan Arata's murder reveals, lynching victims were not always Black. Yet the phenomenon of "terror lynchings" committed by whites against African Americans simply has no parallel in the American story. In the short span between 1897 and 1906, at least 884 Black people were murdered by whites in lynching crimes. White Americans justified lynching Black Americans for a variety of reasons, ranging from minor social transgressions to retaliation for resistance to mistreatment. Black people like Jim Eastman could certainly be lynched for physical altercations with whites. Lynchings based upon fears of interracial sex were among the most common. Lynchings like Lee Walker's that involved allegations of rape and descended into horrific spectacles of mass collective violence were yet another variety. As "public spectacle lynchings" became normalized, some were treated as carnival-like events, featuring food vendors, and pre-publicity, and printers who produced postcards with pictures of the corpse against the backdrop of smiling crowds. The most authoritative study, completed in 2017 by the Equal Justice Initiative (EJI), has uncovered 4,084 confirmed instances of Black people being lynched in the American South between the end of Reconstruction and 1950.[2]

Within this broader context, it is difficult to say to what extent the racial terror that plagued Shelby County—or even a particular section of the county like the Northeast Shelby Triangle—was unique compared to the racial terror that plagued other locales around the South. And yet, the historical record *does* unquestionably paint a damning picture of the specific world inhabited by the Davies family and the many African American families who connected with them, either directly or tangentially. Along with Lee Walker and Jim Eastman, at least eighteen other African Americans were lynched in Shelby County between 1877 and 1950. These victims included Ell Persons, who was hung, burned alive, and dismembered in a 1917 public spectacle lynching near Bartlett attended by an estimated five thousand people; Tommie Williams, lynched near the community of Rosemark in 1927;* and Jesse Lee Bond, lynched in broad daylight in the Arlington town square in 1939 after Bond reportedly disputed a financial matter at the S. Y. Wilson Store.†

---

* Tommie Williams's grandson, James Williams, grew up near Brunswick and was among those interviewed in 2010 for the Davies Manor Association's oral history project.

† Bond, a twenty-year-old sharecropper, was a descendant of Joseph "Free Joe" Harris (the co-founder with Simon Price of Gray's Creek Baptist Church), and an acquaintance and/or relative of people who were part of the African American community living on and around the Davies family's estate through the early twentieth century. One of Bond's younger cousins, Sylvester Lewis, attended Jesse Lee Bond's 1939 funeral at Gray's Creek as a boy. In a 2017 interview with the author, Lewis recalled that Gray's Creek Baptist Church was "overflowing" for the funeral. "People came out from Memphis and other counties, Fayette, some from Tipton County, because they had heard about this," he said. Lewis, who died in 2022 at the age of ninety-two, served for years on the Davies Manor Association Board of Directors alongside a descendant of Charles R. Wilson, who had been charged and quickly acquitted for the murder. Before their deaths,

The 2017 EJI study has determined that Shelby County saw more lynchings during the 1877 to 1950 period than any other county in Tennessee. Moreover, Shelby County was one of twenty-five counties in the larger South that experienced at least nineteen documented lynchings during that same span.*[3]

Today, none of the surviving records in the DMA Archives show members of the Davies family discussing lynching crimes or commenting more generally on the racially motivated violence that permeated their community through the late nineteenth and early twentieth centuries. Looking elsewhere, however, the record does reveal just how closely the family's experience intersected with some of the worst instances of lynchings and mob violence in Shelby County history. From the public support that Dr. Will Davies gave to the Lee Walker lynching and the law enforcement officers who allowed it to happen, to the central role that Gillie Davies's brother-in-law Bond Beaty played in leading a vigilante party in the days leading up to the jail invasion,† to the social, business, and political ties between the Davies family and the various men involved with Jim Eastman's lynching and coverup, it is evident that the Davieses were never far removed from the racial terror that plagued their community through the Jim Crow-era and beyond. Furthermore, evidence that Gus Davies himself perpetrated an extrajudicial murder in

---

Lewis and his cousin Charlie Morris (Jesse Lee Bond's brother) were responsible for leading a renewed research effort that led to a short documentary on Jesse Lee Bond's lynching and an ongoing effort by the Lynching Sites Project of Memphis to place a historical marker at the site of the crime.

* This figure does not account for the previously discussed 1869 lynching of Wash Henley, nor the other known (and unknown) victims of lynchings in Shelby County between 1865 and 1877. On a national level, and citing a figure that "is likely thousands below the true figure," the EJI has documented at least two thousand lynching victims in America during the twelve years of Reconstruction.

† Given the fact that Mollie McCadden was Bond Beaty's adopted daughter, and given how prominently newspapers covered Bond Beaty's role in leading a vigilante posse between July 18 and Walker's murder, it is hard to imagine that Beaty did not either participate in or directly observe the lynching outside the Memphis jail. In the weeks and months that followed the lynching, Beaty's name (perhaps because he was a lawman himself) disappears from the coverage of the public meetings held around the county to show support for the crime and oppose efforts to prosecute the sheriff and the mob.

1907 reveals the most direct link of all between a member of the family and a specific lynching crime.* That summer, according to newspaper reports from Hernando, Mississippi, Gus, along with a small "posse," tracked down an unidentified Black man near Walls who had allegedly broken into the home of a local white farmer. During the "scuffle" that ensued, the Black man reportedly shot at the party, leaving Davies and one other man "slightly wounded with No. 3 shot." Gus and the others then fired upon and killed the man, who was said to have been "buried where he fell."[4]

Regardless of how the Davies family members themselves perceived the lynching crimes that occurred around them—and regardless to what extent certain members of the family can or cannot be linked to those crimes as participants or observers or indirect supporters—the backdrop of domestic racial terror (or more specifically, the implicit understanding that such a fate was always possible if one stepped out of line in certain ways) was the reality that the Black community who worked the Davieses' land would have been forced to live with, day in and day out, from the time of emancipation into the twentieth century. It was a reality based in fear, in a sense of powerlessness, and in the insidious awareness that no matter the horror, there was no reason to hope that justice would be had. For the Davies family and other white landowners, this was the reality that they used to their benefit as they kept their grips tight on the reins of economic control.

On June 8, 1894, Logan Davies died of cancer at the age of sixty-nine. Dr. Will Davies had done all he could for his uncle through the final stages of his illness, often consulting with medical contacts in Memphis about treatment options. Ultimately, though, there was little that could be done. Even as he helped treat Logan through his final days, Will found himself shifting into a caretaker role for his own father. Along with a nervous disorder, James suffered from chronic asthma and digestive problems that only grew worse the further he travelled into his seventies. Not long after the turn of the twentieth century, James

---

* Brief accounts of the crime are found in news summaries from the June 15 and June 22, 1907, editions of the *Times-Promoter* newspaper in Hernando, Mississippi.

became permanently bedbound, causing Will to "[give] up a very large practice to nurse his aged father"—an act that he was said to have done with "loving devotion."[5]

The events that followed in rapid succession between 1903 and 1904 would transform the complexion and future of the Davies family and the log house itself. On November 4, 1903 (after bearing six children to Bond Beaty between 1887 and 1902), Linnie Lee (Davies) Beaty died on the cusp of middle age. Just nine days later, Gillie and Frances Ina Davies welcomed the birth of their daughter, Ellen. The following year, on June 17, seventy-nine-year-old James Davies died. The obituary, written by a family friend and local minister, described James as "one of the best known and thought to be the oldest citizen in the Eighth civil district—not in years, but in length of residence."[6]

James was buried in the Morning Sun Cumberland Presbyterian Church cemetery a few plots away from his brother Logan. Next to them were the plots of their spouses, Frances and Almeda, as well as their closest friends and acquaintances—the Ecklin, Crenshaw, Feild, and Royster families among them. Though the old church itself remained, the Morning Sun community was a much changed place from the days when Logan and James had first arrived. Before long, the Memphis to Somerville Road would be widened and improved to accommodate the coming automobile revolution. Modern homes equipped with the latest comforts were emerging. The oldest homes built in the style of Davies Manor were coming down. The character and complexion of rural Northeast Shelby County was markedly changing.[7]

As Will Davies observed such changes, he continued to reside in the log house as its sole occupant. He also now controlled some six hundred acres (half of the total size of the plantation) that his father had left to him.* During this period, as he returned to concentrating on his medical practice, Will developed a close bond with his young cousin Ellen. A precocious and intelligent child, Ellen would come to demonstrate the same curiosity and love of learning that Will valued so dearly. Meanwhile, the agricultural operation that Gillie primarily managed continued to thrive. And, as had always been the case at the Davies family's

---

* The other half of the estate had been inherited by Gillie and Linnie in 1894. After Linnie's death, Gillie had inherited her portion.

estate, an African American labor force drove the day-to-day work and production schedules.

By the early 1900s, many changes had taken place within the Black community that worked Gillie and Will Davies's land as hired field hands and sharecroppers. As best can be determined, the size of the labor force—approximately thirty-five people—had remained relatively constant through most of the late nineteenth century. The community's makeup, however, had changed notably. Most of the families and younger workers who lived on the estate had moved there just prior to or after the turn of the century. Some of these people (such as Sol and Georgia Nelson) resided along "Smokey Road," which connected the log house to the Memphis to Somerville Road. Quite a few of the African American families with the oldest ties to the Davies remained in other nearby sections of the county. For instance, Richmond and Sarah Jane Bennett and their family had by 1910 relocated to Civil District Nine, south of the Memphis to Somerville Road. So also had Tom and Susan Cartwright and their family. Near the Cartwrights were the farms of Wat Davis and family, and Mat Davis and his.*[8]

The Tucker and Gray clans—two of the Black families believed to have been closest to the Davies family in the years before and just after emancipation—continued to own their own farms beyond the turn of the twentieth century. At some point around 1910, however, a year after Ben Gray died, the rest of the family lost the estate under circumstances that are not entirely clear. Various Tuckers, meanwhile, persisted as landowners. The now quite elderly and widowed Mary Tucker still owned the 150-acre farm (adjacent to Will Davies's property) that she had inherited after the death of Wilcher sometime in the mid or late 1880s.† Mary, or "Aunt Mary," as she was called by members of the white Davies family, had been known through all these years as a "highly respected" midwife who "delivered many . . . babies" on and around her farm. In 1903, when Ellen Davies was born, it had been Mary who served as the midwife to

---

* Both Wat and Mat had been born into slavery on the Davies brothers' plantation during the Civil War. Wat and Mat's father, Joe Davis, is believed to have died in 1875, according to receipts for coffins kept by Logan and James. The identity of Wat and Mat's mother is less clear.

† Very little about Wilcher Tucker is known following his appearance in the 1880 census.

Frances Ina and Gillie. Years later, Ellen would recall, "To 'Aunt Mary' I was known as her 'white child'—she had brought many Negro babies into the world but I was her first white baby!"[9]

When Mary Tucker died around 1910, she was buried in the cemetery connected to Morning Grove Church, a short distance east of Morning Sun.* In 1913, when Sarah Jane (Tucker) Bennett died, she was buried there also. Two years later, when he succumbed to asthma, Richmond Bennett joined his wife and in-laws in the ground of Morning Grove Church Cemetery. Although much of Mary Tucker's land was sold in the years after her death, her son and daughter-in-law, Amos and Pleasant Tucker, and their descendants, would continue to own an adjacent forty-seven-acre farm through most of the twentieth century.[10]

Beyond the Tucker and Bennett families, the Morning Grove Church Cemetery became the final resting place for numerous other African American individuals and families who worked for the Davies family through the subsequent generations and lived on or nearby their estate. Among them were Ida Mae Moss and Valerie Moss, both of whom would become especially close with Davies-Rodgers between the mid to late twentieth century.† Two others were Lucinda Herron, who worked in a domestic capacity at The Oaks and Davies Manor, and Lucinda's son,

---

* It is presumed that Mary Tucker would have been buried alongside Wilcher in the Morning Gove Church Cemetery. No evidence of their graves remains today. In *Turns Again Home*, Ellen Davies-Rodgers wrote the following of Mary Tucker: "During my childhood, 'Aunt' Mary often came to see us. She loved me very much as her 'white child,' which she called me. For a number of years efforts have proved futile in trying to locate her grave in Morning Grove Church Cemetery in order to place a tombstone at her grave. Determined to honor 'Aunt' Mary, when the roads were given names in Davieshire a road was named the *Mary Tucker Drive* in memory of this dear soul who helped me to be born!"

† Both Ida Mae Moss and Valerie Moss received lengthy sketches by Davies-Rodgers in the "Back Porch Court" chapter of *Turns Again Home*. Ida Mae was described as a "splendid Christian woman" and the "plantation secretary." Valerie worked as the primary cook and housekeeper at Davies-Rodgers's home, The Oaks, and "became famous" for her dishes. Davies-Rodgers also described Valerie's battle with breast cancer and the financial assistance she had provided Moss during her treatment. The long-standing connections between various members of the Moss family, the Davieses, and a branch of the family of Roscoe McVay, interviewed by Davies Manor staffers in 2012, date to the nineteenth century, and were among the most notable research findings stemming from the Mose Frazier Committee's work.

Lawrence, a skilled farmhand, gardener, and livestock specialist.* Mose Frazier, the long-time "caretaker" for Davies Manor and a close friend of Lawrence Herron's, would be buried in Morning Grove after his death in 1969.†

Of course, these above-named individuals, each of whom were described by Davies-Rodgers in her final book, were only a small fraction of the larger Black community whose presence had been a constant at the Davies family's plantation for well over a century beginning around 1849. As Davies-Rodgers and Will Davies before her knew all too well, the identities of these other people, this larger Black community who "whether slave or free" was "probably fewer than a hundred" people, had for the most part been lost following their burials in the anonymous plots in the "Davies Plantation Cemetery." And so, in the absence of that basic knowledge, both Will Davies and his younger cousin had made efforts, in their own ways, to memorialize the site. For Dr. Will Davies, memorialization had taken the form of his "omitted in mass" marker, which he is believed to have placed just before his 1931 death.‡ For Davies-Rodgers, it would come in the form of a wooden marker that she placed in 1987 and dedicated as a "memorial to these loyal people." Ultimately though, those efforts would be erased. Today, no traces of the memorials that were placed at the site have been discovered. And as for the cemetery itself, it would disappear a few years after Davies-Rodgers's death when the land was sold for development, plowed over, and turned into a subdivision of single-lot homes.[11]

---

* Lucinda Herron appears on the porch of Davies Manor in the background of this book's cover photo.

† In 2014, acting on recommendations in the final report from the Mose Frazier Committee (chaired by the local researcher Barbara Williams) the DMA purchased a headstone to commemorate Mose Frazier's grave and held a dedication ceremony for the stone with Frazier's family at Morning Grove Missionary Baptist Church Cemetery.

‡ Though it is not certain that Dr. Davies did place the memorial, the historian for the Morning Sun Church, writing in the 1960s, would make the assertion that "the Davies built a nice house with a dairy barn on what was the old slave graveyard. . . . They said Dr. Will kept the spot sacred." It's worth noting that the line about the dairy barn referred to El Hill, a small home that Ellen Davies-Rodgers had constructed shortly after Will's death either on the edge of, or over a portion of, the Davies Plantation Cemetery.

The Lynching Sites Project of Memphis is among the groups working to shine a long overdue light on the legacy of lynching crimes in Shelby County. In 2018, the organization partnered with the National Park Service and the Shelby County Historical Commission to place this marker on Front Street in Memphis near the location of the old Shelby County Jail where Lee Walker was lynched. Photo by Andrew C. Ross

Sylvester Lewis, pictured here during a 2017 interview with the author, served on the Shelby County Historical Commission and the Davies Manor Association Board of Directors until his death in 2022. Lewis was a dedicated local historian whose research has proven critical to preserving narratives about the African American history of Northeast Shelby County. Photo by Andrew C. Ross

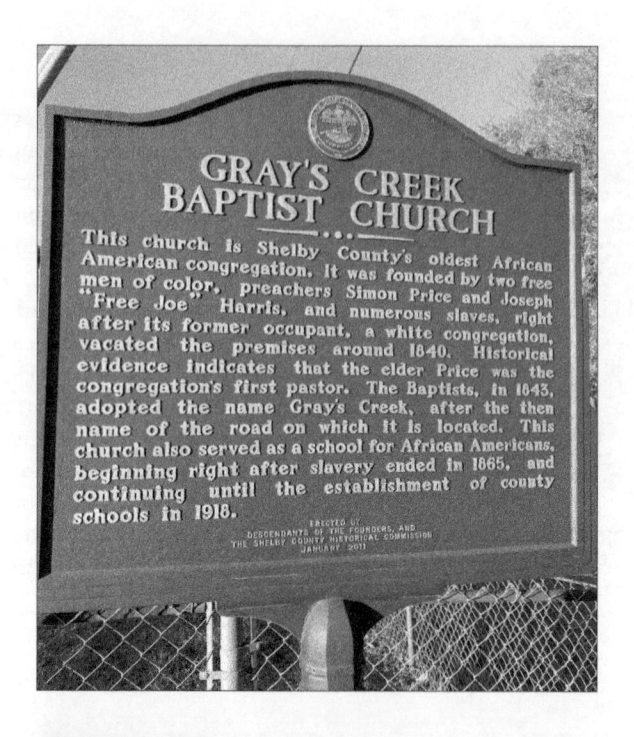

GRAY'S CREEK BAPTIST CHURCH

This church is Shelby County's oldest African American congregation. It was founded by two free men of color, preachers Simon Price and Joseph "Free Joe" Harris, and numerous slaves, right after its former occupant, a white congregation, vacated the premises around 1840. Historical evidence indicates that the elder Price was the congregation's first pastor. The Baptists, in 1843, adopted the name Gray's Creek, after the then name of the road on which it is located. This church also served as a school for African Americans, beginning right after slavery ended in 1865, and continuing until the establishment of county schools in 1918.

ERECTED BY
DESCENDANTS OF THE FOUNDERS, AND
THE SHELBY COUNTY HISTORICAL COMMISSION
JANUARY 2011

GRAY'S CREEK CEMETERY

This cemetery, believed to have been established in the 1830's, is one of the earliest in Shelby County. Originally the Royster family burial ground, the land was acquired by African Americans around 1840. Buried here are many of northeast Shelby County's earliest citizens, including the founders of Gray's Creek Baptist Church, and many of their descendants. The remains of some Caucasians buried here, including members of the Royster family, were transferred to the nearby Morning Sun Presbyterian Cemetery. Others still rest here.

ERECTED BY
DESCENDANTS OF THE FOUNDERS, AND
THE SHELBY COUNTY HISTORICAL COMMISSION
JANUARY 2011

Two related historic markers that help preserve the story of Gray's Creek Baptist Church and Gray's Creek Cemetery, located roughly three miles east of Davies Manor Historic Site. Photos by Andrew C. Ross

Morning Sun Cumberland Presbyterian Cemetery, located less than a mile from Morning Grove Church Cemetery, is a well-preserved historic cemetery holding the remains of Logan and Frances Davies, James and Almeda Davies, William Little Davies, and Julius Augustus Davies. Hillman and Ellen Davies-Rodgers are buried in Pleasant Hill Cemetery in Brunswick. Photo by Elizabeth Brooks

After its founding in the 1880s, Morning Grove Church, located a short distance south of Davies Plantation, became an important community hub for many African Americans who worked for the Davies family. The cemetery attached to the church is still preserved today and holds the remains of members of the Tucker and Bennett families, as well as Mose Frazier and others. In most cases, the headstones have not survived or have deteriorated beyond recognition. Photo by Elizabeth Brooks

This headstone for Mose Frazier was placed by the DMA during a ceremony in 2014 attended by Frazier's family that marked the completion of the Mose Frazier Committee's report. Photo by Elizabeth Brooks

Headstone for Richmond Bennett (1833–1915) in the Morning Grove cemetery, with the inscription: "Gone but not forgotten." Photo by Andrew C. Ross

Amos Tucker (1855–1912) was one of the sons of Wilcher and Mary Tucker who was born into slavery on the Davies brothers' plantation. He is the sole member of his family whose burial plot in the Morning Grove cemetery remains marked with a headstone. Photo by Elizabeth Brooks

Street sign in the Davies Plantation Estates subdivision commemorating Mary Tucker. Photo by Andrew C. Ross

Following the death of Gus Davies in 1924, Mose Frazier moved from Walls, Mississippi, to the Davies family's Shelby County estate. After his first cabin burned, Frazier resided in this simple structure until the 1960s when his daughter Annie Mae "stole [him] off the plantation" against the objections of Ellen Davies-Rodgers. The cabin is still preserved and interpreted today by the Davies Manor Historic Site. Photo by Andrew C. Ross

ALONG THE OLD STAGE-COACH ROAD

Morning Sun and Brunswick
Shelby County, Tennessee

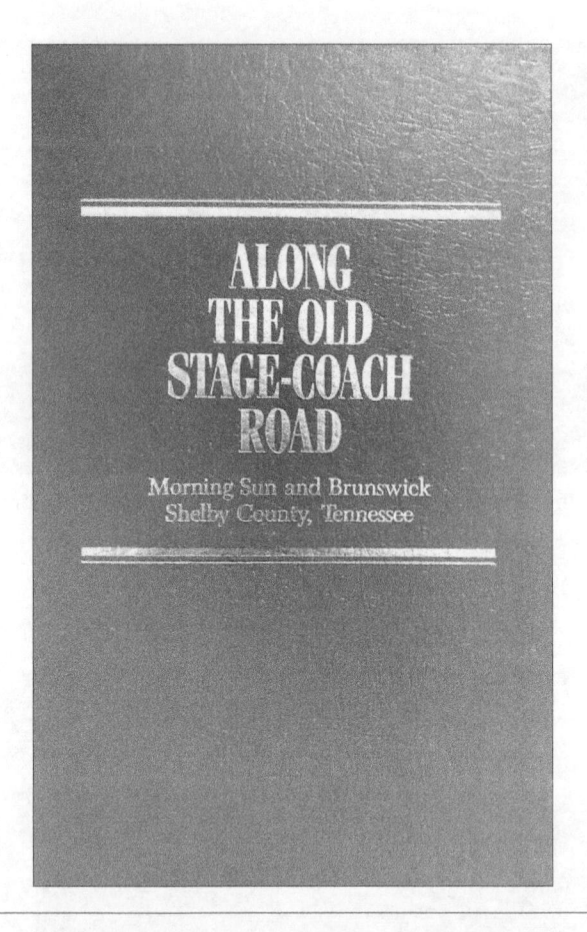

DAVIES PLANTATION CEMETERY, 1855–1910

On this spot were buried family members—workers employed by Logan Early Davies and James Baxter Davies, owners of the plantation in 1855, and following throughout the Civil War era to the turn of the century. There are probably fewer than a hundred unmarked graves. The whole area has been kept undisturbed as a wooded section and as a memorial to these loyal people.

Marker placed by Davies Manor Association, 1987
South of El Hill, 9574 Highway 64

In her 1990 book *Along the Old Stage-Coach Road*, Ellen Davies-Rodgers included the text of a "plain wooden" historical marker that she had placed three years earlier in the cemetery that held the remains of African Americans who had worked for and/or been enslaved by her family between 1855–1910.

Through the decades that followed Dr. Will Davies's 1931 death, as Ellen Davies-Rodgers converted her inherited estate into a historic attraction, she successfully leveraged her work in preservation in order to develop political connections and wield influence within local government and education circles. Meanwhile, building off the knowledge passed down to her from Will and others in her family, she created defining historical narratives about her ancestors, estate, and the wider community. Her ability to disseminate those narratives and enshrine them into the collective public memory became especially pronounced as she started her own press, wrote and published books with that press, and assumed the role of Shelby County Historian. The culmination of her life-long work in history would come about through the creation of the Davies Manor Association, the organization charged with carrying her family's historic home and the narratives contained within it into the future.

Davies-Rodgers's passionate work as a preservationist and public historian made a lasting mark. Her legacy, taken in its entirety, is best understand through a lens of paradox. Along with the paternalistic racism and narrowly conceived perspectives that imbued her approach to shaping collective memory, her career *also* resulted in the preservation of a great deal of invaluable local history—including African American history—that would have otherwise been lost. The survival of the Davies Manor home is certainly a triumph of historic preservation in and of itself.

Still, though, even if she acknowledged in basic terms the links between her family's story, and those of the many African American families who had been enslaved by and worked for her forebears, Davies-Rodgers never demonstrated the ability to objectively grapple with the enormous implications of those links. Never, in any of her writings, did she approach the subjects of white supremacy, slavery, and Black exploitation—much less acknowledge the degree to which her own family, for five consecutive generations, had relied on those forces to build, maintain, and pass on their wealth. If such a limited perspective was not unique to Davies-Rodgers, she was unique in the lasting impact that her sanitized, nostalgia-driven approach to studying the past had on Shelby County history—and, of course, on Davies Manor itself.

Perhaps the most penetrating critiques of Ellen Davies-Rodgers would emerge through the memories of Mose Frazier's daughter, Annie Mae

Frazier Blackwell Myles. Contrasting Davies-Rodgers's published accounts of Mose Frazier as "a great soul" whose "loyalty and service . . . can never be forgotten," Myles remembered the trials and tribulations that her father endured through his many decades working for the Davies family. In a 2017 interview with the author, while recounting those trials in detail—memories that centered on her father living in "semi-slavery," as she put it—Myles stated, "I don't know if I've talked too much but I've told the truth." Pausing, she then added, "You can't tell all the good parts unless you bring in some of that bad part."[12]

PROFILES OF ENSLAVED PEOPLE, 1773-1865

The following pages reflect this author's best effort to present core biographical information about the people enslaved between 1773 and 1865 by three subsequent generations of the Davis/Davies family. Brief introductory notes appear for each grouping of individuals; the notes are intended to contextualize the key records used to draw the profile sketches, the time periods they cover, and the confirmed, presumed, and potential blood relationships between people and families. With a few exceptions, valuations and/or sale figures assigned to enslaved people have not been used in the profiles. However, such figures have been used to inform general understandings about individuals, their ages, and their relationships to others in the enslaved community. I have been as precise as possible with the verbiage used to differentiate between what can be confirmed, what can be presumed, and what may be true when it comes to family networks and the identities of people whose names appear, oftentimes with slightly different spellings, in scattered pre-emancipation and post-emancipation records. In cases where more than one person through the generations shares the same first name, numerals have been used as a differentiator. Although data found in post-emancipation records has been utilized to retroactively determine biographical details about people whose surnames are known, the sketches themselves are focused for the most part on slavery times, and have been conceived as a reflection of the chronological timeline at the core of this book. Rather than being viewed as definitive, the profiles should be understood as works in progress; much opportunity exists to continue developing genealogical and personal information on these people—especially through the late nineteenth and twentieth centuries. Any mistakes or omissions are mine alone.

The first ten sketches detail what has been learned up to this point about the earliest group of people known to have been enslaved by Zachariah Davis in Lunenburg County, Virginia. The sketches have been drawn primarily by using a combination of tax records for Zachariah, Zachariah's 1794 deed of trust, Davies family correspondence, and Lunenburg County fiduciary book records, land deed records, marriage records, and legal records connected to the *Neal v. Davis* lawsuits. The term "1794 Nine" is the author's; it has been devised as shorthand to reflect the way subsequent generations of people enslaved by Zachariah were described in inventory records for his estate, as a group and for reasons of identification, as being the "increase" of the nine individuals named in the 1794 deed of trust.

1794 NINE

*Brister	*Sampson	*Nelly	*Dilcy/Dilcey	*Grace
**Tom	**Tabb	**Hannah	**Nancy	

*adult in 1794; **child in 1794

Peter (1) – Peter was likely born ca. 1750–1758 (no later than 1758). He was enslaved (along with Brister) by Zachariah Davis in Lunenburg County, VA, by 1774. Because he is believed to have died or escaped or been sold or advanced away by Zachariah at some point between 1786 and 1794, the author does not include him among the 1794 Nine.

Brister – Brister was likely born ca. 1750–1758 (no later than 1758). He was enslaved (along with Peter) by Zachariah Davis in Lunenburg County, VA, by 1774. He continued to be enslaved by Zachariah for the remainder of his life. Brister died in October 1820 of illness at Zachariah's estate along with five other bondspeople (Richard, Vilet, Charles, and Rody) and Zachariah's wife, Diana Davis.

Sampson – Sampson's presumed birthdate range is unknown. However, he almost certainly was born no later than 1776. He was enslaved by Zachariah by the late 1780s or early 1790s. He may have come to the estate around the same time as Peter's death or sale or advancement or escape. Sampson's appearances in later records suggest that he formed a union with Nelly. If so, he may have been the father of Jinny. After Zachariah's 1828 death, Sampson was purchased in Zachariah's estate sale (along with Nelly, Dilcy/Dilcey, Tom, Peter, and Sam) by Zachariah's son-in-law Jeremiah Burnett (brother of William Early Davies's first wife, Joanna "Anna" Burnett).

Nelly – Nelly is believed to have been born ca. 1759–1769. In 1785, when she was at least sixteen, she appears in tax records as being enslaved by Zachariah Davis in Lunenburg County. Nelly was likely purchased or acquired by Zachariah around the same time as Dilcy/Dilcey. Records suggest that Nelly formed a union with Sampson. Furthermore, she can be confirmed as the mother of Jinny, who was described as "increase of Nelly's" in Zachariah's 1828 estate. (The estate sale records also confirm that in 1826, Jinny was "carried away" from Lunenburg County by Zachariah's son-in-law Joel Neal and sold in Hickman County, TN.)

Dilcy/Dilcey – Dilcy/Dilcey is believed to have been born ca. 1770–1778. In 1785, when she was still under the age of sixteen, she appears in Zachariah Davis's tax records for the first time as being enslaved in Lunenburg County. She was likely purchased or acquired by Zachariah at that time. Dilcy/Dilcey was described as "a woman" in the 1794 deed of trust. She was purchased by Jeremiah Burnett in Zachariah's 1828 estate sale alongside Nelly, Sampson, Tom, Peter, and Sam.

Grace – Grace appears for the first time in Zachariah Davis's records in the 1794 deed of trust. She was described at that time as "a woman," meaning she was presumably born no later than 1778. In 1816, along with her "youngest child" (probably a boy, born ca. 1806), Grace was advanced by Zachariah Davis to Robert Davis, who took her and the child that same year to Robert's home in the city of Franklin, in Williamson County, TN. She is believed to have remained enslaved at Robert's estate in Franklin with her youngest child until at least the late 1830s.

Tom – Tom appears for the first time in Zachariah Davis's records in the 1794 deed of trust. He was described at that time as "a small boy." Based on that description and his assigned value relative to other children named in the trust, he was presumably born ca. 1787–1792. In 1828 (alongside Sampson, Nelly, Dilcy/Dilcey, Peter, and Sam), Tom was purchased by Jeremiah Burnett at Zachariah's estate sale.

Tabb – Tabb appears for the first time in Zachariah Davis's records in the 1794 deed of trust. She was described at that time as a "small girl." Based on that description and her assigned value relative to other children named in the trust, she was presumably born ca. 1789–1792. Tabb does not reappear in any subsequent records.

Hannah – Hannah appears for the first time in Zachariah Davis's records in the 1794 deed of trust. She was described at that time as a "small girl." Based on that description and her assigned value relative to other children named in the trust, she was presumably born ca. 1789–1792. In 1828, along with her two sons, James and Isaac, Hannah was purchased by Reuben Vaughan at Zachariah's estate sale.

Nancy – Nancy appears for the first time in Zachariah Davis's records in the 1794 deed of trust. She was described then as "a child." Based on that description and her assigned value relative to other children named in the trust, she was presumably born ca. 1790–1794. In 1807, Nancy was advanced as a wedding gift to Zachariah's daughter, Diana, and her new husband, Jeremiah Burnett (brother of William Early Davies's first wife, Joanna "Anna" Burnett). That same year, she was "carried away" by Jeremiah Burnett to an unknown location and sold to an unknown buyer.

The next section that appears below is a reconstructed outline of a tree believed to reflect basic genealogical lines for Booker and Dolly, both of whom are confirmed descendants of the female members of the "1794 Nine." (According to legal records from *Neal v. Davis*, "Both Booker and Dolly are part of the increase of female slaves conveyed in the deed of 13th February 1794.") Based on the manner in which Booker and Dolly are listed and described in Zachariah Davis's final will, in subsequent documents recording the sale of Zachariah's estate (found in *Neal v. Davis* legal records), and in Lunenburg County fiduciary book records, I have made the assertion that Booker and Dolly formed a union resulting in two generations of descendants that totaled at least nineteen people. Fiduciary book records following Henrietta (Davis) Neal's death in 1864 confirm Dolly's status as "the mother and grandmother of all the others." This sketch of Booker and Dolly's descendants (seven named and twelve unnamed) has been drawn based on the scattered references to individual people named in the trust that was managed for more than three decades for the benefit of Henrietta (Davis) Neal.

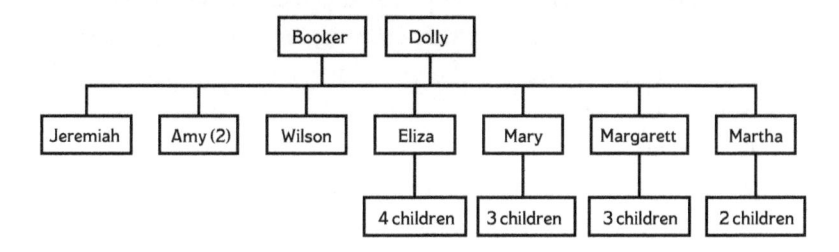

```
                    ┌─────────┬─────────┐
                    │ Booker  │  Dolly  │
                    └─────────┴─────────┘
   ┌──────────┬──────────┬──────────┬──────────┬──────────┬──────────┬──────────┐
 Jeremiah   Amy (2)    Wilson     Eliza      Mary     Margarett   Martha
                                    │          │          │          │
                               4 children  3 children  3 children  2 children
```

Booker – Booker was presumably born no later than 1811. In *Neal v. Davis* legal records, he was described as "a man" by 1829. He was also described as being the son of one of the six female individuals included in the "1794 Nine" (Nelly, Dilcy/Dilcey, Grace, Tabb, Hannah, and Nancy). (According to *Neal v. Davis* records, "both Booker and Dolly are part of the increase of female slaves conveyed in the deed of 13th February 1794.") Although presumed paternal lineage has not been determined, Booker's father may have been Peter, or one of the other male individuals named in the 1794 deed of trust (Sampson, Brister, and Tom). Based on legal records, Zachariah Davis's final will, and the totality of fiduciary book records, Booker is believed to have entered into a union or marriage with Dolly by 1827. In 1828, per the terms of Zachariah Davis's final will, Booker was placed (along with Dolly) in a trust designed to be managed by executors for the support of Zachariah's daughter Henrietta (Davis) Neal. Further research is necessary to trace Booker as he was managed in that trust over the next three-plus decades. In 1863, in the final known mention of Booker in Lunenburg County fiduciary book records, he was being hired out to David Bragg for the benefit of Henrietta Neal.

Dolly – Dolly was presumably born no later than 1812. She was likely born ca. 1805. In 1829, she was described in *Neal v. Davis* legal records as being "a woman" at that time. Dolly had one child by 1829. Dolly was also described in legal records as being the daughter of one of the six female individuals named in the 1794 deed of trust (Nelly, Dilcy/Dilcey, Grace, Tabb, Hannah, and Nancy). Although paternal lineage has not been determined, Dolly's father may have been Peter, or one of the three male members named in the 1794 deed of trust (Booker,

Sampson, and Tom). Dolly is believed to have formed a union with Booker by 1827. In 1828, per the terms of Zachariah Davis's final will, Dolly (along with Booker) was placed in a trust designed to be managed for the support of Henrietta (Davis) Neal. Further research is necessary to trace Dolly as she was managed in that trust over the next three-plus decades. In 1863, "Dolly, Margarett and 3 children" are listed as being under the care of William Tucker as part of the management of the estate to benefit Henrietta Neal: "Dolly, Margarett & 3 children to Wm. Tucker for finding clothing and nursing (the best bid that could be had)." In January 1865, following the death of Henrietta Neal, Dolly and fifteen other members of her family were appraised by Lunenburg County officials at $38,500. Dolly was described as the "mother and grandmother of all the others."

The following sketches are for individuals who are confirmed descendants, presumed descendants, and possible descendants of one or more individuals in the "1794 Nine." These sketches have been drawn from information found in Zachariah Davis's final will, and from the property inventory lists and estate sale documents found in *Neal v. Davis* records. Rather than being listed in chronological order, the list has been arranged based loosely upon the degree to which their status as descendants of the "1794 Nine" group of people can be confirmed.

James – James was a son of Hannah. He was presumably born ca. 1818–1828 in Lunenburg County on Zachariah Davis's estate. In 1828, James was purchased (along with his mother Hannah and brother Isaac) by Reuben Vaughan during Zachariah's estate sale.

Isaac – Isaac was a son of Hannah. He was presumably born ca. 1818–1828 in Lunenburg County on Zachariah Davis's estate. In 1828, Isaac was purchased (along with his mother Hannah and brother James) by Reuben Vaughan during Zachariah's estate sale.

Jinny – Jinny was a daughter of Nelly. She was presumably born ca. 1814–1822 in Lunenburg County on Zachariah Davis's estate. Jinny was described in records as being "a girl" in 1826, when she was "carried away to the west by Joel Neal" and sold in Hickman County, TN, for three hundred dollars.

Grace's youngest child – Grace's youngest child, whose name is unknown, is believed to have been a boy, born ca. 1806 in Lunenburg County on Zachariah Davis's estate. (The assertion about being a boy is based on extrapolations from the information enumerated in the 1820 and 1830 census for Robert Davies.) Grace's youngest child was advanced by Zachariah to Robert Davis in 1816 and taken by Robert to Franklin, TN. Grace's youngest child, along with Grace, is believed to have remained enslaved at Robert's estate in Franklin until at least the late 1830s.

Vincy/Viney/Vina – Vincy/Viney/Vina is believed to have been a descendant of people in the "1794 Nine" group. She was presumably born ca. 1812 in Lunenburg County on Zachariah Davis's estate. She was advanced by Zachariah in 1816 at the age of four to William E. Davis and taken in 1817 by William to Maury County, TN. Vincy/Viney/Vina is believed to have been taken by William to Fayette County in 1843. She is believed to be the same Vina who was allotted (along with Daniel, Enoch, Emeline, and Ann) in 1862 (shortly after William's death) to William's daughter Mariah (Davies) Lockridge, who was still living in Maury County.

Lewis (2) – Lewis is believed to have been a descendant of people in the "1794 Nine" group. He was presumably born ca. 1806–1814 in Lunenburg County on Zachariah Davis's estate. He was advanced as "a boy" in 1816 to Paschal Davis. Lewis is believed to have remained enslaved at Paschal's Lunenburg County estate until 1822, when he was sold by Paschal to an unknown buyer.

Judy – Judy is believed to have been a descendant of people in the "1794 Nine" group. She was presumably born ca. 1806–1816 in Lunenburg County on Zachariah Davis's estate. She was advanced as "a girl" in 1816 to Baxter Davis and "carried away" around the same time to Baxter's estate in Orange County, NC.

Amy (1) – Amy is believed to have been a descendant of people in the "1794 Nine" group. She was presumably born ca. 1804 in Lunenburg County on Zachariah Davis's estate. She was advanced by Zachariah in 1816 at the age of "about twelve" to Sterling Davis, who was then living in Williamson County, TN, but had temporarily returned to Lunenburg County. When Amy was "carried away" by Sterling in 1816 to Williamson County, she "left 2 children" behind, both of whom were later "carried away" at a date "not recollected." According to an account penned later by Sterling (found in *Neal v. Davis* and referencing the year 1816), Amy was "sickly soon afterwards and some years afterwards died." Amy may have been the mother of "William," the boy alleged by Joel Neal in his lawsuit against the Davis family to have been fathered by Sterling and an enslaved woman before being sold by Sterling at an unknown date.

Sarah – Sarah's presumed birth date and origins are unclear, though she may have been a descendant of people in the "1794 Nine" group. She was probably enslaved by Zachariah Davis by the mid-1790s. In Zachariah's final will he stated that he had given Sarah to his own daughter Sarah Davis around the time of Sarah Davis's marriage in 1795 to Thomas C. Anderson. Sarah has not been located in records other than Zachariah's final will.

Hall – Hall is believed to have been a descendant of people in the "1794 Nine" group. Hall's birthdate is unclear, but Hall was presumably born in Lunenburg County on Zachariah Davis's estate. In 1828, per the terms of Zachariah's final will, Hall was placed in a trust (along with Lucy [1] and Lucky) that would be managed by trustees for the benefit of Zachariah's daughter, Martha Davis. Further research is necessary to trace what can be learned of Hall between Zachariah's death in 1828 and 1851, when Martha Davis died, leading to the sale of the people who had been loaned to her in trust by her father. Those people were: "1 ... woman & 2 children" sold to Hatcher Clarke; "1 ... boy" to Edward Stokes; "1 ... boy & 1 girl" to Peter Stokes and L. Jones; and "1 ... girl" to Zachariah D. Burnett.

Lucy (1) – Lucy is believed to have been a descendant of people in the "1794 Nine" group. She was presumably born ca. 1820–1827 in Lunenburg County on Zachariah Davis's estate. In 1828, per the terms of Zachariah's final will, she was placed in a trust (along with Hall and Lucky) to be managed by trustees for the benefit of Zachariah's daughter, Martha Davis. Lucy was described in records documenting the estate sale as "a girl [who] has fit[t]s." Further research is necessary to trace what can be learned of Lucy between Zachariah's death in 1828 and 1851, when Martha Davis died, leading to the sale of the people who had been loaned to her by Zachariah. Those people were: "1 ... woman & 2 children" sold to Hatcher Clarke; "1 ... boy" to Edward Stokes; "1 ... boy & 1 girl" to Peter Stokes and L. Jones; and "1 ... girl" to Zachariah D. Burnett.

Lucky – Lucky is believed to have been a descendant of people in the "1794 Nine" group. Lucky's birthdate is unclear. Lucky was presumably born in Lunenburg County on Zachariah Davis's estate. In 1828, per the terms of Zachariah's final will, Lucky was placed in a trust (along with Hall and Lucy [1]) for the benefit of Zachariah's daughter, Martha Davis. Further research is necessary to trace what can be learned of Lucky between Zachariah's death in 1828 and 1851, when Martha Davis died, leading to the sale of the people who had been loaned to her by Zachariah. Those people were: "1 ... woman & 2 children" to Hatcher Clarke; "1 ... boy" sold to Edward Stokes; "1 ... boy & 1 girl" to Peter Stokes and L. Jones; and "1 ... girl" to Zachariah D. Burnett.

Mary (1) – Mary is believed to have been a descendant of people in the "1794 Nine" group. She was presumably born ca. 1820–1828 in Lunenburg County on Zachariah Davis's estate. She was described as "a girl" when she was sold to Henry Tisdale during the 1828 sale of Zachariah's estate.

Mike – Mike is believed to have been a descendant of people in the "1794 Nine" group. He was presumably born ca. 1818–1824 in Lunenburg County on Zachariah Davis's estate. He was described as "a large boy" in 1828 when he was purchased by Paschal Davis in Zachariah's estate sale. Mike was presumably enslaved afterward at Paschal's Lunenburg County estate.

John (1) – John is believed to have been a descendant of people in the "1794 Nine." He was presumably born ca. 1800–1812 in Lunenburg County on Zachariah Davis's estate. He was described as "a man" when he was purchased in 1828 by Baxter Davis in Zachariah's estate sale. John was presumably enslaved afterward at Baxter's estate in Orange County, NC.

Fanny – Fanny is believed to be a descendant of people in the "1794 Nine" group. She was presumably born ca. 1818–1826 in Lunenburg County on Zachariah Davis's estate. She was described as "a girl" when she was purchased in 1828 by Baxter Davis in Zachariah's estate sale. Fanny was presumably enslaved afterward at Baxter's estate in Orange County, NC.

Abraham – Abraham is believed to be a descendant of people in the "1794 Nine" group. He was presumably born ca. 1818–1828 in Lunenburg County on Zachariah Davis's estate. He was described as "a boy" when he was purchased in 1828 by William E. Coleman at Zachariah's estate sale.

Rebecca – Rebecca was possibly a descendant of people in the "1794 Nine" group. She was presumably born ca. 1818–1828 and enslaved by Zachariah Davis in the 1820s. She was described as "a girl" when she was purchased in 1828 by Paschal Davis in Zachariah's estate sale. Rebecca was presumably enslaved afterward at Paschal's Lunenburg County estate.

Patience – Patience was possibly a descendant of people in the "1794 Nine" group. She was presumably born ca. 1818–1826 and enslaved by Zachariah Davis in the 1820s. She was described as "a girl" when she was purchased in 1828 by Baxter Davis in Zachariah's estate sale. Patience was presumably enslaved afterward at Baxter's estate in Orange County, NC.

Frank (2) – Frank was possibly a descendant of people in the "1794 Nine" group. He was presumably born ca. 1820–1828 and enslaved by Zachariah Davis in the 1820s. He was described as "a boy" when he was purchased in 1828 by Baxter Davis in Zachariah's estate sale. Frank was sold by Baxter to an unknown party at some point between 1828 and 1833, probably after being taken to Baxter's estate in Orange County, NC.

Peter (2) – Peter was possibly a descendant of people in the "1794 Nine" group. He was presumably born ca. 1818–1828 and enslaved by Zachariah Davis in the 1820s. He was described as "a boy" when he was purchased in 1828 by Jeremiah Burnett in Zachariah's estate sale. Peter was presumably enslaved afterward at Jeremiah and Diana (Davis) Burnett's Lunenburg County estate.

Sam (1) – Sam was possibly a descendant of people in the "1794 Nine" group. He was presumably born ca. 1824–1828 and enslaved by Zachariah in the 1820s. He was described as "a small boy" when he was purchased in 1828 by Jeremiah Burnett in Zachariah's estate sale. Sam was presumably enslaved afterward at Jeremiah and Diana (Davis) Burnett's Lunenburg County estate.

William – William was possibly a descendant of people in the "1794 Nine" group. His presumed birthdate cannot be determined. He was alleged by Joel Neal (writing in the early 1830s in *Neal v. Davis*) to have been fathered by Sterling Davis and an enslaved woman. (One possibility based on circumstantial evidence is that Amy (1) was the mother of William.) William was sold by Sterling for 350 dollars in Williamson County, TN, at an unknown date.

Frank (1) – Frank was possibly a descendant of people in the "1794 Nine" group. Frank's presumed birthdate and parentage cannot be determined. Frank was alleged by Joel Neal to have been sold by Sterling Davis in Williamson County, TN, at an unknown date.

Richard – Richard's presumed birthdate and possible ancestral connection to people in the "1794 Nine" group cannot be determined. He was enslaved by Zachariah Davis at the time he died in October 1820 of illness (along with Brister, Vilet, Charles, Rody, and Zachariah's wife, Diana Davis) at Zachariah's Lunenburg County estate. The only known record that lists Richard's name is a letter from Zachariah that confirmed the above deaths.

Vilet – Vilet's presumed birthdate and possible ancestral connection to people in the "1794 Nine" group cannot be determined. She was enslaved by Zachariah Davis at the time she died in October 1820 of illness (along with Brister, Richard, Charles, Rody, and Zachariah's wife, Diana Davis) at Zachariah's Lunenburg County estate. The only known record that lists Vilet's name is a letter from Zachariah that confirmed the above deaths.

Charles – Charles's presumed birthdate and possible ancestral connection to people in the "1794 Nine" group cannot be determined. He was enslaved by Zachariah Davis at the time he died in October 1820 of illness (along with Brister, Richard, Vilet, Rody, and Zachariah's wife, Diana Davis) at Zachariah's Lunenburg County estate. The only known record that lists Charles's name is a letter from Zachariah that confirmed the above deaths.

Rody – Rody's presumed birthdate and origins are unknown. His possible ancestral connection to people in the "1794 Nine" group cannot be determined. He was enslaved by Zachariah Davis at the time he died in October 1820 of illness (along with Brister, Richard, Vilet, Charles, and Zachariah's wife, Diana Davis) at Zachariah's Lunenburg County estate. The only known record that lists Rody's name is a letter from Zachariah that confirmed the above deaths.

Lewis (1) – Lewis was born ca. 1781. His presumed ancestry is unclear. He came to be enslaved by Zachariah Davis at some point between 1795 and 1808. Lewis was given by Zachariah to William E. Davis in 1808. Later, in 1817, he was taken by William to Maury County, TN. Lewis died in Maury County in August 1821 around the age of forty.

The following sketches are for people who are directly named in the surviving pages of the "1804, The ages of the Blacks" ledger kept by William E. Davis/Davies. William is believed to have started the ledger in 1804, the same year that he married Joanna "Anna" Burnett and inherited five people (Patta, Anthona, Fanna, Abraham, and Frankey) from Joanna's father. Except for the first three individuals who appear in the ledger (Patta, Anthona, and Fanna; it is unclear why Abraham and Frankey's births were not recorded), the rest of the individuals are presumed to have been born into the ownership of William, either in Lunenburg County, Virginia; Maury County, Tennessee; or Fayette County, Tennessee. Although the birth ledger was not always maintained by William in chronological order, the entries have been rearranged that way here.

Patta – Patta was born February 10, 1792. She was presumably born in Lunenburg County, VA, on the estate of Jeremiah Burnett. Patta was given by Jeremiah to William E. Davis/Davies in 1804 following William's marriage to Jeremiah's daughter Joanna "Anna" Burnett. Patta is believed to be the same woman alternately referred to through the subsequent decades as "Pat," "Patty," and "Aunt Pat." Patta was taken by William to Maury County, TN, in 1817. In 1843, she was taken by William to the new estate William established in Fayette County, TN. In 1862, shortly after William's death, Patta was allotted by Fayette County commissioners to William's youngest son Henry N. Davies.

Anthona – Anthona was born September 15, 1795, presumably in Lunenburg County on the estate of Jeremiah Burnett. Anthona was given by Jeremiah to William E. Davis/Davies in 1804 following William's marriage to Jeremiah's daughter Joanna "Anna" Burnett. Anthona has not been located in records beyond Jeremiah Burnett's final will but was most likely taken by William to Tennessee in 1817.

Fanna – Fanna was born November 17, 1798, presumably in Lunenburg County on the estate of Jeremiah Burnett. She was given by Jeremiah to William E. Davis/Davies in 1804 following William's marriage to Jeremiah's daughter Joanna "Anna" Burnett. Fanna has not been located in records beyond Jeremiah Burnett's final will but was most likely taken by William to Tennessee in 1817.

Elva – Elva was born January 12, 1811, presumably in Lunenburg County on the estate of William E. Davis/Davies. Elva has not been located in records beyond William's birth ledger but was most likely taken by William to Tennessee in 1817.

Zinna – Zinna was born February 17, 1811, presumably in Lunenburg County on the estate of William E. Davis/Davies. Zinna has not been located in records beyond the birth ledger but was most likely taken by William to Tennessee in 1817.

Rachel – Rachel was born April 10, 1811, presumably in Lunenburg County on the estate of William E. Davis/Davies. Rachel has not been located in records beyond the birth ledger but was most likely taken by William to Tennessee in 1817.

Jordin – Jordin was born November 11, 1812, presumably in Lunenburg County on the estate of William E. Davis/Davies. Jordin has not been located in records beyond the birth ledger but was most likely taken by William to Tennessee in 1817.

Ivey – Ivey was born December 10, 1812, presumably in Lunenburg County on the estate of William E. Davis/Davies. Ivey has not been located in records beyond the birth ledger but was most likely taken by William to Tennessee in 1817.

Lucy (2) – Lucy was born in 1813, presumably in Lunenburg County on the estate of William E. Davis/Davies. Lucy has not been located in records beyond the birth ledger but was most likely taken by William to Tennessee in 1817.

Burrell – Burrell was born September 10, 1814, presumably in Lunenburg County on the estate of William E. Davis/Davies. Burrell was taken by William to Maury County, TN, in 1817, and later, in 1843, to Fayette County, TN. In 1862, shortly after William's death, Burrell was allotted (along with Emely, Coleman, Linda, and Hannah [2]) by Fayette County commissioners to the heirs of William's late daughter Sally Jane (Davies) Walker and her late husband Robert Walker.

Bozwell – Bozwell was born September 17, 1814, presumably in Lunenburg County on the estate of William E. Davis/Davies. Bozwell has not been located in records beyond the birth ledger but was most likely taken by William to Tennessee in 1817.

Chonna – Chonna was born July 10, 1816, presumably in Lunenburg County on the estate of William E. Davis/Davies. Chonna has not been located in records beyond the birth ledger but was most likely taken by William to Tennessee in 1817.

Nelson Harrison – Nelson Harrison was born August 31, 1816, presumably in Lunenburg County on the estate of William E. Davis/Davies. Nelson Harrison has not been located in records beyond the birth ledger but was most likely taken by William to Tennessee in 1817.

John (2) – John was born January 1, 1818, in Maury County, TN, presumably on the estate of William E. Davis/Davies. John has not been located in records beyond the birth ledger but may have been taken by William to Fayette County, TN, in 1843.

Wilshire – Wilshire, more commonly spelled "Willshire" (and by the 1860s "Wilcher"), was born January 4, 1818, in Maury County, TN, presumably on the estate of William E. Davis/Davies. Later legal records would describe Willshire as biracial, as having been "raised" by William, and as being a person of "great value"—all part of the larger trail of circumstantial evidence suggesting that he may have been the child of William and an unknown enslaved woman. In 1827, Willshire was advanced (along with Washington) by William as a wedding gift to William's daughter Eliza (Davis) Mitchell and William Mitchell. Willshire was subsequently "abused" by Mitchell before being sold by Mitchell to Hardy Sellars. Litigation against Hardy Sellars resulted in Willshire returning to the estate and control of William E. Davis/Davies. In 1842, Willshire became embroiled (along with Josh/Joshoway/Joshua) in events that led to a violent altercation between white and Black people from the Davis estate and white and Black people from the estate owned by William's neighbor, Dickey Chappell. In 1843, Willshire was taken by William to Fayette County. Between the mid- to late 1840s, he is believed to have married and started a family with an enslaved woman named Mary, also enslaved at William's estate. In 1862, shortly after William's death, Wilcher was allotted (along with his children: Lucious, Margrett, Amous,

Anthony, Pricilla, and Mary) to Gabe and Elizabeth (Davies) Finney. After the Civil War, Wilcher, his wife Mary, and their family officially adopted the surname Tucker. In 1872, Wilcher purchased a 150-acre farm directly adjacent to the northeast corner of Logan and James Davies's estate. Wilcher Tucker is believed to have died in the late 1880s. Afterward, and well into the twentieth century, Mary Tucker, followed by her children and grandchildren, continued to own and farm on a portion of the original land Wilcher purchased.

Aleck – Aleck was born September 5, 1818, presumably in Maury County on the estate of William E. Davis/Davies. Aleck has not been located in records beyond the birth ledger but may have been taken by William to Fayette County in 1843.

Lucinda – Lucinda was born in September 1819 (on the same day as her twin sister Ellen), presumably in Maury County on the estate of William E. Davis/Davies. She has not been located in records beyond the birth ledger but may have been taken by William to Fayette County in 1843.

Ellen – Ellen was born in September 1819 (on the same day as her twin sister Lucinda), presumably in Maury County on the estate of William E. Davis/Davies. She has not been located in records beyond the birth ledger but may have been taken by William to Fayette County in 1843.

Mourning – Mourning was born August 4, 1820, presumably in Maury County on the estate of William E. Davis/Davies. Mourning has not been located in records beyond the birth ledger but may have been taken by William to Fayette County in 1843.

Ezekiel – Ezekiel was born December 22, 1820, presumably in Maury County on the estate of William E. Davis/Davies. Ezekiel has not been located in records beyond the birth ledger but may have been taken by William to Fayette County in 1843.

Washington – Washington, also known as "Wash," was born October 4, 1821, presumably in Maury County on the estate of William E. Davis/Davies. In 1827, Washington was advanced (along with Willshire) by William as a wedding gift to Eliza (Davis) Mitchell and William Mitchell. Washington is believed to have returned to William's control by 1828. In the 1830s, Washington was advanced (along with Elcey and Elcey's son Samuel) to Eliza and her second husband, Elijah Hanks. Washington (along with Elcey and Samuel) was taken to Nacogdoches, TX, in 1835 by Elijah and Eliza Hanks. After Eliza's death in August 1835 (and the death of Samuel around the same time), Washington was sold (along with Elcey) by Elijah Hanks to a buyer named "Isles" in Louisiana. Washington then returned to Elijah Hanks's control but was later resold (along with Elcey) to a man named "Smith" in Avoyelles Parish. Washington has not been located in records beyond letters in 1838 from one of William's sons confirming the situation in Louisiana involving Smith.

Betsy C. – Betsy C. was born September 18, 1822, presumably in Maury County on the estate of William E. Davis/Davies. Betsy C. has not been located in records beyond the birth ledger but may have been taken by William to Fayette County in 1843.

Alsa – Alsa was born September 13, 1824, presumably in Maury County on the estate of William E. Davis/Davies. In the mid-1830s, Alsa (along with Anderson and Joshua) was given by William to his son William Wesley "W. W." Davies. In 1837, Alsa (along with Anderson and Joshua) was sold by W. W. Davies back to William. Alsa has not been located in additional records after 1837 but may have been taken by William to Fayette County in 1843.

Joshua – Joshua (alternately known as "Josh" and "Joshoway") was born December 31, 1824, "about the brake of day," presumably in Maury County on the estate of William E. Davis/Davies. In the mid-1830s, Joshua (along with Anderson and Alsa) was given by William to his son William Wesley "W. W." Davies. In 1837, Joshua (along with Anderson and Alsa) was sold by W. W. Davies back to William. In 1842, Joshua (along with Willshire) became embroiled in events that led to a violent altercation between white and Black people from the Davis estate and white and Black people from the estate owned by William's neighbor, Dickey Chappell. In 1843, Joshua was taken by William to Fayette County. By the mid-1840s, Joshua is believed to have formed a union with a woman named Mitzi/Meize who had come to be enslaved by William (but does not appear in surviving birth ledger pages). In 1849, Joshua (along with Mitzi/Meize and Yateman) was advanced by William to William's son James B. Davies. Shortly thereafter, Joshua (along with Mitzi/Meize and Yateman) is believed to have been taken to the Shelby County estate jointly owned by Logan and James B. Davies. Joshua (along with Mitzi/Meize and Yateman) is believed to have remained enslaved at the Davies brothers' estate through the end of the Civil War. (In May 1865, Joshua appears in a note about cotton written to Logan by James's second wife, Polly [Little] Davies.) By at least December 1865, Joshua and Mitzi/Meize and their family had assumed the surname Davies/Davis (spelled "Davies" in plantation records and "Davis" in the 1870 census). By that time, Joshua and his family were farming for wages at the Davies brothers' estate. In 1870, Joshua, Mitzi/Meize, and their now four children—Perry, Martha, Archie, and Joe—were enumerated in a household directly adjacent to the Davies brothers' log house. By at least 1880, Joshua and Mitzi/Meize had changed their family's surname to Hadley. Joshua is believed to have died in 1882, according to information in a receipt for a coffin.

Allin – Allin was born in January 1827, presumably in Maury County on the estate of William E. Davis/Davies. Allin has not been located in records beyond the birth ledger but may have been taken by William to Fayette County in 1843.

Janson – Janson was born February 28, 1827, presumably in Maury County on the estate of William E. Davis/Davies. Janson has not been located in records beyond the birth ledger but may have been taken by William to Fayette County in 1843.

Susan – Susan was born February 28, 1827, presumably in Maury County on the estate of William E. Davis/Davies. Susan died on May 1, 1838. Other than her birth and death dates, which are listed in the ledger, she has not been located in records.

Emily (1) – Emily was born February 4, 1828, presumably in Maury County on the estate of William E. Davis/Davies. Emily is believed to have been taken by William to Fayette County in 1843. She is believed to be the same "Emely" whom Fayette County commissioners allotted (along with Coleman, Linda, Hannah, and Burrell) in 1862 to the heirs of William's late daughter, Sarah Jane (Davies) Walker, and William's late son-in-law Robert Walker. Prior to 1865, Emily is believed to have given birth to Elias, Linda, Green, Coleman, and Alich. (Green was allotted by Fayette County commissioners after William's death to Mary [Davies] Scantlin). Emily was likely the same "Emily" who appears in plantation records as being hired out in Shelby County by Logan and James Davies for the years 1863 and 1864. Emily is believed to have married a man named William Cartwright at an unknown date. She was enumerated in the 1870 census along with William Cartwright and seven children: Elias, Linda, Green, Coleman, Alich, Will, and Lucious.

Robert T. – Robert T. was born April 6, 1828, presumably in Maury County on the estate of William E. Davis/Davies. Robert T. has not been located in records beyond the birth ledger but may have been taken by William to Fayette County in 1843.

Anjaline – Anjaline was born April 14, 1829, presumably in Maury County on the estate of William E. Davis/Davies. Anjaline has not been located in records beyond the birth ledger but may have been taken by William to Fayette County in 1843.

Anders – Anders was born December 7, 1829, presumably in Maury County on the estate of William E. Davis/Davies. Anders has not been located in records beyond the birth ledger but may have been taken by William to Fayette County in 1843.

Yateman – Yateman (also spelled "Yeatman") was born August 28, 1830, presumably in Maury County on the estate of William E. Davis/Davies. In early 1843, Yateman is described in Robert Walker's letters to William as suffering from illness at the Maury County estate (alongside Patta and John [3]). According to the letters, Yateman recovered after a treatment of castor oil and bloodletting. He was taken to William's Fayette County estate later that same year. In 1849, Yateman was advanced (along with Joshua/Joshoway/Josh and Mitzi/Meize) by William to James B. Davies. Shortly thereafter, Yateman is believed to have been taken (along with Joshua/Joshoway and Mitzi/Meize) to Logan and James's Shelby County estate.

Sam (2) – Sam was born April 27, 1832, presumably in Maury County on the estate of William E. Davis/Davies. Sam has not been located in records beyond the birth ledger but may have been taken to William's Fayette County estate in 1843.

Hyrum – Hyrum was born August 13, 1832, presumably in Maury County on the estate of William E. Davis/Davies. Hyrum has not been located in records beyond the birth ledger but may have been taken to William's Fayette County estate in 1843.

Mandy Green – Mandy Green was born February 21, 1833, presumably in Maury County on the estate of William E. Davis/Davies. Mandy

Green has not been located in records beyond the birth ledger but may have been taken by William to Fayette County in 1843.

Francina – Francina was born April 27, 1833, presumably in Maury County on the estate of William E. Davis/Davies. Francina has not been located in records beyond the birth ledger but may have been taken by William to Fayette County in 1843.

Jacob – Jacob was born February 1, 1835, presumably in Maury County on the estate of William E. Davis/Davies. Jacob has not been located in records beyond the birth ledger but may have been taken by William to Fayette County in 1843.

John (3) – John was born October 27, 1840, presumably in Maury County on the estate of William E. Davis/Davies. John is believed to be one and the same with the child "John" who was described in Robert Walker's letters as dying from illness in early 1843 in Maury County. John is believed to have been buried on William's land in Maury County shortly before it was acquired by Gideon Johnson Pillow.

Paray Lee – Paray Lee was born October 27, 1842, presumably in Maury County on the estate of William E. Davis/Davies. Paray Lee has not been located in records beyond the birth ledger but was presumably taken to William's Fayette County estate in 1843.

Martha Aaline – Martha Aaline was born September 16, 1844, presumably in Fayette County on the estate of William E. Davis/Davies. Martha Aaline is believed to be "Adaline," who (along with her child and George) was allotted by Fayette County commissioners in 1862 (shortly after William's death) to William Wesley "W. W." Davies (then living in Texas). Afterward, Martha Aaline probably remained in Shelby County, where she was hired out by Logan and James Davies for W. W.'s benefit.

Thomas – Thomas (alternately spelled "Thom") was born June 11, 1847, presumably in Fayette County on the estate of William E. Davies. Following William's death, Thomas was allotted in 1862 by Fayette County commissioners to Mary (Davies) Scantlin, who was living in Texas. Thomas remained in Shelby County through the Civil War years. In 1862, he was hired out for Mary Scantlin's benefit to Gabe and Elizabeth (Davies) Finney. Thomas was hired out in 1863 for Mary's benefit to John Reave. Thomas is believed to be one and the same with "Tom Cartwright," who appears in post-emancipation commissary records kept by Logan and James Davies. Tom Cartwright was enumerated near the Davies brothers in the 1870 census alongside wife Susan and their four children.

Gorge – Gorge was born November 27, 1847, presumably in Fayette County on the estate of William E. Davies. Gorge is believed to be one and the same with "George," who was allotted in 1862 (along with Adaline and her child) to William Wesley "W. W." Davies by Fayette County commissioners. Afterward, Gorge probably remained in Shelby County, where he was hired out by Logan and James Davies for W. W.'s benefit.

Sarah Jane – Sarah Jane was born in August 1848, presumably in Fayette County on the estate of William E. Davies. Although questions remain about her parentage and blood connection to Willshire and Willshire's wife, Mary (based on chronology and what is known of Mary, it does not seem possible that she gave birth to Sarah Jane), Sarah Jane is presumed to be Willshire's daughter. Sarah Jane may very well have been named after William E. Davies's daughter, Sarah Jane (Davies) Walker, who died in 1847. By the late 1850s, if not earlier, Sarah Jane was probably taken to Logan and James Davies's Shelby County estate. At some point between the early 1860s and 1865, she is believed to have formed a union with Richmond, who had come to the Davies brothers' estate as a result of James's marriage to Almeda Little in 1854. Sarah Jane may have given birth to her first child, a daughter named Hattie, around 1862. Sarah Jane is believed to have married Richmond by 1865. After the Civil War, Richmond and Sarah Jane would formally adopt the surname Bennett. Sarah Jane Bennett continued to reside in Shelby County for the rest of her life with her husband and children, who numbered twelve in total. She is believed to have died after 1920.

Lius Polk – Lius Polk was born February 27, 1849, presumably in Fayette County on the estate of William E. Davies. Lius Polk has not been located in records beyond the birth ledger but may have been taken to Logan and James Davies's estate (or Henry Davies's estate) in Shelby County in the 1850s.

Perry – Perry was born April 9, 1849, presumably in Fayette County on the estate of William E. Davies. Perry is believed to have been born to Joshua and Mitzi/Meize and taken to Logan and James Davies's estate (or Henry Davies's estate) in Shelby County in the 1850s. After

1865, Perry's parents adopted the surname Davis (spelled in some records as "Davies"). Perry was enumerated in Joshua and Mitzi/Meize Davis's household in 1870.

Katherine E. – Katherine E. was born September 15, 1849, presumably in Fayette County on the estate of William E. Davies. She has not been located in records beyond the birth ledger but may have been taken to Logan and James Davies's estate (or Henry Davies's estate) in Shelby County in the 1850s.

Lucious Wilks – Lucious Wilks was born February 27, 1851, presumably in Fayette County on the estate of William E. Davies. He is believed to have been among the children of Willshire/Wilcher and Mary. In 1862, Lucious was allotted (along with Wilcher, Margrett, Amous, Anthony, Pricilla, and Mary) to Gabe and Elizabeth (Davies) Finney. After emancipation, Lucious's family adopted the surname Tucker. Lucious worked after the Civil War as a sharecropper on Logan and James Davies's estate. In 1870 he married and began a family with Alice Williams. The couple would have at least eight children. Lucious is believed to have moved with his family to Prairie County, AR, in the early 1890s. After Alice's death in 1904, he remarried. Lucious died between 1910 and 1920 and is believed to be buried in Harris Cemetery in Prairie County.

Harriot I. – Harriot I. was born April 16, 1851, presumably in Fayette County on the estate of William E. Davies. She is believed to be the same "Harriet" whom Fayette County commissioners allotted in 1862 (along with Ben, Mary, and Sealy) to the heirs of William's late daughter, Nancy (Davies) Davidson. Harriot I. was hired out in 1863 and 1864 in Shelby County to unknown parties for the benefit of the Davidson heirs.

Emeline Pettilar – Emeline Pettilar was born September 6, 1851, presumably in Fayette County on the estate of William E. Davies. In 1862, she was allotted (along with Daniel, Vina, Eanoch/Enoch, and Ann) by Fayette County commissioners to William's daughter, Mariah (Davies) Lockridge, who was still living in Maury County. Emeline Pettilar has not been located in additional records. She may have been taken to the Lockridge estate in Maury County.

Alford – Alford was born September 23, 1851, presumably in Fayette County on the estate of William E. Davies. Alford has not been located in records beyond the birth ledger but may have been taken to

Logan and James Davies's estate (or Henry Davies's estate) in Shelby County in the 1850s.

Celine – Celine was born December 2, 1852, presumably in Fayette County on the estate of William E. Davies. She died September 17, 1853.

Margrett – Margrett was born May 30, 1853, presumably in Fayette County on the estate of William E. Davies. In 1862, Margrett (along with Wilcher, Lucious, Amous, Anthony, Pricilla, and Mary) was allotted by Fayette County commissioners to Gabe and Elizabeth (Davies) Finney. Margrett has not been located in additional records and further research is necessary to confirm if she was a blood relative of the Tucker family (as the circumstances of her 1862 allotment indicate).

Eanoch – Eanoch was born June 30, 1854, presumably in Fayette County on the estate of William E. Davies. In 1862, Eanoch (spelled "Enoch" at this time) was allotted (along with Daniel, Vina, Emeline, and Ann) to William's daughter, Mariah (Davies) Lockridge, who was still living in Maury County. Eanoch/Enoch has not been located in additional records. He may have been taken to the Lockridge estate in Maury County.

Amous – Amous, also known as "Amos," was born November 6, 1855, presumably in Fayette County on the estate of William E. Davies. He is believed to have been among the children of Willshire/Wilcher and Mary. In 1862, Fayette County commissioners allotted Amous (along with Wilcher, Lucious, Margrett, Anthony, Pricilla, and Mary) to Gabe and Elizabeth (Davies) Finney. After emancipation, Amous's family adopted the surname Tucker. Amos Tucker is believed to have worked as a sharecropper for Logan and James Davies after the Civil War. He married Pleasant Carter in 1874, and their first child, Maggie, was born in 1875. Amos and his family came to own and farm a portion of the land originally purchased by Wilcher. Amos died in 1912 and was buried in Morning Grove Cemetery, where his headstone still stands today.

Melinda – Melinda was born May 16, 1856, presumably in Fayette County on the estate of William E. Davies. Melinda has not been located in records beyond the birth ledger but may have been taken to Logan and James Davies's estate (or Henry Davies's estate) in Shelby County in the 1850s.

Anthony – Anthony was born March 17, 1858, presumably in Fayette County on the estate of William E. Davies. He is believed to be among the children of Willshire/Wilcher and Mary. In 1862, Fayette County commissioners allotted Anthony (along with Wilcher, Lucious, Margrett, Amous, Pricilla, and Mary) to Gabe and Elizabeth (Davies) Finney. After emancipation, Anthony's family adopted the surname Tucker. In 1880, Anthony Tucker married Sophia Gray. At the time, Anthony was living in his parents' household and working on the farm they owned directly beside the farm owned by his brother Amos Tucker.

Green – Green was born June 23, 1858, presumably in Fayette County on the estate of William E. Davies. Green is believed to have been the son of Emily/Emely (later enumerated in census records as Emily Cartwright after she married William Cartwright). In 1862, Green was allotted (along with Thomas/Tom—later enumerated in census records as Tom Cartwright) to Mary (Davies) Scantlin, who was then living in Texas. Green appears in records from 1863 and 1864 as being hired out by James Davies to P. Ellis in Shelby County for the benefit of Mary Scantlin.

Rachel (2) – Rachel was born November 18, 1860, presumably in Fayette County on the estate of William E. Davies. Rachel has not been located in records beyond the birth ledger. She was most likely taken shortly after her birth to Logan and James Davies's estate (or Henry Davies's estate) in Shelby County.

The following sketches are for individuals who have been identified as being enslaved by William E. Davis/Davies during his lifetime but do not appear in the surviving pages of his "1804, The ages of the Blacks" ledger. The sketches have been drawn primarily based on these individuals' appearances in other scattered records from the DMA Archives, including bills of sale, probate records, and personal correspondence between William's offspring. The profiles loosely reflect the order in which people are discussed in the text of the book.

Abraham – Abraham's presumed birthdate has not been determined. Abraham is believed to have been born in Lunenburg County on the estate of Jeremiah Burnett. In 1804, Abraham was given by Jeremiah to William E. Davis/Davies following William's marriage to Jeremiah's daughter, Joanna "Anna" Burnett. Abraham has not been located in records beyond Jeremiah's final will but may have been taken by William to Maury County, TN, in 1817.

Frankey – Frankey was presumably born ca. 1790–1800 in Lunenburg County on the estate of Jeremiah Burnett. In 1804, Frankey was given by Jeremiah to William E. Davis/Davies following William's marriage to Jeremiah's daughter Joanna "Anna" Burnett. Frankey was taken by William to Maury County in 1817. In 1843, Frankey was taken by William to the Davies family's new estate in Fayette County. In 1862, shortly after William's death, Fayette County commissioners allotted Frankey to Gabe and Elizabeth (Davies) Finney. Frankey has not been located in subsequent records but was presumably enslaved after 1862 at the Finney's Shelby County estate.

Elcey – Elcey was born ca. 1808 in Lunenburg County, presumably on the estate of William E. Davis/Davies. Elcey was taken by William in 1817 to Maury County. In 1827, she was almost given by William to his daughter Eliza as a wedding gift. The argument that ensued resulted in William instead giving Willshire/Wilcher (and Wash/Washington) to Eliza and her new husband, William Mitchell. Elcey gave birth to a son, Samuel, ca. 1833. Around 1835, Elcey (along with Samuel and Wash/Washington) was given by William to Eliza and her second husband, Elijah Hanks, just prior to the couple's move to Texas. Elcey (along with Samuel and Wash/Washington) was taken to Bosque County, TX. Samuel died at some point during the trip or shortly after arrival. Following Eliza's death in 1835, Elcey (and Wash/Washington) was sold by Elijah Hanks to a buyer named "Isles" in Louisiana. Elcey and Wash/Washington were briefly returned to Hanks but later resold to a man named "Smith" in Avoyelles Parish. Neither Elcey nor Wash has been located in additional records beyond letters from W. W. Davies to his father William confirming the chain of events in Louisiana.

Samuel – Samuel was born ca. 1833, presumably in Maury County on the estate of William E. Davis/Davies. Samuel's mother was Elcey. Around 1835, Samuel (along with Elcey) was given by William to Elijah and Eliza (Davies) Hanks prior to the couple's move to Bosque County, TX. Samuel died either during the trip to Texas or shortly after arrival.

Anderson – Anderson was born ca. 1824. His presumed birthplace is unclear. It is possible he was born in Maury County on the estate of William E. Davies but also possible he was born elsewhere. By the 1830s, Anderson was enslaved by William in Maury County. In the mid-1830s, Anderson (along with Josh/Joshua/Joshoway and Alsa) was given by William to his son W. W. Davies. In 1837, Anderson (along with Josh/Joshua/Joshoway and Alsa) was sold by W. W. back to his father just prior to W. W.'s move to Texas. Anderson has not been located in additional records but may have been taken by William to Fayette County in 1843.

London – London was born ca. 1817. His birth location cannot be determined but he may have been born in Kentucky. It is quite possible that he was enslaved on the Younger family's plantation in Hopkins County, KY, by the mid-1830s, if not well before. In 1838, at the age of twenty-one, London was sold by John W. Younger to William E. Davis/Davies. It is unclear where the sale took place, but some evidence suggests it happened in Kentucky. Afterward, London was presumably enslaved by William at his Maury County estate until an unknown date. London has not been located in additional records but he may have been taken by William to Fayette County in 1843.

Ben – Ben was born no earlier than 1815 (probably ca. 1815–1825). His birthplace is unclear. In 1850, Ben was purchased (along with Mary, Amanda, and a child "about twelve") by William E. Davies and his son James B. Davies from Milton Draper and Ridley Roberts. Ben is believed to have been taken to Logan and James Davies's Shelby County estate shortly after the purchase. He is believed to be one and the same with the "Ben" who was later allotted (along with Mary, Sealy, and Harriet) by Fayette County commissioners in 1862 to the heirs of the late Nancy (Davies) Davidson. Afterward, Ben was hired out by Logan and James Davies for the benefit of the Davidson heirs. Ben is believed to be the same "Ben" who is listed (along with Mary) in multiple promissory notes between 1862 and 1864 relating to being hired out by the Davies brothers to neighboring planters.

Mary (2) – Mary was probably born no earlier than 1824 (likely ca. 1824–1830). In 1850, when she was described as "not exceeding twenty-six," she was purchased (along with Ben, Amanda, and a child "about twelve") by William E. Davis/Davies and James B. Davies from Milton

Draper and Ridley Roberts. Mary is believed to have been taken to Logan and James Davies's Shelby County estate shortly after the purchase. She is believed to be the same "Mary" who was allotted in 1862 (along with Ben, Sealy, and Harriet) by Fayette County commissioners to the heirs of the late Nancy (Davies) Davidson. Afterward, she was hired out for the benefit of the Davidson heirs by the Davies brothers. She is believed to be the same "Mary" who appears (alongside Ben) in multiple promissory notes between 1862 and 1864 relating to being hired out to neighboring planters. One possibility is that Mary (2) is one and the same with the "Mary" (Mary Tucker) whom Wilcher married and started a family with beginning around 1850. Because of the questions that remain about this assertion, however, Mary (2) will receive a separate entry from Mary Tucker. (See below.)

Amanda – Amanda was born ca. 1836; her birthplace is unknown. In 1850, at the age of "about fourteen," she was purchased (along with Ben, Mary, and a child "about twelve") by William E. Davies and James B. Davies from Milton Draper and Ridley Roberts. Amanda is believed to have been taken to Logan and James Davies's Shelby County estate shortly after the purchase. Beyond the bill of sale that documented the above details, she has not been located in additional records.

Child "about twelve" – Born ca. 1838 at an unknown birthplace, the child "about twelve" was purchased (along with Ben, Mary, and Amanda) in 1850 by William E. Davis/Davies and James B. Davies from Milton Draper and Ridley Roberts. The child is believed to have been taken to Logan and James Davies's Shelby County estate shortly after the purchase. Beyond the bill of sale for the purchase, the child has not been located in additional records.

Mary (3) – Mary (later Mary Tucker) was born in May 1826 in South Carolina. As stated above, it is a possibility that Mary (3) being described here was one and the same with Mary (2), who was purchased in 1850 (along with Ben, Amanda, and the child "about twelve") by William E. Davies and James B. Davies. However, because of certain questions that remain about this assertion, Mary (3) is being given a separate biographical sketch to leave open the possibility that she was a different woman. (To briefly touch on the questions, uncertainty exists about the parentage of Sarah Jane. According to the latest research, Sarah Jane is understood as being among the children of Wilcher and Mary Tucker. Yet Sarah Jane was born in 1848, prior to Mary (2) being purchased by William E. Davies. One speculative possibility that would address this discrepancy is that Sarah Jane was indeed Wilcher's daughter, only by a different woman, which would explain the pre-1850 date of birth.) Mary is believed to have given birth to Lucious Wilks on February 27, 1851. Other children that followed included Amos, Mary (4), Andy, Anthony, Pricilla, and Amy. In 1870, Mary Tucker was enumerated in the Shelby County census with her husband Wilcher and their children, Lucious, Mary, Amos, Pricilla, Amy, Noah, and Andy Tucker. At that time, the family is believed to have been sharecropping another family's land near the Davies's estate. In 1872, Wilcher Tucker purchased land adjacent to the northeast corner of Logan and James Davies's estate. Mary and Wilcher and their children operated their own farm on this property. After Wilcher's death, most likely in the 1880s, Mary would continue to own a portion of the land. She became well known as a midwife in the community. Ellen Davies-Rodgers, in *Turns Again Home*, described Mary Tucker as the midwife at her own birth. Mary Tucker is believed to be buried in Morning Grove Cemetery in a plot whose location has been lost. Ellen Davies-Rodgers named "Mary Tucker Cove" in the Davies Plantation Estates subdivision in honor of Mary.

Mary (4) – Born ca. 1853, Mary is believed to be the daughter of Wilcher and Mary (3)/Mary Tucker. She is believed to be the same "Mary" whom Fayette County commissioners allotted in 1862 (along with Wilcher, Lucious, Margrett, Amous, Anthony, and Pricilla) to Gabe and Elizabeth (Davies) Finney. Mary was enumerated in the 1870 census in the household of Wilcher and Mary Tucker. Additional research is necessary to trace her beyond 1870.

Mitzi/Meize – Mitzi/Meize was born ca. 1832. Her birthplace origins are unclear, but post-emancipation census records confirm her mother was born in South Carolina and her father born in Georgia. Evidence suggests a connection to the Hadley family, who were originally from Georgia. By the 1840s, if not from the time of her birth, Mitzi/Meize is believed to have been enslaved by William E. Davies in Maury County. She is believed to have married Josh/Joshua/Joshoway by the late 1840s. In 1849, Mitzi/Meize was advanced by William (along with Yateman/Yeatman and Josh/Joshua/Joshoway) to James B. Davies.

She and Yateman and Joshua were taken to the Shelby County estate jointly owned by Logan and James B. Davies and are believed to have remained there through the Civil War. By at least December 1865, if not earlier, she and Joshua had assumed the surname Davis/Davies and were farming for wages at the Davies brothers' estate. In 1870, Mitzi/Meize and Joshua Davis and their four children—Perry, Martha, Archie, and Joe—were enumerated in a household directly adjacent to the Davies brothers' log house. By 1880, Mitzi/Meize and Joshua's family had changed their surname from Davis to Hadley.

Sealy – Sealy's presumed birthdate and place of birth is unknown. Sealy was enslaved by William E. Davies at the time of Davies's death in 1861 and afterward was advanced (along with Ben, Mary, and Harriet) by Fayette County commissioners to the heirs of William's late daughter, Nancy (Davies) Davidson. Sealy has not been located in additional records.

Adaline's child – Adaline's child was presumably born ca. 1858–1862 in Fayette County on the estate of William E. Davies. In 1862, Adaline's child was allotted (along with Adaline) by Fayette County commissioners to W. W. Davies, who was then living in Texas. Rather than being taken to Texas, Adaline and her child are believed to have remained in Shelby County during the Civil War years at the estate of Logan and James Davies. Neither of them have been located in additional records.

Hannah (2) – Hannah's presumed birthdate is unknown. She was enslaved by William E. Davies at the time of his death in 1861 and afterward was advanced (along with Emily/Emely, Coleman, Linda, and Burrell) to the heirs of William's late daughter, Sarah Jane (Davies) Walker. Hannah probably remained enslaved at Logan and James Davies's estate in Shelby County through the Civil War years. She has yet to be identified in additional records.

Coleman – Coleman was born ca. 1861 in Fayette County shortly before William E. Davies's death. He is believed to be the son of Emily/Emely (b. Feb. 4, 1828), who was enslaved by William (and after 1865 known as Emily Cartwright). In 1862, Coleman was allotted (along with Emily/Emely, Linda, Hannah [2], and Burrell) to the heirs of William's late daughter, Sarah Jane (Davies) Walker. He is believed to have remained in Shelby County at the estate of Logan and James Davies (or possibly Henry Davies) through the Civil War years. In 1870

Coleman was enumerated in the household of Emily Cartwright and her husband William Cartwright, which was located in close proximity to the Davies brothers' home.

Linda – Linda is believed to have been born ca. 1856, presumably in Fayette County on the estate of William E. Davies. She is believed to be the daughter of Emily/Emely (b. Feb. 4, 1828). In 1862, Linda was allotted (along with Emily/Emely, Coleman, Hannah [2], and Burrell) by Fayette County commissioners to the heirs of William's late daughter, Sarah Jane (Davies) Walker. Linda likely remained in Shelby County through the Civil War at the estate of Logan and James Davies (or possibly Henry Davies). In 1870, Linda was enumerated in the household of Emily Cartwright and her husband William Cartwright, which was located in close proximity to the Davies brothers' home.

Daniel – Daniel's presumed birthdate and place of birth is unknown. He may have been born in Fayette County on the estate of William E. Davies. Daniel was enslaved by William at the time of William's death in 1861 and afterward was advanced (along with Vina, Enoch, Emeline, and Ann) to William's daughter, the widowed Mariah (Davies) Lockridge, who was then living in Maury County. He may have been taken to Maury County. Daniel has not been identified in additional records.

Ann – Ann's presumed birthdate and place of birth is unknown. She may have been born in Fayette County on the estate of William E. Davies. Ann was enslaved by William at the time of his death in 1861 and afterward was advanced (along with Vina, Enoch, Emeline, and Daniel) to William's daughter, the widowed Mariah (Davies) Lockridge, then living in Maury County. Ann may have been taken to Maury County. She has not been identified in additional records.

Alee – Alee's presumed birthdate and place of birth is unknown. She may have been born in Fayette County on the estate of William E. Davies. Alee was enslaved by William by the 1850s if not before. Around 1856, she was advanced by William (along with a girl named Frank and a girl named Lece) to William's daughter Mary (Davies) Scantlin. Alee was described as being "a woman" at the time of the advancement. In 1856, Alee was taken (along with Frank and Lece) by Mary and her husband J. D. Scantlin to Clifton, TX. In late 1861, Alee was briefly referenced by Mary in a letter to her brother James Davies. Alee is believed to have remained in Clifton through the Civil War at the estate owned by the widowed Mary Scantlin.

Frank (3) – Frank was born ca. 1846–1856. She may have been born in Fayette County on the estate of William E. Davies. Frank was described as being "a girl" in 1856 when she was advanced (along with Alee and Lece) by William to Mary (Davies) Scantlin prior to Mary's migration with her husband J. D. Scantlin to Clifton, TX. Frank is believed to have remained in Clifton through the Civil War at the estate owned by the widowed Mary Scantlin.

Lece – Lece was born ca. 1846–1856. She may have been born in Fayette County on the estate of William E. Davies. Lece was described as being "a girl" in 1856 when she was advanced (along with Alee and Frank) by William to Mary (Davies) Scantlin prior to Mary's migration with her husband J. D. Scantlin to Clifton, TX. Lece is believed to have remained in Clifton through the Civil War at the estate owned by the widowed Mary Scantlin.

Pricilla – Pricilla was born in November 1863. She is believed to be the daughter of Wilcher and Mary (Tucker). It is unclear where she was born but it may have been on the estate jointly owned by Logan and James Davies. Following William E. Davis's death, Pricilla was allotted (along with Wilcher, Lucious, Margrett, Amous, Anthony, and Mary) by Fayette County commissioners to Gabe and Elizabeth (Davies) Finney. Pricilla is believed to have remained enslaved during the Civil War at either the Finney's farm or Logan and James Davies's estate (or possibly Henry Davies's adjacent estate). Pricilla, like the rest of her family, formally adopted the surname Tucker after 1865. In 1881, she married and began a family with Charles B. Royster. By the 1890s, their family was living in Memphis. Pricilla died November 8, 1942.

The next section of individuals appear in birth records for enslaved people that were recorded by brothers Logan and James Davies between 1852 and 1861. These are the only known birth records for bondspeople to have been kept by Logan and James. It is presumed that most if not all of these people were born at the plantation jointly owned by the brothers. It is likely that a number of these individuals (if not most) were buried at the "Davies Plantation Cemetery" located adjacent to the Memphis to Somerville Road (later US 64).

Martha – Martha was born February 14, 1852. She is believed to be the same Martha Davis who was enumerated (at age nineteen) in 1870 in the household headed by Joshua and Mitzi/Meize Davis.

Jacob (2) – Jacob was born September 1, 1855. His presumed parentage has not been determined and he has not been located in additional records.

Emily (2) – Emily was born March 10, 1856. Her presumed parentage has not been determined and she has not been located in additional records.

Harry – Harry was born July 18, 1857. His presumed parentage has not been determined. He died the following year in 1858 and was presumably buried in Davies Plantation Cemetery.

Archa – Archa was born March 27, 1858. He is believed to be the same Archie Davis who was enumerated (at age twelve) in 1870 in the household headed by Joshua and Mitzi/Meize Davis.

Amos (2) – Amos was born November 9, 1858. He is believed to be the same Amos Davis who was later enumerated in 1870 (at age twelve) in the household headed by Joe and Maria Davis. (Also enumerated in the Davis household in 1870 was ten-year-old Mat Davis.)

Arominta – Arominta was born February 4, 1852. Her presumed parentage has not been determined. She died April 24, 1859, and was presumably buried in Davies Plantation Cemetery.

Elias – Elias was born October 31, 1859. His presumed parentage is unclear. (Based on his age, he is not the Elias enumerated in 1870 in William and Emily Cartwright's household.)

Young – Young was born July 27, 1860. Young is believed to be the same Young Cartwright who was enumerated (at age ten) in 1870 in the household headed by Tom and Susan Cartwright. (Also enumerated in the same household in 1870 was Polly Cartwright, age eight).

Madison – Madison was born December 20, 1861. Madison's presumed parentage has not been determined. Based on the birthdate, however, Madison would seem to be a twin sibling of Mat's. (Madison does not appear with Mat and Amos in Joe and Maria Davis's household in 1870). Madison has not been located in additional records.

Mat – Mat was born December 20, 1861. Based on his birthdate, he seems to have been a twin sibling of Madison's. Mat is believed to be one and the same as Mat Davis, who was enumerated (at age ten) in 1870 in the household headed by Joe and Maria Davis. (Also enumerated in the household was twelve-year-old Amos Davis.)

Polly – Polly was born January 1, 1862. Polly is believed to be the same Polly Cartwright who was enumerated (at age eight) in 1870 in the household headed by Tom and Susan Cartwright. (Also enumerated in the household was Young Cartwright, age ten).

The following sketches are for individuals who have been identified as being enslaved by James and Logan Davies but do not appear in the surviving birth ledgers they kept for enslaved people. The sketches have been drawn based on these individuals' appearances in records from the DMA Archives and, in the case of Richmond Bennett, US Census data.

Nice – Nice's presumed birthdate is unknown. Nice appears in records for the first and only time in a September 1865 note from James Davies to Logan Davies that referenced Nice's knowledge of property that had been stolen from the brothers' plantation by Federal soldiers during the Civil War. In his note, James said that he was bringing Nice with him to Memphis in order to "prove the claim against the government for property taken by the Federals." It is presumed but by no means certain that Nice had been enslaved by the brothers during the Civil War, if not well before.

Celia – Celia's presumed birthdate is unknown. She appears in records for the first and only time in a December 1863 note between the overseer at Thomas B. Crenshaw's plantation and Logan Davies. The note confirms Celia, along with her parents, was enslaved by Logan and James Davies. It confirms that Celia had been hired out to the overseer for the year 1863, and also that she and her parents were expected to be hired out to the overseer for the year 1864.

Richmond – Richmond was born ca. 1833, presumably into the ownership of William Little shortly before or after William Little and his family migrated from North Carolina to Shelby County, TN, near Fisherville. According to later census records, Richmond's father had been born in Virginia, and his mother in North Carolina. Following William Little's death in 1851, Richmond was allotted to one of Little's sons. When that son died, Richmond was then allotted in 1854 (through a process of drawing straws) to one of William's daughters, Almeda Penelope Little. In December 1854, when Almeda married James B. Davies, Richmond was taken by Almeda to her new husband's plantation in Morning Sun. At some point between the early to mid-1860s, Richmond is believed to have formed a union with Sarah Jane, the presumed daughter of Wilcher. Richmond was taken to the Civil War in 1862 by James for the purpose of serving as James's "body servant." After the war, Richmond married Sarah Jane Tucker, and the couple and their family assumed the surname Bennett. A later account from William Little Davies would claim the following: "[Richmond] was the body guard of James Baxter Davies during the Civil War and was in the war when the surrender occurred after a career of many battles during that period. Captured by the Federals once escaped and returned home and to the army." In 1870, Richmond and Sarah Jane Bennett and their family were enumerated two households away from Logan and James Davies's log house. In 1880, the Bennett family (now with eight children) were enumerated nine households away from Logan and James Davies's log house. The Bennetts appear in the Davies brothers' commissary records through these two decades as sharecropping Davies-owned land. Richmond and his family remained in the vicinity of the Davies brothers' estate through 1910. They probably continued to farm via sharecropping arrangements. Richmond had twelve children in total with Sarah Jane. He died May 15, 1915, of "asthma, acute phthisis, and anemia," according to Dr. William Little Davies. Richmond was buried at Morning Grove Cemetery, where his headstone still stands today. According to Ellen Davies-Rodgers, "annually, on July 4, for many years Dr. William Little Davies, son of Uncle Jim, placed a flag on [Richmond Bennett's] grave."

DAVIES FAMILY TREE

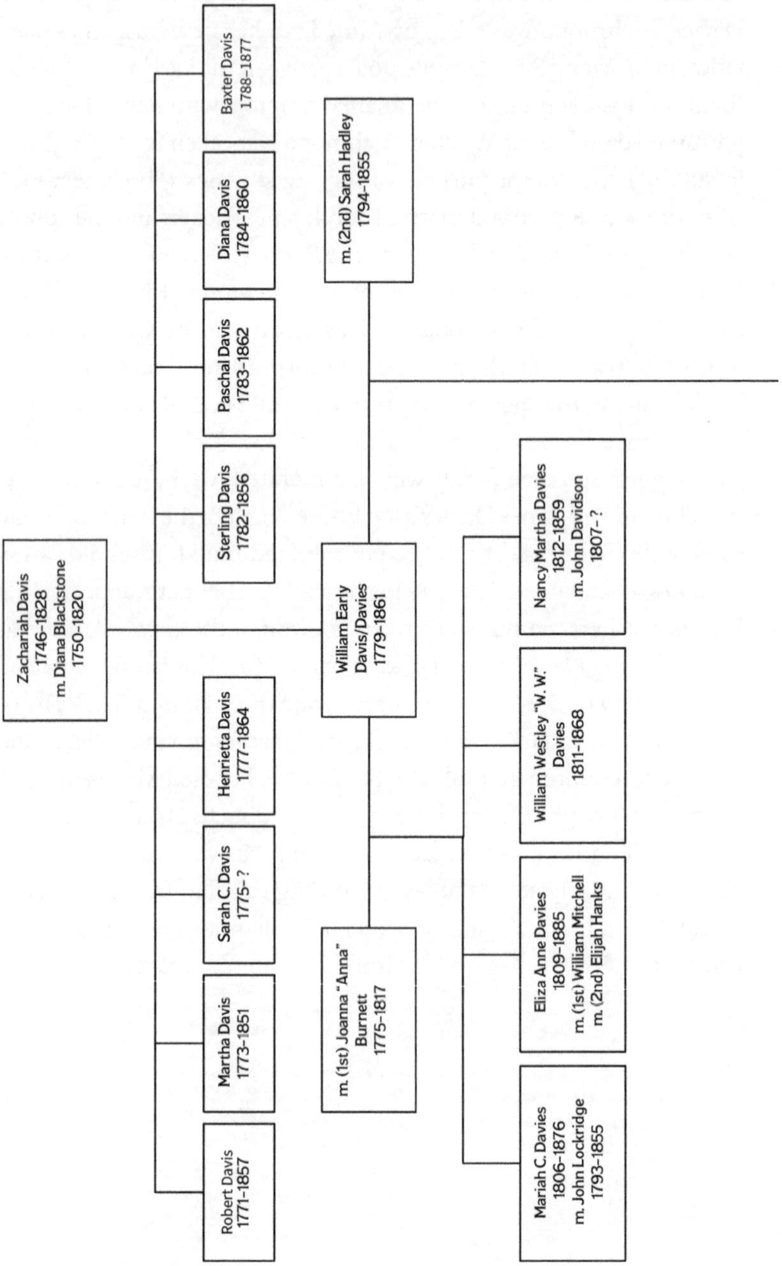

Zachariah Davis 1746–1828 m. Diana Blackstone 1750–1820
Robert Davis 1771–1857
Martha Davis 1773–1851
Sarah C. Davis 1775–?
Henrietta Davis 1777–1864
Sterling Davis 1782–1856
Paschal Davis 1783–1862
Diana Davis 1784–1860
Baxter Davis 1788–1877
William Early Davis/Davies 1779–1861
m. (1st) Joanna "Anna" Burnett 1775–1817
m. (2nd) Sarah Hadley 1794–1855
Mariah C. Davies 1806–1876 m. John Lockridge 1793–1855
Eliza Anne Davies 1809–1885 m. (1st) William Mitchell m. (2nd) Elijah Hanks
William Westley "W. W." Davies 1811–1868
Nancy Martha Davies 1812–1859 m. John Davidson 1807–?

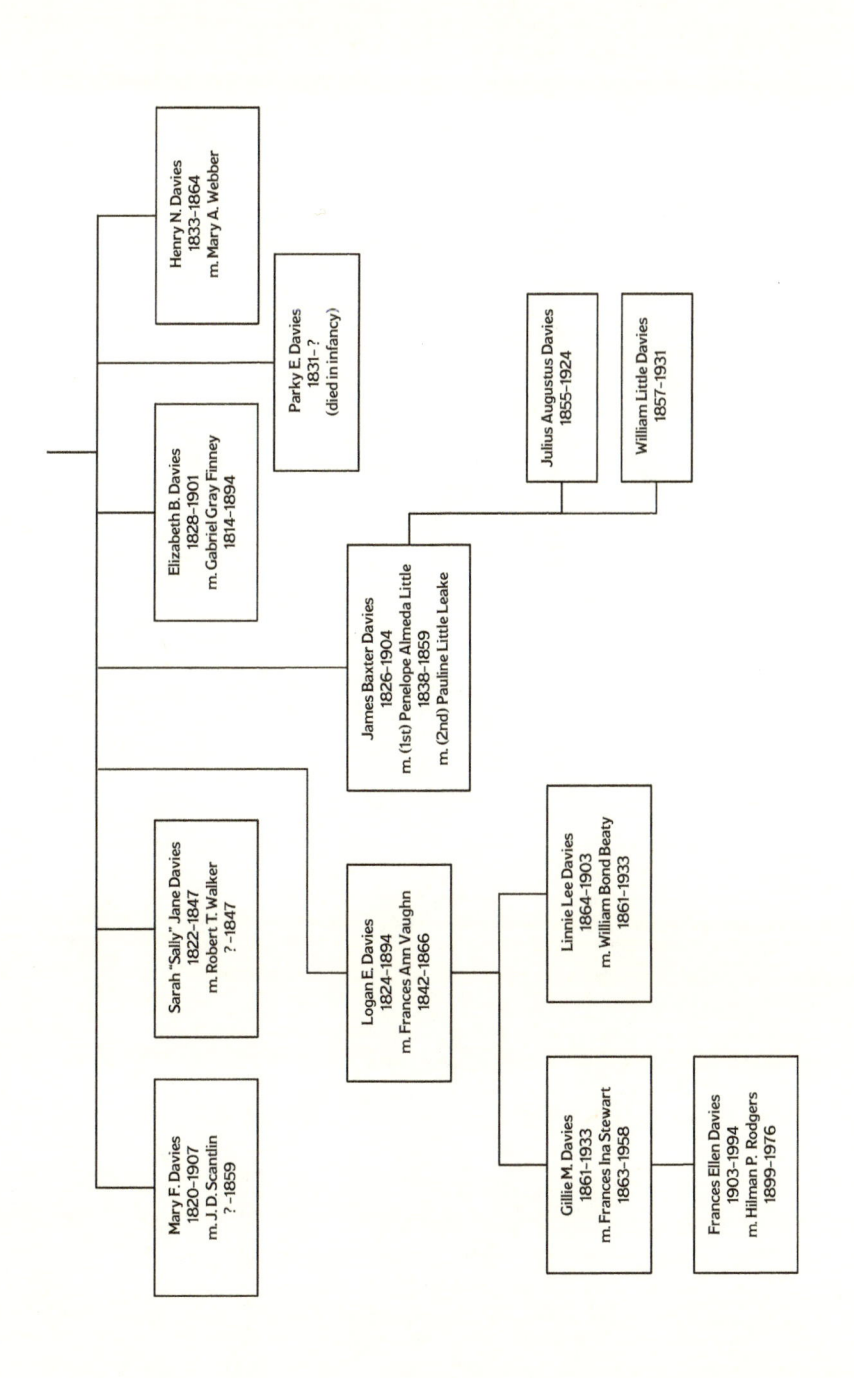

```
                                                                    ┌─────────────────┐
                                                                    │ Henry N. Davies │
                                                                    │    1833-1864    │
                                                                    │ m. Mary A. Webber│
                                                                    └─────────────────┘
                                              ┌──────────────────┐
                                              │  Parky E. Davies │
                                              │      1831-?      │
                                              │(died in infancy) │
                                              └──────────────────┘
                        ┌─────────────────────┐
                        │ Elizabeth B. Davies │
                        │      1828-1901      │
                        │m. Gabriel Gray Finney│
                        │      1814-1894      │
                        └─────────────────────┘
                                                                              ┌──────────────────────┐
                                                                              │ Julius Augustus Davies│
                                                                              │       1855-1924       │
                                                                              └──────────────────────┘
                                                                              ┌──────────────────────┐
                                                                              │ William Little Davies │
                                                                              │       1857-1931       │
                                                                              └──────────────────────┘
                        ┌──────────────────────────────┐
                        │     James Baxter Davies      │
                        │         1826-1904            │
                        │m. (1st) Penelope Almeda Little│
                        │         1838-1859            │
                        │m. (2nd) Pauline Little Leake │
                        └──────────────────────────────┘
                                       ┌──────────────────┐
                                       │ Limmie Lee Davies│
                                       │     1864-1903    │
                                       │m. William Bond Beaty│
                                       │     1861-1933    │
                                       └──────────────────┘
     ┌──────────────────────┐
     │ Sarah "Sally" Jane Davies│
     │       1822-1847      │
     │  m. Robert T. Walker │
     │        ?-1847        │
     └──────────────────────┘
                        ┌──────────────────┐
                        │  Logan E. Davies │
                        │    1824-1894     │
                        │m. Frances Ann Vaughn│
                        │    1842-1866     │
                        └──────────────────┘
                                       ┌──────────────────┐
                                       │ Gillie M. Davies │
                                       │    1861-1933     │
                                       │m. Frances Ina Stewart│
                                       │    1863-1958     │
                                       └──────────────────┘
                                                 ┌──────────────────────┐
                                                 │ Frances Ellen Davies │
                                                 │      1903-1994       │
                                                 │ m. Hilman P. Rodgers │
                                                 │      1899-1976       │
                                                 └──────────────────────┘
┌──────────────────┐
│  Mary F. Davies  │
│    1820-1907     │
│  m. J.D. Scantlin│
│      ?-1859      │
└──────────────────┘
```

NOTES

PREFACE

1. Shirley Downing, "Birthday Party for 'Miss Ellen' to Celebrate 90th," *Commercial Appeal*, November 11, 1993; Shirley Downing, "Five Hundred Honor 'Miss Ellen' at 90th Birthday Fete," *Commercial Appeal*, November 14, 1993; Shirley Downing, "Ellen Davies-Rodgers Dies at 90; County Trailblazer, Philanthropist," *Commercial Appeal*, March 18, 1994.
2. Andy Meek, "The Belle of the (Wrecking) Ball: Davies Manor Land in Lakeland Area Gives Way to Gated Development," *Daily News*, July 27, 2006 (quote); Downing, "Birthday Party for 'Miss Ellen'" (quote); Kenneth Neill, "Mr. Crump: The Making of a Boss, *Memphis Magazine*, April 10, 2019 ("Godfather of Tennessee politics" quote), https://memphismagazine.com/features/mr-crump/; John H. Harkins, *Historic Shelby County: An Illustrated History* (San Antonio, TX: Historical Publishing Network, 2008), 22, 24; Shirley Downing, "Indelible Mark Left on Area by Colorful Davies-Rodgers," *Commercial Appeal*, March 24, 1994; Ellen Davies-Rodgers, *Along the Old Stage-Coach Road* (Brunswick, TN: Plantation Press, 1990) 81–82; Richard Lentz, "General's Campaign Mounts Line Attack," *Commercial Appeal*, April 10, 1969; Clay Bailey, "Landowner Pushing for Incorporation," *Commercial Appeal*, February 23, 1987, Memphis Information Files, Memphis and Shelby County Room, Memphis Public Library.
3. Downing, "Five Hundred Honor "Miss Ellen'"; John Branston, "Progress Bends for 'Miz Ellen,'" *Commercial Appeal*, July 1, 1990; Downing, "Ellen Davies-Rodgers Dies at 90."
4. Ellen Davies-Rodgers, *Turns Again Home: Life on an Old Tennessee Plantation Trespassed by Progress* (Brunswick, TN: Plantation Press, 1992), 26–59, 83–110, 201–205, 301–347. Regarding the subject of lore, see page 13–14, and the claim she "was descended from the founding fathers of the nation,

maternally and paternally." Similarly, Davies-Rodgers claimed she was a descendent of ancient kings through "The Davies of Gwysany," who "ranked for centuries among the first families of North Wales"; "Four Pilgrimages to Davies Manor in August," *Press Scimitar*, August 8, 1957; Alice Fulbright, "Event at Davies Manor Beckons Carnival Visitors," *Commercial Appeal*, May 27, 1979. The Memphis press coverage on Davies-Rodgers between the 1940s and the late 1990s is extensive. See the larger compilation of newspaper clippings found in the "Shelby County–Davies Plantation" folder, Memphis Information Files, Memphis and Shelby County Room, Memphis Public Library; Blackburn, N.C. to Mrs. Hillman P. Rodgers, February 11, 1948, Box 4, Folder 15, Ellen Davies-Rodgers Papers, Special Collections Department, University of Memphis; Mrs. H. W. Cooper to Paul Coppock, typescript (undated), Box 1, Old Stage Road Folder, Ida Cooper Collection, Memphis and Shelby County Room, Memphis Public Library; Historic American Buildings Survey, "Davies Manor: Photographs, Written Historical and Descriptive Data," HABS No. TN-183 (Washington, DC: National Park Service, 1972; edited 1985), 2. The cited information on the Historic American Buildings Survey is drawn from Antoinette G. van Zelm, Lydia B. Simpson, and Robert Katz, *Davies Manor Plantation Historic Structure Report*, prepared by the MTSU Center for Historic Preservation and submitted to the Davies Manor Association on October 1, 2021, 37, https://irp.cdn-website.com/2c253136/files/uploaded/Final-Davies-Manor-Report-with-All-Elements.pdf. This report was completed following a fifteen-month research initiative conducted via a Professional Services Partnership project between the CHP and the Davies Manor Historic Site. The "Historical Background and Context" section of the report resulted in a thirty-seven-page analysis of the DMA's institutional history and Ellen Davies-Rodgers that together marked the most authoritative treatment of Davies-Rodgers and the site's history to date. This comprehensive research that went into the report provided a crucial foundation for many of the conclusions and interpretations that appear in the preface and subsequent Chapters of this book. The author is especially indebted to the research and historical analysis provided by van Zelm, who, along with the CHP's director Dr. Carroll Van West, has a long history of researching Davies Manor; Brenda B. Watson, "'Miss Ellen': Ellen Davies-Rodgers," Tennessee Society, National Society Daughters of the American Revolution *Women in History* Project, 2003, last updated April 10, 2006, https://www.tndar.org/~zachariahdavies/missellen.htm.

5. Davies-Rodgers, *Turns Again Home*, 178–266; "Davies Plantation," Tennessee Century Farms Application, April 30, 1976, MTSU Center for Historic Preservation Files, Albert Gore Research Center at MTSU. Copy

of report accessed in Davies Manor Office Files. See also van Zelm, *Davies Manor Plantation Historic Structure Report*, 5; "'Cousin Ellen': Versatile, Controversial Shelby Leader Is Always Involved and 'Lives It Up,'" *Press Scimitar*, October 10, 1973, ("fiefdom" quote), Memphis Information Files, Memphis and Shelby County Room, Memphis Public Library.
6. Downing, "Five Hundred Honor."
7. Downing, "Ellen Davies-Rodgers Dies at 90."
8. Downing, "Indelible Mark"; James Chisum, "Miss Ellen Joins Other Shelby Pioneers in Hallowed Ground She Cherished," *Commercial Appeal*, March 20, 1994.
9. Downing, "Ellen Davies-Rodgers Dies at 90"; Davies-Rodgers, *Along the Old Stage-Coach Road*, 22–37; Davies-Rodgers, *Turns Again Home*, 198; "80-Year-Old Caretaker Mose Frazier Stands Proud Guard over the House Known to History As . . . Davies Manor," *Commercial Appeal Mid-South Magazine*, July 25, 1965, "Shelby County-Davies Manor" folder, Memphis Information Files, Memphis and Shelby County Room, Memphis Public Library.
10. Barbara Williams, "Mose Frazier Committee Report" and related files, 2012, Davies Manor Association Office Files; "Centuries Old Documents Reveal Connections to Historic Property," *Action 5 News*, May 11, 2012, https://www.actionnews5.com/story/18311997/old-documents-name-slaves-tied-to-mid-south/; van Zelm, "*Davies Manor Plantation Historic Structure Report*," 43. Between 2008 and 2012, the subcommittee formed by the DMA board, the Mose Frazier Committee, was chaired by volunteer researcher and Davies Plantation Estates resident Barabara Williams. Williams, working with DMA staffers and volunteers, interviewed more than two dozen African American individuals whose lived experiences and family histories intertwined with the Davies family either directly or tangentially. Along with discovering more about the twentieth-century African American experience at the Davies family's estate and in the surrounding communities, the committee worked to locate descendants of people the Davies family enslaved and establish a dialogue with them about the DMA's project. In a few cases, descendants (or people who were potentially descendants) were identified and initial contact was made. In the case of interviewee Roscoe McVay, whose family sharecropped land near Davies Plantation between the early 1900s and the 1940s, the committee's research resulted in the conclusion that one of McVay's enslaved ancestors, a woman named Lucinda, was the same "Lucinda" who appears (born in 1819) in William Early Davies's "1804, The ages of the Blacks" birth ledger, found in the DMA archives. This assertion and related information about McVay's ancestral connections to the Davies family were discussed in the *Action 5 News* story referenced above. Roscoe's son, Kevin McVay, participated at length in the genealogical research

efforts. (The younger McVay would later continue to work with myself and DMA staffers on genealogical research and serve on the DMA board of directors.) Beginning in 2017, I, along with Williams and other DMA staffers and volunteers, began to resume contact with certain individuals who were previously interviewed in order to expand those interviews, continue mapping African American genealogical threads, and, hopefully, definitively locate descendants of known people the Davies enslaved. Follow-up interviews were recorded with previously recorded subjects and added to the existing collection of African American oral histories held by the DMA. In two other instances, interviews were recorded with new subjects who shed more light on the African American community who worked on or immediately surrounding the Davies family's estate between the late nineteenth and mid-twentieth century. The goal of establishing contact with a wider network of people descended from the community enslaved by the Davies family in Shelby County remained a work in progress at the time the author left the DMA in 2022.

11. Jeanne C. Crawford, *The Davies Family: West Tennessee Pioneers* (Bartlett, TN: Davies Manor Association, 2009), 14. Along with the conclusions I drew through years of researching the DMA archives and DMA office files, and reviewing old minutes from the DMA board of directors meetings, my assertions are based on my firsthand experiences taking docent-led tours of the Davies Manor house museum and reviewing docent scripts during my initial months working for the DMA.

12. Paul Matthews to Harold Crawford (Jeanne Crawford), printout of email interview by Jeanne Crawford, August 19, 2009, Mose Frazier Committee files, DMA office files; Telephone Interview with Edward F. Williams III, Shelby County Historian, interview by Jeanne Crawford, October 12, 2009, typed transcript, Mose Frazier Committee files, DMA office files.

13. Davies-Rodgers, *Turns Again Home*, 178–199 (quote on interracial relationships, 178).

14. "Bridge Salutes Pioneers, Preservationists," *Memphis Press-Scimitar*, December 12, 1981. The quote in this article referencing *Gone with the Wind* was used in Emily Rosalind Schwimmer's 2011 University of Memphis MA thesis, *A Tale of Two Plantations: The Comparative Development of the Ensley and Davies Plantations in Shelby County, Tennessee, and the Museums that Interpret Them*, University of Memphis Digital Commons, https://digital commons.memphis.edu/etd/380/; Davies-Rodgers, *Along the Old Stage-Coach Road* ("workers employed" quote, 47); Davies-Rodgers, *Turns Again Home* (interracial relationships quote, 178; "faithful helper[s]" quote, 197; "days of innocence" and "citadel" quotes, 363).

15. Laurie B. Green, *Battling the Plantation Mentality* (Chapel Hill: University of North Carolina Press, 2007) (quote taken from title); Annie Mae

Frazier Blackwell Myles, interview by Andrew Ross, Nancy McDonough and Barbara Williams, August 25, 2017, "Oral History with Annie Mae," transcript, DMA archives and DMA office files; Andy Payne, Interview by Samantha Gibbs, Fall 2010, "Andy Payne Interview" transcript, DMA archives and DMA office files. In 2022, Payne accompanied me on a driving tour around the Davies Plantation Estates neighborhood and general vicinity. In the context of identifying former boundaries and notable landscape features of the Davies family's plantation, Payne discussed aspects of Ellen Davies-Rodgers's character and managerial style in terms that aligned closely with his 2010 recorded interview with the DMA. Along with the memories shared by Myles and Payne, the broader assertion about the exploitative climate at Davies-Rodgers's estate is based on comments made in other recorded oral histories and, in some cases, reading between the lines of memories about Davies-Rodgers shared with the Mose Frazier Committee or, more informally, in conversations with the author.
16. Annie Mae Frazier Blackwell Myles, interview by Andrew Ross, Nancy McDonough and Barbara Williams, August 25, 2017, DMA archives and DMA office files; Davies-Rodgers, *Turns Again Home*, 180.
17. Meek, "The Belle of the (Wrecking) Ball," *Daily News*, July 27, 2006; Perre Magness, *Past Times: Stories of Early Memphis* (Memphis, TN: Parkway Press, 1994), 131–34; Harkins, *Historic Shelby County*, 22, 24, 53–55, 60, 76, 110–11; Paul A. Matthews, ed., *Early Families of the Memphis Area* (Memphis, TN: Descendants of Early Settlers of Shelby and Adjoining Counties, 2008), 163–66.
18. "Mission Statement," Davies Manor Association, www.daviesmanor.org.
19. Noah Caldwell and Audie Cornish, "Where Do Confederate Monuments Go after They Come Down," *National Public Radio*, August 5, 2018, https://www.npr.org/2018/08/05/633952187/where-do-confederate-monuments-go-after-they-come-down.
20. Tiya Miles, *All That She Carried: The Journey of Ashley's Sack, a Black Family Keepsake* (New York: Random House, 2021), quote on 300.
21. Watson, "'Miss Ellen,'" ("Each of us is history" quote); Steve Gaither, "Guests Honor Rodgers for Serving 25 Years in County Historian Post," *Commercial Appeal*, October 11, 1990; Daina Ramey Berry, *The Price for Their Pound of Flesh* (Boston, MA: Beacon Press, 2017) 6–7, 61.

INTRODUCTION

1. "Short Illness Fatal to Dr. W. L. Davies," *Commercial Appeal*, May 5, 1931; "Century and a Half of Gracious Living," *Tennessee Conservationist*, December 1957. Article reprinted in Davies-Rodgers, *Turns Again Home*.

2. "Short Illness Fatal"; Dr. WLD Day Books, DMA archives; B. F. O'Daniel to Dr. W. L. Davies, December 6, 1882, W. L. Davies Correspondence 1865–1890, DMA archives; B. F. O'Daniel to Dr. W. L. Davies, February 23, 1883, W. L. Davies Correspondence 1865–1890, DMA archives; *Along the Old Stage-Coach Road*, 11, 130; *Turns Again Home*, 40–41. The day books for Dr. Davies contain frequent references to formerly enslaved people he administered treatments to. Among those listed in May 1912, for example, are Richmond Bennett and his family, Amos Davis, Arthur Ecklin, and Absolem Fields. The broader characterizations about Davies's medical practice have also been drawn based on references across his correspondence. The letters, most of which are addressed to Davies, are loosely organized in "W. L. Davies Correspondence 1865–1890," "W.L. Davies Correspondence 1891–1907," "W. L. Davies Correspondence 1908–1931," and "W.L. Davies Correspondence, Miscellaneous."

3. B.F. O'Daniel to Dr. W. L. Davies, February 23, 1883, DMA archives; Julia Ward to W. L. Davies, October 13, 1883, DMA archives; Julia Ward to W. L. Davies, January 1884, DMA archives; "Short Illness Fatal."

4. W. L. Davies to Julia Ward, March 1883, DMA archives; "Hotel Arrivals," *Memphis Daily Appeal*, July 17, 1885; Davies-Rodgers, *Turns Again Home*, 87.

5. "W. L. Davies to Suzy Gardiner," May 1891, DMA archives; Davies-Rodgers, *Turns Again Home*, 86–87; Lillian M. Harlow to W. L. Davies, September 1907, DMA archives.

6. W. L. Davies Correspondence 1865–1890, DMA archives; Sallie Hadley Finney to W. L. Davies, March 18, 1906, DMA archives; Sara Hadley Finney to W. L. Davies, July 2, 1908, DMA archives; W. L. Davies Correspondence 1908–1931, DMA archives. In particular, see L. E. Foster to W. L. Davies, August 18, 1917; L. E. Foster to W. L. Davies, September 8, 1917; and L. E. Foster to W. L. Davies, October 31, 1917.

7. W. L. Davies Correspondence, 1865–1890, DMA archives; W. L. Davies Correspondence, 1908–1931, DMA archives. In particular, see Sara (Sallie) Hadley Finney to W. L. Davies, July 2, 1908; Haddie Finney (Sallie Hadley Finney) to W. L. Davies, March 13, 1909; and Cousin Sallie (Sallie Hadley Finney) to W. L. Davies, August 31, 1918; Dr. William Little Davies, "Genealogical Notes, Queries and Answers," *Richmond Times Dispatch*, May 6, 1917; Davies-Rodgers, *Along the Old Stage-Coach Road*, 33.

8. Davies-Rodgers, *Turns Again Home*, 26–49.

9. Davies, "Genealogical Notes, Queries."

10. W. L. Davies Correspondence 1865–1890, DMA archives; W. L. Davies Correspondence 1891–1907, DMA archives; W. L. Davies Correspondence 1908–1931; W. L. Davies to unknown cousin (probably Sallie Hadley Finney), October 27, 1930, W. L. Davies Correspondence Miscellaneous, DMA archives. This lengthy letter written by Dr. Davies forms the basis for

much of the book's Introduction, including the assertion about the connections between the Davies and the Ecklin, Crenshaw, Feild, and Thurman families. Although the letter's first four pages have been lost, a close study of contextual clues throughout pages 5–14 (and cross-referencing those clues with Memphis newspapers from October 1930) have allowed me to reconstruct the date. The assertion that Sallie Hadley Finney was the probable recipient is based on the content and tone of numerous other letters known to be written by Finney to Davies.

11. Davies-Rodgers, *Turns Again Home*, 197; W. L. Davies to unknown cousin (probably Sallie Hadley Finney), October 27, 1930, DMA archives; W. L. Davies Correspondence 1908–1931, DMA archives; W. L. Davies letter draft, Brunswick, TN, to [Custodian of "Morning Grove Church and Cemetery], Lenow, TN, May 1929, DMA archives; "Genealogical Report for the Mose Frazier Committee, Richmond Bennett 1833–1915 by Tina Sansone," 2012, DMA office files; "Tucker Family Tree," compiled by Tina Sansone, Ancestry.com. The most up-to-date understandings of the Bennett and Tucker families and the connections between them comes from research conducted by the Memphis genealogist Tina Sansone on behalf of the Mose Frazier Committee, and later, in collaboration with the author and DMA volunteers during and following the development of the *Omitted in Mass* exhibit. I have used Sansone's research, in conjunction with the oral history–related findings compiled by Barbara Williams, who chaired of the Mose Frazier Committee, as a foundation for conducting additional research into the Bennett and Tucker families in the Shelby County Archives. My conversations (between 2017–2022) about the Tucker family with Sylvester Lewis, a member of the Shelby County Historical Commission and DMA board of directors also contributed to my general understanding of these two families in question.

12. Mrs. H. W. Cooper, "Stage Road," unpublished notes, (undated), Box 1, Old Stage Road Folder, Ida Cooper Collection, Memphis and Shelby County Room, Memphis Public Library; Davies-Rodgers, *Along the Old Stage-Coach Road*, 47.

13. United States Agricultural Census, 1860, Shelby County, Tennessee; United States Slave Schedule, 1860, Shelby County, Tennessee; "JBD Notebook with WLD Additions," 1861, DMA archives.

14. W. L. Davies Correspondence 1865–1890, DMA archives; Davies Rodgers, *Turns Again Home* 197; W. L. Davies to unknown cousin (probably Sallie Hadley Finney), October 27, 1930, DMA archives; W. L. Davies letter draft, Brunswick, TN, to [Custodian of "Morning Grove Church and Cemetery], Lenow, TN, May 1929, DMA archives.

15. W. L. Davies to unknown cousin (probably Sallie Hadley Finney), October 27, 1930, DMA archives; "Letter to Aunt Sallie from Your

Devoted niece Martha," August 10, 1917, W. L. Davies Correspondence 1908–1931, DMA archives.
16. W. L. Davies to unknown cousin (probably Sallie Hadley Finney), October 27, 1930, DMA archives; "Dr. William L. Davies Certificate of Commission as Assistant Surgeon-In-Chief, Sons of Confederate Veterans," June 6, 1931, certificate on display in Davies Manor house museum, Davies Manor Historic Site; Kevin Levin, *Searching For Black Confederates: The Civil War's Most Persistent Myth* (Chapel Hill: University of North Carolina Press, 2019).
17. "Tried to Try the Sheriff," *The Memphis Commercial*, October 20, 1893.
18. "Short Illness Fatal"; W. L. Davies to unknown cousin (probably Sallie Hadley Finney), October 27, 1930, DMA archives.
19. "Short Illness Fatal"; W. L. Davies Correspondence 1908–1931, DMA archives; Davies-Rodgers, *Turns Again Home*, 28.
20. W. L. Davies Correspondence, 1908–1931, DMA archives; Margarit (unknown) to W. L. Davies, January 22, 1931, DMA archives; W. L. Davies Death Certificate, May 5, 1931, Mississippi State Department of Health Vital Records.
21. W. L. Davies to unknown cousin (probably Sallie Hadley Finney), October 27, 1930, DMA archives.
22. W. L. Davies to unknown cousin.
23. W. L. Davies to unknown cousin.
24. W. L. Davies to unknown cousin.
25. W. L. Davies to unknown cousin.
26. W. L. Davies to unknown cousin; Davies-Rodgers, *Turns Again Home*, 87.
27. W. L. Davies to unknown cousin.
28. W. L. Davies to unknown cousin
29. W. L. Davies to unknown cousin
30. W. L. Davies Death Certificate, May 5, 1931, Mississippi State Department of Health Vital Records; Davies-Rodgers, *Turns Again Home*, 26–59; Davies-Rodgers, *Along the Old Stage-Coach Road*, 65–131.

CHAPTER 1

1. Richard R. Beeman, *The Evolution of the Southern Backcountry: A Case Study of Lunenburg County, Virginia 1746–1832* (Philadelphia: University of Pennsylvania Press, 1984) 14, 15–24; Landon C. Bell, "The Pioneers: Settlement and Development," in *The Old Free State: History of Lunenburg Cunty and Southside Virginia*, vol. 1 (Baltimore, MD: Genealogical Publishing Co., 1974; originally published 1927); Gareth Mark, "Mark Family Tree, Profile of Zachariah Davis (Ab. 1746–1828)," Ancestry.com. The genealogical profile of Zachariah Davies and his descendants that

forms the foundation for Part I was constructed following a series of email exchanges and document-sharing research conducted in 2021 between the author and Gareth Mark, a professional genealogist and distant descendant of Zachariah. I am indebted to Mark for his expertise working with eighteenth-century Virginia sources and for his extensive review of Lunenburg County records. Mark's finding that Zachariah Davis married Diana Blackstone (rather than Diana Abernathy, as Ellen Davies-Rodgers believed and claimed in her books) is the first time that assertion has appeared.

2. Beeman, *The Evolution of the Southern Backcountry*, 18; Landon C. Bell, *Cumberland Parish Lunenburg County, Virginia, 1746–1816 and Vestry Book, 1746–1816* (Richmond, VA: William Byrd Press, 1930), 527–28.
3. "Mark Family Tree, Profile of Zachariah Davis (Ab. 1746–1828)," Ancestry.com; Landon C. Bell, *Sunlight on the Southside: List of Tithes, Lunenburg County, Virginia, 1743–1783* (Philadelphia, PA: George S. Ferguson Co., 1931), 298, 333.
4. Beeman, *Evolution of the Southern Backcountry*, 120–139.
5. Beeman, *Evolution of the Southern Backcountry*, 129; John H. Wells, *Lunenburg's Unsung Heroes of the American Revolution: "A Peek through a Door Barely Left Ajar!,"* unpublished, n.d., 8. Accessed in Ripberger Public Library local history room, Lunenburg County Public Library System.
6. Davies Family Birth Records, n.d, DMA archives; "Mark Family Tree, Profile of Zachariah Davis (Ab. 1746–1828)"; Deed Book 13, p. 241–42, July 8, 1779, Lunenburg County, Virginia Circuit Court; Public Service Claim for Zachariah Davis, July 12, 1781, Box 1, DMA archives. The original Public Service Claims Court Booklets are housed in Public Service Claims, Record Group 48, Library of Virginia.
7. *Lunenburg County, Va. Tax Lists 1783 & 1784* (Melber, KY: Simmons Historical Publications, 1988) 6, 34; Gordon S. Wood., *The Radicalism of the American Revolution* (New York: Random House, 1992), 6–7.
8. Wood, *Radicalism of the American Revolution*, 6–8, 186; Joseph J. Ellis, *American Creation: Triumphs and Tragedies at the Founding of the Republic* (New York: Afred A. Knopf, 2007) 10.
9. Ellis, *American Creation*, 11.
10. Deed Book 15, pp. 331–33, December 13, 1788, Lunenburg County, Virginia Circuit Court; Deed Book 15 pp. 408–9, June 11, 1789, Lunenburg County, Virginia Circuit Court; Deed Book 15, pp. 409–11, June 11, 1789, Lunenburg County, Virginia Circuit Court; Deed Book 15, pp. 411–13, June 8, 1789, Lunenburg County, Virginia Circuit Court; Deed Book 16, p. 179, August 12, 1790, Lunenburg County, Virginia Circuit Court; Deed of Trust, Deed Book 16, pp. 427–29, February 13, 1794, Lunenburg County, Virginia Circuit Court.

11. Deed of Trust, Deed Book 16, pp. 427–29, February 13, 1794, Lunenburg County, Virginia Circuit Court.
12. Deed of Trust, Deed Book 16, pp. 427–29; *Lunenburg County, Virginia Personal Property Tax Lists 1782 & 1785* (Miami Beach, FL: T. L. C. Genealogy, 1992), 47; "An Inventory and appraisement of the Estate of Zachariah Davis deceased taken this the 14th day of November, 1828," Will Book 9, pp. 44, Lunenburg County, Virginia Circuit Court; "A Statement of the Slaves and Other Property Conveyed in Deed of Trust of 13 February 1794 and Its Value at That Time," Joel Neal & Wife vs. Zachariah Davis exrs., Chancery Records Index No. 1836–024, Virginia Memory, Library of Virginia, Microfilm Reel No. 104; "A Statement of the Increase of the Slaves up to the Year 1828 and What they Sold for then," Joel Neal & Wife vs. Zachariah Davis exrs., Chancery Records Index No. 1836–024, Virginia Memory, Library of Virginia, Microfilm Reel No. 104; "A Statement of Slaves of Increase Sold by the exers. in 1828," Joel Neal & Wife vs. Zachariah Davis exrs., Chancery Records Index No. 1836–024, Virginia Memory, Library of Virginia, Microfilm Reel No. 104.
13. Deed of Trust, Deed Book 16, pp. 427–429, February 13, 1794, Lunenburg County, Virginia Circuit Court.
14. Zachariah Davis Final Will, Will Book 9, pp. 337–339, June 6, 1827, Lunenburg County, Virginia Circuit Court.

CHAPTER 2

1. Zachariah Davis Final Will. Along with the information contained in his final will, my understandings about Zachariah's record of advancing enslaved people to his children are based on scattered references found in the depositions, property inventories, and other legal records associated with Joel Neal & Wife vs. Zachariah Davis exrs., and Joel Neal vs. Trst(s) of Zachariah Davis, Chancery Records Index No. 1847–013, Virginia Memory, Library of Virginia, Microfilm Reel No. 124.
2. "Coroner's Inquisition," March 9, 1809, Lunenburg County, Virginia Circuit Court.
3. Zachariah Davis to Robert Davis, June 21, 1821, Box 1, DMA archives. DMA archives
4. Ibid.
5. Earnestine Lovelle Jenkins, *Race, Representation & Photography in 19th-Century Memphis* (Surrey: Ashgate, 2016) 64.
6. Beeman, *Evolution of the Southern Backcountry*, 97–101, 113. Chapter 4, "The Evangelical Revolt in the Backcountry," provided crucial contextual understanding of the local religious environment in Lunenburg County.

7. Beeman, *Evolution of the Southern Backcountry*, 107; Bell, *The Old Free State*, 385; Fred Anderson, ed., *Baptists in Early America*, vol. 6: *Meherrin, Virginia* (Macon, GA: Mercer University Press, 2019) vii; Richard Beeman, "Social Change and Cultural Conflict in Virginia: Lunenburg County, 1746–1744," *William and Mary Quarterly* 35 (1978): 469.
8. Anderson, *Baptists in Early America*, viii, 27, 36, 1–173. Part II of *Baptists in Early America*, vol. 6, features a full transcription, with footnotes, of the Meherrin Baptist Church's record book between 1771–1844. The original record book is housed at the Virginia Baptist Historical Society; Bell, *The Old Free State*, 385; Beeman, "Social Change," 469–71.
9. Beeman, *Evolution of the Southern Backcountry*, 109–13.
10. Beeman, *Evolution of the Southern Backcountry*, 111. The Albert Raboteau quote that appears in Beeman's book comes from Raboteau's book *Slave Religion: The "Invisible Institution" in the Antebellum South* (New York: Oxford University Press, 2004); Berry, *The Price for Their Pound of Flesh*, 6–7, 61.
11. "The Petition of the Inhabitants of the County of Lunenburg," December 1, 1785, Library of Virginia, Microfilm; Beeman, *Evolution of the Southern Backcountry*, 145–50.
12. Beeman, *Evolution of the Southern Backcountry*, 188–94, 218–22; Fredrika Teute Schmidt and Barbara Ripel Wilhelm, "Early Proslavery Petitions in Virginia," *William and Mary Quarterly* 30 (1973): 133–46.
13. "To the Honorable the General Assembly of Virginia, The Remonstrance and Petition of the free Inhabitants of the County of Lunenburg," November 29, 1785, Library of Virginia, microfilm; Francis Asbury, *Journal of Rev. Francis Asbury: Bishop of the Methodist Episcopal Church*, vol. 3, from January 1, 1801 to December 7, 1815 (New York: Lane & Scott, 1852), 169.
14. John Wigger, "The Unexpected Leader," *Christian History Magazine*, no. 114 (2015): 4–11.
15. *Journal of Rev. Francis Asbury*, vol. 3, 169; Robert Davis to William E. Davis, October 16, 1801, DMA archives. This letter from Robert Davis is addressed to "William Davis, Preacher of the Gospel, Hanover Circuit"; "Mrs. Eleanor Davis," *Genealogical Information from The Western Methodist, 1833–1834*, compiled by Jonathan Kennon Thompson Smith, 2003. The obituary for Eleanor Davis, dated July 11, 1834, states that she became a member of the Methodist Episcopal Church in Williamson County, Tennessee, in 1803 and was living there with her husband Robert Davis by that point; "License as a Minister," September 8, 1803, DMA archives; Davies-Rodgers, *Turns Again Home*, 12.
16. Zachariah Davis to William Davis, January 11, 1804, DMA archives; Zachariah Davis to William Davis, November 17, 1823, DMA archives.
17. Donald Scott, "Evangelicalism, Revivalism, and the Second Great Awakening," National Humanities Center, October 2000, https://nationalhumanitiescenter.org/tserve/nineteen/nkeyinfo/nevanrev.htm.

18. Daniel Walker Howe, *What Hath God Wrought* (New York: Oxford University Press, 2007) 140; Adam Rothman, *Slave Country: American Expansion and the Origins of the Deep South* (Cambridge, MA: Harvard University Press, 2005) 4; Scott, "Evangelicalism, Revivalism," 2000.
19. "Mrs. Eleanor Davis," *Genealogical Information from The Western Methodist, 1833–1834*, Compiled by Jonathan Kennon Thompson Smith, 2003; Bell, *The Old Free State*, 389; Howe, *What Hath God Wrought*, 177; Mark Holloway, *Heavens on Earth: Utopian Communities in America, 1680–1880* (United Kingdom: Dover Publications, 1966), 69; Paul K. Conkin, *Cane Ridge: America's Pentecost* (Madison: University of Wisconsin Press, 1990), 115.
20. Robert Davis to William E. Davis, October 16, 1801, DMA archives.
21. John Berry M'Ferrin, *History of Methodism in Tennessee: vol. 2, 1804–1818* (Nashville, TN: Southern Methodist Publishing House, 1872) 279–281; "Mrs. Eleanor Davis," *Genealogical Information from The Western Methodist, 1833–1834*, compiled by Jonathan Kennon Thompson Smith, 2003; Williamson County Tax Book, 1803, p. 40, Maury County Archives.
22. John Berry M'Ferrin, *History of Methodism in Tennessee, vol. 3: From the Year 1818 to the Year 1840* (Nashville, TN: Southern Methodist Publishing House, 1873), 9, 263.
23. Charity R. Carney, *Ministers and Masters: Methodism, Manhood, and Honor in the Old South* (Baton Rouge: Lousiana State University Press, 2011), 4, 119–126.
24. "The separate answer of William E. Davis to the Bill of complaint . . . ," Joel Neal & Wife vs. Zachariah Davis exrs., Chancery Records Index No. 1836-024, pp. 11–14, Library of Virginia; "The separate answer of Sterling Davis to the Bill of Complaint . . .," Joel Neal & Wife vs. Zachariah Davis exrs., pp. 15–20, Library of Virginia; Zachariah Davis Final Will, Will Book 9, pp. 337–339, Lunenburg County, Virginia Circuit Court. An understanding of the advancements made by Zachariah Davis to his children in 1816 comes about from cross referencing the above two depositions from William E. Davis and Sterling Davis, Zachariah's final will, and other scattered references found in Joel Neal & Wife vs. Zachariah Davis exrs.
25. Zachariah Davis Final Will, Will Book 9, pp. 337–39, June 6, 1827, Lunenburg County, Virginia Circuit Court; "The separate answer of William E. Davis," Joel Neal & Wife vs. Zachariah Davis exrs.; "The separate answer of Sterling Davis," Joel Neal & Wife vs. Zachariah Davis exrs.; "A Statement of the Increase of the Slaves up to the year 1828 and What they sold for then," Joel Neal & Wife vs. Zachariah Davis exrs., p. 11.
26. Annette Gordon-Reed, *The Hemingses of Monticello* (New York: W. W. Norton, 2008) 293.

Notes to Pages 41–46   319

CHAPTER 3

1. William E. Davis to Robert Davis, May 1, 1803, DMA archives; Robert Davis to William E. Davis, August 14, 1803, DMA archives.
2. United States Census, 1820, Franklin County, Tennessee.
3. United States Census, 1830, Franklin County, Tennessee; Tax Records, 1838, Williamson County, Tennessee; M'Ferrin, *History of Methodism in Tennessee: vol. 2, 1804–1818*, 279–81; Rev. Robert Davis obituary, *Western Weekly Review*, April 23, 1857, Williamson County Obituary Records, Book 18, p. 239, Williamson County Archives.
4. Berry, *The Price for Their Pound of Flesh*, 11.
5. Davies Family Birth Records, n.d., DMA archives; Davies-Rodgers, *Turns Again Home*, 14; Beeman, *Evolution of the Southern Backcountry*, 35–37, 60, 167–170; Gay Weeks Neale, *The Lunenburg Legacy* (Lunenburg, VA: Lunenburg County Historical Society, 2005) 42–46.
6. Ann M. Vaughan to William Davis, November 12, 1801, DMA archives.
7. "Office of Deacon Recommendation," March 2, 1802, DMA archives; "License as a Minister," September 8, 1803, DMA archives; Bell, *The Old Free State*, 397; Davies-Rodgers, *Turns Again Home*, 12–13; Jeremiah Burnett Final Will, December 18, 1812, Will Books, pp. 73–75, Lunenburg County, Virginia Circuit Court; "1804, The ages of the Blacks" DMA archives; William Davis vs. Zachariah Davis, Chancery Records Index No. 1816–019, Microfilm Reel No. 77, Library of Virginia.
8. William Davis vs. Zachariah Davis, Chancery Records Index No. 1816–019, Microfilm Reel No. 77, Library of Virginia; Jeremiah Burnett Final Will, December 18, 1812, Will Books, pp. 73–75, Lunenburg County, Virginia Circuit Court.
9. William Davis vs. Zachariah Davis, Chancery Records Index No. 1816–019, Microfilm Reel No. 77, Library of Virginia; "The separate answer of Sterling Davis . . . ," Joel Neal & Wife vs. Zachariah Davis exrs.
10. Davies-Rodgers, *Turns Again Home*, 12–13; Deed Book 24, pp. 462–63, November 11, 1818, Lunenburg County Virginia, Circuit Court. The approximate timeline of Joanna Burnett Davies's death and William E. Davies's relocation to Tennessee has been reconstructed by cross referencing the above two sources with circumstantial evidence and clues found in the depositions recorded in Joel Neal and Wife vs. Zachariah Davis exrs lawsuit. Additionally, the January 4, 1818, birthdate for Wil[l]shire (Tucker), which William recorded in his "1804, The ages of the Blacks" ledger, lists "Mury County" as the location of Wil[l]shire's birth. And a brief account of the Davies Family, penned by the Fayette County genealogist William S. Farley, and found in the local history room of the Fayette County Library, states, "William Earl Davies was born in Lunenburg County,

320 Notes to Pages 47–51

Virginia in 1779. After the death of his first wife he moved to Maury County, Tennessee where he met and married Sarah Hadley in 1819."

11. "1804, The ages of the Blacks," DMA archives.
12. Davies-Rodgers, *Turns Again Home*, 11–14; William E. Davies and Sarah Hadley, December 14, 1819, Maury County Marriage Records, Maury County Archives; United States Census, 1820, Maury County, Tennessee; Samuel D. McMahon to William E. Davis, Deed Book G-1, p. 528, September 12, 1818, Maury County Archives; William Early Davies Correspondence, DMA archives; Receipt for delivery of cotton to James P. Peters, May 27, 1827, DMA archives.
13. Zachariah Davis to William Davis, January 11, 1804, DMA archives.
14. United States Census, 1820, Lunenburg County, Virginia; Joel Neal & Wife vs. Zachariah Davis exrs., p. 7; Southside Virginia Genealogical Society, *The Heritage of Lunenburg County, Virginia 1743–2009* (Marceline, MO: Walsworth Publishing Co., 2009), 309.
15. Zachariah Davis to Robert Davis, June 21, 1821, DMA archives; Zachariah Davis to William Davis, November 17, 1823.
16. Bell, *The Old Free State*, 420; United States Census, 1820, Lunenburg County, Virginia; Joel Neal & Wife vs. Zachariah Davis exrs. The background information and assertions about Joel Neal are based on Joel's own depositions and letters, as well as references to his character scattered throughout other parties' depositions included in the case. Henrietta is discussed in both William and Sterling Davis's depositions.
17. Joel Neal & Wife vs. Zachariah Davis exrs., p. 7–9; "The deposition of Henry Tisdale," Joel Neal & Wife vs. Zachariah Davis exrs. In addition to the information found in these two documents, references to Jinny being taken to Tennessee by Joel Neal are made throughout the depositions, inventory, and financial records included in the case.
18. Joel Neal & Wife vs. Zachariah Davis, pp. 20–23; "The deposition of Henry Tisdale," Joel Neal & Wife vs. Zachariah Davis.
19. Zachariah Davis Final Will; Joel Neal & Wife vs. Zachariah Davis exrs., pp. 20–23.
20. Zachariah Davis Final Will; "An Inventory and appraisement of the Estate of Zachariah Davis Dec'd, taken this the 14th day of November 1828," Will Book 9, pp. 444–49, Lunenburg County, Virginia Circuit Court; "An account of the Sales of the Estate of Zachariah Davis dec'd made 26 of November 1828 by James Bagley & Thomas Keeton, executors," Will Book 10, pp. 174–86, Lunenburg County, Virginia Circuit Court.
21. Zachariah Davis Final Will, Will Book 9, pp. 337–39, June 6, 1827, Lunenburg County, Virginia Circuit Court.

Notes to Pages 53–58   321

CHAPTER 4

1. Eliza Anne Davis by William E. Davis her guardian vs. Hardy Sellars, Maury County Circuit Court, 1828, Microfilm, pp. 1–50, Loose Records from Maury Couty Circuit Court, Maury County Archives. The page numbers associated with this lawsuit are based on my scans from the loose records folder as they appear in the county's microfilm rolls.
2. "1804, The ages of the Blacks," DMA archives; Eliza Anne Davis by William E. Davis, her guardian vs. Hardy Sellars, pp. 1–6; Davies-Rodgers, *Turns Again Home*, 113, 198; Davies-Rodgers, *Along the Old Stage-Coach Road*, 29.
3. State of Tennessee vs. William D. Mitchell, Maury County Circuit Court, 1828, microfilm, pp. 1–36, Maury County Archives.
4. State of Tennessee vs. William D. Mitchell, pp. 25–27, Maury County Archives; Eliza Anne Davis by William E. Davis, her guardian vs. Hardy Sellars, pp. 1–50, Maury County Archives.
5. Eliza Anne Davis by William E. Davis, 7–15, 40–50.
6. Eliza Anne Davis by William E. Davis, 40–50; George S. Yerger, *Reports of Cases Argued and Determined in the Supreme Court of Tennessee during the Year 1833*, vol. 4 (Nashville, TN: Hall and Heiskell, State Printers, 1834), 503–6.
7. Paschal W. Davis to William E. Davis, October 13, 1828, DMA archives; Davies, "Genealogical Notes, Queries"; "A Statement of the Increase of the Slaves up to the Year 1828 and What they Sold for then," Joel Neal & Wife vs. Zachariah Davis exrs.; "A Statement of Slaves of Increase Sold by the exers. in 1828," Joel Neal & Wife vs. Zachariah Davis exrs.
8. Joel Neal & Wife vs. Zachariah Davis exrs.
9. "The separate answer of William E. Davis . . . ," Joel Neal & Wife vs. Zachariah Davis exrs.; "The separate answer of Sterling Davis . . . ," Joel Neal & Wife vs. Zachariah Davis exrs. See also Joel Neal & Wife vs. Zachariah Davis, pp. 123–30.
10. Joel Neal to James Neal, undated, Joel Neal & Wife vs. Zachariah Davis exrs. Joel Neal's quotes and characterizations of the Davis family primarily come from three of his letters to James Neal, penned between 1832–1833. The documents that are part of the Joel Neal & Wife vs. Zachariah Davis exrs. lawsuit are unnumbered as they appear in the scanned microfilm records. I captured the records in 148 scanned pages. These letters from Joel appear in pp. 30–36 of 148.
11. Joel Neal to James Neal, undated.
12. Joel Neal to James Neal, undated, pp. 134–48.
13. Joel Neal vs. Trustees of Zachariah Davis, Index No. 1847-013, LVA Microfilm No. 124, pp. 1–14.
14. Joel Neal & Wife vs. Zachariah Davis exrs, pp. 103–48; Joel Neal vs. Trustees of Zachariah Davis, pp. 1–14; Lunenburg County Fiduciary Book

No. 2, 1855–1859, pp. 82–83, 88–91, 154–58, 218–19, 403–10, 562; Lunenburg County Fiduciary Book, No. 3, 1859–1863, pp. 19–20, 77, 208, 230, 321, 359, 479, 497–98; Lunenburg County Fiduciary Book No. 4, 1864–1868, pp. 101, 108.

CHAPTER 5

1. United States Census, 1830, Maury County, Tennessee; Maury County Tax Records, 1836; The assertion about the approximate size of William Davis's landholdings in 1830 is based on a review of land deed records prior to 1830 and the 1836 tax records.
2. William Davis His Book, August, 9, 1809, Lunenburg, Box 9, Loose Papers, DMA archives.
3. *Maury County Tennessee History and Families* (Columbia, TN: Maury County Historical Society, 1998). See section on Maury County early history by Bob Duncan; Marise P. Lightfoot, "Maury County," October 8, 2017, Tennessee Encyclopedia, Tennessee Historical Society.
4. Nathaniel Cheairs Hughes, *The Life and Wars of Gideon J. Pillow* (Knoxville: University of Tennessee Press, 1993), xvii–xviii; James M. Pukl Jr., "James K. Polk's Early Congressional Campaigns of 1825 and 1827," *Tennessee Historical Quarterly* 39 (1980): 440–58; Samuel D. McMahon to William E. Davis, Deed Book G-1, pp. 528, September 12, 1818, Maury County Archives; William E. Davis vs. Dickey Chappel, 1843, Maury County Circuit Court, Microfilm, Maury County Archives.
5. Anonymous Informant to William E. Davis, 1836, transcribed letter, DMA office files. The transcribed version of the original letter is included in a DMA office files folder that contains a loosely organized selection of key correspondence and business records from the DMA archives. The records in the folder were compiled and transcribed in the early 2000s by DMA staffers and volunteers. The location of the original letter is unclear; W. W. Davis to William E. Davis, October 13, 1838, DMA archives; Census Report of San Augustine, Blake Collection, vol. XIX, pp. 328–339, Nacogdoches Archives, vol. 85, pp. 301–16, 1835, web.
6. Anonymous Informant to William E. Davis, 1836.
7. William W. "W.W." Davies to Wm. E. Davies, Bill of Sale, February 1, 1837, DMA archives.
8. W.W. Davies to Wm. E. Davies, October 13, 1838, DMA archives.
9. John W. Younger to William E. Davis, Bill of Sale, November 13, 1838, DMA archives.
10. United States Census, 1830, Hopkins County, Kentucky; United States Census, 1840, Hopkins County, Kentucky; Chase C. Mooney, *Slavery in Tennessee* (Westbrook, CT: Negro Universities Press, 1957), 18–19, 38–39, 44; Lester C. Lamon, *Blacks in Tennessee, 1791–1970* (Knoxville: Tennessee

Historical Commission and University of Tennessee Press, 1981), 9, 22; Clayton E. Jewett and John O. Allen, *Slavery in the South: A State-by-State History* (Westport, CT: Greenwood Press, 2004), 229.
11. United States Census, 1840, Maury County, Tennessee; William E. Davis vs. Dickey Chappel, 1842, Maury County Circuit Court Loose Files, Maury County Archives; Dicky Chappel vs. William E. Davis, 1842, Maury County Circuit Court Loose Files, Maury County Archives; State vs. Dicky Chappel, 1842, Maury County Circuit Court Loose Files, Maury County Archives; State vs. William E. Davis, et al, 1842, Maury County Circuit Court Loose Files, Maury County Archives.
12. Fragment of deposition by William E. Davis, 1842, Box 6, Lawsuits folder, DMA archives. This document has been damaged by time, is very difficult to decipher, and has not been located in the Maury County archives. Yet it appears to reference 1832, and to have been penned by William E. Davis during the 1842 court proceedings.
13. Deposition by William E. Davis, William E. Davis vs. Dickey Chappel, 1842.
14. Deposition by Dickey Chappell, Dickey Chappel vs. William E. Davis, 1842.
15. Stephanie M. H. Camp, *Closer to Freedom: Enslaved Women and Everyday Resistance in the Plantation South* (Chapel Hill: University of North Carolina Press, 2004), 6.
16. Deposition by Dickey Chappell, Dickey Chappel vs. William E. Davis, 1842.
17. Camp, *Closer to Freedom*, 1–2.
18. Gideon J. Pillow to Rev. William E. Davis, April 29, 1843, DMA archives; Gideon J. Pillow to William E. Davis, June 6, 1843, DMA archives; Gideon J. Pillow to William E. Davis, August 28, 1843; DMA archives; Gideon J. Pillow to William E. Davis, Deed, October 21, 1843, Deed Book L, pp. 458, Fayette County Archives. This land deed recorded in Fayette County confirms that Davies and Pillow originally entered into an article of agreement about the land swap in January 1843.
19. Robert Walker to William E. Davies, March 1843, DMA archives; Gideon J. Pillow to William E. Davis, Deed, October 21, 1843.
20. Robert Walker to William E. Davies, June 8, 1843, DMA archives.
21. Robert Walker to William E. Davies.
22. Robert Walker to William E. Davies.

CHAPTER 6

1. Gary T. Edwards, "In and Out of the Chickasaw Cession: Understanding Migrational Pressure and Economic Transition on Tennessee's Final Frontier, 1818–1860," *Tennessee Historical Quarterly* 65, no. 2 (2006): 106–29.
2. John R. Finger, *Tennessee Frontiers: Three Regions in Transition* (Bloomington: Indiana University Press, 2001), 6–7, 240; Joseph S. Williams, *Old Times in*

West Tennessee (Memphis, TN: W. G. Cheeney, 1873), 273–74; Samuel Cole Williams, *Beginnings of West Tennessee: In the Land of the Chickasaws, 1541–1841* (Johnson City, TN: The Watauga Press, 1930) 95–97.
3. Williams, *Beginnings of West Tennessee*, 84–86, 102; Edwards, "In and Out of the Chickasaw Cession," 116, 121–22.
4. Cailin Elise Meyer, "Landscape and the Planter Ideal: Planter Class Formation in Fayette County, 1825–1860," BA Honors Paper, Rhodes College, 2010, 13; Edwards, "In and Out of the Chickasaw Cession," 108, 114; Williams, *Old Times in West Tennessee*, 273–74.
5. Edwards, "In and Out of the Chickasaw Cession," 118–22; Polk Memorial Association Collection of James Knox Polk (1795–1849) Papers 1780–1972, Tennessee State Library and Archives, Finding Aid, pp. 3; Sean Wilentz, *The Rise of American Democracy: Jefferson to Lincoln* (New York: W. W. Norton, 2005), 770.
6. Mooney, *Slavery in Tennessee*, 101–22, 189, 201.
7. "United States Census, 1840, Maury County, Tennessee; "1804, The ages of the Blacks," DMA archives; United States Slave Schedule, 1850, Fayette County, Tennessee; Mooney, *Slavery in Tennessee*, 189.
8. "The ages of the Blacks," DMA archives; Jeremiah Burnett Final Will, December 18, 1812, Will Books, pp. 73–75, Lunenburg County, Virginia Circuit Court; "Fayette County commissioners to allot off the Negroes belonging to William E. Davies," February 7, 1862, DMA archives. These are among the key records that have been used to make the assertions about Patta and Frankey's continued presence at William Davies's estate between the late eighteenth and mid-nineteenth centuries. See also Robert Walker correspondence to William E. Davies, DMA archives, and 1860 Federal Slave Schedule and Population Census data for William E. Davies's household; Edward E. Baptist, "Stol' and Fetched Here": Enslaved Migration, Ex-slave Narratives, and Vernacular History," in *New Studies in the History of American Slavery*, ed. Edward E. Baptist and Stephanie M. H. Camp, 243–266 (Athens: University of Georgia Press, 2006).
9. Baptist, "Stol' and Fetched Here," 243, ("explosive expansion," 248).
10. Baptist, "Stol' and Fetched Here" ("devastating separation," 245; "spoke a history," 243).
11. Baptist, "Stol' and Fetched Here" ("who they were," 249; "interpreters and synthesizers," 264);
12. Gideon J. Pillow to Willam E. Davies, April 29, 1843, DMA archives.
13. Gideon J. Pillow to Willam E. Davies, April 29, 1843, DMA archives; Gideon J. Pillow to Willam E. Davies, June 6, 1843, DMA archives; Gideon J. Pillow to William E. Davis, deed, October 21, 1843, Deed Book L, pp. 458, Fayette County Archives.

14. William E. Davies Cotton Receipt, Mosby and Hunt, December 11, 1843, DMA archives. A general understanding of William's business activities and preferred consignment firms for his cotton has been gleaned from a holistic reading of the many cotton receipts in the DMA archives.
15. William E. Davies Receipt, Mosby and Hunt, September 21, 1848, DMA archives; William E. Davies receipts, 1840s, DMA archives.
16. William E. Davies Cotton Receipts, Mosby and Hunt, January 1847, April 1, 1847, April 24, 1847, DMA archives; Camp, *Closer to Freedom*, 6, 12–20; Andrew C. Ross, Exhibit Consultation meeting with Susan O'Donovan, 2018.
17. Carolyn Pittman, "Memphis in the Mid-1840's: Memphis Before the Mexican War," *West Tennessee Historical Society Papers* 23 (1969): 30–44; Andrew S. Edson, "How Nineteenth Century Travelers Viewed Memphis Before the Civil War," *West Tennessee Historical Society Papers* 24 (1970): 30–40.
18. Gene Dattel, *Cotton and Race in the Making of America* (Chicago: Ivan R. Dee, 2009), 46; Pittman, "Memphis in the Mid-1840's," 42; Edson, "How Nineteenth Century Travelers," 35–37.
19. *Memphis Daily Eagle*, April 26, 1847, see advertisements; *Daily Enquirer*, April 23, 1847, see advertisements.
20. *Appeal*, April 24, 1847.
21. Pittman, "Memphis in the Mid-1840s," 41–44; Jenkins, "Before Photography"; G. Wayne Dowdy, *Enslavement in Memphis* (Columbia, SC: The History Press, 2021).
22. Dowdy, *Enslavement in Memphis*; "NEGROES! NEGROES!," *Daily Enquirer*, February 27, 1847.
23. Milton Draper and Ridley Roberts to William E. Davies, bill of sale, April 22, 1850, DMA archives.
24. Milton Draper and Ridley Roberts to William E. Davies, bill of sale, April 22, 1850, DMA archives.

CHAPTER 7

1. Van Zelm, "Davies Manor Plantation Historic Structure Report," 4–11. The 200-acre tract purchased by Logan Davies in 1849 had previously been surveyed for one George E. Hunter in 1838. For more background on this piece of land, see entry number 572 in Shelby County Survey Book B., pp. 77, 207. See also Shelby County Deed Book D, p. 281, Shelby County Register of Deeds. Referring to the 1849 purchase by Logan, Van Zelm, Simpson, and Katz write in their report, "This transaction took place in response to a recent law passed by the State of Tennessee in an effort to

correct some fraudulent claims and confusion over occupancy claims. The law allowed occupants to lay claims to lands which they had been living on or improving, suggesting that Logan Davies (and possibly his younger brother James, as well as enslaved people) had been working on the property while still members of their father's household in Fayette County. Further insight into this land comes from a mortgage indenture made by George E. Hunter in 1833, which describes the 'land on which he now lives' along with a bed and bedstead, a press, a clock, and livestock as securities for a loan to be paid by January 1, 1834. If he failed to pay the loan on time, trustee William A. Bryan was to sell the property at public auction. The description indicates Hunter likely had a house on the property, which the Davies brothers may have been living in while improving the land in the 1840s." For the likelihood that Joel W. Royster would have utilized enslaved labor for construction of his home(s) and related work after arriving in Shelby County, see his household's data as enumerated in the 1830, 1840, and 1850 U.S. population census, and in the 1850 slave schedule.

2. William E. Davies's cotton and business receipts, 1846–1851, DMA archives; Partial note in William E. Davies's handwriting regarding previous advancements of slaves, n.d., DMA archives. See a transcription of this note in the DMA office files summary of records binder; United States Slave Schedule, 1850, Shelby County Tennessee; United States Slave Schedule, 1860, Shelby County, Tennessee; United States Agricultural Census, 1850, Shelby County, Tennessee.

3. United States Census, 1870, Shelby County, Tennessee; "Davies Family Birth Records"; "Tucker Family Tree."

4. United States Slave Schedule, 1850, Fayette County, Tennessee; "1804, The ages of the Blacks."

5. William E. Davies to M. L. Williams, promissory note, January 14, 1851, DMA archives; United States Census, 1850, Shelby County, Tennessee.

6. United States Census, 1850, Shelby County, Tennessee; United States Census, 1860, Shelby County, Tennessee; Logan Davies to Matthew W. Webber, promissory note, December 25, 1859, DMA archives; United States Census, 1840, Shelby County, Tennessee; United States Census, 1860, Fayette County, Tennessee. See data on Matthew W. Webber in 1840 and 1850 Shelby County census records and the 1860 household location of Webber in Fayette County in proximity to William E. Davies's estate. See Jane Howles Hooker, *Neighbors along the Wolf: History of Bethany Christian Church* (Memphis: Self-Published, 2004), 27–34, for a sketch on Webber and more general information about the Fisherville community; Frederick Arthur Hodge, *The Plea and the Pioneers of Virginia: A History of the Rise and Early Progress of the Disciples of Christ Church in Virginia* (Richmond, VA: Everett Waddey Co., 1905), 49; E. C. Leake and M. L. Williams to Logan

Davies, promissory note, January 1, 1863, DMA archives; Matthews, ed., *Early Families of the Memphis Area*, 245–50; Ida Cooper Collection, Box 2, Folders 10, 8, 21, 28; Box 5, Folder 33; Box 12, Folders 10, 44. These folders from Boxes 2, 5, and 12 primarily cover the Leake and Royster families and were crucial in helping me reconstruct the local world surrounding the Davies family. However, beyond these above-named folders, references and information found throughout Ida Cooper's extensive fifteen box collection have been used to inform my general understanding of the historical communities of northeast Shelby County, in particular, Morning Sun. See also folders pertaining to the Crenshaw family, Davies Manor and the Davies family, the Ecklin family, the Feild family, the Gray family, Morning Sun Cemetery and Morning Sun Cumberland Presbyterian Church, and "Stage Road-Old road"; References to Markum, Robert, and Charles Williams are scattered throughout business records, receipts, and scraps of notes in the DMA archives. The information about the roles Charles and Markum Williams played as guardians for Almeda Little after William Little's death (subjects that are discussed in Chapters 8 and 9) came from the probate records of William Little, found in the Shelby County Archives. See also Little, *The Family History and Genealogy of William Little*. A sampling of the more obscure secondary texts that informed my understanding of northeast Shelby County, helped me develop Chapters 8 and 9, and, more generally, feel confident in building a narrative that emphasizes the importance of the business and personal relationships that existed between the Davies family and those families who appear in this book (and likewise, the Black families that each of these white planter families enslaved) includes: *A History of Fisherville and A History of the Fisherville Civil Club*, compiled by Suzanne Schaeffer (Self-published, 1981); Dr. Catherine Wilson, *A History of Chambers Chapel United Methodist Church and Cemetery* (Self-published, 1998); Catherine Wilson, *The Story of Orion Hill* (Arlington, TN: Self-published, 2019); Davies-Rodgers, *Along the Old Stage-Coach Road* and *Turns Again Home*; Perre Magness, *Good Abode: 19th Century Architecture in Memphis and Shelby County, Tennessee* (Memphis, TN: Junior League of Memphis, 1983); Earnest Edward Lacey, *The Search for Free Joe* (Memphis, TN: Free Joe Publications, 1999).
7. Ann C. Royster Thurman Probate Records, 1842, Shelby County Archives; Wilson, *The Story of Orion Hill 18–26, 44–53*; Joel W. Royster, land deed records, Shelby County Archives; United States Census, 1830, Shelby County, Tennessee; Ida Cooper Collection, Royster family folders.
8. My assertions about Morning Sun in this section are based on a holistic study of the DMA archives in conjunction with more general understandings drawn from a range of secondary sources, in particular, Camp, *Closer to Freedom*, 1–11; Dylan C. Penningroth, "My People, My People: The

Dynamics of Community in Southern Slavery," in Baptist and Camp, *New Studies in the History of American Slavery*, 167.

9. Penningroth, "My People, My People," 167.

CHAPTER 8

1. Wilentz, *The Rise of American Democracy*, 319–21, 375–79, quotations on 644–46.
2. Howe, Daniel Walker, *What Hath God Wrought*, see chapter 6, "Overthrowing the Tyranny of Distance"; see "JBD" (James Baxter Davies) notebooks, Book 1–6, DMA archives for mentions of his travels by train to Texas.
3. Darlene Hooker Sawyer and James A. Waddell, *Forgotten Days of Farms, Flowers and Fellowship in Cordova, Tennessee* (Collierville, TN: InstantPublisher.com, 2015); My understanding of the day-to-day business activities that concerned the Davies family and other planter families they intersected was informed by files in the Quarterly Court Loose Papers Index, 1820–1865, Shelby County Archives. See index number files associated with "ML Williams," "R. Field," "JB Davis," "Logan Davis," "HN Davis," "Henry N Davis," "Joel W Royster," and "Thomas B Crenshaw," among others.
4. See promissory notes and receipts for hiring and hiring out enslaved people, 1851–1865, in DMA archives. Some notes/receipts are found in the "Slave Records" folder, while others are scattered in folders containing cotton receipts. Notations about hiring and hiring out enslaved people are also scattered in JBD Books 1–7, DMA archives.
5. Berry, *The Price for Their Pound of Flesh*, 78–80; Gordon-Reed, *The Hemingses of Monticello*, 318–20 (quotation on 319).
6. Stephanie M. H. Camp, "The Pleasures of Resistance: Enslaved Women and Body Politics in the Plantation South, 1830–1861," *Journal of Southern History* 68, no. 3 (Aug., 2002), 533–72, 535. https://doi.org/10.2307/3070158. 88.
7. W. L. Davies to unknown cousin (probably Sallie Hadley Finney), October 27, 1930, DMA archives; See endnote 8 in the previous chapter for more on the sources that informed my understanding of planter families from Morning Sun. My understanding of political sentiments, including Thomas B. Crenshaw's, was drawn largely from people's appearances in Memphis newspapers during the debates over secession and after the Civil War; Robert Ecklin to Sallie Ecklin, November 19, 1850, John P. and Sallie Ecklin Thurman Papers, Folder 2 ("multiply and replenish"); For connections between the mentality of Southern planters and notions of Manifest Destiny, see Howe, *What Hath God Wrought*, 702–8, 752,762, and Amy S.

Greenberg, *A Wicked War: Polk, Clay, Lincoln, and the 1846 U.S. Invasion of Mexico* (New York: Vintage Books, 2012), 55, 62.

8. Davies-Rodgers, *Turns Again Home*, 41, 46, 49; Wilson, *The Story of Orion Hill*, 19, 45 (quote on Orion Hill, 19, is taken by Wilson from Davies-Rodgers, *The Holy Innocents*, 43); Ida Cooper Collection, Box 2, Folders 21 & 28 and Box 12, Folder 44. For more on Royster, see van Zelm, "Davies Plantation Historic Structure Report," 7–9.

9. Matthews, ed., *Early Families of the Memphis Area*, 247–48 (quotes on 247); da Cooper Collection. See folders on Royster and Leake families.

10. See endnote 8 in previous Chapter for more on the sources that informed my general understandings of the relationships between the Davies and other families; Roscoe Feild served in the same Confederate regiment as James Davies during the Civil War. After the war, Feild took his loyalty oath in Memphis with Logan Davies, subjects that are discussed more at length in subsequent pages. See Thomas B. Crenshaw [in Acct. with] Logan Davies, January 1862, DMA archives for account of Thomas B. Crenshaw paying Logan to track an enslaved man named Simon who escaped. During the Civil War, Logan hired out an enslaved woman named Celia and Celia's parents to the overseer at Crenshaw's plantation. Other clues indicating business connections with Crenshaw are found scattered in the DMA archives; Carolyn Bazemore, "The History of Cordova Is the History of Cordova Presbyterian Church," March 2016, accessed 2022. The history page on the website that featured the Basemore article and mention of Calaveras County has since been removed; United States Slave Schedule, 1850, Shelby County, Tennessee; see Ida Cooper Collection, Wash family folders for Wash's Store and Box 3, Folder 21 for Cooper's detailed notes on the Old Stage Road and important establishments alongside it; see United States Census, 1860, Shelby County, Tennessee for enumeration data showing the proximity of Washington Bolton to the Davies brothers .

11. Camp, *Closer to Freedom*, 7–10, 16, see chapter 1, "A Geography of Containment."

12. Sylvester Lewis, "Gray's Creek Missionary Baptist Church," *West Tennessee Historical Society Papers*, 2002, 119–21; G. Wayne Dowdy, "Gray's Creek Missionary Baptist Church," *The Best Times*, March 31, 2018; Sylvester Lewis, Interview with Andrew C. Ross, January 20, 2017; David Royster Final Will, 1842, Shelby County Archives; Ann C. Royster Thurman Probate Records, Shelby County Archives. Information in David Royster's final will about Kitty Price, combined with mentions of Kitty, Royal, Jim, Young, in Ann Royster Thurman's probate records, allowed me to make the assertions about the Price family. See also text for Gray's Creek Baptist Church historical marker, erected at the church in 2011 by descendants of

the founders, and the Shelby County Historical Commission; enumeration of Ann Thurman's household in United States Census, 1850, Shelby County, Tennessee; Ida Cooper Collection, Leake and Royster family folders; and Lacey, *The Search for Free Joe*. Information provided by the local historian Sylvester Lewis about Simon Price and Joseph Harris and the Gray's Creek Community more generally proved crucial to this Chapter. Lewis disagreed with some of the conclusions about Joseph Harris drawn by Lacey, which I have taken into account.

13. Ida Cooper Collection, Royster and Leake family folders; Sylvester Lewis, Interview with Andrew C. Ross; Lewis, "Gray's Creek Missionary Baptist Church"; Wilson, *The Story of Orion Hill*, 45.

14. Henry Louis Gates Jr., *The Black Church: This Is Our Story, This Is Our Song* (New York: Penguin Press, 2021), 42–43, 63–64; Lewis, "Gray's Creek Missionary Baptist Church"; Dowdy, "Gray's Creek Missionary Baptist Church"; Gray's Creek Baptist Church historical marker.

15. Beverly Breene Bond, *Millie Swan Price: Freedom, Kinship, and Property, Tennessee Women: Their Lives and Times*, vol. 1 (Athens: University of Georgia Press, 2009), 47–48. It has not been determined if connections exist between Millie Swan Price and the Price family researched by Bond, and Simon and Kitty Price and family that appear in this narrative.

16. Lacey, *The Search for Free Joe*. The primary documents Lacy relied upon and featured in his text are found in the Shelby County Archives; Sylvester Lewis, interview with Andrew C. Ross; see enumeration data for the household of Joseph Harris in United States Census, 1840, 1850, and 1860, Shelby County, Tennessee.

17. United States Census, 1860, Shelby County, Tennessee; Lacey, *Freejoe: A Story of Faith, Love and Perseverance* (Memphis, TN: Free Joe Publications, 1996).

18. Blassingame, *The Slave Community*, 305–15; Camp, *Closer to Freedom*, 9; United States Census, 1860, Shelby County, Tennessee. A close study of the households enumerated in Shelby County across Civil Districts Eight and Nine reveals how unique Harris was within his community; the quote is standard language used in bills of sale during slavery times but is drawn in this case from John W. Younger to William E. Davis, Bill of Sale, November 13, 1838, DMA archives.

19. United States Census, 1860, Shelby County, Tennessee; United States Slave Schedule, 1860, Shelby County, Tennessee. The conclusion that purchases were made was informed by comparing 1860 population census and slave schedule data for James and Logan with similar data from their father's estate in Fayette County; "James B, Davies, Book" (with WLD additions), DMA archives. This book lists the names and birthdates of enslaved children born between 1852 and 1862 and also features additions and notations

related to family history made by William Little Davies after James's death.
20. Robert Williams to Logan Davis, receipt, March 12, 1855, DMA archives; Logan Davies to Matthew W. Webber, promissory note, December 25, 1859, DMA archives; Ann C. Royster Thurman Probate Records, Shelby County Archives.
21. Logan Davies to Matthew W. Webber, promissory note, December 25, 1859, DMA archives; W. L. Daley to J. B. Davies, promissory note, February 13, 1862, DMA archives; E. C. Leake and M. L. Williams to Logan Davies, promissory note, January 1, 1863, DMA archives; W. L. Daley to J. B. Davies, promissory note, January 1, 1865, DMA archives.
22. Mooney, *Slavery in Tennessee*, 29–33; Quarterly Court Loose Papers Index, 1820–1865, Shelby County Archives. See the many index number files for road and bridge work; Bill Carey, *Runaways, Coffles and Fancy Girls: A History of Slavery in Tennessee* (Nashville, TN: Clearbrook Press, 2018), 153–60.
23. Burrel Keynes in Acct. with L. E. Davies, August 12, 1858, Logan E. Davies Book #1, DMA archives; D. H. Branch to L. E. Davies for Hunting, August 24, 1858, Logan E. Davies Book #1, DMA archives; John Farabee to L.E. Davies for hunting Negro by Request of Edward, June 14, 1859, Logan E. Davies Book #1, DMA archives; Thomas B. Crenshaw to L. E. Davies for hunting Simon, January 11, 1862, Logan E. Davies Book #1, DMA archives.

CHAPTER 9

1. James B. Davies and Penelope A. Little marriage certificate, December 18, 1854, Shelby County Archives; Pauline L. Little, *The Family History and Genealogy of William Little, Shelby County, TN, 1790–1851* (Spring Hill, TN: Self-published, 2008), 44–49. The records reproduced in Pauline L. Little's genealogy book are just a portion of the files that compose William Little's estate records. For more records that shed light on Almeda, see files for both William Little and William W. Little in Shelby County Probate Court Loose Papers Index 1820–1900.
2. H N Davis (Henry Newton Davies) and Mary A Webber marriage certificate, May 5, 1857, Shelby County Archives; "Married," *Tennessean*, July 8, 1857.
3. William Little Property Inventory, August 25, 1851, Shelby County Probate Court Loose Papers Index 1820–1900, Shelby County Archives. This record from William Little's estate records is reproduced and transcribed in Little, *The Family History and Genealogy of William Little*, 28. For the records that confirm Almeda inherited Richmond, see 1854 files in Shelby County Probate Court Loose Papers for Almeda's brother, Julius A. Little. In

particular, see the document recording the division of slaves, December 4, 1854.
4. William Little Property Inventory, August 25, 1851, Shelby County Archives.
5. Thavolia Glymph, *Out of the House of Bondage: The Transformation of the Plantation Household* (New York: Cambridge University Press, 2008), 100, 130.
6. Andrew C. Ross, Revised Davies Family Tree; "James B, Davies, Book" (with WLD additions), DMA archives; H N Davis (Henry Newton Davies) and Mary A Webber marriage certificate, May 5, 1857, Shelby County Archives; LE Davies and Frances A. Vaughan marriage certificate, November 27, 1860, Shelby County Archives.
7. "James B, Davies, Book" (with WLD additions), DMA archives. The reference to Sarah's burial location was made in this notebook by William Little Davies; Little, *The Family History and Genealogy of William Little*, 40; Andrew C. Ross, Revised Davies Family Tree; See also van Zelm, "Davies Manor Plantation Historic Structure Report," 15–16 for more details on the sources that have informed a revised understanding of Almeda's life. Although Almeda's birthdate has sometimes been given as 1833, a review of census data, her gravestones, and notes from her son William Little Davies reveal 1838 as her true birthdate.
8. Little, *The Family History and Genealogy of William Little*, 19; Almeda Little Essays, 1853, DMA archives; van Zelm, "Davies Manor Plantation Historic Structure Report," 14–16.
9. "James B, Davies, Book" (with WLD additions), DMA archives; "26 slaves," October 8, 1861, JB Davies Book #2, DMA archives; United States Census, 1860, Shelby County, Tennessee; United States Slave Schedule, 1860, Shelby County, Tennessee.
10. United States Census, 1860, Shelby County, Tennessee; United States Agricultural Census, 1860, Shelby County, Tennessee.
11. United States Slave Schedule, 1860, Shelby County, Tennessee.
12. United States Slave Schedule, 1860, Shelby County, Tennessee; United States Slave Schedule, 1860, Fayette County, Tennessee; van Zelm, "Davies Manor Plantation Historic Structure Report," 17.
13. United States Slave Schedule, 1860, Shelby County, Tennessee; United States Census, 1860, Shelby County, Tennessee; United States Agricultural Census, 1860, Shelby County, Tennessee; United States Slave Schedule, 1860, Fayette County, Tennessee; United States Census, 1860, Fayette County, Tennessee; United States Agricultural Census, 1860, Fayette County, Tennessee.
14. Dattel, *Cotton and Race*, 36; Bruce Levine, *The Fall of the House of Dixie: The Civil War and the Social Revolution That Transformed the South* (New York: Random House, 2013), 4.

15. W. Raymond Cooper, "Four Fateful Years, Memphis, 1858–1861," *West Tennessee Historical Society Papers*, 1957, 36–75; Frederic Bancroft, *Slave Trading in the Old South* (Columbia, SC: J. H. Furst Company, 1931) quotes on 250.
16. Gerald M. Capers Jr., *The Biography of a River Town: Memphis Its Heroic Age* (Chapel Hill: University of North Carolina Press, 1939) 76, 79, 110; Dattel, *Cotton and Race*, quote and statistics, 46; see United States Census, 1860, Shelby County, Tennessee for data and household location of Washington Bolton.
17. Wilentz, *The Rise of American Democracy*, 767; Cotton Receipts, October 1860, DMA archives.
18. Levine, *The Fall of the House of Dixie*, 35–43; Wilentz, *The Rise of American Democracy*, 758, 763–65; Ken Burns, "The Cause," episode 1, *The Civil War*, 1990. See also October 1860 issues of the *Memphis Bulletin* and *Daily Argus* for an understanding of local coverage of the presidential election.
19. Wilentz, *The Rise of American Democracy*, 765–67 (quotation on 646).
20. *Memphis Daily Appeal*, November 18, 1860.
21. Derek W. Frisby, "The Vortex of Secession: West Tennesseans and the Rush to War," in *Sister States Enemy States: The Civil War in Kentucky and Tennessee*, ed. Kent T. Dollar, Larry H. Whiteaker and W. Calvin Dickinson, 46–71 (Lexington: University of Kentucky Press, 2009).

CHAPTER 10

1. "The Meeting at Raleigh on Yesterday," *Memphis Daily Appeal*, April 2, 1861.
2. "Union Convention at Raleigh," *Memphis Daily Argus*, April 2, 1861.
3. "The Meeting at Raleigh on Yesterday," *Memphis Daily Appeal*, April 2, 1861.
4. Stanley F. Horn, ed., "The Volunteer State Volunteers - For the Confederacy," *Tennessee Historical Quarterly* 5, no. 1 (March 1946): 58–59.
5. "Public Meeting at Morning Sun," *Memphis Daily Appeal*, April 24, 1861; JB Davis, Home Guard, File No. 1861-45-000, Quarterly Court Loose Papers Index, Shelby County Archives.
6. "Meeting of the People of Fayette," *Memphis Daily Appeal*, April 24, 1861.
7. "Mary F. Scantlin to James B. Davies," May 15, 1861, DMA archives; Wilentz, *The Rise of American Democracy*, 779.
8. Hughes, *The Life and Wars of Gideon J. Pillow*, 167–73; Larry J. Daniel, *Conquered: Why the Army of Tennessee Failed* (Chapel Hill: University of North Carolina Press, 2019), 12, 28; John Harkins, *Metropolis of the American Nile* (Oxford, MS: Guild Bindery Press, 1982), 72; Fold3, "B.S. Thurman," *Compiled service records of Confederate soldiers Who Served in Organizations from the State of Tennessee, 1861–1865*, National Archives and Records Administration (NARA); Fold3, "J.B. Ecklin," *Compiled service records*, NARA; Fold3 "D.R. Royster," *Compiled service records*, NARA.

9. "JBD Notebook with WLD Additions," DMA archives; "Family History" notes by William Little Davies, DMA archives; William Little Davies letter draft, Brunswick, TN, to [Custodian of Morning Grove Church and Cemetery], Lenow, TN, May 1929, DMA archives; David R. Royster Final Will, June 2, 1861, Shelby County Archives; an understanding of Young Price's role as a body servant for Beverly S. Thurman is drawn largely from letters in the John P. and Sallie Ecklin Thurman Papers, 1844–1896, Southern Historical Collection, Wilson Library, University of North Carolina at Chapel Hill, and A. J. Vaughan, *Personal Record of the Thirteenth Regiment, Tennessee Infantry, C.S.A.* (Toof, 1897).
10. "The Meeting at Raleigh on Yesterday," *Memphis Daily Appeal*, April 2, 1861.
11. Mary F. Scantlin to James B. Davies, May 15, 1861, Box 2, DMA archives.
12. Mary F. Scantlin to James B. Davies.
13. Mary F. Scantlin to James B. Davies.
14. Beverly S. Thurman to Sallie Ecklin Thurman, June 30, 1861, Folder 7, John P. and Sallie Ecklin Thurman Papers.
15. "Prosecution of the War," *Memphis Daily Avalanche*, July 25, 1861.
16. Mary F. Scantlin to James B. Davies, November 21, 1861, Box 2, DMA archives.
17. Mary F. Scantlin to James B. Davies, December 5, 1861, Box 2, DMA archives.
18. Mary F. Scantlin to James B. Davies, December 5, 1861.

CHAPTER 11

1. Donald L. Miller, *Vicksburg: Grant's Campaign That Broke the Confederacy* (New York: Simon & Schuster, 2019), 52–55.
2. Partial note to James B. Davies, February 8, 1862, Box 8, DMA archives.
3. "Fayette County commissioners to allot off the Negroes belonging to William E. Davies," February 7, 1862, DMA archives.
4. "1804, The Ages of the Blacks," DMA archives; John W. Younger to William E. Davis, bill of sale, November 13, 1838, DMA archives; Milton Draper and Ridley Roberts to William E. Davies, bill of sale, April 22, 1850, DMA archives; Jeremiah Burnett final will, December 18, 1812, Will Books, pp. 73–75, Lunenburg County, Virginia Circuit Court; William E. Davies to M. L. Williams, promissory note, January 1, 1851, DMA archives.
5. Gabriel G. Finney to James B. Davies, promissory note, March 8, 1862, DMA archives.
6. "Fayette County commissioners to allot," February 7, 1862, DMA archives; R. H. Johnson and E. C. Leake to Logan Davies, promissory note, January 1, 1863, DMA archives.

7. "Fayette County commissioners to allot," February 7, 1862, DMA archives; W. L. Daley to James B. Davies, promissory note, February 13, 1862, DMA archives; W. L. Daley to James B. Davies, promissory note, January 1, 1865, DMA archives.
8. W. W. Davies to James B. Davies, [illegible] 11, 1867, DMA archives; William Leon Davies to James B. Davies, September 17, 1868, DMA archives. See James B. Davies correspondence folder for other letters from William Leon Davies to his uncle written in the years just after the Civil War.
9. "1804, The ages of the Blacks," DMA archives; "Fayette County commissioners to allot," February 7, 1862, DMA archives.
10. Berry, *The Price for Their Pound of Flesh*, 6, 61.
11. "Fayette County commissioners to allot," February 7, 1862, DMA archives; United States Census, 1870, Shelby County, Tennessee; Davies-Rodgers, *Turns Again Home*, 113, 198; "Tucker Family Tree," Ancestry.com; Davies-Rodgers, *Along the Old Stage-Coach Road*, 29. See also land deed records for Wilcher Tucker, Shelby County Archives, and entries documenting Wilcher, Amos, and Lucious Tucker in post-Civil War commissary ledger books, DMA archives.
12. United States Agricultural Census, 1860, Shelby County, Tennessee; United States Slave Schedule, 1860, Shelby County, Tennessee; United States Census, 1860, Shelby County, Tennessee.
13. "Fayette County commissioners to allot," February 7, 1862, DMA archives; "1804, The ages of the Blacks," DMA archives; Robert Walker to William E. Davies, June 8, 1843, DMA archives.
14. "Fayette County commissioners to allot," February 7, 1862, DMA archives.

CHAPTER 12

1. Levine, *Fall of the House of Dixie*, 68–69.
2. Fold3, "J.B. Davis," *Compiled service records*, NARA; W. L. Davies letter draft, Brunswick, TN, to [Custodian of Morning Grove Church and Cemetery], Lenow, TN, May 1929, DMA archives; "James B. Davies, Book" with WLD addition, DMA archives; Genealogical Report for the Mose Frazier Committee, Richmond Bennett 1833–1915 by Tina Sansone," 2012, DMA office files; "Bennett Family Tree," compiled by Tina Sansone, Ancestry.com; Davies-Rodgers, *Turns Again Home*, 113, 197–98; Davies-Rodgers, *Along the Old Stage Coach Road*, 29.
3. Fold3, "F.B. Crenshaw," *Compiled service records*, NARA; Fold3, "M.H. Crenshaw," *Compiled service records*, NARA; Fold3, "R. Feild," *Compiled service records*, NARA; Fold3, "W.C. Little," *Compiled service records*, NARA.
4. "James Baxter Davies," obituary, *Memphis Morning News*, June 17, 1904 (quotation); John P. and Sallie Ecklin Thurman Papers.

5. Folders 8 and 9, John P. and Sallie Ecklin Thurman Papers. For quotes, see Beverly Thurman to Sallie Ecklin Thurman, March 30, 1862, and J. P. Thurman to Sallie Ecklin Thurman, April 3, 1862.
6. Daniel, *Conquered*, 19–22 (quote on 20); Levin, *Searching For Black Confederates*, 1–11.
7. Levin, *Searching For Black Confederates*, 61; Bruce Levine, "In Search of a Usable Past," in *Slavery and Public History: The Tough Stuff of American Memory*, ed. James Oliver Horton and Lois E. Horton, 187–211 (New York: The New Press, 2006).
8. Levin, *Searching For Black Confederates*, 28; Levine, Bruce, "In Search of a Usable Past," 187–211.
9. J. P. Thurman to Sallie Ecklin Thurman, April 9, 1862, Folder 9, John P. and Sallie Ecklin Thurman Papers.
10. J. P. Thurman to Sallie Ecklin Thurman, April 15, 1862 and J. P. Thurman to Sallie Ecklin Thurman, April 16, 1862, Folder 9, John P. and Sallie Ecklin Thurman Papers.
11. J. P. Thurman to Sallie Ecklin Thurman, April 15, 1862 and J. P. Thurman to Sallie Ecklin Thurman, April 16, 1862, Folder 9, John P. and Sallie Ecklin Thurman Papers.
12. Fold3, "J.B. Davis," *Compiled service records*, NARA; Daniel, *Conquered*, 28.
13. Wm Griffin, *The Memphis Daily Avalanche*, May 17, 1862; "How Beautiful, How Holy Is Charity," *Memphis Daily Avalanche*, May 9, 1862.
14. Sallie Ecklin Thurman to J. P. Thurman, May 18, 1862.
15. Sallie Ecklin Thurman to J. P. Thurman, May 18, 1862.
16. Sallie Ecklin Thurman to J. P. Thurman, May 18, 1862.

CHAPTER 13

1. Daniel, *Conquered*, 30.
2. John H. Harkins, *Metropolis of the American Nile* (Oxford, MS: Guild Bindery Press, 1982). 75–76.
3. John Cimprich, *Slavery's End in Tennessee, 1861–1865* (Tuscaloosa: University of Alabama Press, 1985). See chapter "Master and Slave after Federal Occupation"; Levine, *The Fall of the House of Dixie*, 102–3; John Bordelon, "'Rebels to the Core': Memphians under William T. Sherman," *Rhodes Journal of Regional Studies*, 2005: 6–36.
4. Harkins, *Historic Shelby County*, 67; Steven V. Ash, *When the Yankees Came: Conflict and Chaos in the Occupied South* (Chapel Hill: University of North Carolina Press, 1995), 99.
5. DMA office files; Davies-Rodgers, *Along the Old Stage Coach Road*, 78; See also National Register of Historic Places Application for Mt. Airy, National Park Service, January 4, 2002, p. 6.

6. Field family files, Box 2, 5, 10 & 12, Ida Cooper Collection. See also Davis family folders and "Dr. Charley Davis Version, Commercial Appeal, 1940," in Cooper's typed notes. Although the full name of the woman at the center of this story was not listed by Cooper, I concluded that the identity of the "niece of the Chambers family" was Virginia "Jennie" Vaughan Gardiner (1838–1921).
7. Davies-Rodgers, *Along the Old Stage-Coach Road*, 43–44.
8. James B. Davies to Logan Davies, September 5, 1865, Box 8, DMA archives.
9. Miller, *Vicksburg*, 201.
10. Miller, *Vicksburg*, 199–200; Levine, *The Fall of the House of Dixie*, 124–127; John Cimprich, "Slave Behavior during the Federal Occupation of Tennessee, 1862–1865," *Historian*, no. 3 (May 1982): 335–46.
11. Cimprich, "Slave Behavior," 339–42; Cheri LaFlamme Szcodronski, "From Contraband to Freedmen: General Grant, Chaplain Eaton, and Grand Junction, Tennessee," *Tennessee Historical Quarterly*, no. 2 (Summer 2013): 106–27.
12. Miller, *Vicksburg*, 205–11.
13. Miller, *Vicksburg*, 205–11; Szcodronski, "From Contraband to Freedmen," 109.
14. Miller, *Vicksburg*, 206; "Register of Freedmen, Camp Shiloh," 1864, www.lastroadtofreedom.org; Thomas B. Crenshaw to L. E. Davies for hunting Simon, January 11, 1862, Logan E. Davies Book #1, DMA archives; Fold3, "Royal Price," *Compiled Military Service Records of Volunteer Union Soldiers Who Served with the United States Colored Troops: Artillery Organizations, 1861–1865*, NARA; For Jim Price, service records have not been located; information on his service comes instead from 1890 Veterans Schedules of the U.S. Federal Census. See "Special Schedule, Surviving Soldiers, Sailors, and Marines, and Widows, etc.," Shelby County, Tennessee, 9th Civil District, p. 2, Ancestry.com.
15. "James B. Davies, Book" with WLD addition, DMA archives; James B. Davies to Logan Davies, September 5, 1865, DMA archives; James B. Davies to Logan Davies, November 14, 1865, DMA archives.

CHAPTER 14

1. Fold3, "W.C. Little," *Compiled service records*, NARA; Fold3, "F.B. Crenshaw," *Compiled service records*, NARA; Daniel, *Conquered*, 29.
2. Daniel, *Conquered*, 30–45; Fold3, "JB Davis," *Compiled service records*, NARA; Fold3, "M.H. Crenshaw," *Compiled service records*, NARA; Fold3, "R. Feild," *Compiled service records*, NARA.
3. Fold3, "JB Davis," *Compiled service records*, NARA; Fold3, "J.B. Ecklin," *Compiled service records*, NARA; Vaughan, *Personal Record of the Thirteenth*

Regiment, 80; United States Census, 1870, Shelby County, Tennessee. See Arthur Ecklin household enumeration in the Ninth Civil District.

4. Fold3, "J.B. Ecklin," *Compiled service records*, NARA; Darlene Hooker Sawyer, "Morning Sun's Beginnings," May 2016. (Web link is no longer active. See printed article in author's and church's files); "Joshua Bryan Ecklin," n.d., Find a Grave, https://www.findagrave.com/memorial/7475762/joshua-bryan-ecklin.

5. Linnie Lee Davies's birthdate is alternately recorded as 1863 and 1864. Her gravestone reads 1864. I have relied upon an entry in Logan E. Davies, Book No. 1, DMA archives, that lists her birthdate as March 15, 1864; "Tuition Receipt, Payment of L. E. Davies as Administrator for James Walker in Full of His Tuition," December 2, 1863, DMA archives.

6. Levine, *The Fall of the House of Dixie*, 150–70; 194–95, 200–202; Cotton and grocery receipts, October and November 1863, DMA archives. In particular, see Logan Davies, twelve bales cotton on consignment, October 13, 1863; Tuition payment receipt for "Augustus and Willie Davis," December 29, 1863, DMA archives; Unknown to Logan E. Davies, promissory note, 1863, DMA archives; E. C. Leake and M. L. Williams to Logan Davies, January 1, 1863, promissory note, DMA archives.

7. E. C. Leake and M. L. Williams to Logan Davies, January 1, 1863, promissory note, DMA archives; Unknown to Logan E. Davies, 1863, promissory note, DMA archives; W. L. Daley to James B. Davies, January 1, 1864, promissory note, DMA archives.

8. Madison H. Chambers to Logan E. Davies, September 1863, DMA archives.

9. Cotton receipt, October 13, 1863, DMA archives; Travel Permit to Logan E. Davies, October 21, 1863, DMA archives; Cotton receipt, November 5, 1863, DMA archives.

10. Levine, *The Fall of the House of Dixie*, 159; "54th Massachusetts Regiment," National Park Service, n.d., https://www.nps.gov/articles/54th-massachusetts-regiment.htm.

11. "Tennessee USCTs," Tennessee Civil War Trails Brochure, n.d., https://www.civilwartrails.org/docs/TN-brochure.pdf; Lamon, *Blacks in Tennessee*, 31; "Battle of Moscow" marker, Tennessee Civil War Trails, The Historical Marker Database, n.d., https://www.hmdb.org/m.asp?m=37273.

12. Lamon, *Blacks in Tennessee*, 31–33; Beverly Thurman to Sallie Ecklin Thurman, n.d., Folder 18, John P. and Sallie Ecklin Thurman Papers; 1890 Veterans Schedules of the U.S. Federal Census, "Special Schedule, Surviving Soldiers, Sailors, and Marines, and Widows, etc..," Shelby County, Tennessee, 9th Civil District, p. 2, Ancestry.com; Fold3, "Royal Price," *Compiled Military Service Records*, NARA; "Tennessee USCTs," Tennessee Civil War Trails Brochure, n.d., web.

13. Cimprich, "Slave Behavior," 340–45; Ira Berlin, Barbara J. Fields, Steven F. Miller, Joseph P. Reidy and Leslie S. Rowland, eds., *Free at Last: A Documentary History of Slavery, Freedom, and the Civil War* (New York: The New Press, 1993), 185–200.
14. Thos. W. Coulter to Logan E. Davies, December 25, 1863, DMA archives.
15. Thos. W. Coulter to Logan E. Davies, December 25, 1863; Camp, *Closer to Freedom*, 9; Exhibit consultation meeting between Andrew C. Ross and Susan O'Donovan, 2018.
16. Daniel, *Conquered*, 70–80; Fold3, "JB Davis," *Compiled service records*, NARA.
17. "M.H. Crenshaw," *Compiled service records*, NARA; Fold3, "F.B. Crenshaw," *Compiled service records*, NARA; Fold3, "W.C. Little," *Compiled service records*, NARA; Fold3, "R. Feild," *Compiled service records*, NARA; Fold3, "J.P. Thurman," *Compiled service records*, NARA; Fold3, "J.B. Ecklin," *Compiled service records*, NARA; Beverly Thurman to Sallie Ecklin Thurman, July 31, 1863, Folder 12, John P. and Sallie Ecklin Thurman Papers.
18. Daniel, *Conquered*, 290–300; Fold3, "R. Feild," *Compiled service records*, NARA.
19. Beverly Thurman to Sallie Ecklin Thurman, August 16, 1864, Folder 15, John P. and Sallie Ecklin Thurman Papers; Fold3, "Beverly S. Thurman," *Compiled service records*, NARA.
20. Vaughan, *Personal Record of the Thirteenth Regiment, Tennessee Infantry, C.S.A*, 80–81.
21. Vaughan, *Personal Record of the Thirteenth Regiment, Tennessee Infantry, C.S.A*, 80–81.
22. Levin, *Searching for Black Confederates*, 72, 74. See also chapter "Camp Slaves and The Lost Cause"; my general understanding of the role of body servants in Lost Cause literature was also informed by David W. Blight, *Race and Reunion: The Civil War in American Memory* (Cambridge, MA: Harvard University Press, 2001).
23. Sawyer, "Morning Sun's Beginnings," May 2016, Morning Sun Cumberland Presbyterian Church, web. (Web link for church is no longer active. See printed article in author's files and church's files.)

CHAPTER 15

1. S. C. Gwynne, *Hymns of the Republic: The Story of The Final Year of the American Civil War* (New York: Scribner, 2019) 184–85, quotation on 123.
2. Stanley F. Horn, *The Army of Tennessee* (Norman: University of Oklahoma Press, 1953), 379–80; Daniel, *Conquered*, 315–20.
3. Horn, *The Army of Tennessee*, 379–80; Daniel, *Conquered*, 315–20; Fold3, "J.P. Thurman," *Compiled service records*, NARA; Fold3, "Henry M [N.] Davies," *Compiled service records*, NARA.

4. Daniel, *Conquered*, 322–24; Horn, *The Army of Tennessee*, 394–404; Lamon, Blacks in Tennessee, 31, 33.
5. "James B. Davis Book" (with William Little Davies additions), DMA archives.
6. Fold3, "Henry M. [N] Davies," *Compiled service records*, NARA; "H.N. Davies," Selected Records of War Department relating to Confederate Prisoners of War, 1861–1865, NARA, Ancestry.com. See also "H.N. Davis," Camp Chase Hospital Records, p. 92–93, NARA, Accessed in DMA office files, and Fold3, "H.N. Davis," Graves Registration Card, Camp Chase Ohio, Grave No. 1557. There are some discrepancies about the date of Henry's capture. His service records indicate he was captured on Dec. 16, 1864, the second day of the Battle of Nashville. However, the Camp Chase hospital records say he was captured on Dec. 10, 1864. I have chosen to rely on his service records; James Baxter Davies Obituary, June 17, 1904, *Memphis Morning News*.
7. W. H. Webber to James B. Davies, January 1, 1865, promissory note, DMA archives; W. L. Daley to J. Davies, January 1, 1865, promissory note, DMA archives; "J.B. Davis" license to marry "Mrs. PL Leake," January 14, 1865, Book 3, p. 324, Shelby County Marriages, Shelby County Archives.
8. There are no official records related to James's discharge. The information about his surrender comes from notes by William Little Davies, and from James's obituary; Daniel, *Conquered*, 323–25; Levine, *The Fall of the House of Dixie*, 244.
9. J. P. Thurman to Sallie Ecklin Thurman, January 14, 1865, Folder 16, John P. and Sallie Ecklin Thurman Papers.
10. J. P. Thurman to Sallie Ecklin Thurman, March 6, 1865, Folder 17, John P. and Sallie Ecklin Thurman Papers; Sallie Ecklin Thurman to J. P. Thurman, March 16, 1865, Folder 17, John P. and Sallie Ecklin Thurman Papers.
11. Sallie Ecklin Thurman to J. P. Thurman, March 16, 1865, Folder 17, John P. and Sallie Ecklin Thurman Papers; J. P. Thurman to Sallie Ecklin Thurman, undated, Folder 18, John P. and Sallie Ecklin Thurman Papers. References to events made in this letter make it clear it was written in the spring of 1865.
12. "Confederate Law Authorizing the Enlistment of Black Soldiers, as Promulgated in a Military Order," General Orders No., 14, March 13, 1865, transcript text reproduced for Freedmen and Southern Society Project, Maintained by Stephen F. Miller, https://freedmen.umd.edu/csenlist.htm.
13. Levin, *Searching for Black Confederates*.
14. "Bennett Place Surrender," n.d., American Battlefield Trust, https://battlefields.org/learn/articles/bennett-place-surrender.
15. "James Baxter Davies," obituary, *Memphis Morning News*, June 17, 1904; "James B, Davis Book," (with William Little Davies additions), DMA archives; Davies-Rodgers, *Turns Again Home*, 197.

16. "Bennett Family Tree" by Tina Sansone, Ancestry.com; "James Baxter Davies," obituary, *Memphis Morning News*, June 17, 1904.

CHAPTER 16

1. "Negro Mass Meeting," *Memphis Argus*, May 25, 1865.
2. "The Final March: Grand Review of the Armies," National Park Service, n.d., https://www.nps.gov/cane/the-final-march-grand-review-of-the-armies.htm; "Telegraph Report," *Memphis Bulletin*, May 25, 1865.
3. "Negro Mass Meeting," *Memphis Argus*, May 25, 1865.
4. Fold3, "Royal Price," *Compiled Military Service Records*, NARA; Stephen V. Ash, *A Massacre in Memphis: The Race Riot That Shook the Nation One Year after the Civil War* (New York: Hill and Wang, 2013), 75–76.
5. "Negro Mass Meeting," *Memphis Argus*, May 25, 1865.
6. "The Procession Yesterday," *Memphis Bulletin*, May 25, 1865.
7. "A Speck of a Riot," *Memphis Argus*, May 25, 1865; "A Desperate Fracas," *Memphis Bulletin*, May 25, 1865.
8. "Negro Mass Meeting," *Memphis Argus*, May 25, 1865.
9. "Oath of Allegiance Affidavit, L. E. Davies, No. 1749," May 24, 1865, microfilm, Memphis and Shelby County Room, Memphis Public Library; "Oath of Allegiance Affidavit, R Fields, No. 1751," May 24, 1865, microfilm, Memphis and Shelby County Room, Memphis Public Library; Richard White, *The Republic for Which It Stands: The United States during Reconstruction and the Gilded Age, 1865–1896* (New York: Oxford University Press, 2017), 35–63, quote on 35.
10. "Oath of Allegiance Affidavit, Joshua Ecklin, No. 1381," May 24, 1865; "Oath of Allegiance Affidavit, Thos. W. Coulter, No. 1301," May 20, 1865; "Oath of Allegiance Affidavit, Sarah W. Bolton, No. 938," May 19, 1865; "Oath of Allegiance Affidavit, Virginius Leake, No. 629," May 18, 1865; "Oath of Allegiance Affidavit, Mary O. Williams, No. 64," May 17, 1865; "Oath of Allegiance Affidavit, Mrs. Pauline L. Davies, No. 66," May 17, 1865; "Oath of Allegiance Affidavit, J. P. Thurman," May 1865. All of the above affidavits are found on microfilm in the Memphis and Shelby County Room, Memphis Public Library.
11. Pauline L. Davies to Logan E. Davies, May [15], 1865, James Baxter Davies Correspondence, DMA archives. Although Pauline "Polly" Davies does not explicitly address James's whereabouts in her letter to Logan, contextual clues indicate that James had not yet made it home from the war; "Coming In," *Memphis Bulletin*, May 25, 1865.
12. Levine, *The Fall of the House of Dixie*, xviii. Quote used by Levine comes from the *Memphis Argus*, 1865, and was used in Eugene D. Genovese, *Roll, Jorda, Roll: The World the Slaves Made* (New York, 1974), 110; Ida Cooper

Collection, Royster family files, Boxes 2, 12, Memphis and Shelby County Room, Memphis Public Library; Davies-Rodgers, *Along the Old Stage-Coach Road*, 73.

13. Guy Gugliotta, "New Estimate Raises Civil War Death Toll," *New York Times*, April 2, 2012; the 750,000 Figure I have used comes from the findings of the demographic historian J. David Hacker, discussed in this article; Drew Gilpin Faust, *This Republic of Suffering: Death and the American Civil War* (New York: Vintage Books, 2008), xi–xviii, quotes on xiii.
14. Eric Foner, *A Short History of Reconstruction* (New York: Harper & Row, 1990), 1–14, quote on 5.
15. "News Reports," *Memphis Bulletin*, May 24, 1865; William G. Brownlow, "A Proclamation By William G. Brownlow, Governor of Tennessee," *American Historical Magazine* (1898) 151–54.
16. Foner, *A Short History of Reconstruction*, 19–20, 86–87, 116; Gregory P. Downs, *After Appomattox: Military Occupation and the Ends of War* (Cambridge, MA: Harvard University Press, 2019) 120, 148, 154–55; Robert Tracy McKenzie, "Reconstruction," Tennessee Encyclopedia, Tennessee Historical Society, October 8, 2017, http://tennesseeencyclopedia.net/entries/reconstruction.
17. "News Reports" *Memphis Bulletin*, May 24, 1865; "General Orders No. 58," *Memphis Bulletin*, May 24, 1865.
18. "News Reports" *Memphis Bulletin*, May 24, 1865; Ash, *A Massacre in Memphis*, 119.
19. Brower Harnwell, "Editorial," *Memphis Argus*, May 24, 1865; Anonymous, "Letter to the Editor," *Memphis Argus*, May 24, 1865.

CHAPTER 17

1. "Report on Countryside," *Memphis Argus*, November 10, 1865.
2. Lamon, *Blacks in Tennessee*, 37; United States Census, 1870, Shelby County, Tennessee; Logan E. Davies and James B. Davies agreement with Ben Goodlett and A Hicks, February [?], 1870, DMA archives; Ledger Books 1869–1870 Ledger, DMA archives; James B. Davies agreement with Joshua Davies and family, December 21, 1865, James B. Davies Book No. 3, DMA archives.
3. "1804, The ages of the Blacks," DMA archives; United States Census, 1870, Shelby County, Tennessee; W. W. Davies to Wm. E. Davies, bill of sale, October 13, 1838, DMA archives; James B. Davies agreement with Joshua Davies and family, December 21, 1865, James B. Davies Book No. 3, DMA archives.

4. United States Census, 1870, Shelby County, Tennessee; "James B, Davies, Book" (with WLD additions), DMA archives. See entries in this book documenting the births of Young and Polly (Cartwright).
5. United States Census, 1870, Shelby County, Tennessee.
6. Foner, *A Short History of Reconstruction*, 78–81, quotes on 78–79.
7. Foner, *A Short History of Reconstruction*, 69–81, quotes on 69, 78.
8. White, *The Republic for Which It Stands*, 80–81.
9. Steven Hahn, Steven F. Miller, Susan E. O'Donovan, John C. Rodrigue, and Leslie S. Rowland, ed., *Freedom: A Documentary History of Emancipation, 1861–1867*, Series 3: Volume I, Land and Labor, 1865 (Chapel Hill: University of North Carolina Press, 2017). See "Proceedings of a Meeting of Employers in Shelby County, Tennessee," November 23, 1865, 934–36.
10. Hahn et al., *Freedom*.
11. Foner, *A Short History of Reconstruction*, 59; Ash, *A Massacre in Memphis*, 41.
12. Hahn et al., *Freedom*, see "Letter from White Tennesseans to the Freedmen's Bureau Superintendent of the Sub District of Memphis - Shelby Depot, TN," November 25, 1865, 849–50.

CHAPTER 18

1. Cotton Receipts, 1865–1870, DMA archives; W. L. Daley to James B. Davies, receipt, DMA archives; Davies-Rodgers, *Turns Again Home*, 85.
2. United States Census, 1870, Shelby County, Tennessee.
3. United States Census, 1860, Shelby County, Tennessee; United States Census, 1870, Shelby County, Tennessee; James B. Davies to Logan Davies, September 5, 1865, DMA archives; James B. Davies to P. Ellis "for Board of Boy Green" for 1864 and 1865, November 1865, DMA archives. See additional notes from November 1865 recording James receiving payment for having hired out Harriet and Emily in 1863 and 1864; James Baxter Davies, obituary, *Memphis Morning News*, June 17, 1904.
4. News brief on Thomas B. Crenshaw's Death, *Memphis Daily Appeal*, July 26, 1867.
5. Snowden Maddox to L. E. Davies, receipt [for 1865, for December 15, 1865 for "visit wife prescription & meds"], DMA archives; Snowden Maddox to L. E. Davies, receipt, January 1866; Logan Davies and L. H. and J. B. Fuller, receipt for headstone for Fannie A. Davies, June 27, 1873, DMA archives. This receipt includes the inscription text for the headstone that confirms Fannie's death date; Davies-Rodgers, *Along the Old Stage-Coach Road*, 140.
6. James B. Davies to Logan Davies, September 5, 1865, DMA archives. This note is part of the evidence supporting the assertion that James, Will, and

Gus Davies were living on Pollie's estate in the years immediately after the Civil War. See also the Pollie's oath of allegiance affidavit, May 17, 1865, which indicates she had retained property from her inheritance and/or first marriage; Depositions (transcriptions) of M. L. Williams, W. M. Williams, Mrs. Mary O. Williams, and Mrs. Hallie Falwell in case of *Pauline L. Davis v. James B. Davis*, Chancery Court, Memphis, February 20, 1868, photocopies in Lawsuits Folder, DMA archives; Little, *The Family History and Genealogy of William Little*, 59.

7. Depositions (transcriptions) of M. L. Williams, W. M. Williams, Mrs. Mary O. Williams, and Mrs. Hallie Falwell in case of Pauline L. Davis v. James B. Davis, February 20, 1868, photocopies in Lawsuits Folder, DMA archives. See also deposition of Redford Hall, February 23, 1868, DMA archives.
8. Pauline L. Davis v. James B. Davis, divorce bill, Chancery Court, Memphis, TN, September 25, 1867, Lawsuits Folder, DMA archives; R. R. R. Hall and Mrs. P Leake, January 5, 1870, Book D, p. 333, Shelby County Marriages, Shelby County Archives.
9. "James Baxter Davies," obituary, *Memphis Morning News*, June 17, 1904.
10. Mary Scantlin to James B. Davies, April 7, 1867, DMA archives.
11. Mary Scantlin to James B. Davies, June 28, 1867, DMA archives.
12. Mary Scantlin to James B. Davies, September [?], 1867, DMA archives.
13. Mary Scantlin to James Davies, January 20, 1868, DMA archives; Mary Scantlin to James Davies, February 27, 1868, DMA archives.
14. Davies-Rodgers, *Along the Old Stage-Coach Road*, 11, 70; University of Nashville Catalogue, 1877–1878 Session, 23–24, *U.S. School Catalogs, 1765–1935* [database online], Provo, UT: Ancestry.com.
15. "Dr. J. A. Davis, of Raleigh . . . is now prescribing for the inmates of the poorhouse," newspaper clipping, n.d. [1881], DMA archives; Davies-Rodgers, *Along the Old Stage-Coach Road*, 70; Julius Augustus Davies Certificate, University of the City of New York, 1881, Degrees Folder, DMA archives; Andrew C. Ross, "A Most Unusual Collector: The Forgotten Story of Julius Augustus Davies," *Delta Magazine*, July 8, 2019, https://deltamagazine.com/a-most-unusual-collector.
16. Julius A. Davies to William L. Davies, November 6, 1881, W. L. Davies Correspondence 1865–1890, DMA archives. See other correspondence for scattered information that informed an understanding of Dr. Davies's practice; Davies-Rodgers, *Turns Again Home*, 41.
17. United States Census, 1870, Shelby County, Tennessee; United States Census, 1880, Shelby County, Tennessee.
18. United States Census, 1880, Shelby County, Tennessee; James B. Davies to J. R. Matthews, receipt, January 22, 1882, DMA archives.
19. J. B. & L. E. Davies to J. R. Matthews, receipt for "1 Coffin Emily Cartwright," May 9, 1875, DMA archives; J. B. & L. E. Davies to J. R.

Matthews, receipt for "1 Coffin for Cartwright's son," June 1, 1875, DMA archives; United States Census, 1880, Shelby County, Tennessee.
20. United States Census, 1880, Shelby County, Tennessee; United States Agricultural Census, 1880, Shelby County, Tennessee; George Cherry to Wilcher Tucker, January 1, 1872, Book 91, p. 237, Shelby County Register of Deeds, Shelby County Archives. For the location of the Tucker family farm, see description in the land deed in conjunction with "Map of Shelby County, Tennessee, 1888, Carefully compiled from the Records and other authentic sources, and published by M. T. Williamson, Memphis, Tenn," Shelby County Archives. This map shows detailed plat boundaries with the names of landowners and acreage marked. See also scattered entries for Tucker family members in commissary ledger books, 1867–1880, DMA archives.

CHAPTER 19

1. Foner, *A Short History of Reconstruction*, 69–77, 109–11, 116; Henry Louis Gates Jr., *Stony the Road: Reconstruction, White Supremacy, and the Rise of Jim Crow* (New York: Penguin Press, 2019) 6–11; *Reconstruction: America after the Civil War*, directed by Julia Marchesi, hour 2, PBS (McGee Media, 2019); Paul A. Cimbala and Randall M. Miller, ed., *The Freedmen's Bureau and Reconstruction: Reconsiderations* (New York: Fordham University Press, 1999), xvi–xix.
2. Eric Foner, "Rooted in Reconstruction: The First Wave of Black Congressmen," *The Nation*, October 15, 2008, https://www.thenation.com/article/archive/rooted-reconstruction-first-wave-black-congressmen/; Gates, *Stony the Road*, xv–xvii, 8, 16; *Reconstruction: America after the Civil War*; Foner, *A Short History of Reconstruction* (W.E.B. Du Bois quote on 254).
3. Lamon, *Blacks in Tennessee*, 38–46; Harkins, *Historic Shelby County*, 80–82.
4. Beverly Greene Bond, "Memories of a Massacre: Memphis in 1866," n.d., https://www.memphis.edu/memphis-massacre; Ash, *A Massacre in Memphis*, 4, 187–96; Foner, *A Short History of Reconstruction*, 117–19.
5. Foner, *Reconstruction*, 261–71; White, *The Republic For Which It Stands*, 70–75; Gates, *Stony the Road*, 7.
6. Foner, *A Short History of Reconstruction*, 146, 184–91; Gates, *Stony the Road*, 9–15; "Memphis," *Chicago Tribune*, October 3, 1868; Lamon, *Blacks in Tennessee*, 39.
7. "Found Dead," *Public Ledger*, January 18, 1869; "A Beautiful Young Lady Runs Away with a Black Paramour," *Public Ledger*, January 15, 1869; "The Lynching of Wash Henley," historical marker, erected in 2019 by the Lynching Sites Project, National Park Service, and the Shelby County

Historical Commission, Historical Marker Database, https://www.hmdb.org/m.asp?m=146805.
8. Foner, *Reconstruction*, 421–422; Lamon, *Blacks in Tennessee*, 46–48; F. Wayne Binning, "The Tennessee Republicans in Decline, 1869–1876: Part I," *Tennessee Historical Quarterly* 30, no. 4 (Winter 1980): 471–84.
9. "Anti-Radical Convention of Shelby County," *Daily Memphis Avalanche*, June 5, 1874.
10. "Ho! For Bartlett," *Public Ledger*, June 26, 1874.
11. "Saturday June 17," *Daily Memphis Avalanche*, June 7, 1876; "Democratic-Conservative Convention," *Public Ledger*, June 6, 1876; "The Crops - Good Times Coming - Growth and Prosperity of Shelby Depot - A Most Gratifying Exhibit," *Memphis Daily Appeal*, June 9, 1875; "Editorial," *Public Ledger*, November 8, 1876.
12. "Democratic Executive Committee of Shelby County," *Daily Memphis Avalanche*, August 2, 1876.
13. "Editorial," *Public Ledger*, November 8, 1876.
14. Gates, *Stony the Road*, 6.
15. J. Herron to J. B. Davis, July 29, 1880, DMA archives.
16. "Restoration of Radical Rule," *Memphis Daily Appeal*, July 30, 1880; "Final Struggle," *Memphis Daily Appeal*, July 31, 1880; Harkins, *Historic Shelby County*, 82–83; Roger L. Hart, *Redeemers, Bourbons & Populists: Tennessee 1870–1896* (Baton Rouge: Louisiana State University Press, 1975), 39.
17. "To-Morrow," *Memphis Daily Appeal*, August 4, 1880; "Editorial," *Memphis Daily Appeal*, August 6, 1880; "The Election of the Negro Shaw," *Memphis Daily Appeal*, July 30, 1880; "Marines," *Public Ledger*, August 4, 1880.
18. "A Rousing Gathering," *Public Ledger*, August 3, 1880; "The Democratic Rally," *Memphis Daily Appeal*, August 5, 1880.
19. "Election Returns," *Public Ledger*, August 6, 1880; "The Triumph of Justice, Decency and Intelligence," *Public Ledger*, August 6, 1880.
20. "Petrowski to Shelby County," *Memphis Daily Appeal*, August 7, 1880.
21. Hart, *Redeemers, Bourbons & Populist*, 40.
22. Harkins, *Historic Shelby County*, 83.
23. Foner, *A Short History of Reconstruction*, 254.

CHAPTER 20

1. Davies-Rodgers, *Along the Old Stage Coach Road*, 119, 130; "James Baxter Davies," obituary, *Memphis Morning News*, June 17, 1904; B. F. O'Daniel MD to William L. Davies, December 6, 1882, WLD Correspondence, 1865–1890, DMA archives.
2. United States Agricultural Census, 1880, Shelby County, Tennessee; Davies-Rodgers, *Along the Old Stage Coach Road*, 119; "The Renowned

Jack, Mammoth," advertisement, June 10, 1883, DMA archives; "Davies & Young," 1881, advertisement, framed in Davies Manor Historic Site house museum.
3. Davies-Rodgers, *Turns Again Home*, 15, 83; Abie Earle Beaty, Application for Membership, March 28, 1960, U.S. Sons of the American Revolution Membership Applications, 1889–1970 [web database], Ancestry.com; W. B. Beaty and Miss Linlie Lee Davies, marriage license, June 6, 1886, Book L, p. 236, Shelby County Marriage Records 1820–1977, Shelby County Archives [web database]; United States Federal Census, 1900, Shelby County, Tennessee. See enumeration for Bond Beaty.
4. *Appeal-Avalanche*, July 19, 1893; United States Census, 1860, Shelby County, Tennessee. See enumeration for Abel Beaty; "JB Davis," Home Guard, Quarterly Court Loose Papers Index, 1820–1865, File No. 1861-45-0000, Shelby County Archives," [web database]; "One of the Best Known Practitioners," *Commercial Appeal*, June 20, 1897. See also Ida Cooper Collection files on various branches of the Bond family, Boxes 1, 2, 3, 7, 12, Memphis and Shelby County Room, Memphis Public Library.
5. "Saved by Her Sister," *Memphis Commercial*, July 19, 1893; Van Zelm, "Davies Manor Plantation Historic Structure Report," 27–29.
6. Davies-Rodgers, *Turns Again Home*, 15–17; "The Cock Will Fight," *Memphis Daily Avalanche*, November 11, 1888.
7. Davies-Rodgers, Turns Again Home, 87; "Hotel Arrivals," *Memphis Daily Appeal*, July 17, 1885; "Morning Sun," *Memphis Avalanche*, March 24, 1886.
8. "Morning Sun," *Memphis Avalanche*, March 24, 1886.
9. Van Zelm, "Davies Manor Plantation Historic Structure Report," 28; Gates, *Stony the Road*, 14–17; "Saturday June 17," *Daily Memphis Avalanche*, June 7, 1876; "Civil District Lists," *Public Ledger*, June 7, 1876; "Miss Eva Griffin Gave a Delightful Musicale . . .," *Memphis Avalanche*, December 9, 1888; "The Cock Will Fight," *Memphis Daily Avalanche*, November 11, 1888; "JM Bond Wife Margret E. Bond First District & Squire Bond & Witherington, Ledger Entry," n.d., James B. Davies Books, Book 3, DMA archives; "C.G. Hughes, Justice," *Memphis Daily Appeal*, November 2, 1886; Davies-Rodgers, *Turns Again Home*, 29–30. The primary sources listed above all shed light on the Davies family's interactions with others in their community. These sources, along with those that undergird the remainder of Chapter 20, have informed my assertions about the leading figures in the Brunswick community, and the social, political, and business circles that the Davies family moved within through the late nineteenth century.
10. "Shelby Depot," *Memphis Daily Appeal*, June 9, 1875; "Brunswick Election Results," *Memphis Avalanche*, November 2, 1890.
11. "C.G. Hughes Mentions," *Memphis Daily Appeal*, April 17, 1884; "A Call on the Sheriff," *Public Ledger*, April 12, 1880; "Suspended from the Ministry,"

Memphis Commercial, June 8, 1893; Davies-Rodgers, *Turns Again Home*, 30; "The Cock Will Fight," *Memphis Daily Avalanche*, November 11, 1888.

12. "W. H. Bond Mentions," *Memphis Daily Appeal*, April 14, 1887; "Democratic-Conservative Convention," *Public Ledger*, June 6, 1876; "News in Brief," *Memphis Daily Avalanche*, November 11, 1884; "Golly Bond in Bondage," *Memphis Daily Appeal*, November 11, 1877.

13. United States Census, 1860, Shelby County, Tennessee; United States Census, 1870, Shelby County, Tennessee; United States Census, 1880, Shelby County, Tennessee. See Charles B. English enumeration data; "Shelby Depot," *Memphis Daily Appeal*, June 9, 1875; "Brunswick Items," *Memphis Daily Avalanche*, May 28, 1882; "Map of Shelby County, Tennessee, 1888, Carefully compiled from the Records and other authentic sources, and published by M. T. Williamson, Memphis, Tenn," Shelby County Archives. See Charles B. English's landholdings; "It Was a Foul Murder," *Memphis Avalanche*, September 4, 1887.

14. "It Was a Foul Murder," *Memphis Avalanche*, September 4, 1887.

15. "It Was a Foul Murder," *Memphis Avalanche*, September 4, 1887; "Heinous Crime," *Weekly Public Ledger*, September 13, 1887.

16. "A Peculiar Potentate," *Weekly Public Ledger*, October 11, 1887; "Retribution for a Governor," *Memphis Avalanche*, September 28, 1888.

17. "A Jury Packer," *Daily American*, November 13, 1887; "Bond out on Bond," *Public Ledger*, November 14, 1887; "Beginning of the Coffman Case," *Memphis Avalanche*, November 16, 1887.

18. "Beginning of the Coffman Case," *Memphis Avalanche*, November 16, 1887; "He Killed a Negro," *Chicago Tribune*, November 23, 1887; "The Acquittal of W. P. Coffman . . . ," *Weekly Public Ledger*, November 29, 1887.

19. "List of Registrars," *Weekly Public Ledger*, May 6, 1890; "Brunswick, Tenn," *Memphis Avalanche*, September 23, 1888.

20. "Brunswick, Tenn," *Memphis Avalanche*, September 23, 1888; "English and Stewart as Business Partners," *Memphis Avalanche*, September 9, 1888; Davies-Rodgers, *Turns Again Home*, 41; Davies-Rodgers, *Along the Old Stage-Coach Road*, 11–12.

21. "The Sentiment at Brunswick," *Memphis Commercial*, July 29, 1893.

22. "Saved By Her Sister," *Memphis Commercial*, July 19, 1893; "Still He Survives," *Memphis Commercial*, July 20, 1893.

23. "Saved By Her Sister," *Memphis Commercial*, July 19, 1893; "Vengeance Afoot!," *Public Ledger*, July 19, 1893.

24. "Still He Survives"; "Charley Martin Shot," *Leaf-Chronicle*, July 20, 1893; "It Is Thought That He Will Die . . . ," *Appeal-Avalanche*, July 23, 1893.

25. "Still He Survives," *Memphis Commercial*, July 20, 1893; "Rope For Rapist," *Appeal-Avalanche*, July 21, 1893.

26. "Captured and Confessed," *Memphis Commercial*, July 22, 1893.

27. "Lee Walker," Lynching Sites Project, n.d., https://lynchingsitesmem.org/lynching/lee-walker.
28. "Lynched and Burned," *Memphis Commercial*, July 23, 1893.
29. "The Negro Walker Lynched," *New York Times*, July 7, 1893; "Lynched and Burned," *Memphis Commercial*, July 23, 1893; "Done For!," *Public Ledger*, July 24, 1893.
30. "Lynched and Burned," *Memphis Commercial*, July 23, 1893.
31. "Lynched and Burned," *Memphis Commercial*, July 23, 1893.
32. "The Negro Walker Lynched," *New York Times*, July 7, 1893; "Mob Law Cannot Rule," *Appeal-Avalanche*, July 25, 1893; "Lynched and Burned," *Memphis Commercial*, July 23, 1893; "But Bones," *Cincinnati Enquirer*, July 24, 1893.
33. "Mob Law Cannot Rule," *Appeal-Avalanche*, July 25, 1893; "To Be Investigated," *Memphis Commercial*, July 24, 1893; "Brunswick Will Indignate," *Public Ledger*, July 26, 1893.
34. "Lynchers in Limbo," *Memphis Commercial*, July 25, 1893; "Under Which King?," *Memphis Commercial*, July 29, 1893.
35. "First District Heard From," *Appeal-Avalanche*, August 8, 1893; "Resolutions on the Lynching," *Memphis Commercial*, August 5, 1893; "Sheriff M'Lendon Indorsed," *Appeal-Avalanche*, August 1, 1893.
36. "The Sentiment at Brunswick," *Memphis Commercial*, July 29, 1893.
37. "Tried to Try the Sheriff," *Memphis Commercial*, October 20, 1893.
38. "Lynchers Go Scott Free," *Memphis Commercial*, November 1, 1893.

EPILOGUE

1. "The Year's Record," *Lake Geneva Herald*, December 29, 1893; *Reconstruction: America after the Civil War*, hour 4; Gates, *Stoney the Road*, 247.
2. David W. Blight, *Race and Reunion: The Civil War in American Memory* (Cambridge, MA: Harvard University Press, 2002), p. 334 for "884" figure; Equal Justice Initiative, *Lynching in America: Confronting the Legacy of Racial Terror*, 3rd ed. (Montgomery, AL: Equal Justice Initiative, 2017), p. 40 for "4,084" figure.
3. "Ell Persons," Lynching Sites Project, n.d. web, https://lynchingsitesmem.org/lynching/ell-persons; "Jesse Lee Bond," Lynching Sites Project, n.d., https://lynchingsitesmem.org/lynching/jesse-lee-bond. These Lynching Sites Project web pages contain additional links to primary source material related to the Persons and Bond lynchings; Margaret Vandiver, *Lethal Punishment: Lynchings and Legal Executions in the South* (New Brunswick, NJ: Rutgers University Press, 2005), 59–65, 200; Equal Justice Initiative, *Lynching in America*, 41, 43.
4. Old Hughey, "Poplar Corner Pick-Ups," *Times-Promoter*, June 15, 1906; Old Hughey, "Poplar Corner Pick-Ups," *Times-Promoter*, June 22, 1906. Both

articles accessed in Chronicling America database, Library of Congress, https://chroniclingamerica.loc.gov/.

5. "Logan E. Davies," Find a Grave, n.d., https://www.findagrave.com/memorial/7592442/logan_early_davies; "James B, Davies, Book" (with WLD additions), DMA archives; "James Baxter Davies," obituary, *Memphis Morning News*, June 17, 1904. See also references to Logan's illness in "W.L. Davies Correspondence 1891–1907."

6. van Zelm, "Davies Manor Plantation Historic Structure Report," 29; Davies-Rodgers, *Turns Again Home*, 18; "James Baxter Davies," obituary, *Memphis Morning News*, June 17, 1904.

7. Cooper, "Stage Road – Old road," See pages of numbered notes describing sections of the "Old Stage Road," n.d., Box 3, Ida Cooper Collection, Memphis and Shelby County Room, Memphis Public Library; Davies-Rodgers, *Along the Old Stage Coach Road*, 14–39, 64–117.

8. United States Census, 1900, Shelby County, Tennessee; United States Census, 1910, Shelby County, Tennessee; Davies-Rodgers, *Turns Again Home*, 28–29, 179–180; Louella Kerr, telephone interview with Andrew C. Ross, transcript, July 2020.

9. United States Census, 1910, Shelby County, Tennessee; Davies-Rodgers, *Turns Again Home*, 113, 198; "Amos Tucker," Book 493, p. 84 and Book 373, p. 422, Shelby County Register of Deeds; The Gray Family, Interview by Andrew Ross and Evelyn Jackson, September 1, 2020, DMA archives.

10. "Bennett Family Tree," by Tina Sansone, Ancestry.com; "A Tucker Family Tree," by Tina Sansone, Ancestry.com; "Amos Tucker," Book 493, p. 84 and Book 373, p. 422, Shelby County Register of Deeds.

11. Davies-Rodgers, *Turns Again Home*, 184–187, 189–192; W. L. Davies to unknown cousin (probably Sallie Hadley Finney), October 27, 1930, DMA archives; "Richmond Bennett," Find A Grave, https://www.findagrave.com/memorial/80368620/richmond-bennett; "Mrs. Lucinda Herron," Find A Grave, https://www.findagrave.com/memorial/80378380/lucinda-herron; Davies-Rodgers, *Along the Old Stage-Coach Road*, 30, 47, 58.

12. Annie Mae Frazier Blackwell Myles, Interview by Andrew Ross, Nancy McDonough and Barbara Williams, August 25, 2017, "Oral History with Annie Mae," transcript, DMA archives and DMA office files.

ACKNOWLEDGMENTS

I'd like to begin this accounting of debts by acknowledging the lessons I absorbed and the people I encountered early on in my career working for small-town newspapers. Those jobs left me with a deep-seated belief in the power of local history and local storytelling, and the importance of tapping into ground-level perspectives from unexpected angles as a means to reach for larger truths. I am certain that I would not have had the ability to take on much less finish this project without those initial experiences in community journalism. Thanks to James Jennings for taking a chance and hiring me at the *Clarksdale Press Register* when I had yet to publish a word. Among the blessings that stemmed from working in that storied corner of the Mississippi Delta was the chance to assist Vladimir Alexandrov with the research for his book *The Black Russian*. Joining the search for the obscure figure at the heart of that story helped trigger a lightbulb about the type of archival-based research and writing I wanted to one day tackle, so thank you Vladimir for helping plant that seed. Thanks to Cyndy Wright at the *Bastrop Advertiser* and the editorial department at the *Killeen Daily Herald* for opportunities at those publications. My time in Texas made be a better reporter but it also led in a roundabout way to a stint as a research assistant in New York for the investigative journalist Wayne Barrett. Wayne was as close to a professional mentor as I have ever had, and the skills I learned in that role were never far away from me throughout the length of this project. Your kind is missed nowadays, Wayne.

Moving to Memphis for graduate school turned out to be another critical turn in the long and winding path that led me to this book. Thank you to my cohorts in the MFA Creative Writing Program at the University of Memphis and to my primary instructors there—Cary Holladay, John Bensko, and Tim Johnston. I learned about craft and revision during my time in the program but most importantly to have more confidence in my creative instincts. Thanks to Joseph Jones for helping me find my footing in the teaching realm, and to Donal Harris, Darryl Domingo, Laura Wright, and Josh Phillips for always having friendly words in Patterson Hall. Others who enriched my time at U of M included Leslie Luebbers, Neil O'Brien, Robert Connolly, and Warren Perry—all of whom I encountered through the Museum Studies Graduate Certificate Program. Warren showed me that I wasn't entirely delusional for trying to find a new career path somewhere between writing work and museums; I only wish there could have been more happy hours at R. P. Tracks before the cruel illness came that took him far too soon.

I appreciate Rosalind Withers for the opportunity at the Withers Collection Museum & Gallery in 2015, and Caroline Mitchell Carrico and Louella Weaver at the Pink Palace Museum for creating a wonderful research and script-writing project that allowed me to immerse myself in the treasure chest of stories that is the Memphis and Shelby County Room at the Benjamin L. Hooks Central Library. Thanks also to Bill Patton and Meagan May at Backbeat Tours for hiring me as a historic tour guide during the period when I was piecing together an income with more gig jobs than I care now to remember. It was not lost on me then, nor is it now, just how lucky I have been to find my way into the field of public history in a city as soulful and layered and vital to the American story as Memphis.

The years I spent at the Davies Manor Association presented unique challenges, some of which were expected, others that were less so, but throughout it all, it was a deeply rewarding and educational experience in more ways that I could ever name here. Regardless if there are those who have taken issue with my decision to tell this story in this form, and regardless if there are those with whom I have disagreed over larger matters of interpretation and the role of museums, I appreciate the many people I worked with and came to know there, both inside and outside the organization. The story that unfolds in this book is intended to stand independently of Davies Manor. Yet it is my sincere hope as well that the book can inform work connected to the historic site for many years to come.

First, thanks to Henry Boyd, who has been a major asset to the DMA for many years. His leadership on the board of directors resulted in the formation of the Mose Frazier Committee project in 2008, and led to numerous other positive developments that followed. Thanks to former executive director Nancy McDonough for her work on the original oral history initiative, for her long history of dedication to Davies Manor, and for creating the position that allowed me to come on board in 2017. Jimmy Ogle, former Shelby County historian and DMA board president, is a walking encyclopedia of knowledge on all things Memphis and Shelby County history and taught me a great deal. Others who have made real contributions to the DMA in recent years include Chris Mock, Cyndy Osborne, Katrina Hansen, Ryan Parry, Nick Gotten, Jack Smith, Sylvester Lewis, Judy Mills, Susie Sally, John Charles Wilson, Kevin Quinn, and Julie Sefton. Going back well before my time, thanks is due to Ed Williams, Jeanne Crawford, and Marilyn Van Eynde. Ed Williams was the Shelby County historian who followed Davies-Rodgers, and although I never knew him, I know that he helped keep the organization going through uncertain times. The same is true of Van Eynde and Crawford and plenty of others who have thanklessly given their time and energy through the years. Simply keeping a small historic site running, much less doing good history work there, is a more difficult task than most realize. I must also acknowledge the debt owed to Ellen Davies-Rodgers. However difficult it has been at moments to navigate the legacy she left behind, there is no question that she documented an enormous amount of historical data that would have otherwise disappeared. Similarly, her preservation of the Davies Manor home and surrounding site has resulted in the survival of a unique toehold into the past—and one whose true potential, I believe, is in only beginning to be tapped.

A huge thank you is owed to Barbara Williams. Barbara chaired the Mose Frazier Committee project in a volunteer capacity and paved the way for so much of what I and others would later pick up on in the effort to expand Davies Manor's story. The knowledge that has been gleaned about the African American community connected to Davies Manor's twentieth-century history would not have been possible without her. More generally, Barbara's innate curiosity and appreciation for nuanced thinking have been sources of inspiration throughout the length of the project. In many ways, my involvement with the project can all be traced back to that initial meeting I had with Barbara in 2017 when she explained to me her fascination with the story of Richmond Bennett. Katherine Memmott was another volunteer researcher who put in many thankless hours of skilled genealogical sleuthing during the time we were working to get the exhibit that became *Omitted in Mass* off the ground. Thanks as well to Tina Sansone, who Barbara and I both enlisted at different points to work on the genealogical threads connected to Richmond and Sarah Jane Bennett and Wilcher and Mary Tucker.

Deep gratitude is owed to all those, either living or now deceased, who participated in Davies Manor's African American oral history initiative and related research through the subsequent years. Along with the interviews Barbara documented, my conversations with Altoria Prince, Louella Nelson Kerr, Randi Gray and his family, and Shirley Herron Alexander proved to be especially helpful. The late Annie Mae Frazier Blackwell Myles and her daughter Ella Blackwell Pitts both sat for multiple interviews. Annie Mae's candid recollections were every bit as illuminating as they were difficult to hear. Never did Annie Mae express bitterness, however. Instead, she was always generous, kind, and full of humor, and beyond the memories she shared about life at the Davies family's estate, I learned many other things through our conversations. Thanks to Andy Payne for taking me on a highly informative driving tour that helped me understand the route of the long-vanished "Smokey Road" and glimpse the historical terrain of Davies Plantation as it would have looked before being converted into a golf course and subdivisions. Thanks to Tom Edwards for providing an authoritative, firsthand understanding of the location of the Davies Plantation Cemetery along US 64. I can only hope that I have handled this story in a way that gives proper respect to all the unknown souls who were buried there between 1855 and 1910.

Kevin McVay and Dwight Fryer offered valuable knowledge, context, and perspective about African American history in northeast Shelby County and West Tennessee. Both were generous with their time participating in programming events. One of my regrets in the book was that I was not able to bring in more discussion of the genealogical research that Kevin has worked on with the DMA through the years related to his family. Thanks to Evelyn Jackson for her help during a renewed oral history effort that we began in 2020 with the help of a Tennessee Humanities Grant. Aram Goudsouzian at the University of Memphis connected me to Evelyn, and has been a source of encouragement and inspiration in other ways himself. Kim Short assisted as a volunteer researcher and docent at Davies Manor during my time there. Kim always asked questions that needed to be asked and I appreciate the opportunity she facilitated in 2019 to discuss Davies Manor at the Morton Museum of Collierville History.

I consider it a blessing to have known Sylvester Lewis, who, before his passing in 2022 at the age of ninety-two, served on the DMA board and on the Shelby County Historical Commission. Sylvester was an invaluable well of knowledge about local African American history, in particular the history of the Gray's Creek/Eads community near Davies Manor where he grew up. He patiently answered my questions on many phone calls and sat for multiple recorded interviews. The chance to ride northeast Shelby County's backroads with Sylvester was one of the highlights of my time at Davies. Without Sylvester's research into Simon and Kitty Price, Gray's Creek Baptist Church, and his own ancestor, Joseph "Free Joe" Harris, the sections of the book dealing with those interrelated topics would not have been possible.

I benefited greatly from consultations with historians specializing in American slavery, public history, and nineteenth-century life. I owe an especially large debt to Antoinette van Zelm, assistant director of the Center for Historic Preservation at Middle Tennessee State University. Antoinette and her team there devoted much time and energy to a public partnership project with Davies Manor that resulted in a renewed deep dive into the Davies Manor archives and early land deed records at the Shelby County Archives. The final report and family history section that Antoinette wrote for that project helped shape my thinking in new and important ways. Antoinette was also kind enough to read a full draft of this manuscript shortly before publication and provided crucial feedback on improving the text. Thanks to Earnestine Jenkins, Beverly Bond, and Susan O'Donovan at the University of Memphis, and Tim Huebner at Rhodes College for consultations on the *Omitted in Mass* exhibit development. I must also acknowledge the debt owed to the professional historians whom I have never met but whose books proved so crucial to expanding my thinking about the history of American slavery and enslaved people, and the evolving historiography of slavery studies. At points in this project I relied especially heavily on the incredible scholarship of Tiya Miles, Stephanie M. H. Camp, Daina Ramey Berry, Annette Gordon-Reed, and Edward E. Baptist. Works by Eric Foner, Sean Wilentz, Richard White, Daniel Walker Howe, and Henry Louis Gates Jr. were among the other critical secondary sources that I relied upon to expand the narrative lens beyond the local level.

I am deeply appreciative of the assistance I received from the archivists, librarians, public historians, county clerks, and others I encountered at the outside collections, courthouses, and historic sites I visited. In Lunenburg County, Virginia, the county clerk Gordon Erby was generous with his time helping me locate the earliest records related to Zachariah Davis and the Black families Davis and his children enslaved. Erby's tip about the location of the abandoned "Love's Mill" site resulted in an especially beneficial excursion one afternoon during my stay there. Cookie Curren provided insightful general knowledge about early Lunenburg County history that helped me get a feel for that very particular place. Willard Hazlewood also generously assisted me from afar on a number of occasions with research in the county clerk's office. The staff at the Library of Virginia in Richmond were helpful locating obscure petition documents and tax records. In Maury County, Tennessee, thank you to county archivist Thomas Price and his staff who patiently helped me work my way through the legal records that shed so much light on the events from the 1830s and 1840s. Closer to home, Frank Stewart at the Shelby County archives was always generous with his time answering my many emails and requests for scans of records. Wayne Dowdy and his team at the Memphis and Shelby County Room never failed to point me in the right direction during my visits there. That place is a tremendous resource to the Greater Memphis community. Gerald Chaudron, Jim Cushing, and the staff at the Special Collections Department at the University of Memphis were also enormously helpful as I researched the Ellen Davies-Rodgers Papers. The excellent staff in the interlibrary loan department at U of M's McWherter Library were a great help locating more obscure secondary sources and facilitating my ability to acquire microfilmed legal records from the Library of Virginia. Finally, thank you to Gareth Mark, who I had the good fortune to intersect with through Ancestry.com. A descendant of the Davies family, and a professional genealogist to boot, Gareth provided invaluable expertise and advice during my dive into eighteenth-century Virginia.

Acknowledgments

Thank you to Gianna Mosser, Betsy Phillips, Joell Smith-Borne, Patrick Samuel, Alissa Faden, and the rest of the team at Vanderbilt University Press. I could not have asked to find a better home for this project than VUP. I owe an especially large debt to Betsy Phillips, who saw the potential for what the book could become in my initial proposal and has remained a steadfast supporter ever since. Betsy's correspondence and editing assistance at various points in the manuscript's development proved to be critical. I deeply appreciate the anonymous readers who agreed to peer review the manuscript on behalf of VUP. The recommendations and critiques that I received through that process were eye-opening in the best possible way. Thanks as well to Duvall Osteen for providing general support and advice on the contractual details, and to Ann Morrison for generously offering an amazing work space in New Orleans on multiple occasions.

There are plenty of others who have directly and indirectly influenced my thinking throughout the writing of the book and shown their support in ways both large and small. A short list includes Brandon Dahlberg, Chris Moyer, Ashley Roach-Frieman, Clay Cantrell, Magda Sakaan, Jimmy Rout, Brigette Jones, and Ramiro Hinojosa. Thanks also to Michael Kuntzman and the good folks at The Cove, and to the staff at City and State for the years of excellent service and early morning smiles. Thanks to Kimberly Horton, president and CEO at The Blues Foundation, and my co-workers there. Thanks to Garrett Jue, Jackson Huffman, Jay Everett, Erick Alcaraz, Katelyn Quador, Julia Osmond, Jennifer Osmond, and the rest of the soccer crew for their friendship and for the outlet that helps keep me sane. Thank you to Elizabeth Brooks. I couldn't have done this without your support. Finally, thank you to my parents, siblings, and the rest of my extended family for providing the foundation that makes all else possible.

INDEX

Enslaved individuals who appear in the narrative prior to 1865 are alphabetized by their first name. In instances where post-emancipation surnames for these same people can be confirmed, those names are provided in brackets. All individuals who make their first appearance in the narrative after 1865 are listed alphabetically by their last name.

Page numbers in *italic* refer to illustrations.

Abernathy, Diana, 21n, 314n1
Abraham (1), 55, 280
Abraham (2), 45–47, 143, 282, 293–94
Adaline, 145. *See also* Martha Aaline
Albert, 71, 73–74
Aleck, 285
Alee, 138, 141, 299–300
Alford, 291–92
Allin, 287
Alsa, 69, 286, 295
Amanda, 92–94, 143, 295–96
amnesty oaths, 195–98
Amos [Davis], 108, *120*, 205, 217, 301–2, 312n2
Amos/Amous [Tucker], 146, 174–75, 284, 291–93, 297, 300
  post-emancipation, 205, 218, 259, 266, 297
Amy (1), 39, 277–78, 281
Amy (2), 55, 69, 275
Anders, 288
Anderson, 69, 286, 295
Anderson, Thomas C., 278
Andrews, Mark L., 42
Anjaline, 288

Ann, 145–46, 277, 291–92, 299
Anthona, 45–47, 282
Anthony [Tucker], 146, 174–75, 218, 285, 291–93, 297, 300
Arata, Dan, 253
Archer/Archie/Archa [Davies] [Hadley], 108, *120*, 203–4, 217, 286–87, 298
Arominta, 108, *120*, 301
Arthur/Artie [Ecklin], 7, 136, 152–54, 167, 312n2
Asbury, Francis, 32–34, 38, 61
Ash, Stephen V., 160
Astrop, Henry, 27
Athy, Phil R., 226–27
Atlanta, 177–80

Baptist, Edward E., 85
Baptists, 30–32, 36, 96, 102, 112
Barrett, James Hill, 251
Beaty, Abel, 156, 230
Beaty, Linnie Lee (Davies), 168, 204, 214, 230–31, 233, *238*, 245–46, 257
Beaty, William "Bond" ("W. B."), 230–31, 233, *238*, 239, 244–47, 250–51, 255

Beauregard, P. G. T., 159
Bell, Jim, 217
Bell, John C., 128–29
Bell, Rachel, 217
Ben, 92–94, 143, 144, 168, 183, 291, 295–96. *Possibly same as* Gray, Ben
Bennett, Steve, 204
Bennett Place, 186, 187n
Berry, Daina Ramey, xxxvi, 31, 146
Betsy C., 286
Black citizenship, 199–200, 219, 221. *See also* Fourteenth Amendment
Blackstone, John, 20
Black suffrage, 193, 200, 219–21, 227–28. *See also* Fifteenth Amendment
Bob [Davis], 128, 205n. *See also* Green, Bob
Bode, Phil, 251
Bolton, Isaac, 91
Bolton, Sarah, 196, 211
Bolton, Wade H., 91
Bolton, Washington, 91, 104, 117, 128, 196, 211
Bolton and Dickens (slave trading firm), 91–92, 104, 108, 117
Bond, Golly, 240
Bond, Jesse Lee, 254
Bond, John Priddy, 251
Bond, Mary Lucinda, 230
Bond, William H. ("W. H."), 224, 227, 239, 240n, 241–43
Booker, 50–51, 55, 57–58, 274–76
Bozwell, 46n, 284
Bragg, Braxton, 177
Bragg, David B., 57, 275
Bragg Hospital, 177
Branch, D. H., 110
Breckenridge, John C., 128–29
Brister, 20–25, 28–29, 48, 62–63, 272, 275, 281
Brown, John, 129
Brownlow, William "Parson," 194, 197–99, 220, 223

Bunch, Lonnie G., III, xxxivn
Burnett, Jeremiah, 44–45, 55, 95, 143, 273–74, 280, 282–83, 293–94
Burnett, Zachariah D., 278–79
Burrell, 46n, 144–45, 168, 183, 283, 287, 298–99

Calhoun, John C., 100
Camp, Stephanie M. H., 74
Camp Chase, 178, 182–83, 340n6
Camp Douglas, 167
Camp Shiloh, 165, 176. *See also* Shiloh, Battle of
Cane Ridge, 36
Cartwright, Alich, 205, 288
Cartwright, Caroline, 204
Cartwright, Elias, 205, 218, 288
Cartwright, Lucious, 205, 288
Cartwright, Lucy, 204
Cartwright, Mariah, 218
Cartwright, Susan, 204–5, 217, 258, 290, 301–2
Cartwright, Will, 205, 288
Cartwright, William, 205, 218, 288, 293, 299
Celia, 172, 196, 302
Celine, 292
Chambers, Madison H., 169
Chandler, Walter, *xix*
Chappell, Dickey, 54, 70–76, 81, 86, 116, 148, 203, 284, 286
Charles, 28–29, 48, 272, 281
Cherry, George, 218
Chickasaw/Chickasaw nation, 35, 82, 116, 124n
Chonna, 46n, 284
Christianity, 29–30, 36, 88, 178, 239
    and Davis/Davies family, 29–38, 40, 41–45, 47, 61, 231–32
    and issues of slavery and race, 30–38, 105–8, 146
    See also individual sects and churches
Civil Rights Act of 1866, 219

Clarke, Hatcher, 278–79
Clinton, Dewitt, 251
Cloe, 27
Cobb, Howell, 154
Coffman, William P., 240–42, *241*, *243*
Coke, Thomas, 32
Coleman, William E., 280
Coleman [Cartwright], 145, 205, 283, 287–88, 298–99
Coll, 72–74
Collins Chapel African Methodist Episcopal Church, 191, 193
contraband camps, 164–65, 171, 176, 191
Cooper, H. W. "Ida," xiiin
Coppock, Paul, xiiin
Corinth, Mississippi, 152–53, 155–56, 159, 182
cotton, xxxiv, 1, 36, 48, 101, *116*, 126–27, 207
 on Davies plantation (Shelby County), xiv, xxxn, 6–7, 13, 87–90, 97–99, 124–28, 142, 168–70, 210, 229, 287
 on Davis/Davies plantation (Fayette County): 75, 81–83, 86–90, 94
 on Davis plantation (Maury County), 46–47, 60, 76
 and enslaved labor, 1, 7, 36, 47, 88, 98, 102, 124–28, 135, 168–70, 287
 in Memphis and Shelby County, xxxn, 9, 87–91, 102, *122*, 126–28, 157, 169–70, 202, 218
 and sharecropping, 216, 229
Coulter, Thomas W., 172, 196
Crenshaw, Florian, 135, 151–52, 166, 177
Crenshaw, Merritt, 135, 151–52, 166, 177
Crenshaw, Thomas B., 102, 104, 110, 126–27, 133–35, 196, 212, 302
 during Civil War, 151, 165, 172
Crump, Edward Hull "Boss," Jr., xi, *xvii*, *xix*

Daley, W. L., 145, 168, 183, 210
Daniel, 145–46, 277, 291–92, 299
Davidson, Nancy (Davies), 144, 291, 295–96, 298

Davies, Almeda Penelope (Little), 5–6, 112–15, *117*, 178, 183, 290, 303
 death and burial, 123, 151, 212, 257, *263*
Davies, Frances "Fanny" Anna Vaughn, 119, 123, 140, 167–68, 212, 257, *263*
 confrontation with Union officer, *xix*, 160–62, *173*
Davies, Frances Ina (Stewart), *238*, 243–44, 257, 259
Davies, Gillie Mertis, xiii, *xvii*, 12, 168, 214, 230–32, *238*, *239*, 255, 257, 259
 and operation of Shelby County plantation, 230–31, 244, 257–58
 and politics, 231, 233, 243
Davies, Henry Newton, 59, 88, 97, 112, 115, 143
 during Civil War, 137, 340n6, 182–83, 211–12
 as slaveholder, 125–26, 148, 282, 298
Davies, James Baxter, 5, 59, 71–72, 88, 100–104, *117*, 137–39
 and Davies Manor, xiii, *xix*, 103, 214, 231
 death and burial, 256–57, *263*, *268*
 during Civil War, 150–52, 154–56, 162, 166–68, 177–78, 181–84, 186–87, 329n10
 during Civil War aftermath, 196, 210–15, 229
 and politics, 133–35, 223, 225–27, 229
 and settlement of father's estate, 140–45
 and Shelby County plantation, xxxn, 2, 5–7, 92–99, *117*, *121*, 202–6, 210–18, 229–32, *237*
 as slaveholder, 6–7, 94, 108–15, *120–21*, 124–26, 147, 150, 165, 183, 203–5, 286–93, 295–303
 See also Davies Manor; Davies plantation (Shelby County)
Davies, Julius Augustus ("Gus"), 7, 115, *117*, 168, 204, 212–16, 230, *236*
 death and burial, 9, *263*, *267*
 in Walls, Mississippi, 9, 10, 216, 255–56

Davies, Logan Early, 59, 71–72, 86–88, 100–4, *118*, 123–28, 183, 194–98, 212, 230
　and Davies Manor, xiii, *xix*, 103, 214, 231
　death and burial, 256–57, *263*, 268
　during Civil War, 139–40, 142–45, 162, 167–72
　and politics, 12, 133, 223–27, 229, 239
　and Shelby County plantation, xxxn, 2, 5–7, 92–99, *117*, *121*, 202–6, 210–18, 229–32, *237*
　as slave catcher, 110–11, 151n, 165
　as slaveholder, 6–7, 92, 108–15, 120–21, 124–26, 147, 165, 171–72, 203–5, 286–93, 295–303
　See also Davies Manor; Davies plantation (Shelby County)
Davies, Mary A. (Webber), 112, 115n, 183, 212
Davies, Mattie, 212
Davies, Pauline "Polly" Little (Leake), 112–13, 178, 183, 196, 213, 215, 287, 341n11
Davies, William Little, *ii*, *xvii*, 1–9, 10–11, 102, 115, *117*, 168, 204, 212–14, 231–33, 252, 255–57
　death and burial, *263*, 269
　as head of Davies plantation (Shelby County), *xxi*, 6, 12, 15, 257–58
　as local and family history source, xiii, xxxiii, 4–5, 12–15, 102, 151n, 154, 182, 186, 303
　as physician, 2, 215–16, 230, *236*, 244, 257, 312n2
　views on race, 7–9, 13–14, 260
Davies Manor, *ii*, *x*, *xxiii*, xxix–xxx, *11*, 115, 144, 168, 210, 214–17, 229–32, 244, 259–60
　acquisition by Davies family, 93, 97, 103
　construction of, xiii, *xviii*, *xix*, 103, 307n4
　as historic attraction, xiv, *xvii*, *xx–xxi*, xxv–xxvii, xxxi–xxxiii, 161, 269

　and nearby households, 204, 298, 303
　restoration of, xiii, *xvii*
　See also Davies Manor Historic Site; Davies plantation (Shelby County)
Davies Manor Association, xxv, xxx–xxxiii, 254n, 260n, *261*, *264*, 309n10
　archives, xvi, xxv, 4n, 255
　creation of, xiv, xxx, 269
Davies Manor Historic Site, *viii*, xi–xiii, xxiv, *xviii*, xxv–xxvi, 124n, *262*, *267*
Davies plantation (Shelby County), 95, 124, 144, 161–62, 167–70, *173*, 186, 196n, *238*, *239*, *267*
　acquisition by Davies family, 93, 97, 103, 325n1
　cemetery, 260, 268, 301
　diversification after Civil War, 229–30, *237*
　enslavement at, xxv–xxxvii, 2–3, 6–7, 14, 94–99, 105, 108–15, 120–21, 124–26, 143–47, 150, 165, 170–71, 183, 203–5, 211, 217–18, 229, 258n, *266*, 286–93, 295–303, 309n10
　establishment, xiii, *xviii*, *xix*
　sharecropping at, xiv, xvi, xxv–xxviii, 7, 202–6, 217, 229, 258, 298, 303, 309n10
　under Ellen Davies-Rodgers, *xix–xx*, xxiv, 15, 260n, *267*
　under James and Logan Davies, xxxn, 2, 5–7, 92–99, *117*, *121*, 202–6, 210–18, 229–32, *237*
　under William Little Davies, 5–6, *11*, 12–13, 15, 257
　See also Davies Manor; *individual enslaved persons and family members*; Oaks, The
Davies-Rodgers, Frances "Ellen," xi–xvi, *xii*, *xvii–xxiv*, xxx–xxxi, xxxiv, 12, 15, *238*, 257–60, *263*, *267*
　Along the Old Stage-Coach Road, 4n, 94n, 124n, 268
　birth, 257, 258–59

as historian, xiv, *xxii–xxiii*, xxxvi, 3, 4n, 14n, 21n, 124n, 154, 161–62, 186, 197, 303
Holy Innocents, The, xxii
and issues of ancestry, xiv, xxv–xxvi, 4n, 307n4
and plantation mentality, xxvi–xxix, 310n15
Romance of the Episcopal Church in West Tennessee, 1832–1964, The, xiv, *xxii*
Turns Again Home, xxvii, xxix, 4n, 186–87, 259n, 297
Davis, Ann, 44
Davis, Baby, 205
Davis, Baxter, 39, 55–56, 277, 279–80
Davis, Carry, 217
Davis, Clifford, *xix*
Davis, Cora, 217
Davis, Delia, 204–5
Davis, Diana (Blackstone), 20, 21n, 22, 24, 30–31, 35, 41, 61, 272, 281
death, 27, 48
Davis, Dianna (Burnett), 50, 274, 280
Davis, Eleanor, 35–37, 42
Davis, George W., 218
Davis, Gordon, 204–5
Davis, Jefferson, 185, 192, 198
Davis, Joanna "Anna" (Burnett), 44–46, 59, 65–66, 148, 273–74, 282–83, 294
Davis, Joe, 205, 217n, 258n, 301–2
Davis, Maria, 205, 217n, 301–2
Davis, Martha, 20, 50–51, 278
Davis, Mary Asbury, 59, 101
Davis, Paschal, 39, 55, 277, 279–80
Davis, Robert, 20, 27–28, 41–42, 46–47, 51, 56–57, 63–64
as Methodist preacher, 27, 33–38, 43–44, 61, *101*
as slaveholder, 35, 37–39, 42–43, 273, 277
Davis, Sarah (Anderson), 20, 50, 278
Davis, Sarah (Hadley), 47, 53, 59, 87, 123, 217

Davis, Sterling, 38–39, 46, 56, 63, 277–78, 281
Davis, William Early, 22, 33–37, 41, 52–56, 59–60, 63, 66, 112, 122, 128
change of family name to Davies, 86
death and estate of, 140–49, *173–75*
feud with Dickey Chappell, 54, 70–76, 81, 86, *116*, 148, 203, 284, 286
as Methodist minister, 4, 33–34, 41, 43–44, *61*
move to Fayette County, 74–75, 81, 83–88, *116*
as possible father of Willshire, 53, 56, 95, 147, 284
as slaveholder, 4–5, 14, 39, 43–48, 52–54, 59, 65, 67–77, 84–96, 121, 125–26, 142–49, 174–75, 277, 282–300
See also Davis/Davies plantation (Fayette County); Davis plantation (Maury County)
Davis, William Wesley ("W. W."), 45, 68–69, 294, 298
as slaveholder, 68–69, 72, 145, 203, 286, 289–90, 295
Davis, Zachariah, xiv, xxvi, 4, 19–35, 38–40, 45–46, 48–52, 56, *61–63*
and Christian faith, 29–35, 40, 43, *61*
death and estate of, 54–58, 64, 272–81
as slaveholder, 4, 20, 22–29, 33–35, 38–41, 45–51, 55, 62–63, 69, 97, 149, 272–82
See also Davis "manor plantation" Reedy Creek estate (Lunenburg County)
Davis (Lockridge), Mariah, 45, 145, 277, 291–92, 299
Davis "manor plantation" Reedy Creek estate (Lunenburg County), 20, 22, 33, 43–44, 45, 48, 54, *61*
enslaved individuals connected with, 20, 23–24, 27–29, 35, 39–41, 43–44, 49, 85–86, 272–82
Davis (Mitchell/Hanks), Eliza Ann, 45, 52–54, 67–69, 284–86, 294

Davis plantation (Maury County), 46–47, 66, 75, 85–87
    enslaved individuals at, 46–47, 59, 67–77, 85–87, 267, 269–70, 277, 282–89, 294–95, 297
    See also Davis, William Early
Davis/Davies plantation (Fayette County), 81–88, 92–95, 115, *116–17*, 123, 145, 168, 210
    enslaved individuals at, 81, 92, *116*, *121*, 125, 142–49, 203, 277, 282–300
    See also Davis, William Early
Davis/Davies/Hadley, Joe, 203–4, 217, 287, 298
Davis/Davies/Hadley, Josh, 217
Davis/Davies/Hadley, Perry, 203–4, 287, 290–91, 298
Dianna, 108
Dickens, Thomas, 91
Dickson, Alex, xv–xvi
Dilcy/Dilcey, 23–25, 28, 55, 57, 62–63, 272–73, 275
Dolly, 50–51, 55, 57–58, 64, 274–76
Donelson, Alex, 103, 133, 211
Donelson, Jane (Royster), 103
Donelson, Kate (Royster), 103, 211
Donelson, Samuel, 103
Douglas, Stephen A., 128–29
Draper, Milton, 92, 94, 295–96
Du Bois, W. E. B., 220

Eastman, Jim, 240–42, *241*, *243*, 253–55
Eaton, John, 164
Ecklin, Charl, 13
Ecklin, Joshua, 196
Ecklin, Joshua B., 135–37, 139, 150, 152, 155, 167, 178, 211
Ecklin, Robert, 103, 134–35, 161
Elcey, 52–53, 67–69, 285–86, 294
Elias, 108, 120, 301
Eliza [Price], 137n, *176*
Elizabeth, 108
Ellen, 285
Ellis, Joseph J., 23
Ellis, P., 293
Elva, 46n, 283
Emancipation Proclamation, 163, 193–94
Emeline Pettilar, 145, 277, 291–92, 299
Emely/Emily [Cartwright], 144, 205, 218, 283, 287–88, 293, 298–99
Emily (2), 108, *120*, 301
English, Charles B., 224, 227, 239–43, 251–52
Enoch/Eanoch, 145, 277, 291–92, 299
Equal Justice Initiative, 254–55
Ezekiel, 285

Fanna, 45–47, 282–83
Fanny, 279
Fanny [Harris], 55, 107
Farabee, John, 110
Feild, Emily (Ecklin), 161
Feild, Roscoe, 104, 133–34, 194–95, 212
    during Civil War, 151–52, 156, 161, 166, 177–78, 329n10
Fifteenth Amendment, 221
Fifty-Fourth Massachusetts Infantry, 170
Fifty-Ninth Colored Heavy Artillery, 171, 192
Finney, Elizabeth Blanche "E. B." (Davies), 146–48, *173*, 218, 285, 289, 291–94, 297, 300
Finney, Gabe, 144, 146–47, 150, *173*, 218, 285, 289, 291–94, 297, 300
Foner, Eric, 206
Forrest, Nathan Bedford, xxxii, 181–82, 184, 224
Fort de Russey, 139
Fort Donaldson, 142, 150
Fort Henry, 142, 150
Fort Pickering, 165, *176*, 191–92, 221
Fort Pillow, 136
Fort Wagner, 170
Fourteenth Amendment, 199, 221
Fowlkes & Co., *122*, 128
Frances, 165
Francina, 289

Frank (1), 56, 281
Frank (2), 280
Frank (3), 138, 141, 299–300
Frankey, 45–47, 84–85, 95, 125, 143, 148–49, 282, 294
Franklin, Battle of, 182
Frayser, Harry M., 251–52
Frazier, Mose, x, xvi, xxi, xxix, 216, 260, 264, 267, 269–70
Freedmen's Bureau, 207–9, 219
Fugitive Slave Act, 100, 129

Gabe [Little], 7, 151–54, 166, 177
Gardiner, Jennie, 161, 169
Gardiner, Suzy, 2–3
Gates, Henry Louis, 221
George (1), 95, 145, 289–90
George (2), 109
Glymph, Thavolia, 115
Gordon-Reed, Annette, 39, 102
Grace, 24–25, 28, 39, 42, 57, 62–63, 272, 275, 277
Grant, Ulysses S., 142, 163–65, 170, 186, 226
Gray, Ben, 204–5, 217, 258. *Possibly same as* Ben
Gray, Bennie, 204
Gray, Celia, 204
Gray, Cora, 204
Gray, Jim (1), 106n
Gray, Jim (2), 204
Gray, Joe, 204
Gray, John, 106n
Gray, Louis/Lewis, 204–5, 217
Gray, Virginia, 204
Gray's Creek, 88, 96, 106–7, 113n, 254n
Gray's Creek Baptist Church, 105–8, 136n, 254n, 262
Gray's Creek Cemetery, 262
Green, Bob, 205. *See also* Bob [Davis]
Green, Elnora, 205
Green, Fanny, 205
Green, Geo, 205
Green, Lizzie, 205

Green (Cartwright), 144, 150, 205, 287–88, 293

Hall, 50–51, 278–79
Hall, Redford, 213
Hamlin, Charles, Jr., 20, 22–23, 27, 32–33, 98
Hanks, Elijah, 67–69, 285–86, 294
Hannah (1), 24–25, 55, 62–63, 272–76
Hannah (2), 144–45, 168, 183, 283, 287–88, 298–99
Harkins, John, xxx
Harnwell, Brower, 200
Harper's Ferry, 129
Harriet/Harriot I., 144, 168, 291, 295–96
Harris, Isham G., 134, 136, 150, 198
Harris, John, 105
Harris, Joseph "Free Joe," 105–8, 136n, 254n
Harris, Mollie, 217
Harris, Peter, 217
Harry, 108, 120, 301
Hart, Roger L., 228
Hattie [Bennett], 151, 290
Hayes, Josephine, 210–11
Hayes, Robert Butler, 210–11
Hayes, Rutherford B., 225
Hayes, Samuel Jackson, 126–27, 211n
Henley, Wash, 222–23, 255n
Herron, James, 225
Herron, Lawrence, 260
Herron, Lucinda, 259
Hood, John Bell, 181–82, 191
Horton, Henry, 12
Hughes, C. G., 239, 241, 252
Hunter, George E., 325n1
Hunter, Lem, 217
Hunter, Minnie, 217
Hurlbut, Stephen, 171
Hyrum, 288

Inge, Richard, 239, 252
Isaac, 274, 276

Island No. 10, 150, 153, 155
Ivey, 46n, 283

Jackson, Andrew, 60, 82, 103, 126
Jackson, Rachel Donelson, 103
Jacob (1), 289
Jacob (2), 108, 120, 301
James, 276
Janson, 287
Jenkins, Earnestine, 176
Jeremiah, 55
Jim [Price], 106, 137n, 157, 165, 171, 176, 222
Jinny, 24, 49–50, 55, 69, 273, 276
John (1), 55, 279
John (2), 284
John (3), 75–76, 288–89
Johnson, Andrew, 150, 195–96, 199, 221
Johnston, Albert Sidney, 152–53
Johnston, Joseph, 183–84, 186
Jones, John W., 83
Jones, L., 278–79
Jones, Philip T., 222
Jordin, 46n, 283
Joshua/Josh/Joshoway [Davies] [Hadley], 68, 72, 74, 94, 284, 286–88, 290–91, 295, 297–98
    post-emancipation, 165, 203–6, 217, 287, 291, 298
Judy, 39, 277

Katherine E., 291
Keynes, Burrell, 110–11
King, Martin Luther King, Jr., xxxii
Kitty [Price], 105–6, 109, 136n, 176
Ku Klux Klan, *xix*, *xxxii*, 222, 224, 240–41. *See also* white supremacy

Leake, Edward Curd, 96, 112, 135, 144, 168, 178, 183, 212–13
Leake, Richard, 96
Leake, Samuel "Colonel," 96, 103–5, 107, 112

Leake, Virginius, 96, 133, 196
Lece, 138, 141, 299–300
Lee, Robert E., 170, 181, 185–86
Levin, Kevin, 180
Lewis (1), 46–47, 282
Lewis (2), 39, 277
Lewis, Sylvester, 254n, *261*
Lincoln, Abraham, 128–29, 133–35, 150, 162–63, 181, 192, 194–95
Linda [Cartwright], 145, 205, 283, 287–88, 298–99
Little, Watt, 151, 166, 177–78
Little, William, 114, 302–3
Lius Polk, 290
London, 70, 92, 143, 295
Lone Hill, 104, 110, 126, 165, 172
Looney, Robert, 155
Louisa [Price], 137n, *176*
Lucinda, 285, 309n10
Lucious Wilks [Tucker], 146, 174–75, 205, 218, 284, 291–93, 297, 300
Lucky, 50–51, 278–79
Lucy (1), 50–51, 278–79
Lucy (2), 46n, 283
lynchings, 8, 223, 233, *238*, 245–48, *249*, 250–56
    Lynching Sites Project, *261*

Maddux, Snowden Craven, 156, 209, 212, 215–16, 223–24, 227, 236, 239, 244
Madison, 108, *120*, 165, 301
Magness, Perre, xxx
Mandy Green, 288–89
Margarett, 275–76
Margrett [Tucker], 146, 174–75, 284, 291–93, 300
Mariah (Gray), 204
Martha Aaline, 145, 289–90
Martha [Davis] [Davies] [Hadley], 108, *120*, 203–4, 298, 301
Martin, Charley, 245
Mary (1), 55, 279
Mary (2), 92–95, 143–44, 168, 183, 295–98

Mary (3) [Tucker], xvi, 5–6, *173*, 187n, 205, 218, 258–59, *266–67*, 285, 290–93, 296–97, 300. *Possibly same as* Mary (2)
Mary (4) [Tucker], 146, 174–75, 205, 285, 291–93, 297, 300
Mat [Davis], 108, 165, 205, 258, 301–2
Matthews, J. R., 217
Matthews, Paul A., xxx
McCadden, Katie, 244
McCadden, Mollie, 231, 233, *238*, 244–46, 255n
McClendon, A. J., 246, 250–52
McDaniel, Robert, 75n
McMahon, Al, 241–42, *243*
McVay, Kevin, 309n10
McVay, Roscoe, 259n, 309n10
Meherrin Baptist Church, 30–31
Melinda, 292
Memphis, *viii*, xi–xv, xix, xxix–xxxii, 12, 94, 104, 107–9, 131, *189*, 202, 224, 276, 300, 302
 and Civil War, 129–30, 139, 142, 150, 159–65, 169–70, *173*, 176, 177, 192–200
 and cotton trade, 81, 87–90, 122, 127–28, 142, 160, 169–70, 210
 growth of, 89–91, 107, 127, 191, 207
 lynchings and racial violence, 8, 193–94, 220–23, 241–47, *248*, 249–55, 281
 massacre, 220–23, *235*
 and slave trade, xxxii, 91–92, 96, 104, 108, *117*, 127–28, 193, 207, 224
 William Little Davies in, 2–3, 9, 232, 256
Memphis Cotton Carnival (Association), xiii, *xvii*
Methodism, 4, 27, 36, 42, 44–45, 61, 64
 and issues of slavery, 32–35, 37–38
Mike, 55, 279
Miles, Tiya, xxxv
Miller, S. J., 253
Mills, 75–77, 86, 148
Mima, 165
Mincy, 165
Mitchell, Robert, 67

Mitchell, William D., 52–54, 59, 67, 284–85, 294
Mitzi/Meize [Davies] [Hadley], 94, 203–4, 206, 217, 286–87, 290–91, 297–98
Molly, 108
Morning Grove Church cemetery, 5, 259–60, *263–66*, 292, 297, 303
Morning Sun, 1–2, 13, 210, 223, 229–33, 237, 257, 259
 during Civil War, 134, 153–57, 160–61, 166, 169, 172, 177, 182n, 186, 195–97
 prior to Civil War, 88, 96–97, 102–6, 110, 112–13
 See also Davies plantation (Shelby County)
Morning Sun Cumberland Presbyterian Church, xiiin, *79*, 157, 231
 cemetery, 180, 257, *263*
Morning Sun home guard, 134–35, 139–40, 142, 150–51, 230
Morris, Bill, xv
Morris, Charlie, 255n
Morris Island, 170
Mosby and Hunt, 87–88, 90
Mose Frazier Committee, xxv–xxvi, 259n, 260n, *264*, 309n10, 310n15
Moss, Ida Mae, 259
Moss, Valerie, *xxi*, 259
Mourning, 285
Mt. Airy, 104, 161, 178
Myles, Annie Mae Frazier Blackwell, xxix, *267*, 269–70

Nancy, 24–25, 50, 62–63, 272, 275
Nashville, Battle of, 182–83, 340n6
Neal, Henrietta (Davis), 48–51, 55–57, 64, 274–76
Neal, Joel, 25, 48–50, 52, 55–57, 273, 276, 278, 280–81
Neal, John, 49
Nelly, 23–25, 49, 55, 57, 62–63, 272–73, 275–76
Nelson, Georgia, 258

Nelson, Sol, 258
Nelson Harrison, 46n, 284
New Orleans, 3, 71, 73, 87, 90, 221
Nice, 162, 165, 211, 302

Oaks, The, xiii, xiv, *xx–xxi*, xxix, 259. *See also* Davies Manor Historic Site; Davies plantation (Shelby County)
Onetti, Jake, 251
Orange, 110–11
Orion Hill, 103

Park, 72, 74
Park, John, 223–24
Patience, 55, 280
Patta ("Aunt Pat," "Patty"), 45–47, 76–77, 84–85, 95, 125, 148–49, 282, 288
Payne, Andy, xxviii–xxix, 310n15
Payne, R. G., 134, 137
Penningroth, Dylan C., 97
Perryville, Battle of, 166
Persons, Ell, 254
Peter (1), 20, 22, 24–25, 28, 272–73, 275
Peter (2), 55, 280
Petrowski, 227
Pillow, Gideon Johnson, 60, 71, 74–75, 83, 86–87, 116, 136, 289
Pleasant Hill Cemetery, 5, 263
Pleasant Hill Church, 156
Pleasant Hill School, 215
Polk, James K., 60, 83
Polk, William Julius, 60
Polly [Cartwright], 108, 120, 165, 204, 301–2
Price, Simon, 105–9, 136n, 176, 254n
Pricilla [Tucker], 146, 174–75, 205, 218, 285, 291–93, 297, 300

Raboteau, Albert, 31
Rachel (1), 46n, 283
Rachel (2), 143, 293
Rachel (3), 165
Randle [Feild], 7, 151–54, 166, 177–78
Rebecca, 55, 280

Reconstruction, 195, 196n, 198, 206, 219–25, 228, 254, 255n
Red River Revival, 36
Reedy Creek. *See* Davis "mannor plantation" Reedy Creek estate (Lunenburg County)
Reedy Creek Baptist Church, 30–31, 44
Reubin, 30
Richard, 28–29, 48, 272, 281
Richmond [Bennett], 6–7, 113–15, *265*, 290, 302–3, 312n2
  as body servant to James Davies, 6, 150–56, 166–67, 177, 182–84, 186, 196
  post-emancipation, 187, 204–5, 212, 217, 258–60, 290, 303
Robert T., 288
Roberts, Ridley, 92, 94, 295–96
Rodgers, Hillman, xi, *xx–xxi*, xxv, xxviii–xxix, 263
Rody, 28–29, 48, 272, 281
Royal [Price], 106, 137n, 157, 165, 171, 176, 192, 221n, 222, *235*
Royster, Charles B., 300
Royster, David Richard ("Dick"), 97, 105
  during Civil War, 136–37, 139, 152, 155, 177, 197, 211
Royster, Joel W., xiiin, 93, 97, 103, 105, 133, 196–97, 211, 212
Rutherford Creek plantation. *See* Davis plantation (Maury County)

Sally, 168
Sam (1), 55, 273, 280
Sam (2), 288
Sampson, 24–25, 49, 55, 62–63, 272–73, 275–76
Samuel, 67–69, 285–86, 294
Sarah (1), 30
Sarah (2), 50, 278
Sarah Jane (Tucker) [Bennett], 94–95, 147, 151, 173, 290, 296–97
  post-emancipation, 187, 204–5, 217, 258–59, 290, 303

Scantlin, J. D., 138, 299–300
Scantlin, Mary (Davies), 137–42, 144, 214–15, 287, 289, 293, 299–300
Sealy, 144, 291, 295–96, 298
secession, 8, 129, 133–37, 139, 157, 198–99, 212
Second Confiscation Act, 163–64
Second Great Awakening, 35–36, 64, 135
Sellers, Hardy, 53–54, 60, 70, 284
Separate Baptists, 30–32
sharecropping, *xxi*, 1, 9, 205–8, 214, 216–19, 254n, 297
    at Davies plantation, xiv, xvi, xxv–xxviii, xxxv, 7, 9, 202–6, 217, 229, 258, 291–92, 298, 303
Shaw, Ed, 220, 222–23, 225–28
Shelby County Anti-Radical Convention, 223–24
Shelby County Democratic-Conservative Convention, 224, 239
Shelby County Historical Commission, *xxiii*, *261*
Shelby Depot, 6, 113n, 156, 202, 208–16, 223–27, 230, *236*
Sherman, William T., 177–78, 183–84, 191
Shiloh, Battle of, 153, 155–57, 166, 177, 197. *See also* Camp Shiloh
Simon, 110–11, 151n, 165
Simon [Crenshaw], 7, 151–54, 166, 177
Sisy, 95–96, 143
slavery
    agency exercised by enslaved individuals, xxxiv, 73–74, 89, 107–8, 115, 171–72
    body servants in Civil War, 6–7, 136–39, 150–56, 166–67, 177–87, 303
    and cotton production, 1, 7, 36, 47, 88, 98, 102, 124–28, 135, 168–70, 287
    rape and sexual exploitation of, 101–2, 172
    runaways and escape from enslavement, 24, 73, 89, 110–11, 140, 143, 151n, 157n, 158n, 159–60, 163–65, 170–71, 176, 272

separation of enslaved family members, 26, 29–31, 39–41, 46, 49–51, 67, 77, 84–86, 95, 114
slave trading, xxxii, 91–92, 96, 104, 108, 112–14, 117, 127–28, 143, 193, 196, 207, 211, 224
See also contraband camps; Fugitive Slave Act; *specific enslaved individuals, plantations, and slaveholders*
Sons of Confederate Veterans, xxxi–xxxii
Stanton, Edward, 170
States Rights Secession Party of Shelby County, 133–34
Stewart, James Rufus, 244
Stokes, Edward, 278–79
Stokes, Peter, 278–79
Stones River, Battle of, 167, 177
Strickland, Jim, xxxii
Susan, 287
S. Y. Wilson Store, 254

Tabb, 24–25, 62–63, 272–75
Tennessee Historical Commission, *xviii*, *xix*,161
Third USCT Heavy Artillery, 171, 192–94, 221n
Thirteenth Amendment, 198–99, 219, 221
Thirteenth Tennessee, 136, 152, 167, 179
Thirty-Eighth Tennessee Infantry, 150–52, 155–56, 166, 177, 182n
Thomas/Tom ("Thom") [Cartwright], 144, 150, 204–5, 217, 258, 289–90, 293, 301–2
Thurman, Ann (Royster), 105–6, 109, 136, 176, 179n
Thurman, Beverly, 136–37, 139, 150, 152–55, 167n, 171, 177–80, 184, 212
Thurman, Fendal Carr, 105–6, 109, 136, 179n
Thurman, J. P., 180, 196
    during the Civil War, 137n, 152, 155–58, 165, 171, 177, 179n, 181, 183–85

Thurman, Sallie (Ecklin), 13, 103, 137n, 139, 152–61, 165, 171, 178, 179n, 184–85
Tisdale, Henry, 279
Tom, 24–25, 55, 62–63, 272–73, 275–76
Toombs, Robert, 185
Tucker, Alice (Williams), 218, 291
Tucker, Amy, 205, 218, 297
Tucker, Andy, 205, 297
Tucker, Maggie, 218, 292
Tucker, Noah, 205, 297
Tucker, Pleasant (Carter), 218, 259, 292
Tucker, Sophia (Gray), 204, 293

Union Convention of Shelby County, 133
Union Depot, 113n, 207–9, 222, 244, 251
Unionists, 128–29, 133–35, 140, 150, 194, 197–99
US Colored Troops, 157n, 158n, 165, 170–71, 182, 191–94, 200, 221–22, 235. *See also individual regiments*

VanderSchaaf, Claire, xvi
Vaughan, A. J., 167, 179–80
Vaughan, Reuben, 274, 276
Vilet, 28–29, 48, 272, 281
Vincy/Viney/Vina, 39, 45–46, 145–46, 277, 291–92, 299
Virginia [Harris], 107

Waldron, Robert, 194
Walker, Lee, 8, 245–47, 248, 249, 249–55, 261
Walker, Robert, 75–77, 86, 144, 283, 287–89
Walker, Sarah "Sally" Jane (Davies), 59, 94–95, 144–45, 168, 283, 287, 290, 298–99
Walls, Mississippi, xxi, 9, 10, 12, 216, 256, 267
Wash, William, 104
Wash's Store, 134
Washington/Wash, 53, 67–69, 284–86, 294
Wat [Davis], 205, 258
Webber, Matthew W., 96, 109, 112–13
Webber, W. H., 183
Wells, Ida, 246

white supremacy, xxviii, xxxi–xxxvi, 105–7, 129, 135, 200, 220–22, 233, 251, 269. *See also* Ku Klux Klan
Wilcher/Wilshire/Willshire [Tucker], 53, 94–95, 146–48, 173–75, 187, 284–85, 291–94, 297, 300
  death and burial, 5, 259n, 266, 285
  fight with Dickey Chappell's men, 72, 74, 203, 284
  litigation over, 54, 59, 67, 70, 284
  paternity of, 53, 56, 95, 147, 285
  post-emancipation, 6, 147, 205, 218, 285, 292, 296–97
  presumed father of Sarah Jane, 94, 147, 151, 173, 290, 297–98, 303
William, 278, 280
Williams, Barbara, 260n, 309n10
Williams, Charles, 96, 113, 123
Williams, Edward, xxvii
Williams, James, 254n
Williams, Joseph S., 83–84
Williams, Markum L., 95–96, 108, 112–13, 123, 135, 143, 168, 196, 213
Williams, Mary Octavious (Little), 113, 196
Williams, Robert, 96, 108–9, 113, 133
Williams, Tommie, 254
Wilson, Charles R., 254n
Wilson, Sam T., xiv–xv
Woodlawn Plantation, 103

Yateman/Yeatman, 76, 94, 286, 288, 297–98
yellow fever, 123, 218, 226
Young, Alfred, 230
Young [Davies] [Davis] [Cartwright], 108, 120, 204, 301–2
Young [Price], 106, 136–37, 139, 152–54, 167n, 171, 176, 177–80, 184
Younger, John W., 70, 295

Zachariah Davies Chapter of the Daughters of the American Revolution, xiv–xv, xx, 211n
Zinna, 46n, 283

Printed in the USA
CPSIA information can be obtained
at www.ICGtesting.com
CBHW022055170724
11751CB00018B/42